WOMEN OF FORTUNE

Women of Fortune tells the compelling story of mercantile wealth, arranged marriages, and merchant heiresses who asserted their rights despite loss, imprisonment, and murder. Following three generations of the Bennet and Morewood families, who made their fortune in Crown finance, the East Indies, the Americas, and moneylending, Linda Levy Peck explores the changing society, economy, and culture of early modern England. The heiresses – curious, intrepid, entrepreneurial, scholarly – married into the aristocracy, fought for their property, and wrote philosophy. One spent years on the Grand Tour. Her life in Europe, despite the outbreak of war, is vividly documented. Another's husband went to debtors' prison. She recovered the fortune and bought shares. Husbands, sons, and contemporaries challenged their independence legally, financially, even violently, but new forms of wealth, education, and the law enabled these heiresses to insist on their own agency, create their own identities, and provide examples for later generations.

LINDA LEVY PECK is a prizewinning historian who has published extensively on politics, society, and culture in early modern England. She is the author of *Northampton: Patronage and Policy at the Court of James I* (1982), *Patronage and Corruption in Early Modern England* (1990), which won the John Ben Snow prize awarded by the North American Conference on British Studies, and *Consuming Splendor: Society and Culture in Seventeenth-Century England* (2005), awarded Honorable Mention (2006) by the Sixteenth Century Conference. She also edited *The Mental World of the Jacobean Court* (1991). Now Professor of History Emerita at George Washington University and Senior Fellow at the Institute of Historical Research, University of London, she has also served as president of the North American Conference on British Studies.

WOMEN OF FORTUNE

Money, Marriage, and Murder in Early Modern England

LINDA LEVY PECK

CAMBRIDGE
UNIVERSITY PRESS

CAMBRIDGE
UNIVERSITY PRESS

University Printing House, Cambridge CB2 8BS, United Kingdom

One Liberty Plaza, 20th Floor, New York, NY 10006, USA

477 Williamstown Road, Port Melbourne, VIC 3207, Australia

314–321, 3rd Floor, Plot 3, Splendor Forum, Jasola District Centre, New Delhi – 110025, India

79 Anson Road, #06–04/06, Singapore 079906

Cambridge University Press is part of the University of Cambridge.

It furthers the University's mission by disseminating knowledge in the pursuit of education, learning, and research at the highest international levels of excellence.

www.cambridge.org
Information on this title: www.cambridge.org/9781107034020
DOI: 10.1017/9781139524094

First published 2018

Printed in the United Kingdom by TJ International Ltd. Padstow Cornwall

A catalogue record for this publication is available from the British Library.

ISBN 978-1-107-03402-0 Hardback

To my family and friends

Contents

Color Plates

Figures

Acknowledgments

As flowers begin to peek through the snow, they hint that spring is on the way. So too with this book. It is my great pleasure to offer thanks to all those who helped bring it to fruition.

I was the recipient of an Andrew W. Mellon Foundation Fellowship at the Folger Shakespeare Library in 2007–2008 for which I am most grateful. While there I developed the project that became this book and had the great pleasure of being part of the Folger community of scholars.

Historians are dependent on the work of archivists and curators. *Women of Fortune* began with a letter from Grace Bennet to her husband Simon shown to me by Robin Harcourt Williams, Librarian and Archivist to his Grace the Marquess of Salisbury. The Hatfield Archives were invaluable in documenting the lives of the Bennets and Frances, Countess of Salisbury and I wish to express my great thanks to him for all his help. I also wish to thank the Marquess of Salisbury for permission to use and cite the Hatfield House manuscripts and to reproduce Hatfield House paintings.

Georgianna Ziegler, Folger Shakespeare Library Reference Librarian and Deputy Director, and good friend, has engaged in countless discussions of early modern literature, culture, and this book for which I am very grateful. I thank Michael Witmore for permission to quote from Folger manuscripts and reproduce Folger images.

For work with manuscripts, I also wish to thank the librarians of the British Library, The National Archives, the Guildhall, the House of Lords Record Office, History of Parliament, Oxford University, the Nottingham University Library, the Centre for Buckinghamshire Studies, Cambridgeshire Archives, Derbyshire Record Office, London Metropolitan Archives, and the Westminster Archives Centre.

For the illustrations, I had great help from the curators whose images I have used. I especially wish to thank the Earl of Halifax for permission to use the portrait of Elizabeth, Lady Bennet now on loan to Temple Newsam. I also thank Art Resource, the British Library, the Conway Library, the Courtauld, Christ's Hospital, the Folger Shakespeare Library, the Hatfield House Archives and the Marquess of Salisbury, the Heinz Archive of the

National Portrait Gallery, Leeds Museums and Art Galleries (Temple Newsam House) UK/Bridgeman Images, the Metropolitan Museum of Art, The National Archives, the National Gallery, London, the National Gallery of Ireland, the National Maritime Museum, the National Portrait Gallery, the Tate, and the Westminster Archive Centre.

This book benefitted particularly from the advice from many friends and colleagues. I want to thank my wonderful colleagues and graduate and undergraduate students at George Washington University, in particular my chairman, William Becker, who arranged leave from the university for me to work on the book. I was also helped by the comments of scholars at the Midwest Conference on British Studies, seminars at the Folger Shakespeare Library, the Huntington Library, the Institute of Historical Research, University of London, Texas A and M, Princeton University, Johns Hopkins University, and the University of North Carolina where I read early chapters of the book. In particular, I want to thank James Rosenheim, Margaret Ezell, Cynthia Herrup, Nigel Smith, Orest Ranum, Mary Fissell, J. G. A. Pocock, John Marshall, Lois Schwoerer, A. R. Braunmuller, Christine Krueger, Linda Salamon, Dana Greene, Arthur Bienenstock, Jasia Reichardt, Ann Scott, Lindsay Moore, Cynthia Schultes, and Kelsey Flynn for conversations about the book. I am very grateful to Julia Rudolph for discussions of mortgage law in the seventeenth century.

I especially want to thank Stanley G. Engerman, Barbara J. Harris, and Roger Knight, who read the entire manuscript. Stan's breadth of knowledge, ability to pose the right question, and to read work even in its earliest stages has been invaluable to me as to so many others. I cannot thank him enough. Barbara Harris has brought her great knowledge of women's history and medieval precedent to her reading of this manuscript as well as her fine eye for writing and logic. Roger Knight, as an eighteenth-century historian, has helped me to see the larger picture of which my subjects were a part. I also thank the anonymous readers for the Press whose helpful comments helped shape the scope of the manuscript. Finally, I wish to thank my editors, Michael Watson who encouraged me at the beginning of the project and especially Elizabeth Friend-Smith who has been supportive throughout and whose keen reading of the manuscript and advice has been so helpful.

Finally, to those friends who have been towers of strength for so many years – Arline J. Fireman, Joyce Gelb, Barbara J. Harris, Barbara Ballis Lal, Marjorie Lightman, Margaret Staats Simmons – gratitude is not enough.

I alone, of course, am responsible for the errors remaining.

Abbreviations

Add. Mss.	Additional Manuscripts
BL	British Library
CSP Col.	*Calendar of State Papers, Colonial*
CSPD	*Calendar of State Papers, Domestic Series*
EEBO	Early English Books Online
EMLO	Early Modern Letters Online
Folger	Folger Shakespeare Library
HCJ	*Journal of the House of Commons*
HLJ	*Journal of the House of Lords*
HLRO	House of Lords Record Office
HMC	Great Britain. Royal Commission on Historical Manuscripts.
LMA	London Metropolitan Archives
ODNB	*Oxford Dictionary of National Biography*
PROB11	Prerogative Court of Canterbury Wills
TNA	The National Archives
VCH	Victoria County History (series)

THE BENNETS OF CLAPCOT

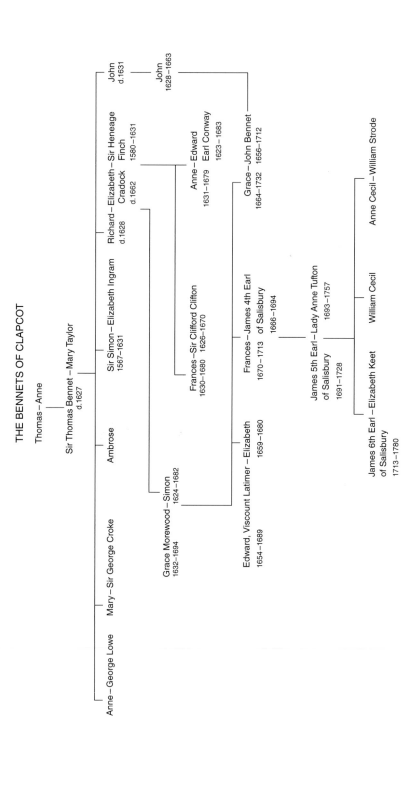

MOREWOODS OF THE OAK

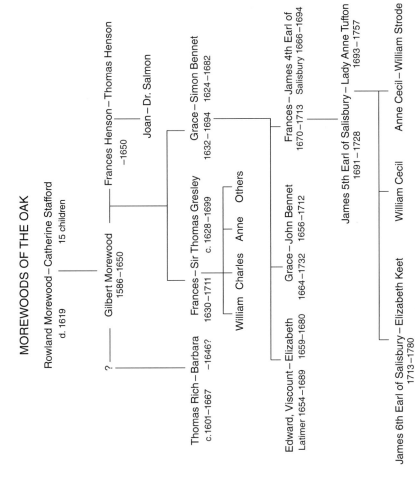

Rowland Morewood — Catherine Stafford
d. 1619   15 children

Gilbert Morewood — Frances Henson — Thomas Henson
1586–1650   –1650

Joan — Dr. Salmon

? ——— Thomas Rich — Barbara
c.1601–1667   –1646?

Frances — Sir Thomas Gresley
1630–1711   c. 1628–1699

William   Charles   Anne   Others

Grace — Simon Bennet
1632–1694   1624–1682

Grace — John Bennet
1664–1732   1656–1712

Edward, Viscount — Elizabeth
Latimer 1654–1689   1659–1680

Frances — James 4th Earl of
1670–1713   Salisbury 1666–1694

James 5th Earl of Salisbury — Lady Anne Tufton
1691–1728   1693–1757

William Cecil

Anne Cecil — William Strode

James 6th Earl of Salisbury — Elizabeth Keet
1713–1780

Introduction
Prologue

At 9 am on Wednesday, September 19, 1694, a butcher named Barnes from Stony Stratford, Buckinghamshire, walked three miles to Calverton House in the neighboring village. Locals gossiped that its widowed owner, Grace Bennet, kept large quantities of gold in the manor house. Finding her alone in the servants' hall Barnes broke her neck so viciously that "her face turned behind her."[1] She may have been the only mother of a peeress to be murdered in the seventeenth century.

This audacious robbery and murder immediately raises many questions. Who was Grace Bennet? What was the larger context for her murder? Why did Thomas, Earl of Ailesbury, call Grace "the most sordid person that ever lived?"[2]

When I read the report of Grace Bennet's murder, I already knew something about her. She appeared in my previous book, *Consuming Splendor: Society and Culture in Seventeenth-Century England.*[3] *Consuming Splendor* examined the ways in which the consumption of luxury goods transformed social practices, gender roles, royal policies, and the economy in seventeenth-century England. Specifically, that book looked at new ways to shop; the Crown's sponsorship of luxury trades and manufactures; new aspirations in building, furnishing, and collecting; the reinvention of identity through new artifacts; and the transformation of meaning as objects moved across cultures and into new contexts.

Grace Bennet was a luxury consumer. Her desires included new cravings for West Indian groceries and the accessories to go with them. In 1662 she

---

[1] Anon., *The Unfortunate Lady: A Brief Narrative of the Life, and Unhappy Death of the Lady Bennet, Late of Buckinghamshire; Who Was Most Barbarously and Inhumanly Murthered at Her Own House, on Wednesday the 19th of September, 1694, by a Butcher of Stony-Stratford . . .* (London: Printed for H. Maston in Warwick-Lane, 1694).

[2] *Memoirs of Thomas, Earl of Ailesbury,* ed. W. E. Buckley, 2 vols., Roxburghe Club Publications (Westminster [London]: Nichols and Sons, 1890), Vol. II, p. 481.

[3] *Consuming Splendor: Society and Culture in Seventeenth-Century England* (Cambridge: Cambridge University Press, 2005).

Figure 0.1 Sugar box, 1673–1674, width 8 in. (20.3 cm.), Gift of Irwin Untermyer, 1968 (68.141.161). © The Metropolitan Museum of Art. Art Resource, NY, British, London. Grace Bennet's silver sugar box may have resembled this one made ten years later.

wrote to her husband in London: "I want a thing; such a one as your mother had to put sugar in: they are to be bought at the goldsmiths; they are made of silver and they used to call them sugar chests. If you buy one let it be of the biggest size as usually made."[4] Grace Bennet's 1662 order for the largest silver sugar chest available in London and her subsequent murder began my investigations. *Women of Fortune* has become a study of social, economic, and cultural change in early modern England through an analysis of the Bennet and Morewood families and their network of connections across city, country, and continents. The book examines the creation of the family fortune from international trade and Crown finance to private banking and shares; the marriage of the families into the country gentry and nobility through a strategy of providing large marriage portions; and the powerful women who added to, invested in, and spent the family fortune while establishing their own independence.

I

Women of Fortune tells the story of three generations of merchant, gentry, and noble families, intertwined by marriage, whose climb to wealth and

[4] Hatfield House Archives, General 72/35, Grace Bennet to Simon Bennet, May 5, 1662.

position played out against the background of a century of economic growth, civil and international war, and domestic upheaval. In particular, the book looks at the women in these families, young heiresses who became baronets, peers, and bankrupts' wives, and City and noble widows who promoted their own property rights and cultural and intellectual interests in the years between 1570 and 1732.

These three generations of the Bennet and Morewood families, and their extended kin – the Finches, Gresleys, Riches, Cliftons, and Cecils – include Yorkshire and Berkshire parish gentry, London merchants, Lord Mayors, lawyers, a Speaker of the House of Commons, a Lord Chancellor, a leading doctor, a well-known philosopher, court officials, and the nobility. Their life trajectories demonstrate the importance of parish gentry aspirations, merchant wealth, and aristocratic need, of upward mobility attained through international trade, the law, court office, and marriage, and downward mobility through overly enthusiastic attempts at agricultural improvement and over-extension of debt. They include Royalists, Parliamentarians, Tories, Whigs, and Jacobites, members of the Church of England, Presbyterians, nonjurors, Roman Catholics, and a Quaker.

The individual stories of the Bennets and Morewoods shed important light on the connections between land, commerce, and finance, changing attitudes toward money as a symbol and as a commodity, including the value of gold and the size of marriage portions, and the benefits of investments in trade, mortgages, and shares. As new forms of investments such as real estate speculation and shares appeared, older forms such as saving gold were deprecated. The Bennets and their kin also illustrate the continuing interest in placing gentlemen as London apprentices in the late seventeenth century and contemporary attitudes toward overseas trade.

Heiresses have often been seen simply as the transmitters of property, footnotes in the larger story of the rise and fall of aristocratic and noble families. Their own lives, before and after marriage, have generally been left unexplored.[5] In contrast, *Women of Fortune* looks at several heiresses to merchant and aristocratic fortunes and examines how they managed their property and promoted their children's advancement. In particular, it analyses the individual identities they created for themselves and the new lives they devised on the continent and in London. Some Bennet women had to

---

[5] See Sir John Habakkuk, *Marriage, Debt, and the Estates System: English Landownership, 1650–1950* (Oxford: Clarendon Press, 1994); Lawrence Stone, *Family and Fortune: Studies in Aristocratic Finance in the Sixteenth and Seventeenth Centuries* (Oxford: Oxford University Press, 1973). For work on seventeenth- and eighteenth-century heiresses, see, for instance, Rosemary O'Day, *Cassandra Brydges (1670–1735), First Duchess of Chandos: Life and Letters* (Woodbridge: Boydell and Brewer, 2007).

accept arranged marriages when they were young teenagers, while others faced legal claims from their husbands and sons who wished to control their estates. Yet as other historians have found, patriarchal practices were increasingly challenged in practice in everyday life and in the courts in the seventeenth century.[6] *Women of Fortune* suggests that elite women's positions improved in the late seventeenth century, including their freedom to travel abroad, to study, to write, and to manage their own money.[7] Over three generations, the Bennet and Morewood women were strong, curious, and independent. They took major roles in their families and as widows carved out fresh starts for themselves.

Despite suggestions that England had a closed elite, the experiences of the Bennets and Morewoods, suggest that England's landed elite in the seventeenth century was open to those whose wealth came from trade and banking if the connections were good enough or the marriage portion large enough.[8] Three Bennet heiresses, in two different generations, married into the upper nobility while two others married into the baronetcy.

II

Women of Fortune begins its story with two younger sons of parish gentry, Thomas Bennet and Gilbert Morewood, who came to London from Berkshire and Yorkshire as gentlemen apprentices to London livery companies. Thomas Bennet and his brother Richard both became members of the Mercers' Company in the middle of Queen Elizabeth's reign. Gilbert Morewood was, remarkably, one of ten Morewoods apprenticed to the Grocers' Company in the seventeenth century. Thomas Bennet and Gilbert Morewood made their fortunes in a variety of different enterprises. Although Thomas, as a mercer, began his career trading in luxury textiles in the 1570s and 1580s, he later diversified his capital into Jacobean Crown finance, money lending, and real estate. He became an alderman and Lord Mayor of London and was knighted by James I in 1604. Morewood, the grocer,

---

[6] Tim Stretton and Krista J. Kesselring, eds., *Married Women and the Law: Coverture in England and the Common Law World* (Ithaca, NY: McGill University, 2013).

[7] On seventeenth-century women writers, see Hilda Smith, *Reason's Disciples: Seventeenth-Century English Feminists* (Champaign-Urbana: University of Illinois Press, 1982).

[8] On the issue of whether or not Britain had an open elite, see Lawrence Stone and Jeanne C. Fawtier Stone, *An Open Elite? England 1540–1880* (Oxford: Oxford University Press, 1984), and more recently Nuala Zahedieh, "An Open Elite? Colonial Commerce, the Country House and the Case of Sir Gilbert Heathcote and Normanton Hall," in *Slavery and the British Country House*, ed. Madge Dresser and Andrew Hann (Swindon: English Heritage, 2013), pp. 71–77, 150–152; Kimberly Schutte, *Women, Rank, and Marriage in the British Aristocracy, 1485–2000: An Open Elite?* (Basingstoke: Palgrave Macmillan, 2014).

made his fortune in the East India Company, importing spices and exporting lead, but he also invested in the Virginia Company and other ventures to the New World, as well as in marine insurance, real estate, and money lending. A strong Presbyterian Morewood became one the leaders of the East India Company in the 1640s.

The importance of credit and risk in the English economy, already growing in the late sixteenth century,[9] continued especially during the English Civil War and the Republic. As a result, new types of banks emerged from the 1640s on. Thomas Bennet's grandson, Simon Bennet, who inherited family wealth from his merchant father, philanthropist uncle, and aunt in the midst of the English Civil War, chose not to invest in international trade but instead invested the family's property holdings in a new venture, the mortgage and loan business. Even as Robert Abbott and later Robert Clayton were establishing their early bank in the late 1640s,[10] Simon Bennet went into private banking. Simon Bennet, however, did not take deposits; he was self-financing. Simon made short-term loans backed either by promissory notes or by mortgages on real estate to a clientele that included both the landed and the city's shopkeepers. Because mortgage law was still developing, borrowers tended to avoid mortgages if they could. Only 2.5 percent of land in England was mortgaged in the 1660s, but by the 1690s the figure was 20 percent.[11] While his business was not as large as Clayton's, his contemporaries called him "Great Bennet." In his twenties he was already one of the richest men in Buckinghamshire and sheriff of the county.

In contrast, his cousin, John Bennet, another grandson of Sir Thomas Bennet, sought to improve the agricultural production of his lands in Cambridgeshire through enclosure, new technology, and further land purchases. He financed his plans through short-term mortgages backed by his land. When he failed to repay on time, he faced foreclosure and prison despite the doctrine of the equity of redemption, which supposedly protected mortgagees.[12] Thus, one cousin, Simon, in finance, increased his fortune through short-term loans, mortgages, and moneylending while the other, in

---

[9] Craig Muldrew, *The Economy of Obligation: The Culture of Credit and Social Relations in Early Modern England* (London: Palgrave Macmillan, 1998).

[10] Frank T. Melton, *Sir Robert Clayton and the Origins of Deposit Banking* (Cambridge: Cambridge University Press, 1986, 2002).

[11] Christiaan van Bochove, Heidi Deneweth, and Jaco Zuijderduijn, "Real Estate and Mortgage Finance in England and the Low Countries, 1300–1800," *Continuity and Change*, 30, 1 (2015), 9–38.

[12] The doctrine of the "equity of redemption" allowed redemption of property even if a payment was missed if the mortgage was repaid within a reasonable amount of time. Heneage Finch, 1st Earl of Nottingham and Lord Chancellor, enunciated it in Newcomb *v.* Bonham in 1681.

agriculture, lost it using the same instruments. At the beginning of the eighteenth century, Simon Bennet's daughter Grace adopted a new form of investment, placing most of her money in stocks in the Bank of England and the East India and South Sea Companies.

Thus the Bennets and Morewoods illustrate the increasing diversity of investments available in the seventeenth century. In the heated economy of the late seventeenth century, wealth, in the form of gold coins, marriage portions, land, rental property, bonds, loans, mortgages and bills of exchange became increasingly important to the well to do regardless of rank or gender. In 1690 Nicholas Barbon attacked those who simply kept their wealth in gold and refused to invest it or spend it.[13]

Over more than a century the Bennet and Morewood fortune grew and their social position increased through the use of large marriage portions, drawn from new sources in international trade with the East and West Indies, North and South America, Crown finance, and banking. That fortune did not come, however, from owning plantations in the West Indies. Furthermore, unlike many rich men, Simon Bennet did not build a new country house. He lived in Calverton Manor, which his grandfather, Sir Thomas, the Lord Mayor, bought for his son and which Simon had inherited. In 1659 Simon put on an extension.[14] By 1732, the Bennets had not gained a title for themselves but their successful marital strategies meant, that with the death of the last heiress, most of their wealth was left to the Earls of Salisbury and went to support Hatfield House.

Economic diversification and social change provided a new context for gender roles in the seventeenth century.[15] Under the traditional common law doctrine of coverture, once married, women's property came under their husband's control during their lifetime. In the seventeenth century, however, legal arrangements made at the time of their marriage could overcome the doctrine of coverture. For instance, fathers created trusts leaving money separately to their daughters and provided timber rights on land that they would inherit. Husbands arranged for their wives to have "pin money," a separate settlement at the time of marriage. Under the "doctrine of necessaries," women could contract for goods if they were appropriate to the status of their husbands. Widows could make prenuptial agreements with their new husbands. Often husbands left elite women their jewelry, household furnishings, coaches and horses. Women also made wills leaving their estate to their

---

[13] Nicholas Barbon, *A Discourse of Trade* (London: Tho. Milbourne for the author, 1690).

[14] Calverton Manor was featured on *Restoration Home* on BBC2, August 2011.

[15] See Jeanne Boydston, "Gender as a Question of Historical Analysis," *Gender and History*, 20 (November 2008), 558–583.

daughters and provided that their sons-in-law were to have no right to control their money.[16]

Women continually asserted their property rights across the century and Bennet women repeatedly used the law to press their property rights from the 1620s to the 1730s. *Women of Fortune* illustrates how women managed their own wealth, often controlled the family economy, and brought lawsuits to protect their property against all contenders, including their husbands and sons. Thus Lady Elizabeth Finch, a wealthy City widow, made a prenuptial agreement to protect both her own and her son Simon's large inheritance. She left money to her married daughters and explicitly tried to prevent her sons-in-law from having any control over it. While married, Lady Frances Gresley asserted her timber rights and pressed to have her younger sons placed as gentlemen apprentices. Grace Bennet the younger demanded from her husband the rents left to her by her father by means of a trust. As a widow, Lady Frances Clifton used an Act of Parliament to provide marriage portions for her daughters. She also sued William Sacheverell for mishandling her affairs even though her brother, Heneage Finch, Earl of Nottingham, Solicitor General, had recommended him. While wealthy widows in the sixteenth and early seventeenth centuries usually remarried, none of the Bennet women, who married in 1650 or later and were predeceased by their first husbands, did so. In this they mirrored a general trend: London women in general did not remarry at the end of the seventeenth century.[17]

Women of Fortune also displays the identities these women created for themselves as cosmopolitan scholars, travelers, London consumers, and investors, going beyond their roles as daughters, wives, widows, and mothers. Their identities were reflected in their choice of geographical location, manners, and cultural interests. The mid and late seventeenth century increasingly offered women opportunities for social and geographical mobility and for female agency that caused anxiety about old and new forms of material culture and behavior. Anne Finch, Viscountess Conway, became a philosopher who wrote a critique of the work of ancient and contemporary philosophers such as Hobbes and Spinoza and maintained an international network of correspondents. Her niece, Frances, Countess of Salisbury, left her small son behind and spent four years in Europe from 1699 to 1703 where she immersed herself in the culture of Italy, France, and the Low Countries.

---

[16] See Amy Louise Erickson, *Women and Property in Early Modern England* (New York: Routledge, 1995).

[17] Jeremy Boulton, "London Widowhood Revisited: The Decline of Female Remarriage in the Seventeenth and Early Eighteenth Centuries," *Continuity and Change*, 5, 3 (1990), 323–355.

London was central to the social life of almost all of the elite women in *Women of Fortune*. While the family began as parish gentry in Berkshire and Yorkshire and some of the Bennets, Morewoods, and their connections had country houses built in the sixteenth and early or middle seventeenth centuries, the capital increasingly became a center for elite life which included shopping, marriage making, visiting, attending parliament and the law courts, and entertaining for longer and longer periods of each year. Almost all of the Bennet women lived in, visited, and maintained ties with friends or relations in London. After living with her merchant husband Richard Bennet in the City of London, Elizabeth, Lady Finch, lived in Kensington House, which later became Kensington Palace, for thirty years. Her daughter Frances, Lady Clifton, once widowed, spent only six months a year in Nottinghamshire, the other six in Bloomsbury. Lady Finch's younger daughter, the philosopher Viscountess Conway, often stayed with her mother at Kensington House. Frances dowager Countess of Salisbury, once back from Europe, lived mainly in London, as did her sister, Grace Bennet, one street away in Mayfair. Even Lady Gresley, who spent much of her time in Drakelowe in Derbyshire, had a decades-long correspondence with her old friend Sir John Moore, the former Lord Mayor of London.

III

Yet despite these examples of women who asserted their power over their property and created their own metropolitan identities, arranged marriages continued in the Restoration even when ideas of companionate marriage had long been in circulation. Thus, *Women of Fortune* looks closely at the arranged marriages of the three Bennet heiresses, daughters of Grace and Simon Bennet. Grace Bennet was the daughter of a well-to-do East India Company merchant, Gilbert Morewood, and she had married Simon Bennet, the rich real estate investor and private banker. They had had seven children together, but only three girls survived to adulthood. Simon and Grace sought to make upwardly mobile marriages for their three daughters: Elizabeth Bennet married Edward, Viscount Latimer, son of Thomas Osborne, Earl of Danby, Lord Treasurer of England; Frances Bennet married James, 4th Earl of Salisbury; and Grace Bennet married her cousin John Bennet, a Member of Parliament.

While heiresses were always sought after, in the 1680s, James Butler, 1st Duke of Ormond, made clear that the monetary value of brides was related to their status: those with what he called a "defect of quality" had to offer larger portions. Presumably the young Frances Bennet, whom he was considering for his grandson, had such a defect of quality because her father was a wealthy banker or moneylender without title, even though their cousin Henry Bennet, Earl of Arlington, who was acting as broker, was Charles II's Lord Chamberlain. Ormond rejected everything about the Bennets – except their money. In the end, the Bennets rejected Ormond.

Women of Fortune tells the story of the Bennet heiresses and their husbands before and after these marriages à la mode. Thus, Elizabeth Bennet, who had married Viscount Latimer in 1674, died after the birth of her second child. Because neither child survived, Latimer had to return her £10,000 portion to Simon Bennet. He was never rich enough to marry well again. Frances Bennet, at the age of thirteen with her £20,000 portion, married James Cecil, 4th Earl of Salisbury, in 1684, rather than the Duke of Ormond's grandson. Salisbury converted to Roman Catholicism in 1687, became a member of James II's Bedchamber in 1688, and was imprisoned in the Tower for Jacobitism after the Glorious Revolution. Grace the younger eloped with her cousin, John Bennet, a Cambridgeshire country gentleman. John Bennet used his in-laws' wealth to attempt to improve his agricultural holdings, failed, and went to debtors' prison in 1698, dying there in 1712. Earlier, in 1694, the girls' mother, Grace Bennet, personally difficult and disliked locally for both enclosing land and failing to pay tithes and poor rates, was murdered by the local butcher searching for gold.

Facing these family losses, Grace Bennet's surviving daughters, one a widowed young countess, the other the wife of the bankrupt Bennet, created new lives for themselves in London and on the continent. Almost all studies of the Grand Tour and the Giro d'Italia in the seventeenth and early eighteenth centuries focus on young men and the role that the tour played in their education and their careers. Little has been written on women travelers before the mid or later eighteenth century. When Frances, Countess of Salisbury left for Paris and then Rome for Jubilee Year in 1699, she began a trip that was one of the longest undertaken by any aristocratic woman in the seventeenth century. Her account book documents her daily visits to see art, architecture, and antiquities, to hear music, visit churches, and view gardens and monuments. She was an indefatigable traveler. Making connections with Roman Catholics and Jacobites, she and her would-be lover, George Jocelyn, who wooed her for fifteen months, evoked gossip from Samuel Pepys and his circle among others. Nevertheless, the countess stayed in Europe after surviving smallpox and remained a step ahead of the clashing armies in the War of the Spanish Succession.

Grace Bennet the younger successfully sued her imprisoned husband for the income from her properties that he continued to collect. Surviving her husband's decade-long sojourn in the Fleet and then the King's Prison, she made a life for herself in Mayfair within a circle of well-to-do single women.

She successfully invested much of her fortune in shares, lent money to her friends, and maintained close ties to her nephew, the 5th Earl of Salisbury, and his family. The sole survivor of her family, she left much of the seventeenth-century merchant wealth made in the East India trade and banking to her great nephew, the 6th Earl of Salisbury, in 1732, reviving that family's fortunes.

IV

Women of Fortune analyzes the connections that linked individuals, families, and groups to their larger environment in city and country. Such connections were especially important in a society in which private relationships provided important access to social and economic resources, political advancement, and intellectual and cultural patronage. Constructed by extended kinship relationships, marital connections, financial and business dealings, as well as religious, political, and intellectual ties, these connections often overlapped. The significance of these connections were the variety of ways in which they enabled people to carry on their businesses, secure loans, gain political advantage, make marriages, and form intellectual and cultural circles.

Two of Sir Thomas Bennet's children married his business associates in the cloth trade and Crown finance, George Lowe and Sir Arthur Ingram. Bennet then worked closely with Ingram on Crown loans, and loans to the nobility. He also helped Ingram take as his third wife a woman whose father was indebted to Bennet. Kin acted as brokers in making marriages as in the case of Henry Bennet, Earl of Arlington, who tried to arrange noble marriages for two daughters of his cousin Simon Bennet. At the same time, Arlington's efforts aimed to reinforce his own political standing with the Lord Treasurer, Lord Danby, and James Butler, Duke of Ormond. Frances, Lady Gresley appealed to her father's former apprentice, a wealthy investor and former Lord Mayor, to place her younger sons as apprentices in the City. Anne, Viscountess Conway became a well-known philosopher, not only because she had tutors at home but also because she maintained a long correspondence with her brothers' Oxford tutor, Henry More.

Networks linked groups as well as individuals. Because the Morewoods of Yorkshire and Derbyshire sent ten of their sons to the Grocers' Company in the seventeenth century, they created a new network of London, Derbyshire, and Yorkshire merchants who became suppliers of lead to the East India Company. Grace Bennet's London social circle included women investors to whom she loaned money. John Bennet used his connections to his brother, his brother's patron, and his cousin who was an MP to gain a seat in parliament. It appears, however, that the Bennets and Morewoods were somewhat less likely to turn to neighbors or directly to political patrons. By looking at networks of connection rather than just at an individual family, *Women of Fortune* encompasses men and women, merchants and nobility, city and country people, friends and relations within its narrative.

V

Women of Fortune is based on wide-ranging archival evidence from Hatfield House, the Folger Shakespeare Library, The National Archives, the British Library, the Guildhall, the House of Lords Record Office, Oxford University, the Nottingham University Library, the Centre for Buckinghamshire Studies, Cambridgeshire Archives, Derbyshire Record Office, London Metropolitan Archives, and Westminster Archives Centre. In particular, it draws on significant new evidence from Hatfield House, including the detailed accounts of Frances, Dowager Countess of Salisbury's four-year travels on the continent from 1699 to 1703 and Simon Bennet's business records. It also makes use of Lady Gresley's correspondence with Sir John Moore, Lord Mayor of London, between the 1670s and the 1690s, now at the Folger Shakespeare Library, and the correspondence of Lady Frances Clifton at the Nottinghamshire University Library. Nevertheless, it lacks correspondence for some of the main women in the story and has to rely on the contemporary writings of others for the reconstruction of their activities from accounts and lawsuits. There are only a few existing portraits of the women discussed in our story. While two Bennet women are buried in Westminster Abbey, there are no surviving funeral monuments for most. This visual erasure of these elite women, several of whose husbands have elaborate tombs, requires bearing witness to their extraordinary stories.

The book is divided into four parts: Money, Marriage, Murder, and Metropolis. Part I, "Money," opens with Chapter 1 on the making of the Bennet fortune between 1570 and 1682. Sir Thomas Bennet, son of a minor gentleman from Berkshire, became a mercer, imported luxury cloth from Europe, and then moved into court finance. His son Richard traded in European and North American goods including tobacco, and his grandson Simon turned to the mortgage and loan business in 1648. Chapter 2 looks at the career of Gilbert Morewood, from Yorkshire, who became a grocer and successful East India Company merchant up to his death in 1650. The Bennets and Morewood diversified their fortunes into real estate and money-lending, bought country property, and invested in marriage portions. Simon Bennet married Grace Morewood bringing together the two fortunes.

Part II, entitled "Marriage," consists of three chapters. Chapters 3 and 4 focus on Bennet and Morewood women of the second generation and their marriages into the aristocracy, from knights to noblemen, the ways in which they protected their own property and that of their children, and how they created singular identities for themselves. Elizabeth Bennet was the widow of the merchant Richard Bennet. Called "the £30,000 widow," after Richard's death, Elizabeth was courted by a number of men of high rank. Choosing Sir Heneage Finch, she made her new home in Kensington House, now Kensington Palace, in 1629. Her daughter Frances married Sir Clifford Clifton, scion of an old Nottinghamshire family much in debt. Once widowed, Frances fought for her own property and her daughter's marriage portions, and tried to ensure her son's marriage to the daughter of the Duke of Newcastle. Lady Finch's other daughter, Anne, studied philosophy with Henry More, the Cambridge Platonist, and married Edward, son of Viscount Conway, whose title he soon inherited, and wrote on vitalism. Lady Frances Gresley, daughter of Gilbert Morewood, married the baronet Sir Thomas Gresley, ruled her family's economy, sought to place her sons as London apprentices, and fought for her own property rights against her husband and son.

Chapter 5 turns to marriage making for the third generation, the three daughters of Simon and Grace Bennet. It examines the contemporary rationale for arranged marriages, marriage brokers and marriage portions, and the price of brides in the 1680s. The candid comments of the Duke of Ormond and Henry Bennet, Earl of Arlington, as they sought to arrange marriages in the 1680s illuminate both the process and the attitudes that underlay it. The chapter also looks at whether these arranged marriages were a success for the noblemen and gentlemen who received the Bennet portions. Part III, "Murder," addresses the murder of Grace Bennet. It examines the murder itself in 1694 and its wider context, Grace's relationship to her neighbors, family, and the changing economy. Grace opposed her minister's claim for tithes on newly developed land. At the same time her reputation for burying gold on her property attracted opprobrium as attitudes changed in favor of new forms of investment. Finally, stereotypes of elderly women may have stigmatized Grace living alone and trying to manage her estate after her husband's death.

Part IV, entitled "Metropolis," focuses on cosmopolitanism in London and on the continent. In four chapters it looks at the Bennet sisters, Frances and Grace the younger, after the murder of their mother. Chapter 7 examines Frances, Countess of Salisbury, before and after her marriage to the 4th Earl of Salisbury and in her early widowhood. It analyzes the four years between 1699 and 1703 that she spent in France, Italy, and the Low

Countries, where she went, what she saw, and who she met. It includes her visits to classical sites, Renaissance villas with painting and sculpture galleries, medieval and Baroque churches, and Roman gardens. She created a new aristocratic identity for herself although one English contemporary sniffed on her return that she was "Mighty Frenchified in her dress."[18]

Chapter 8 traces the parallel trip of her lover, George Jocelyn, who followed her for fifteen months in hopes of marrying her, and the chorus of contemporaries who commented on their romance. Chapter 9 turns its attention to her brother-in-law, John Bennet, who became deeply in debt after trying to improve his estate and went to debtors' prison in 1698. Chapter 10 follows both Frances, Countess of Salisbury and Grace Bennet the younger, her sister, whose husband was in prison, after they returned to London. It provides a glimpse of early Hanoverian London and the social life of these well-to-do single women. With Grace's death in 1732, the Bennet and Morewood property passed to her Salisbury heirs and other family members descended from the Cliftons. The Conclusion opens in 1738, during the final accounting of Grace Bennet's estate, and discusses two pictures by William Hogarth of the same year that surprisingly have connections to the Bennets.

VI Conclusion

Tracing the arc of fortune and the mosaic of family, *Women of Fortune* examines the social and economic challenges that faced entrepreneurs in merchant, gentry, and noble families, and their success and failure in meeting them between 1570 and 1732. It discusses the interconnection of land and trade, social and geographical mobility, political and religious diversity, and the centrality of London to both business and social lives. These central themes helped shape not only the lives of these families but also the history of the long seventeenth century itself.

The Bennet and Morewood family histories help us to understand what changed and what remained static for this London elite living through economic, cultural, and political change. Close ties between the landed elite and the City were maintained as families placed their sons as gentlemen apprentices late in the century. Arranged marriages continued late into the Restoration, despite the spread of companionate marriage, as portions grew in size because of increased trade to the East and West Indies and the New World. Luxury consumption produced a new infrastructure in London in the early seventeenth century and new forms of business appeared by mid-

---

[18] HMC, *Rutland*, Vol. II, p. 176, Lady Rachel Russell to Lady Granby at Belvoir Castle.

century in the forms of banks. By the end of the century, lotteries and shares sold on the London Stock Exchange were in place. The Bennet women took part in this new economy, as they had before as moneylenders, mortgagees, purchasers of real property, and plaintiffs and defendants defending their property. Now they also became investors in shares, depositors in banks, and buyers of lottery tickets. As widows they also chose to live in London rather than in the homes of their families or husbands.[19]

Furthermore, *Women of Fortune* illuminates the new opportunities available to elite women even as they continued to face legal structures and social pressure that tried unsuccessfully to set limits to their aspirations and independence. New forms of wealth, education, travel, and law enabled generations of new Bennet and Morewood heiresses to create their own identities in new ways. From Lady Elizabeth Finch in Kensington House to Anne, Viscountess Conway, the philosopher, to Frances, dowager Countess of Salisbury on the Grand Tour, to her sister Grace, the investor on Albemarle Street, the Bennets and their aunts and other kin, each sought the freedom and space to live their lives as they wished. How well they succeeded is the focus of this book.

---

[19] Barbara Harris points out that some late fifteenth-century widows also chose to live in London. Barbara J. Harris, *English Aristocratic Women 1450–1550: Marriage and Family, Property and Careers* (Oxford and New York: Oxford University Press, 2002).

PART I

Money

CHAPTER I

"The Great Man of Buckinghamshire:" The Lord Mayor, the Benefactor, and the Moneylender
The Bennets

How did you make a fortune in early modern England? The Bennet family began making their money by importing luxury textiles under Queen Elizabeth and then moved into Crown finance under James I. They later diversified into trade to Virginia and the East Indies, real estate, moneylending, and stocks. They spent their capital on country and city property, the largest of which was Kensington House, now Kensington Palace. One member of the family made the most important donation to University College, Oxford, since 1249. Most important, the Bennets invested in large marriage portions that ensured their entrée into the Stuart social elite in the seventeenth and early eighteenth centuries. Bennet women married into the aristocracy and nobility and charted paths of independence for themselves and their children. The Bennets' story reveals the world of trade, credit, consumption, and changing social roles in which they constructed their networks and relationships. This chapter opens with the founder of the Bennet fortune, a younger son of minor provincial gentry, Thomas Bennet, who became Lord Mayor of London in 1604.

Lord Mayors' funerals celebrated achievement in this life and sought salvation in the next. On March 22, 1627, a large procession wound its way from St. Olave Old Jewry to Cheapside, the greatest thoroughfare in the City of London and site of important public spectacles. Two conductors with black staves led formal groups of participants: eighty-six poor men in gowns, great City merchants and Crown financiers preceded by their servants in cloaks; City alderman and their wives; family mourners and Francis White, Bishop of Carlisle and Royal Almoner in his vestments. With penons raised, they escorted the body of Sir Thomas Bennet, mercer, alderman, and Lord Mayor, to his final rest in the Mercers' Chapel on the north side of Cheapside.

This splendid London funeral, a solemn City ritual for one of its much admired officials, displayed both the City elite and major elements of the Jacobean economy, the international cloth trade, the Crown's customs farms, court finance, and Asian and Atlantic ventures. The Elizabethan and Jacobean merchant aristocracy were present that day. Sir Baptist Hicks, the great supplier of luxury silks and large loans to the Crown and aristocracy; Sir Arthur Ingram, customs farmer, Crown financier, and Lionel Cranfield's associate in the cloth trade; and Sir Thomas Myddleton, a founder of the East India Company, Lord Mayor, and Member of Parliament in the 1620s. The one person who was missing was Lionel Cranfield himself. Cranfield, the cloth merchant who became a government advisor and ultimately Lord Treasurer and Earl of Middlesex, had been accused of corruption and impeached by parliament in 1624, King James' last parliament. Although on the verge of being pardoned in 1627, he remained on the margins of City and court life. A clutch of aldermen, who reflected Sir Thomas's long career serving alongside them, took part. Sir Heneage Finch, Recorder of the City of London and Speaker of the House of Commons, was there too.

Finally, the Bennet family and their relations followed the body displaying a network of City and judicial connections that the Bennets had created by strategic marriage alliances. The procession included George Lowe, the European cloth merchant, customs farmer, and alum projector who had married Sir Thomas Bennet's daughter Anne, and Sir George Croke, Justice of the Court of Common Pleas and soon to be Justice of the King's Bench, who had married his daughter Mary. Sir Thomas Bennet's four sons attended, including Simon who had married Elizabeth Ingram, the daughter of Sir Arthur Ingram, and Richard, who was married to Elizabeth Cradock. Unusually, there were two infant mourners, Sir Thomas Bennet's grandsons. One, named Thomas, was the son of Sir Thomas's youngest son John; he died before reaching adulthood. The other, Simon, became even wealthier than his grandfather.

Sir Thomas Bennet's funeral capped his very significant career in the cloth trade, City office, and Crown finance that founded the family fortune.[1] Yet Bennet was by no means the only younger son of minor gentry who successfully made his fortune in those years. As we shall see, it was a prosperous time for younger sons to go into business. English trade in the Mediterranean, the Baltic, Asia, and the New World grew dramatically in the late sixteenth and seventeenth centuries despite political conflict, Civil War, and sporadic battles with European neighbors.

The population of England almost doubled between 1541 and 1651 from 2,774,000 to 5,228,000. While many could not afford foreign goods,

---

[1] BL, Add. Mss. 71131E. The previous year Sir Thomas Bennet attended Sir William Cokayne's funeral, which was even larger. BL, Add. Mss. 71131D.

imports also doubled alongside the increase in population.[2] Members of the great livery companies such as the Mercers who traditionally dealt with cloth were not limited to these trades. Demand for imported goods from Europe and from Asia from the late sixteenth century on created new ventures, new markets, and new products. The Muscovy Company was founded in 1553 followed by the Levant Company in 1581 to trade with the Ottoman Empire. The East India Company in rivalry with the Dutch East India Company was founded in 1600. In addition, colonial trade to the West Indies and the North American colonies, dreamed of in the works of Richard Hakluyt and the projects of Sir Walter Raleigh, began to be realized. First, the Virginia Company undertook its plantations in the first decades of the seventeenth century, followed by projects for other North American tobacco colonies in the 1620s and 1630s. Barbados, claimed for King James, began to be worked by indentured servants. Jamaica, Barbados, and the Caribbean Islands plantations were transformed by the introduction of sugar and African slavery in the late 1640s and 1650s. To become a merchant in international trade opened the door not only to the traditional cloth trade but also to global enterprise. Domestic commerce and manufactures also increased across the century.

Bennet invested his fortune in more than the cloth trade. He embedded his family in social, economic, and political relationships that established it in the Stuart elite, in county society as well as in London. Richard Grassby points out the importance of marriage and inheritance to "capital accumulation."[3] It did even more. Over one hundred years of inherited wealth made in trade, real estate, and moneylending supported upwardly mobile marriages and philanthropy, education, travel, and consumption. The Bennet fortune enabled Bennet women to develop their own interests and assert their legal rights both as wives and as widows although not without a price.

The Lord Mayor

Sir Thomas Bennet was born in 1550 in Clapcot, Berkshire. He and his older brother Richard, both younger sons, were apprenticed to the Mercers' Company. Such apprenticeships were much sought after. After he became free of the company, his nephew, known as Thomas junior, became his apprentice, a member of the company in 1586 and, ultimately, an alderman and a knight himself.

[2] Christopher Clay, *Economic Expansion and Social Change: England 1500–1700*, 2 vols. (Cambridge: Cambridge University Press, 1984), Vol. I, p. 2.

[3] Richard Grassby, *The Business Community of Seventeenth-Century England* (Cambridge: Cambridge University Press, 1995), p. 267.

Elizabethans and Jacobeans loved luxurious textiles. Their portraits displayed their taste for rich silks, finely worked embroideries, deep velvets, and elaborate lace collars and cuffs. Sumptuary laws, which sought to limit luxury fabrics according to status, proved difficult to enforce and lapsed after 1604. Sir Thomas began to trade in cloth in the 1570s and, by the 1580s, was importing luxury textiles from Stade near Hamburg and Flushing in the Low Countries. Between 1587 and 1588, for instance, Sir Thomas imported silk sarcenet, grosgrain, velvet taffeta, camlets – originally costly Eastern fabric combining silk and camel or goats hair, silk and crepe from Cyprus called "sipers," Milan fustian, linen cloth, and buckram from Stade, altogether rated by the customs at £1,638-16-4. The next year he imported velvet, sipers, Holland cloth, "sisters thread," the name for the best-bleached thread, for a total value of £500-17-8.[4] In addition to his wholesale trade, Bennet may also have had a retail shop on Cheapside.[5] The last year in which Sir Thomas traded in cloth was 1604, the year he served as Lord Mayor.[6]

Bennet proved to be an especially civic-minded City official. Beginning in the 1590s, after more than twenty years as a cloth merchant, Bennet moved into City government, becoming alderman for Vintry in 1593/1594, sheriff in 1594/1595 and, later, alderman for Lime Street in 1603/1604 and for Bassishaw from 1611 to 1627. After serving as Lord Mayor in 1603/1604, King James knighted him. Well known for his charity and service to the city, Bennet served as president of Bridewell and Bethlehem Hospitals and patron of St. Bartholomew's Hospital. Plague repeatedly swept London while Bennet served as sheriff and mayor, and again in 1625 while he was alderman. His work on behalf of the capital was remembered in his 1627 funeral certificate, which recorded that "he remained the only father and protector of all the inhabitants of that city in all their extremity to his immortal praise."[7]

At the beginning of King James' reign, Bennet turned from the cloth trade to court finance. The symbiotic relationship between Crown, courtiers, and great City merchants became a feature of early Stuart administration. Several of the most successful cloth merchants turned from trade to customs

---

[4] Robert G. Lang, "The Greater Merchants of London in the Early Seventeenth Century" (unpublished D.Phil. thesis, Oxford University, 1963), p. 390, citing E190/7/8, E190/8/1, and E190/8/6.

[5] Ann F. Sutton, *The Mercery of London: Trade, Goods and People, 1130–1578* (Aldershot: Ashgate, 2005), pp. 470–471 and 471n.

[6] Lang, "The Greater Merchants of London," p. 151, Appendix B, Summaries of Entries in the London Port Books Relating to the Trade of the Merchants in the Sample: pp. 386ff., 390. Imports Mich. 1587 to Mich. 1588 (E190/7/8 and E190/8/1); Imports July 1, 1589 to Mich. 1589 (E190/8/6).

[7] G. E. Cokayne, *Some Account of the Lord Mayors and Sheriffs of the City of London during the First Quarter of the Seventeenth Century* (London: Phillimore and Co., 1897), pp. 16–18.

farming. Forming syndicates that took over the administration of the Crown's revenue on wine, textiles, and other commodities, they paid rent to the Crown for the privilege. The Crown relied on wealthy merchants for short-term loans, while the merchants profited from the privatization of royal authority, the transfer to them of royal power to collect duties, taxes, rents, and fees. George Lowe, Sir Thomas's son-in-law, was among the merchants who had made money in the cloth trade who wanted to become a customs farmer.[8] The very lucrative customs farms created a secondary market in which people bought and sold shares. Sir Thomas held a twenty-fourth share of the French and Rhenish wine farm worth £300; he sold half and kept half for himself.[9]

Crown finance allowed Bennet to diversify his wealth. With his capital from the cloth trade, Bennet joined Sir Arthur Ingram in loaning money to the Crown and, with Lionel Cranfield he took part in the sale of Crown lands between 1607 and 1614. On June 13, 1609, for instance, Bennet was listed as one of the General Contractors for Crown lands along with other leading merchants including Cranfield, Sir Baptist Hicks, and Sir William Cockayne as well as Sir Thomas Lake, the Secretary of State. Bennet invested £3,000 while Cranfield put in £11,000, Lake, £10,000, and Cockayne, £1,100. Together with others, they invested a total of £67,000.[10] Bennet put £500 of the Crown lands in his son Simon's name.[11]

Credit was a key element in the early modern economy. In the absence of a banking system, merchants often lent their surplus capital at interest. Sir Thomas Bennet provided loans to the Crown, to Ingram and Cranfield, noblemen and noblewomen, and other merchants. In 1613 Bennet was one of six aldermen who were willing to lend King James £2,000 despite a delay in the Crown's repayment of the royal loan of 1610.[12] Bennet also provided credit to the wine farm. Charles Howard, Earl of Nottingham, had the royal grant of the custom duties on wine imports that Cranfield and other merchants administered for him. In 1607 Cranfield endorsed as "notes of great importance" a reckoning between himself and William Massam on the one hand and James Cullimore on the other. It showed "the sums to be

---

[8] Hatfield House Archives, General 101/14. G. Lowe & Co. to Richard Bennet, at Antwerp. Lowe wrote to his partner Richard Bennet that he was breaking off their business to undertake "the great farm" of the customs.

[9] Robert Ashton, *The Crown and the Money Market* (Oxford: Clarendon Press, 1960), p. 87.

[10] HMC, *Sackville*, Vol. I, *Cranfield Papers, 1551–1612*, p. 182; Lang, "The Greater Merchants of London," pp. 310, 313.

[11] HMC, *Sackville*, Vol. I, *Cranfield Papers*, p. 185, March 13, 1609–1610.

[12] Ashton, *The Crown and the Money Market*, p. 121n.

charged upon and paid out of the wine account for moneys borrowed and interest due to Sir Thomas Bennet and others."[13]

Sir Thomas Bennet reinforced his close relationship with Sir Arthur Ingram with the marriage of his son Simon to Elizabeth, Sir Arthur's daughter (see Plate 1). Elizabeth brought Simon a £6,000 portion, twice the size of his sister Mary Bennet's portion. Elizabeth's portrait, *c.* 1620, displays her as well-to do, with a beautiful deep lace collar and cuffs on her black dress, a broad brimmed hat with a handsome feather, sitting in an oversize rich red velvet chair. She wears a long double rope of pearls and a shorter diamond or emerald pendant set in gold. Her long earrings have fashionable black ribbons. She resembles a rich merchant's wife more than a Jacobean court lady.[14]

Sir Thomas consistently provided Ingram with substantial financial support. When Ingram needed to pay Robert Cecil, Earl of Salisbury, who held the patent on the customs on silk, Sir Thomas Bennet provided 70 percent of the £1,000 Ingram needed. Ingram wrote to Lionel Cranfield: "If you can with the rest of my good friends make up ... the full £1,000, you may much pleasure me. If you care not to make up Sir Thomas Bennet's £700 ... send me word." In 1611 Ingram wrote to Cranfield just after his son died. "I am not willing to come from Bow as yet, whereby I am deprived of my means to supply my lord of Salisbury his occasions, except it may stand with your great good favour to supply my credit which is deeply in this action engaged to my lord ... Sir Thomas Bennet hath promised me £700."[15] Bennet's financial relationship with Sir Arthur Ingram appears most fully in the case of Sir Edward Grevile, who bought Crown lands and owed Sir Thomas Bennet £10,000. Ingram leveraged Grevile's debts to Bennet to marry Grevile's daughter Mary as his third wife in 1615 and to take over Grevile's estate while paying off Bennet.[16]

Prominent aristocratic women also borrowed money from Sir Thomas Bennet and sometimes used their London furnishings to secure their loans. Thus, Dame Grissell Woodroffe, the widow of Sir Nicholas Woodroffe, Lord Mayor of London and MP, sold the wainscot, glass, and other movables in a property near Brooke Street to Sir Thomas. Lady Mary Chandois

---

[13] HMC, *Sackville*, Vol. I, *Cranfield Papers*, pp. 97–98.

[14] Compare, for instance, contemporary portraits of the Countess of Somerset and the Countess of Arundel.

[15] HMC, *Sackville*, Vol. I, *Cranfield Papers*, p. 235, Ingram to Cranfield. Bennet also loaned £1,000 to Edward Ducket, a mercer. BL, Add. Charter 6221, Bond of Edward Duckett, Mercer of London, to Thomas Bennet, 1615.

[16] Anthony F. Upton, *Sir Arthur Ingram, c. 1565–1642* (Oxford: Oxford University Press, 1961), pp. 157–158, Aug. 24, 13 James I [1615]. ODNB, "Sir Arthur Ingram."

conveyed the furniture of her house in Brooke Street Stepney to him as security for a debt.[17] Some transactions did not end happily. Bennet served as trustee of one-quarter of Sherfield manor for Lady Dorothy Wharton who had inherited it from her father.[18] Lady Dorothy and her husband Philip, Lord Wharton, sued Sir Thomas over manors conveyed to Bennet for money she had borrowed.

In addition to using his capital to lend money to the Crown and the aristocracy, Sir Thomas also invested in property. As Richard Grassby has pointed out, well-to-do seventeenth-century businessmen diversified their holdings and Sir Thomas Bennet was no exception.[19] Real estate investment allowed merchants not only to reallocate their assets but also to invest in properties in the City that were increasing in value, in suburbs in the east or west, or a manor in the neighboring shires. Some merchants returned to their gentry roots or created them. Sir Thomas Bennet invested in property both in London where he lived and in the country. But he did not return to the county of his birth.

Sir Thomas owned a house in St. Olave Old Jewry and had property in St. Martin Ludgate, St. Clement Danes, on Brock Street in Stepney, and Grays Inn Fields. He also owned property in Shelton, Norfolk, Selston, Nottinghamshire, and Salton, Sinnington, and Marton in Yorkshire.[20] Bennet did not always accumulate property through purchase. In 1624 Lord Eure agreed to transfer Salton to him for the debts owing from Lord Eure's father. Because Eure was a recusant, King James served as an intermediary granting Bennet the manor, prebend, and rectory.[21]

Sir Thomas also bought new country houses for two of his sons. Sir Thomas purchased Beachampton and Calverton in Buckinghamshire, which he settled on his son Simon.[22] For his son Richard, he purchased the sixteenth-century manor and manor house of Broad Marston in Pebworth, Gloucestershire, in 1622.[23] Sir Thomas continued to live in the City.

---

[17] Hatfield House Archives, Deeds 74/7, 1604; Deeds 106/20, 1606. Possibly Mary Baroness Chandos of Sudeley, widow of William Brydges, 4th Baron Chandos.
[18] Bodleian, Oxford Ms. Eng. Hist c478/f. 8–9, Lady Wharton to her cousin Sir William Heyricke, Nov. 26, 1617; TNA, C3/390/76, Wharton v. Bennet, Lord Philip Wharton, knight, Dame Dorothy Wharton and others v. Sir Thomas Bennet and Richard Bennet, 1621.
[19] Grassby, *The Business Community of Seventeenth-Century England*, pp. 265–268.
[20] VCH, Nottingham, Vol. II, p. 75; VCH, *York North Riding*, Vol. II, pp. 489–490; VCH, *York North Riding*, Vol. I, p. 552. Lang, "The Greater Merchants of London," p. 433. TNA, C 142/435/116, Sir Thomas Bennet, Inquisition Post Mortem, 1627–1628.
[21] *CSPD, 1623–1625*, p. 299. VCH, *York North Riding*, Vol. I, p. 552, "Salton."
[22] VCH, *Buckingham*, Vol. IV, pp. 149–153, 308–311.
[23] Historic England, Broad Marston Manor, List Entry 1350112.

In his major study of Jacobean aldermen, Robert Lang estimates that Sir Thomas Bennet left an estate of £24,000 in movables besides his real estate. While he was not as wealthy as Sir Baptist Hicks and Sir John Spencer, and the fewer than ten great Jacobean aldermen who left estates worth between £50,000 and £125,000, Bennet ranked in the top twenty-four of Lang's sample of 140 aldermen who served between 1600 and 1624.[24]

Sir Thomas married Mary Taylor, daughter of Robert Taylor who was also a member of the Mercers' Company (see Plate 2). Her *c.* 1590 portrait by the Netherlands artist Hieronymus Custodis shows Lady Bennet wearing a fashionable vest embroidered with the kind of silks imported by the mercers and holding a dog, symbol of loyalty. Sir Thomas and Lady Bennet used education and marriage to ensure that their children and grandchildren became part of a larger Stuart elite that incorporated those who had made their fortunes in land and trade. The couple provided university educations for their sons, all four of whom went to Oxford, and made socially advantageous marriages for their children and grandchildren that in some cases linked their family to the nobility and to the royal court.

The Bennets had two daughters. Anne married first William Duncombe, a member of the Haberdashers' company, and second, George Lowe. Anne's daughter Mary married Sir Ralph Dutton. A younger son with his own estate, Dutton was knighted in 1624, the year of his marriage, and was later named a gentleman of Charles I's Privy Chamber.[25] Sir Thomas's younger daughter Mary married George Croke in 1610, then a highly regarded and well-to-do Inner Temple lawyer. Knighted in 1623, Croke later became one of the Justices of the King's Bench who voted against King Charles in the Ship Money Case in 1637. Sir Thomas provided Mary with a portion of £3,000.[26]

Sir Thomas Bennet's emotional world was geographically broad and generationally rich. In his will he remembered more than fifty people, three London hospitals, and three London prisons. Marked by legacies that went considerably beyond his nuclear family, Sir Thomas provided gifts for sisters and their children, in-laws and their children, extended cousins and their children, and servants, employees, and artisans. For instance, Bennet left £40 to his nephew Anthony Burt, a carrier of Worcester; £13-6-8 to William Bennet of Moulford, Berkshire, a bargeman, who lived close to Sir Thomas's ancestral home; and £5 to James the Joyner "that wainscoted my little parlor."

[24] Lang, "The Greater Merchants of London," pp. 30, 285–286.
[25] Gloucestershire County Council, D678/1 F3/1–5. Sir Thomas Bennet, his son Simon, and George Lowe provided his granddaughter's prenuptial and jointure guarantees.
[26] TNA, PROB11/151/286, Will of Sir Thomas Bennet, Alderman of Saint Olave Old Jewry, City of London, Feb. 20, 1627.

After an optimistic statement of his belief in his salvation and request to be buried next to his wife in the Mercers' Chapel, Bennet turned to his sons, daughters, and grandchildren. Since his wife predeceased him, he divided his personal estate in two according to the custom of London. One-half was divided among his four sons to ensure that each received £3,000. If the estate proved larger, Sir Thomas's daughter Mary, who had already received her £3,000 on her marriage to George Croke, would share equally with her brothers in any additional money. Because Sir Thomas had spent £500 on building, furniture, and plate at Beachampton, Buckinghamshire, which he gave to his son Simon, it would be deducted from Simon's share. Similarly, he had made a £1,000 loan to his son Richard that would be subtracted from his portion.

Bennet left legacies to his daughters' families. He left £100 to his deceased daughter Anne's husband, George Lowe, and £250 more to Anne and George Lowe's son. He left £66-13s-4d to Anne's daughters and £50 apiece to her grandchildren. He provided £200 each to his daughter Mary and her husband, Justice Croke, and £200 each to their four daughters. All of the children were to receive their inheritance when they were 21. As he recalled family and friends, Bennet returned to two of his sons. He added another £500 each to Ambrose and John Bennet. For John's baby son Thomas, his godson, Sir Thomas left £20 "towards the placing of him an apprentice to such a trade or profession as he shallbe found most fittest." He also remembered his godson Thomas Dale.

Bennet's will is marked by charity and hospitality. He left £5 for his parish priest, Thomas Tuke, a moderate puritan, whose sermons were influenced by William Perkins. He provided legacies for three hospitals, Christ Church, St. Thomas in Southwark, and Bridewell, and three City prisons, Newgate, the Counters in Wood Street, and Poultry. Finally, Sir Thomas left money for dinners at the three hospitals (£13-16-6 each), as well as at St. Olave's (£15) and at the Mercers' Company (£40) on the day of his funeral.

In a codicil to his will a year later, Sir Thomas sorted out his real estate. Two of his sons, Ambrose and Simon, were childless. Sir Thomas sought to consolidate most of his real estate in the hands of Simon and Richard and Richard's son Simon, the toddler who attended Sir Thomas's funeral. At the same time, he made sure that if that young boy did not survive, other heirs, particularly his youngest son John's children, including young Thomas, who had also attended the funeral, might inherit. In addition, he gave or confirmed land to Ambrose and John and his grandsons George Lowe and Thomas Croke. Finally, he confirmed his gift of the Bennet home and land in St. Olave Old Jewry to Richard Bennet and his heirs.[27] While a nobleman

[27] TNA, PROB11/151/286.

might create an entail, this wealthy merchant placed his hopes in his very elaborate will and codicil.

Sir Thomas Bennet had acted none too soon. By the early 1630s all of his sons were dead. Ambrose died unmarried in 1631. John, the youngest, became a rich merchant with a house on Barge Court, Bucklersbury, near Cheapside, but died in 1632. John's son Thomas died young, but his younger son John established his family as country gentry with court connections in Cambridgeshire.[28] Another of John's sons, Ambrose, spent several years in Virginia.

The Mercer

Richard Bennet became a mercer and cloth trader like his father after attending Merton College, Oxford. He married Elizabeth Cradock, daughter of William Cradock of Stafford, Sir Baptist Hick's cloth factor in Hamburg. In the 1620s, as his business interests broadened, he began to look to Asia and the New World for new goods. He traded to the East Indies and became a member of the Virginia Company.[29] While investing in the East India Company, he hedged his risk with contracts struck with other investors such as the grocer Edmund Scott. Scott sued Richard's widow Elizabeth over such an agreement in the 1630s.[30] At his death Bennet's warehouse held over 100 pounds of tobacco, the product of his trading with Virginia or elsewhere in the Americas.[31]

Richard died shortly after his father, Sir Thomas Bennet, in 1628. The Inquisition Post Mortem taken at Gloucester Castle that year reveals Richard's expansive real estate holdings, many inherited from his father, others the family's city and country homes. Richard was in the midst of expanding his father's house in St. Olave Old Jewry and his own manor house at Broad Marston. Even today Broad Marston retains its handsome Jacobean staircase, mullioned windows and ceiling beams.[32] The manor of Broad Marston, a hamlet in Pebworth, Gloucestershire, contained 100 acres of pasture, and Richard had also purchased Pebworth's rectory. In London, in addition to the family property in St. Olave Old Jewry, he had property in Candlewick

---

[28] Cokayne, *Some Account of the Lord Mayors and Sheriffs of the City of London*, pp. 16–18.

[29] Hatfield House Archives, Legal 29/21b; Bills 107, 1617; Legal 38/4, 52/10, 237/11, 1620.

[30] Hatfield House Archives, Legal 124/12, Bill of Complaint of E. Scott as to transaction with Richard Bennet in an East Indian Adventure; E. Scott *v.* Dame Elizabeth Finch, 1632.

[31] TNA, E199/28/40, London and Middlesex Schedule of Goods of Richard Bennet, 22 James I. In Shelton and Thorpe he had "10 messuages, 10 cottages, 50 acres of land, 100 acres of meadow, 200 acres of pasture, and 20 acres of wood."

[32] *New York Times*, March 3, 2016.

now Cannon Street. In the country, Richard owned the Calverton and Stony Stratford properties in Buckinghamshire, which his father had purchased. He also held land in Deanshanger and Passenham, in Northamptonshire, and the manor of Shelton and Thorpe, Nottinghamshire, with 370 acres of land, meadow, pasture, and wood and ten cottages. In addition, he had 20 acres of woods in Hasler parish, Warwickshire.

Richard's will of 1627 left his young son Simon his lands in Calverton, Deanshanger, Passenham, and Shelton, his tenement near London, and "dwelling house" in St. Olave in Old Jewry. He gave his wife Elizabeth the two tenements being built next to his house until Simon was 24. Should she remarry, the profits were to go to Simon. During her widowhood, Richard gave Elizabeth his "mansion house of Broad Marston with all its lands," woods, and the rectory and parsonage at Pebworth. After her death or remarriage, all were to go to Simon. Significantly, three-quarters of the lands in Broad Marston were held by knight's service. Therefore, Simon, aged 3 years and 11 months, became a royal ward and heir to a future fortune.[33] Richard left one-third of his estate to Elizabeth, and made her his executor, supervisor of his son's education, and a very wealthy widow.

The Benefactor

Richard's older brother, Sir Simon Bennet, was not a City merchant but a country gentleman. He continued his father's philanthropy but on a grander scale. Sir Simon attended University College, Oxford, married Elizabeth Ingram, and was made a baronet a few months after Sir Thomas's funeral in 1627. Sir Simon emphasized his ties to his sisters and brothers-in-laws and his father in law, Sir Arthur Ingram, in his 1631 will. He provided £100 to be divided among "twenty poor maids that have dwelt in my house or in Beachampton or in Calverton for five years" after their marriages providing his executor, overseers, or the ministers of Beachampton and Calverton approved their matches.[34] The property Sir Simon had inherited from his father was already designated for his nephew, young Simon Bennet.

But Sir Simon wished to make a major donation of his own. In 1630 he paid King Charles £6,000 for Handley Park, 863 acres of royal forest in Whittlewood, Northamptonshire. With the income, timber, and capital

---

[33] TNA, Court of Wards, WARD 7/77/75; Inquisition Post Mortem, Richard Bennet: Gloucester, 4 Charles I, *Abstracts of Gloucestershire inquisitions post mortem in the reign of Charles I*, part 4 no. 80, Vol. 9 (London: British Record Society, 1893–1914), pp. 89–91.

[34] Centre for Buckinghamshire Studies, PR13/25/4, Copy of probate of will of Sir Simon Bennet of Beachampton, Baronet, Aug. 15, 1631; TNA, PROB11/160/369, Sir Simon Bennet's will.

from this large property, Sir Simon proposed to endow University College, Oxford, with new scholarships, new fellowships, and new buildings.[35] University College, a small and poor if ancient Oxford college, had long wanted to expand, like all colleges then and now. Efforts under Master John Bancroft, later Bishop of Oxford, twenty years earlier had gone for naught.[36] Sir Simon left Handley Park to his wife Elizabeth, his executor, for her lifetime with reversion to University College. He made Sir Arthur Ingram, his father-in-law, and Sir George Croke, his brother-in-law, the trustees of his gift. Sir Simon's donation was on a grand scale. With one gesture he increased the college's income by 40 percent. One twentieth-century commentator writes that it was "much the richest benefaction made to the college since 1249, producing over three times as much as any other single endowment and increasing our annual revenue by something between one-third and one-half."[37]

Beginning in 1634, the overjoyed College commissioned architectural models for the new buildings. They held several timber sales of Handley Park oak and rented out the property using the proceeds to begin to build a new hall, chapel, and the main quadrangle. The latter had cost more than £5,200 by 1642, "of which all but £1800 came from Handley timber."[38] This significant legacy, however, was made conditional by his executor Elizabeth, Lady Bennet, on the college's naming the buildings "Sir Simon Bennet's Lodgings and Hall." The college agreed. In his will Sir Simon had been vague about the number of scholarships and fellowships to be established. The trustees of the gift, led in the 1630s and early 1640s by Sir Arthur Ingram and Sir George Croke after the death of Lady Bennet, raised the question of the number of Bennet scholars and fellows, the amount of rent to be had from Handley Park for their support, and their relationship to the eight old foundation fellows.[39]

[35] TNA, Letters Patent to Sir Simon Bennet, Chief Justice of the Forests South of the Trent, Handley within the Forest, Whittlewood Forest, Northamptonshire and Buckinghamshire, March 27, 1629–March 26, 1630.

[36] Nicholas Tyacke, *The History of the University of Oxford*, Vol. IV, *Oxford in the Seventeenth Century* (Oxford: Oxford University Press, 1997); University College Archives, "Oxford Main Buildings," www.univ.ox.ac.uk/college_building/main-quad/ [accessed August 18, 2016].

[37] A. D. M. Cox, "Handley Park," *University College Record*, 6, 1 (1971), p. 57.

[38] Robin Darwall-Smith, *The History of University College, Oxford* (Oxford: Oxford University Press, 2008), pp. 157–173, "Oxford Main Buildings." I am grateful to Robin Darwall-Smith for discussion of the Bennet benefaction and the online catalog of the Handley Wood estate and University College Archives.

[39] TNA, SP16/281, f. 143, "Considerations touching the settlement of Sir Simon Bennett's foundation in University College, Oxford," [undated]; University College Archives, UC: P164/ L2/1, n.d. (late 1630s or early 1640s?), Memorandum from the trustees of Sir Simon Bennet's will on how the land at Handley Park is to be leased, and how it should support eight Fellows and

In 1640, in the midst of political crisis between King Charles and parliament, the college turned to Archbishop Laud who advised that four fellowships and scholarships were the prudent number and the rent from Handley Park should be set at £350 a year. Some trustees, however, wanted to increase the rent to £400 or £500 to support eight Bennet scholars and fellows, with half allocated to Bennet kin or associates. Meanwhile, the guardians of young Simon Bennet, presumably his mother Elizabeth, Lady Finch, and Francis Finch, questioned the benefaction itself. They refused to turn over the property until forced to do so by a court decree in 1639.[40]

During the 1630s the college continued to build, providing the chapel with painted glass windows along Arminian lines and planning its Gothic quadrangle even as it engaged in litigation with the Bennet family and its trustees. With the advent of the Civil War, however, the college stopped building and did not fill the Bennet fellowships at all. In response, William Herbert, Earl of Pembroke, Lord Chancellor of the University of Oxford, wrote in the strongest terms to the college in 1648 that they had failed to fulfill their duty under the terms of the gift. He called it "a great scandal not only upon your particular society but the university also, and a general discouragement to all persons charitably affected, to see so bountiful and eminent a gift so much abused."[41] In 1649 the Court of Chancery decided for the Bennet trustees. Parliament put in a new master who increased the rent on Handley Park and doubled the number of Bennet fellows and scholars to eight each with half reserved for Bennet kin.[42] The Bennets responded by sending letters of recommendation on behalf of relatives and friends for Bennet fellowships.[43]

At the Restoration, the Master of University College sued again and the number of scholars and fellows were reduced and settled once more at four each for fellows and scholars.[44] The College completed its new quadrangle

eight Scholars, with four of the Scholars and Fellows selected from Bennet's kin. UC: P164/L2/2, n.d. (late 1630s or early 1640s?); Case concerning Sir Simon Bennet's will, in which his trustees set out their proposals for eight Fellows and eight Scholars to be supported by his foundation, with four of the Scholars and Fellows selected from Bennet's kin; UC: P164/L2/3; n.d. (late 1630s or early 1640s?); Draft proposals for the execution of Sir Simon Bennet's foundation, up to ten Fellows and ten Scholars.

[40] Darwall-Smith, *History of University College*, p. 161. University College Archives, UC: E14/L1, lawsuit between University College and the trustees of Bennet's will, 1637–1639; UC: E14/L2, lawsuit between University College and the guardians of Simon Bennet the younger, 1638–1639.

[41] Darwall-Smith, *History of University College*, p. 173; UC: MA26/C1/3.

[42] Darwall-Smith, *History of University College*, p. 173; UC: E14/L5, 1649, settlement of the Bennet Estate, 1647–1650.

[43] Darwall-Smith, *History of University College*, p. 173.

[44] Darwall-Smith, *History of University College*, p. 184.

with handsome buildings now facing the High Street. Although the college did not name the new buildings "Sir Simon Bennet's Lodgings and Hall," one side of the quadrangle was named for the donor and a small portrait of Sir Simon Bennet hangs in the Hall. Two Bennet relations, Ambrose and Thomas Bennet, held fellowships in the later seventeenth century. Ambrose managed Handley Park before leaving abruptly for Jamaica and, later, Virginia, while the cleric Thomas Bennet, descended from Sir Thomas Bennet's youngest son John, became Master of the college in 1691 before dying in office a year later.[45] By the later twentieth century, Sir Simon Bennet's gift was still one of the three largest in the history of University College.[46]

The Moneylender

Sir Simon's nephew and namesake, young Simon Bennet, was rich and well connected. Born in 1624, as a three-year-old he had attended his grandfather's funeral in London in his nurse's arms. In 1628 his father died and, a year later, his mother Elizabeth married Sir Heneage Finch, Speaker of the House of Commons. (Her lively courtship, marriage, and family life are discussed in Chapter 3.) Because Simon became a royal ward when he inherited land held directly from the king, the young boy was an attractive financial commodity. Charles I granted his wardship to Walter Steward (c. 1586–1649) who then assigned it to two other courtiers, Sir Richard Wynn, the Queen's Treasurer, and Sir William Uvedale, Treasurer of the Privy Chamber. Simon's mother Elizabeth, now Lady Finch, had to purchase his wardship from Walter Steward and his assignees at a cost of £4,000.[47]

Sir Heneage Finch joined Lady Finch as Simon's guardian until his death in 1631. His brother, Francis Finch, then took his place with the consent of the Court of Wards. Simon's education differed from that of his Finch stepbrothers and sisters. Heneage, Francis, and John Finch went to Oxford and Cambridge as teenagers. Heneage later practiced law and began his judicial career, while John studied medicine and became a diplomat. Frances and Anne were educated at home. In contrast, Simon entered Lincoln's Inn on January 29, 1646, at the age of twenty-two.[48]

---

[45] University College Archives, UC: MA32/L1/1.
[46] Cox, *University College Record*, Vol. 6,1 (1971), p.63. The college held on to Handley Woods until 1971.
[47] Hatfield House Archives, Deeds 160/21, Assignment by W. Steward to Sir R. Wynn and Sir W. Uvedale of wardship and marriage of Simon Bennet, 1628.
[48] *The Records of the Honorable Society of Lincoln's Inn ... Admissions Register*, Vol. I, *Admissions from 1420–1799* ([London] Lincoln's Inn: Printed by H. S. Cartwright, 1896), p. 252.

Figure 1.1 Monument to Simon Bennet, Beachampton, Buckinghamshire, 1680s, by Jasper Latham? Photograph by A. F. Kersting, H 14111. The Conway Library, The Courtauld Institute of Art, London. The funeral monument with its lengthy inscription was paid for with the proceeds of a bad debt.

Simon's accounts along with other evidence shed light on his business, his marriage, his investments, and his politics. Simon had a fortune to look after when he came of age. He was not only his father's heir but also his uncle's. Sir Heneage and Lady Finch provided sureties that they would provide Simon with his legacy and an account of his estate.[49] To that end, they sued the philanthropist Sir Simon Bennet over Sir Thomas Bennet's will. At issue was whether or not as executor Sir Simon was collecting outstanding debts, providing the appropriate share to young Simon, and rendering them a proper account.[50] When Sir Simon Bennet died in 1631, young Simon inherited his fortune and his house in Beachampton, Buckinghamshire, originally purchased by his grandfather, Sir Thomas Bennet.

[49] LMA, Orphans Deeds 33 CLA/002/04/033.
[50] TNA, C3/402/53, Finch *v.* Bennet, Sir Heneage Finch and Dame Elizabeth Finch *v.* Sir Simon Bennet re personal estate of Sir Thomas Bennet, 1631 or before.

Until 1645 Simon was both a royal ward and, as the son of a London merchant, a London orphan whose estate was administered by the Court of Orphans. His mother, Lady Finch, had to pay rent to the king on Simon's lands while he was a minor. In 1645 she sued a group of merchants, who held her bond, to pay the requisite monies into the Court of Wards. Three well-known City merchants, William Courten, Sir Edward Littleton, and David Goubard "stand bound to the said petitioner in the sum of two thousand pounds for the payment of one thousand and forty pounds at a day now past the better to secure the debt of one thousand pounds and more which the said petitioner oweth and is indebted to his Majesty for the rents of the lands of Symon Bennet his Majesty's ward." Lady Finch petitioned the court to accept the bond for her payment, which it did.[51] That same year, when Simon turned twenty-one, he sued his mother to be removed from wardship.

Two years later he demanded an accounting of his inheritance. Even in his early twenties, Simon Bennet was acutely aware of the extent of his fortune and took steps to gain control of it. Although Lady Finch had actively tried to safeguard Simon's estate while he was a minor through lawsuits against Sir Simon Bennet and University College, Oxford, Simon now insisted on an accounting from his mother and Francis Finch.[52] "Coming above two years ago to full age of twenty-one years, and having as yet no accompt from his said guardians of diverse and great sums of money that he conceives to be due to him which they have received during his minority, he himself presents to his said guardians his demands."

Sir Thomas Bennet had left his family a personal estate of £24,000 when he died in 1627. Simon's "demands" reveal that he had inherited an even larger personal fortune from four of his Bennet kin, his father, two uncles, and an aunt. Simon claimed an annual income of over £2,145 a year from real estate and a personal estate of £31,941-19-11.[53] This estate was made up of several income streams. To begin with, Simon was entitled to one-third of his father's personal property amounting to £4,186-14-11 from the time of his father's death sixteen years earlier. Simon's father also left him £500 a year. After sixteen years that now totaled £8,000. His uncle, Sir Simon Bennet, left young Simon £1,500 a year. After paying rent to the king, Simon netted £820 a year, which after fourteen years now amounted to £11,480. Simon's uncle Ambrose left him a legacy of £170 a year that after

[51] University of Nottingham Mss., Clifton Papers, Cl L252, 1, 4, Trinity Term, 21 Charles I, 1645, Court of Wards and Liveries; TNA E44/484, Assignment of an obligation by Lady Elizabeth Finch of Kensington, widow, June 13.

[52] Hatfield House Archives, Legal 247/10.   [53] Hatfield House Archives, Legal 247/10.

fourteen years equaled £2,380. His aunt Elizabeth, Lady Bennet, left him £655 a year, which after nine years provided Simon with another £5,895. In addition, the Court of Wards had ruled that he was entitled to 4 percent a year interest on all the income that his guardians had received on his behalf over the past sixteen, fourteen, and nine years. With interest on his capital Simon's inheritance might have added up to as much as £47,329.[54]

To put Simon's inheritance in perspective, in the middle of the seventeenth century, the median amount a testator might leave was well under £200, and forty years later Gregory King estimated a temporal lord had an income of £2,800 a year.[55] Simon's guardians' accounts have not survived. His fortune, which had been made by his grandfather and father in international trade and court finance between 1570 and 1628, was, by 1647, now invested in land, rents, houses, leases, and loans.

Simon ended on a conciliatory note, asked his guardians for a fair accounting without resort to the law, expressed his willingness to accept amendments, and hoped that they would not blame him for making these claims. "This demandant having for a year and a half and above with all respective patience expected an accompt, and though it hath been often desired by the friends of this demandant of his guardians yet he nor they have not as yet received any accompt at all, and that delay hath forced this demandant to make these demands as aforesaid."[56] Whether his guardians had been able to collect all the income detailed by Simon; whether they were able to deduct expenses such as living costs or the cost of his wardship; and whether Sir Simon's legacy had declined because of his bequest to University College, it is not clear how much money Simon actually received. Nevertheless, Simon Bennet's inheritance was indeed very substantial.

Two years later, on the eve of his marriage in 1649, Simon and his mother, Elizabeth, reached an agreement to release each other from further accounting and suits in regard to his inheritance. The indenture dated October 20, 1649 showed that Simon had already taken up residence at Sir Simon's former house at Beachampton, Buckinghamshire. He had inherited land from his father in Gloucestershire, Nottinghamshire, Norwich, the City of London, and Calverton, Buckinghamshire, as well as manors in Yorkshire. "For the love and affection that he oweth and beareth unto her, as also for that she the said Lady Finch out of her tender love and

---

[54] I am grateful for discussions of interest and annuities with Stanley G. Engerman.

[55] Stephen Broadberry, *British Economic Growth 1270–1870* (Cambridge: Cambridge University Press, 2015), pp. 296–297; Gregory King, "Natural and Political Observations upon the State and Condition of England, 1696," in *Two tracts by Gregory King*, ed. G. E. Barnett (Baltimore: John Hopkins University Press, 1936).

[56] Hatfield House Archives, Legal 247/10.

affection to him . . . hath released him by deed . . . all and every sum that she may any way claim of him upon his marriage of otherwise," he released her of all the sums or accounts owing for Richard Bennet's estate.[57] A few days later, Lady Finch signed a similar release.[58] Nevertheless, Simon sued his mother and Francis Finch over lands in Calverton and Beachampton and Yorkshire in 1650.

In 1648, just as Simon Bennet came into his inheritance, the political world around him exploded. The outbreak of the second Civil War, the political role of the New Model Army, the continuing agitation by the Levelers, and Pride's Purge at the end of the year set the stage for the trial and execution of Charles I in January 1649. Simon's account book for the period 1648–1650 sheds light not only on his business but on his activities in London as it was convulsed with political fervor. Simon's earliest accounts begin in 1648 and show the young businessman buying newsletters and books that sprang from the press in a London no longer fettered by censorship. Politically he accepted office under the Commonwealth, while his Finch stepbrothers were royalists or traveling abroad. Simon moved regularly from Beachampton to his chambers in Lincoln's Inn and to Kensington where his mother lived. His accounts are otherwise frustratingly silent on politics, yielding only rents collected, loans made, and lawsuits filed.

The Marriage of Simon Bennet and Grace Morewood

In the months after the execution of Charles I in 1649, Simon Bennet met and married Grace Morewood, the pretty daughter of Gilbert Morewood, an East India Company merchant. In October of that year, he took a coach to Mr. Morewood's "about perusing the writings."[59] Gilbert Morewood offered Simon a handsome £6,000 portion. In exchange Simon settled on Grace his two Buckinghamshire manors, Beachampton and Calverton, with nearby Stony Stratford and its fairs, markets, and fishing on the Ouse, which Sir Thomas Bennet had originally purchased.[60]

Simon and Grace married on October 20, 1649, at St. Bartholomew the Less. Despite puritan emphasis on simplicity in the new Republic, Simon's accounts show large amounts of money spent on gifts to the bride, ribbons, trumpeters,

[57] Hatfield House Archives, Deed 89/20, Simon Bennet's release for Lady Finch, Oct. 20, 1649.
[58] Hatfield House Archives, Deed 152/9, Lady Finch's release for Simon Bennet, Oct. 25, 1649.
[59] Hatfield House Archives, Accounts 139/3, Oct. 12, 1649.
[60] Hull University Archives, Brynmor Jones Library, Papers of the Forbes Adam/Thompson/Lawley (Barons Wenlock) Family of Escrick U DDFA2/24/1, Marriage Settlement: Symon Benet of Beachampton, co. Bucks. esq. (son and heir of Richard B. of London dec'd) to Gilbert Morewood of London esq. of Symon Benet and Grace Morewood, daughter of Gilbert, Oct. 9, 1649.

and a banquet at Kensington House, the Finch family home. The confectioner charged £23. Ribbons, ribbons, and more ribbons festooned the wedding and the wedding party: 250 yards of silver ribbon for £43-15, 206 more yards of ribbon for £51, and yet another bill for gloves and ribbons, perhaps as gifts. Ribbons played an important part in sixteenth- and seventeenth-century English marriage rituals. Decorating bridal clothes, tied around arms or legs, given as favors to guests, ribbons celebrated the festive occasion of the marriage.[61] In contrast, the amounts paid at the church were small. Simon paid the minister and clerk at St. Bartholomew a pound each with another pound for the poor and something for the bell ringers.

Simon presented Grace with a muff and tippet for which he paid £51 plus a pair of wedding garters and a wedding ring made of angel-gold. He bought a pair of spurs, presumably for himself. Gilbert Morewood paid Simon £4,000 of the £6,000 of Grace's portion and Simon deposited it with Alderman Thomas Vyner, one of England's early bankers. Simon also spent £10 for the drawing up of the deeds of jointure. In December 1649, Gilbert Morewood paid the remaining £2,000 of the dowry and Alderman Vyner returned the £4,000 to Simon.[62]

Finance and Moneylending

At twenty-three Simon Bennet had thought he knew pretty well what his inheritance amounted to, and he did not wait long to put his capital to use. Moneylending and credit took place at all levels of society in medieval and early modern England. Gentlemen wrote to one another requesting £50; women loaned each other money and took out loans from City merchants; bankers backed kings with finance for wars. Suits for debt increased greatly in the late Elizabethan period.[63] Even as moneylending was merely a part of the business activities of many shopkeepers and merchants, it gradually became a profession in itself. Early banking from the 1640s on took two forms centered on goldsmiths like Sir Thomas Vyner and his half-nephew Sir Robert Vyner, and scriveners like Robert Abbott and his son-in-law Sir Robert Clayton. According to Frank Melton, goldsmiths like the Vyners moved into Crown finance, while Sir Robert Clayton worked in private

---

[61] David Cressy, *Birth, Marriage and Death, Ritual, Religion and the Life-Cycle in Tudor and Stuart England* (Oxford: Oxford University Press, 1997), pp. 361–363.

[62] Hatfield House Archives, Accounts 139/3, Oct. 1649.

[63] Craig Muldrew, "Credit and the Courts: Debt Litigation in a Seventeenth Century Urban Community," *The Economic History Review*, ns 46 (1993), 23–38; Marjorie McIntosh, "Money Lending in the Periphery of London, 1300–1600, *Albion*, 20 (1988), 557–571.

finance, lending money especially to country gentry during the 1650s and the Restoration.[64]

Simon Bennet provides a case study in the new kind of private banking that developed after the Civil War, but he found his niche in real estate and private finance not in deposit banking. Simon used his father, uncles' and aunt's legacies as well as Grace's portion of £6,000 to make even more money. He prospered by focusing on one of the areas that Sir Thomas Bennet, Richard Bennet, and Gilbert Morewood invested in too, property and loans. Simon was a property magnate and made short-term loans secured by bonds or mortgages. Although he was in finance, Simon Bennet appears to have taken no deposits. He was self-funding.

Simon's interest rate was regulated by parliamentary statute. While the Elizabethan statute of 1571 expressed doubts about the morality of taking interest, it allowed it, and by 1627 parliamentary legislation permitted interest of 8 percent. In 1651 the Rump parliament, however, drew attention to the problems of debt suffered by those in trade and agriculture:

Divers of this Commonwealth, both for their urgent and necessary occasions for the following their Trades, Maintenance of their Stocks and Imployments, have borrowed, and do borrow divers sums of Money, Wares, Merchandize and other Commodities; but by reason of the said general fall and abatement of the value of Land, and the prizes of the said Merchandize, Wares and Commodities, and Interest in Loan continuing at so high rate, as eight pounds in the hundred pounds for a year, doth not onely make men unable to pay their Debts, and continue the maintenance of Trade, but their Debts daily increasing, they are enforced to sell their Lands and Stocks at very low Rates, to forsake the use of Merchandize and Trade and to give over their Leases and Farms, and so become unprofitable Members of the Commonwealth.[65]

To deal with such indebtedness, the statute reduced the rate of interest to 6 percent. The Interregnum statute was confirmed at the Restoration in 1660. While moral injunctions against borrowing and lending had a long history, expanding trade, agricultural change, and the consumer society in seventeenth-century England made credit a centerpiece of economic life.

As a landlord and a moneylender, Simon Bennet owned and rented out property in as many as twelve counties, cities, and towns and lent money at interest on short-term bonds which were secured either by larger amounts of

[64] ODNB, "Sir Robert Clayton"; Frank T. Melton, *Sir Robert Clayton and the Origins of English Deposit Banking, 1658–1685* (Cambridge: Cambridge University Press, 1986).
[65] C. H. Firth and R. S. Rait, eds., *Acts and Ordinances of the Interregnum, 1642–1660* (London: HMSO, Printed by Wyman and Sons Ltd., 1911); "Act forbidding any person to take above the rate of Six Pounds for the loan of One Hundred Pounds for a year. August 8, 1651."

money or by mortgages. He might loan money at first without a mortgage, but when the debt came due and the debtor wanted to continue the loan or to borrow more money, Simon would ask that the security be backed by a mortgage on property. According to the common law, should the debtor default, Simon had the right to take the property. The risk of the business to Simon lay in the creditworthiness of the debtor, the value of the property, and the legality of the mortgage. At times, Simon Bennet and his heirs found themselves facing debtors who had mortgaged the same piece of property several times over. The risk to the debtor, of course, was the loss of the property securing the mortgage.

Simon first ran his business from London. His associate was Thomas Russell of the Inner Temple who witnessed Simon's marriage settlement and whom his mother called cousin in her will. Later, living in Calverton, Buckinghamshire, Simon sent orders to Roger Chapman, who identified himself as of the "Inner Temple" and coordinated his mortgages and loans. The records of Simon Bennet's business range from the late 1640s to 1680. The records kept by Russell and then by Chapman list the receipts and expenditures of the business by date. They included receipts of interest and rent, payments to Simon's mother, Lady Finch, of the monies due on her jointure, payments in gold to Simon's wife Grace, and money brought by Simon from the country to be placed upon the Exchange at interest.[66]

Simon Bennet's clients ranged widely from London shopkeepers to the king, but most appear to have been the landed. He appears to have loaned money mainly to those who were already in debt and who used the loans to keep afloat rather than using the money for investment in new ventures or new land purchases. Simon built his business from his own properties and securities, adding to his capital from the rents, properties, interest, and mortgages he accumulated.[67]

Early examples from the accounts show small-scale loans to Londoners and actions taken against debtors. In 1648 Thomas Russell recorded that he had received overdue rent from Mr Swale the cheese monger after going to the bailiff and paid £11-9-0 to an attorney for trying to arrest one Gibbons. Russell loaned £200 "by order of my cousin Benet to Mr. Thomas Trotter at the Signe of the Legg in Newgate market upon his bill sealed to be repaid with interest at 6 per cent at 7 days notice."

By November 1650, at the age of just twenty-six, Simon was of sufficient wealth and connections to be appointed sheriff of Buckinghamshire by the

[66] For instance, Hatfield House Archives, Accounts 162/6, June 18, 1657. "Received of my Cousin Bennet which brought with him from Beachampton two hundred pounds."
[67] Hatfield House Accounts, Accounts 162/6.

Council of State. Richard Grenville compiled a list of the yearly estate values of Buckinghamshire gentry in the 1650s. Three men had estates with values higher than Simon Bennet's: Robert Dormer, Earl of Carnarvon, listed by Grenville as having an estate of £7,000 a year, and Sir John Borlase and Sir Thomas Lee, both with £4,000 a year. Borlase and Lee came from leading county families who often sat in the House of Commons. Grenville listed Simon Bennet as having an estate worth £3,000 a year along with Sir William Drake, a lawyer, official, and Member of Parliament, Sir Robert Dormer, and Sir Peter Temple. Dormer and Temple were members of old Buckinghamshire families who often were chosen to represent the county in the House of Commons as knights of the shire. By comparison, Sir Ralph Verney, from another old Buckinghamshire family, had an estate with an annual value of only £1,400. In short, young Simon was one of the richest gentlemen in the county, the economic equal of baronets and knights who were the political leaders of Buckinghamshire.[68]

During the Interregnum, Bennet served not only as sheriff but also as assessor of taxes in 1652 and 1657 under the Rump and the Protectorate. He traveled to France in April 1657, apparently on behalf of the Cromwellian regime, just after the Anglo-French alliance signed in March 1657 against the Spanish culminated in the successful Battle of the Dunes or Dunkirk in June 1658. On April 10, Captain William Whitehorne wrote to Robert Blackborne, Secretary to the Admiralty,

I will transport Simon Bennet to Calais on the arrival of the *Oxford* as there is no other ship now in the Downs but the *Essex*, the ketch having gone to Dover for a bowsprit. I hope the soon going over of the frigates to the other side may prove beneficial to the nation and to trade, annoying the enemy, and securing Charles Stuart and his party on the other side.[69]

Henry More wrote to Simon's half sister Ann Finch, in May 1657, wondering if "French air helps Simon Bennet's consumption."[70] On the eve of the Restoration, Bennet was named to committees to oversee the militia and to raise taxes.[71]

---

[68] A. M. Johnson, "Buckinghamshire 1640–1660, A Study in County Politics" (MA thesis, University of Wales), Appendix II, "A List of Yearly Estate Values as Recorded in Richard Grenville's Ms. Note Book" (1962–1963), Buckinghamshire County Library.

[69] *CSPD, 1657*, p. 337.

[70] Marjorie Nicholson and Sarah Hutton, eds., *The Correspondence of Anne, Viscountess Conway, Henry More and Their Friends, 1642–1684* (Oxford: Clarendon Press, 1930, 1992), p. 143, Henry More to Ann Finch, May 11, 1657.

[71] Firth and Rait, *Acts and Ordinances of the Interregnum*, Vol. II, pp. 658, 1062, 1321, 1364, 1427.

Business knew no politics. Simon Bennet loaned money to royalists and parliamentarians, many of them noblemen in need of money once the wars were over. For instance, on April 15, 1657, Bennet received £90, the annual interest on £1,500 for "Thomas Lord Grey of Groby deceased." Lord Grey of Groby fought with the parliamentary armies, supported Pride's Purge and signed King Charles's death warrant. He made his will on April 4, 1657, and died shortly thereafter with many outstanding debts.[72] In contrast, two months later, on June 6, 1657, Sir Edward Hopton paid Simon £150 on the £2,500 he had borrowed. Hopton had fought with the royalist armies, although his father favored parliament.[73] Hopton paid interest again on the same £2,500 in 1659, this time £76 for six months and thirteen days.

Sir Christopher Hatton (1605–1670), one of Charles I's courtiers who fought on his side, was made Baron Hatton in 1643. He went abroad after the king's defeat returning to England in 1656. Based on Hatton's estate, worth £2,200 a year, Simon Bennet repeatedly loaned him money on his property holdings beginning in 1658. "The Lord Hatton and his sonne upon a mortgage of Hatton House and gardens and the manor of Gretton in Northamptonshire £4000 payable with interest viz 22 August 1659 £240; 22 Aug. 1660 £240; 22 Aug 1661, £4240."[74] Later, in 1663, Hatton, Bennet, and Russell leased a piece of land in Holborn belonging to Hatton House for forty-two years.[75] Bennet also loaned money to his royalist brother-in-law, Sir Clifford Clifton, £30 here, £100 there, as well as loaning £400 to his cousin Ambrose Bennet who was one of the Bennet scholars at University College, Oxford.

In 1659 Charles II issued the Declaration of Breda offering pardons to those who had participated in the Civil War except for the signers of Charles I's death warrant. In June 1660, Simon Bennet declared that he laid hold of the king's pardon granted at Breda and promised future obedience.[76] Once pardoned, Bennet became one of Charles II's moneylenders and was again appointed sheriff of Buckinghamshire in the 1660s. Such a position was not without patronage. When his cousin Sir Henry Bennet, who now held a position at court and later as Earl of Arlington became one Charles II's chief

---

[72] Hatfield House Archives, Accounts 162/6, April 15, 1657. *ODNB*, "Thomas Grey of Groby." The article does not provide a death date, but the Bennet accounts make clear that he was dead by April 15 and no doubt earlier.
[73] Hatfield House Archives, Accounts 162/6, June 6, 1657. *ODNB*, "Sir Edward Hopton."
[74] Hatfield House Archives, Accounts 162/6, Aug. 26, 1658. *History of Parliament, 1660–1690*, "Sir Christopher Hatton."
[75] Derbyshire Record Office, D3 155/7590 Lease, Feb. 4, 1663.   [76] *CSPD, 1660–1661*, p. 38.

ministers, asked to name the under sheriff, Simon regretfully made his excuses saying that he had just named someone himself.[77]

By the late 1650s, Bennet had picked up property in the heart of Westminster. Cannon Row was the site of a series of noble houses in the Elizabethan period.[78] In June 1658, Bennet loaned Edward More £1,000 backed by mortgages on manors in Surrey and property on "Channon" Row. Three months later he lent him another £1,300 with interest on another property.[79] More was apparently unable to keep up his payments and the Cannon Row property came into Bennet's hands. Years later, between 1676 and 1680, lawyers for Emanuel Hospital, an almshouse for poor women established by Ann, Lady Dacre, by her will in 1601, sued Bennet. They claimed that More's grandfather had granted the hospital 40 shillings a year rent out of his mansion house on Cannon Row, which had now been converted into "Bennet's court and held by Simon Bennet." When the City of London subpoenaed Bennet in Buckinghamshire on behalf of the hospital, his attorney repeatedly postponed his answer. Finally, the exasperated attorney for London and the Hospital noted that if Bennet and his attorney asked for further time, "acquaint the court that . . . the suit being but for a charity of 40s per annum and the charges falling upon . . . the poor Hospital they ought not to be delayed by the Exceptant who is a very rich man."[80] Simon's attitude toward the hospital differed from his grandfather's who had been the president of two London hospitals and the benefactor of three.

By 1666 Sir Robert Vyner had taken over Sir Thomas Vyner's goldsmith and banking business and had become one of Charles II's major sources of funds. Indeed, Simon Bennet had deposited £4,000 of Grace Morewood's portion in the Vyner bank in 1650. But the Anglo-Dutch War drained Vyner's finances. On December 2, 1666, Simon Bennet, now a banker himself, ordered Chapman to loan Sir Robert Vyner £2,000.[81]

By 1674, according to Roger Chapman's accounts, Simon Bennet held 155 securities or instruments of debt. In comparison, between 1672 and 1677, Sir Robert Clayton, the leading scrivener banker of the day, had 250 securities for debt on his books.[82] Although Simon Bennet's business was not as large and he is unknown today, his contemporaries referred to him as "Great Bennet" and

[77] *CSPD, 1665–1666*, p. 72, Simon Bennet to Earl of Arlington, Nov. 24, 1665.

[78] John Nichols, ed., *The Progresses, and the Processions of Queen Elizabeth*, 3 vols. ([London]: Printed by and for the editor, 1788–1805), Vol. III, p. 414.

[79] Hatfield House Archives, Accounts, 162/3.

[80] LMA, CLA/071/AD02/001006. In fact the rent had not been paid for seventy-one years beginning long before it came into Bennet's hands.

[81] Hatfield House Archives, Accounts162/3, Dec. 8, 1666; *ODNB*, "Sir Robert Vyner."

[82] Melton, *Sir Robert Clayton and the Origins of English Deposit Banking*, chapter 5.

regularly sought him out for loans. His clients ranged from the greatest to the ordinary, their debts from great sums to small. In 1676 Simon Bennet loaned Charles II £10,000 at 6 percent and in 1678 another £2,000.[83] In contrast, the year before Richard Wooley, citizen and barber surgeon, agreed to a bond for £60 for a loan of £38.[84] After Simon's death, his executor Ralph Lee acknowledged to the Court of Common Pleas that Sir Anthony Chester, Baronet, Sheriff of Buckinghamshire, and Member of Parliament, had satisfied the judgment for his £700 debt to Simon Bennet.[85]

Mortgages were fungible. In 1658 Henry Gooderick paid off the £3,000 principal that Simon had lent to Haycourt Layton on a mortgage in 1655 "whereupon the estate was reconveyed to Mr. Goodericke and Mr. Layton's bond of £6,000 for performance was delivered up to the said Mr. Goodericke."[86] Sir Clement Clark of Ridge in Shropshire and his wife Sarah made a mortgage with Philip Holman on the manor of Hotgrove and adjoining Pledall farm. By an indenture, 23 Charles II, Clark assigned it to Simon Bennet "to whom there is now due £3,640." Simon now lent Clark a further £360.[87]

But Bennet did not always agree to lend. Simon had been an important lender to the Ingoldsby family in Buckinghamshire who had intermarried with the Cromwells as well as a cousin of Bennet's. Francis Ingoldsby, the oldest brother, sat in the Cromwellian parliaments while his brother Richard signed King Charles's death warrant but was pardoned at the Restoration. Francis was deeply in debt and ultimately had to sell the family estate in the 1670s. Before that, he turned to Simon Bennet for a series of large loans in the 1660s. In March 1666–1667, Mr. Ingoldsby paid £1,000 "for £2000 there remaining and for interest £48 for which he and his sonne have given bonds and a new security of lands for the £2000 and a bond of £4000 to perform covenant whereupon the old writings and statute were delivered up according to my Cosens Benet's order."[88] In October 1672, however, Simon Bennet received a request for funds from a Mr. Robinson and asked Roger Chapman's advice in a letter marked "Mr. Ingoldsby's business." Chapman counseled him against immediately providing further loans because in the

[83] BL, Add. Ms. 3057, f. 17, John Bennet to the king. [*c.* 1690?]; *Calendar of State Papers, Treasury Books*, Vol. II, *1667–1668*, ed. W. A. Shaw (London: Longman, 1868–1889), p. 534, March 9, 1667–1668.

[84] Hatfield House Archives, Legal 120/4, Judgment for security of L38, Feb. 11, 1674/1675.

[85] Centre for Buckinghamshire Studies, Chester Family of Chicheley, D-C/3/10, Nov. 26, 1689.

[86] Hatfield House Archives, Accounts 162/6, June 30, 1658.

[87] Hertfordshire Record Office, Skippe Family of Ledbury, B38/132. Quitclaim for the remainder, subject to redemption.

[88] Hatfield House Archives, Accounts 162/6.

previous ten months, from December 17, 1671, to October 2, 1672, Ingoldsby and Robinson had become bound for loans on four different occasions. That totaled £361 plus interest, Chapman sternly wrote, "towards all these we have received towards principal and interest besides charges at several payments £188."[89] Although the sums were not large, the frequency of the requests gave Chapman pause. The refusal of new loans by Bennet and others and the outstanding debts may have led to the sale of the family estate.

"Once a Mortgage, Always a Mortgage"

Mortgage law was undergoing change in the period when Simon Bennet was making his fortune as a moneylender. Court decisions set new limits to the ability of moneylenders to foreclose on debtors. The common law had allowed the holders of mortgages to foreclose when debtors did not pay their debts on time, even when the amount owed was less than the value of the property. From the fifteenth century on, however, but especially in the seventeenth century, Lord Chancellors developed a doctrine called "the equity of redemption" that provided debtors with equitable relief. By the principle of the equity of redemption, the borrowers always had the right to repay their mortgages even when they missed the payment if they repaid it within a reasonable amount of time. Most importantly, in 1681 Heneage Finch, Earl of Nottingham and Lord Chancellor, in his decision in Newcomb *v.* Bonham, stated that "Once a mortgage always a mortgage." Mortgages were taken out to secure loans not to convey property, and with the equity of redemption, the creditor received his money and the debtor kept his land.[90] That Simon Bennet, the Lord Chancellor's stepbrother, was in the mortgage and loan business provides an additional and previously unknown context for Nottingham's views.

In the last years of his life, Simon Bennet was still lending money. Roger Chapman's account book for 1681 shows both the deeds he presented to Simon and the accounts he received and paid out. Thus he delivered deeds to

[89] Hatfield House Archives, General 92/7, Roger Chapman to Simon Bennet, Oct. 2, 1672. On December 17, Mr Ingoldsby, Mr. Robinson, and two associates had become bound for £200 for a payment of £103; on February 8, they had become bound for another £200 for payment of £100 and interest and about the same time Mr. Ingoldsby and others became bound in another bond of £200 for payment of £100 and interest, and not long after Mr Ingoldsby and others became bound in another bond of £100 for payment of £58 and interest.

[90] I am grateful to Julia Rudolph for discussion of "equity of redemption" and for the opportunity to read her article, "Property and Possession: Literary Analyses of Mortgage and Male Folly," in *A Cultural History of Law*, Vol. IV, *A Cultural History of Law in the Age of Enlightenment*, ed. Rebecca Probert and John Snapes (London: Bloomsbury, 2018), which discusses Nottingham's decision.

Simon Bennet from Mary Grey, Countess of Kent, John Tracy, 3rd Viscount Tracy of Rathcoole, Sir Walter Bagott, Baronet and Member of Parliament for Staffordshire, Nicholas Barnes, Mr. Hartley, Mr. Maynard, and others including Franklin's deeds for a shop at Stratford.[91] William Carpender, the rector of Calverton Church, Bennet's local minister, audited the books.

Simon Bennet's large fortune glittered brightly in Buckinghamshire. While Simon brought money to London to invest at interest at the Royal Exchange, his wife Grace received very fine and very valuable gold coins from the business.[92] Grace kept her collection of gold pieces at home in Calverton. Even as new financial instruments appeared, many people still kept gold on hand. Grace Bennet's hoard, however, would have tragic consequences.

Conclusion

Sir Thomas Bennet demonstrated how provincial younger sons could make commercial fortunes in international trade and then diversify assets into Crown finance, property, and moneylending. Two of Sir Thomas's sons, Richard and John, also became City merchants, while two eschewed business and identified themselves as country gentlemen. One, Sir Simon, made an extraordinary donation to University College, Oxford that transformed its architecture and fellowship.

Richard, a mercer like Sir Thomas Bennet, began importing cloth but later expanded his business into the East India trade and new goods such as American tobacco. Richard's son, Simon Bennet, became a private banker in the late 1640s as it was developing in the better-known businesses of Richard Abbott, Robert Clayton, and the Vyners. To his grandfather's wealth from the international trade in luxury fabrics and Jacobean Crown finance, Simon added profits from the East and West Indies inherited from his father Richard and the lands and legacies of his Bennet uncles and aunt. Simon's accounts provide insight into the seventeenth-century mortgage market. His business, based on real estate and moneylending, built on the expanding need for credit by the Crown, the nobility and gentry augmented by City shopkeepers.

Simon's marriage to Grace Bennet, daughter of Gilbert Morewood, grocer and East India merchant, also brought Simon wealth from global trade. How Gilbert Morewood made his fortune is the story, we will turn to in the next chapter. By the third generation, all of Sir Thomas's male descendants

[91] Hatfield House Archives, Accounts 142/12.
[92] Hatfield House Archives, Accounts 142/12A, pp. 22, 24.

identified themselves as country gentleman, even Simon, described as "great Bennet of Buckinghamshire." In the 1670s and 1680s, Simon and Grace Bennet invested their capital in large marriage portions to ensure their daughters married well. Even earlier, the Bennet and Morewood fortunes had begun to underwrite their entry into the Stuart elite, a political and social network including the court, the nobility, as well as the upper gentry that did not reject but most often welcomed their wealth made in trade and finance.[93]

[93] On differing views of the aspirations of gentry in business, see R. G. Lang, "Social Origins and Social Aspirations of Jacobean London Merchants," *The Economic History Review*, ns 27, 1 (Feb. 1974), 28–47; Grassby, *The Business Community in Seventeenth-Century England* and Perry Gauci, *The Politics of Trade: The Overseas Merchant in State and Society, 1660–1720* (Oxford and New York: Oxford University Press, 2001); Susan Whyman, "Land and Trade Revisited: John Verney, Merchant and Baronet," *London Journal*, 22 (1997), 16–32.

CHAPTER 2

"My Personal Estate Which God of His Infinite Goodness Hath Lent Me:" The Grocer's Apprentice

The Morewoods

Gilbert Morewood traced a successful journey from Yorkshire to London, from apprenticeship in the Grocers' Company to success as an East India Company merchant, even during the English Civil War. Like Sir Thomas Bennet, Morewood was a younger son of minor gentry and his career, too, illustrates the many ways in which commercial fortunes could be made in the seventeenth century. International ventures from the East Indies to Virginia to Brazil, some more successful than others, enabled Morewood to become rich. While he identified himself as a merchant and citizen of London, he bought country property linking his family again to the land and to the gentry. Morewood also invested some of his capital in marriage portions aimed at creating important opportunities for social mobility and elite status for his daughters and their descendants. At the same time, his career reflects dramatic changes in the economic and social life of the Morewoods of Yorkshire and Derbyshire in the seventeenth century.

The Morewoods of the Oaks had lived in the Chapelry of Bradfield near Sheffield since the late fourteenth century. Bordering the Pennines, "a bleak, high and mountainous tract of country," Bradfield's pastoral landscape had thin and poor soil. Although other landed families had begun to leave, the Morewoods remained and, in the seventeenth century, they were the principal inhabitants of their eponymous hamlet. Although they were not elected to parliament, they occasionally held appointments as justices of the peace. They usually married into other northern families. The medieval church at Bradfield, where the Morewoods worshipped and buried their dead, welcomed large numbers of communicants on Easter and began recording its curates in 1533 when Henry VIII broke with Rome. Plaques to the Morewoods adorned the church. In the 1670s a Morewood cousin received a coat of arms when he became sheriff of Yorkshire. In the eighteenth century, one John Morewood sold the Oaks. The new owner demolished much of the mansion, leaving only a farmhouse. The Yorkshire Morewoods thereafter, sniffed the nineteenth-century historian Joseph Hunter, had "sunk into the general population."[1]

Yet Hunter's narrative arc ending in social insignificance omits the Morewoods' participation in the dynamic changes that affected English society and the economy over the course of the seventeenth and eighteenth centuries. The initial setting of the Morewoods' story may resemble a Brontë novel with "scenery of a most romantic kind."[2] But in the early seventeenth century, Rowland Morewood and his son John, each with more than a dozen children, chose to connect themselves to the world of London and expanding international commerce. Rowland placed several of his sons as apprentices in the Grocers' Company. Rowland's son Anthony bought an estate at Alfreton, Derbyshire, in 1629. Over the course of the seventeenth century, the Derbyshire Morewoods mined the coal they found on their property and flourished, serving as assessors and sheriffs in the county over several generations.[3] Rowland's son John left money in his will to educate his four youngest sons in trade.[4] All four, Francis, Gilbert, Benjamin, and Joseph, became merchants in London and northern towns. As a result, the northern Morewoods became merchants in the East Indies, the Netherlands, and Atlantic trades in lead and, later, in coal and cotton.

While it was not unusual for younger sons to be placed in trade, following Rowland Morewood's initial example, the Yorkshire and Derbyshire Morewoods, systematically sent their younger sons to London as apprentices. Indeed, they exemplify this seventeenth-century phenomenon. While there had been a Peter de Morewood who was a Nottingham merchant in the fourteenth century, there were no Morewood grocers until 1601. Remarkably, between 1601 and 1650, *ten* Morewoods became gentlemen apprentices in the Grocers' Company.[5] By the end of the seventeenth century, there were fourteen Morewood grocers almost all with Yorkshire and Derbyshire roots, the last in 1690.[6] While a few did not complete their apprenticeships, most did. Their relatives who were already members of the

---

[1] Joseph Hunter, *Hallamshire: The History and Topography of the Parish of Sheffield* (London, 1819), pp. 469–470; Joseph Hunter, *Familiae Minorum Gentium*, Vol. III, ed. John W. Clay, Harleian Society, Vol. 39 (London, 1895), 1062–1067; *Registers of Bradfield in the Diocese of York, 1550–1722*, ed. and transcribed by Arthur B. Browne (Sheffield: A MacDougall and Sons, 1907).

[2] J. S. Fletcher, *A Picturesque History of Yorkshire*, 6 vols. (London: Caxton Publishing, c. 1901), Vol. II, pp. 73, 79–80.

[3] Hunter, *Familiae Minorum Gentium*, Vol. III, p. 1063.

[4] TNA, PROB11/204/281, Will of John Morewood of the Oaks, May 11, 1648.

[5] Guildhall Ms. 11592A, Grocers' Company Admissions Etc. 1345–c. 1670, Alphabet Book.

[6] Guildhall Ms. 11592A/001/002; Ms. 11571/9, Grocers' Company, Wardens' Accounts; Clifton Webb, *London Livery Company Apprenticeship Registers*, Vol. 48, *Grocers' Company, Apprenticeships, 1629–1800* (London: Society of Genealogists Enterprise Limited, 2008).

Grocers' Company helped them. In some cases they became their masters, in others they put up their bonds. Seventeenth-century sons placed in trade now had the opportunity to make larger fortunes because of the expansion of England's global commerce.

As a young man, Gilbert Morewood served as an apprentice to Anthony Morewood, probably a cousin, who had become a freeman of the Grocers' Company in 1601. Gilbert himself became a freeman of the company by 1616.[7] While it has been suggested that apprentices who came to London from long distances were apprenticed to masters with whom they had no connections, this was not the case with most of the Morewoods.[8] Gilbert Morewood himself accounted for several other Morewood merchants, encouraging his sister and brother to apprentice their sons to the Grocers' Company. It is not surprising that after he became a freeman of the company, he brought his nephews to London as his apprentices. In 1631 Reginald Eyre, his sister's son, and in 1646–1647 his brother John's son, Benjamin Morewood, became his apprentices.[9] In addition, Gilbert put up a £500 bond for his nephew Anthony's apprenticeship in 1638 and his nephew Joseph's apprenticeship in 1648.[10]

These younger sons, usually teenagers, did have some choice in whether to become apprentices. Gilbert Morewood's daughter, Lady Frances Gresley, remembered in the 1680s that her father had allowed her cousins to experience the trade for two months or a quarter of a year to see if it was to their liking before they were bound to a master. Gilbert Morewood's most successful apprentice was Sir John Moore who became a great lead merchant, a large investor in the East India Company, and Lord Mayor of London in the 1680s. Enrolled by his Leicestershire father, Moore became free of the Grocers' Company in the late 1640s. Lady Frances reminded Moore in their later correspondence that his father had offered him alternatives too. "Your father gave you your chise to go to the university or be a prentis."[11]

---

[7] Guildhall Ms. 11592a, Grocers' Company Admissions Etc. 1345–c. 1670, Alphabet Book. Morewood is one of two Gilbert Morewoods who had been apprenticed to Anthony Morewood. See also Guildhall Ms. 11571, Grocers' Company, Wardens' Accounts, 1601–1611. The first Gilbert Morewood, apprenticed in 1603, received his freedom in 1610 and died in 1626. The wardens' account of the Grocers' Company refer to the two as Gilbert Morewood senior and junior during the time they overlapped and contributed to the Brotherhood money between 1613 and 1624. See Guildhall Ms. 11571/9, 10, 11, Grocers' Company, Wardens' Accounts.

[8] Guildhall Ms. 11592A, Grocers' Company, Admissions Etc. 1345–c. 1670, Alphabet Book. Patrick Wallis, "Labor, Law and Training in Early Modern London: Apprenticeship and the City's Institutions," *Journal of British Studies*, 51, 4 (2012), 791–819.

[9] Webb, *London Livery Company Apprenticeship Registers*.

[10] Guildhall Ms. 11592A/2, Grocers' Company.

[11] Folger, V. b. 25, Gresley Mss., Letter 12, Frances Gresley to Sir John Moore, April 1687.

Figure 2.1 Wenceslas Hollar, *Ad Londinum Epitome & Ocellium*, [graphic], Part 2 (Amsterdam, 1647). The Folger Shakespeare Library. The engraving shows the importance of shipping on the Thames.

By the 1640s the Morewoods of Yorkshire and Derbyshire were part of a substantial network linking the north to the City of London and international trade. Gilbert Morewood and his brother Andrew were both East Indies merchants; Joseph was a merchant living in Greenwich, Benjamin was a London merchant, John was a manufacturer in London, and Anthony was a merchant in Barbados. At the same time, the network of connections woven between Morewoods in the City and northern towns was reciprocal. Gilbert Morewood's godson Gilbert and his brother Anthony became leading lead merchants in Dronfield, Derbyshire, Hull, and Sheffield. They probably served as suppliers to Morewood and the East India Co.[12]

London

When Gilbert Morewood first came to the City, London was the opposite of Bradfield, Yorkshire: noisy, busy, colorful, and overflowing with people. Rich and poor rubbed shoulders. New building was going up both in the City itself and in the developing West End. Houses were still built of wood, but King James ordered that brick should be used for all new building. The City expanded both westward and eastward. Migrants came to the City seeking work, and the gentry joined the throngs especially during term time when the courts were doing business. Ships sailed up the Thames filled with

[12] VCH, *York East Riding*, Vol. I, p. 142.

Mediterranean and Asian luxury goods and unloaded at the eastern docks. Spices brought in by the East India Company included pepper, nutmegs, cloves, and currants. The Levant Company imported silk and dried fruit from the Mediterranean.[13] Thomas Gresham's Royal Exchange contained a hundred retail shops that displayed expensive wares, especially luxury textiles and clothing. The New Exchange on the Strand, built by the Earl of Salisbury, had more shops filled with luxury goods. By mid-century, exotic groceries, such as coffee and chocolate, joined tobacco in new public spaces like the coffee house. Jacobean and Caroline comedies satirized the new consumer society, the practices of shopping in the Exchanges, and the china shops.

Although traditional attacks on luxury and luxury goods as vice continued into the eighteenth century, the argument that luxury consumption actually promoted economic growth and national welfare began to appear in the 1620s in the works of Thomas Mun and across the century in the writings of William Petty, Nicholas Barbon, and Bernard Mandeville.[14] Their views coincided with the international goods on display in the retail shops across the capital, the quest for improved technology, and the new building in the wake of the Great Fire.

Gilbert Morewood spent his apprenticeship with Anthony Morewood in the parish of St. Sepulchre without Newgate near the Old Bailey. Once he became a freeman of the Grocers' Company, he settled in St. Christopher le Stocks, near Threadneedle Street, close to where the Bank of England is today, where he paid rent of £20 a year. He also had a shop in the parish of St. Bartholomew Exchange where his brother Andrew lived, near the Royal Exchange.[15] Here Gilbert sold pepper, nutmeg, and other spices.

By 1640 Gilbert Morewood had made his fortune. He lived in Cornhill ward containing wealthy Lombard Street and Gresham's Royal Exchange. In May of that year, King Charles and the Privy Council ordered wards of London to list their wealthiest inhabitants for tax purposes. Some wards divided their merchants into four categories of wealth. Cornhill did not subdivide its list in this way, but Gilbert Morewood ranked third in the whole ward. In the 1640 subsidy, Morewood was listed first in his parish. In

---

[13] Christopher Clay, *Economic Expansion and Social Change: England 1500–1700*, 2 vols. (Cambridge: Cambridge University Press, 1984), Vol. II, pp. 129–130.

[14] Linda Levy Peck, *Consuming Splendor: Society and Culture in Seventeenth-Century England* (Cambridge: Cambridge University Press, 2005), pp. 25–72.

[15] T. C. Dale, "Inhabitants of London in 1638: St. Bartholomew Exchange," in *The Inhabitants of London in 1638* (London: The Society of Genealogists, 1931), pp. 36–37. *British History Online*: www.british-history.ac.uk/no-series/london-inhabitants/1638 [accessed April 28, 2018].

contrast, his brother Andrew and Thomas Rich, his future son-in-law, were listed among "the third sort of men" in their wards, Broad Street Ward and Cheap, respectively.[16]

Although Gilbert Morewood's accounts have not survived, other sources document the several ways in which he made his money and diversified his wealth: imports and exports, property purchases in city and country, money-lending, and insurance. Most importantly, Morewood was a member of the East India Company. Between 1619 and 1650, Morewood invested in its ventures, imported pepper and other spices, and exported lead to Amsterdam and Surat. In addition, he became a member of the Virginia Company and owned shares in ships trading to Brazil in South America and, perhaps, Guinea, West Africa.[17] All of his enterprises shed light on the larger context of seventeenth-century English economic change and political challenge.

Gilbert Morewood and the East India Company

Under its royal charter, granted in 1600, the East India Company held the monopoly on trade to an East that was vaguely defined. Membership included merchants who sold Asian commodities at home or reexported its goods abroad as well as aristocrats and office holders who invested in the company's ventures. The trading company proved very profitable in the first two decades of the seventeenth century, had losses in the 1630s, declined in the 1640s, and collapsed in the 1650s until Oliver Cromwell rechartered it.[18] Gilbert Morewood subscribed to the company's series of joint ventures and was selected as one of the twenty-four "committees," or individual commit-tee members, who governed the company in the 1640s. He supplemented his trading activities to the East with membership in the Virginia Company, purchasing two shares in 1622 and actively attending the company's meet-ings between 1622 and 1624.[19] Most East Indies merchants did not trade to the Americas after the dissolution of the Virginia Company. Morewood was one of the few who did.[20]

---

[16] *List of the Principal Inhabitants of the City of London 1640, from Returns Made by the Alderman of Several Wards*, ed. W. J. Harvey (London: Mitchell and Hughes, 1886), pp. 13, 5.

[17] Theodore K. Rabb, *Enterprise and Empire: Merchant and Gentry Investment in the Expansion of England, 1575–1630* (Cambridge, MA: Harvard University Press, 1967), p. 346.

[18] K. N. Chaudhuri, *The English East India Company: The Study of an Early Joint-Stock Company, 1600-1640* ([London and New York]: Frank Cass and Company, 1965), pp. 217, 223.

[19] *The Records of the Virginia Company of London*, ed. Susan Myra Kingsbury, 3 vols. (Washington, DC: Government Printing Office, 1906–1935), Vol. III, pp. 592–594. Jan. 30, 1621–1622.

[20] Robert Brenner, *Merchants and Revolution: Commercial Change, Political Conflict, and London's Overseas Traders, 1550–1653* (Princeton, NJ: Princeton University Press, 1993), p. 103.

Morewood imported Asian goods with the East India Company beginning in 1619,[21] dealing at first in pepper, nutmeg, and cloves. Pepper
from southern India, Java, and Sumatra and spices from the Maluku Islands
in Indonesia were the company's major imports in its first two decades
(see Plate 3).[22] Andrew Morewood, Gilbert's brother, bound to John Wood-
ward of the Grocers' Company in 1619, also became a member of the East
India Company and traded at times with his brother.[23] In one instance, in
1635, Gilbert and Andrew bought one-sixteenth of the cloves brought in by
one Captain Crispe. Gilbert also dealt in gunpowder. In 1632 he offered to
buy 100 barrels of powder to be transported at £4 a barrel.[24]

The East India Company imported more spices from Asia, especially
pepper, than it could sell at home, so it required its merchants to re-export
the excess, most often to Northern Europe, Italy, and the Baltic.[25] Morewood often flouted these rules for which he was fined. For instance, on
January 28, 1625, Daniel Harvey asked the East India Company to accept
Gilbert Morewood's security for seventy hogsheads or barrels of nutmegs.[26]
Two months later, Morewood requested the reduction of his tax for selling
nutmegs in town.[27] Morewood's fine for meeting local demand for spices
was part of a larger debate about the East India Company's trade. The
company was criticized for exporting bullion to pay for its Asian imports.
In reply the company emphasized that they were re-exporting Asian goods
that balanced the treasure sent to the Indies. Thus, the company urged critics
not to focus on a loss of bullion but the country's overall balance of
payments.[28] To support their policy, they fined their members for selling
luxury spices in London.

Exporting spices also supported the price at home and brought profits to
the company by creating more markets than simply bringing back the spices

---

[21] *CSP Col., Vol. III, 1617–1621*, #738, p. 294, Sept. 3, 1619, referred to Morewood's debts. In
1624 he signed a petition with other East India Company merchants against the Dutch embargo
on trade. *CSP Col., Vol. IV, 1622–1624*, pp. 490–493, June 1624.

[22] Chaudhuri, *The English East India Company*, pp. 21, 153–167; Clay, *Economic Expansion and
Social Change*, Vol. II, pp. 127–130.

[23] Guildhall Ms., Grocers' Company, 11592A/001.

[24] *A Calendar of the Court Minutes, etc. of the East India Company, 1635–1639*, ed. Ethel Bruce
Sainsbury (Oxford: Clarendon Press, 1907), p. 63. *CSP Col., Vol. VIII, 1630–1634*, p. 308,
Nov. 9. 1632.

[25] *CSP Col., Vol. VI, 1625–1629*, p. 46; Chaudhuri, *The English East India Company*, pp. 20–21;
Clay, *Economic Expansion and Social Change*, p. 164. Philip Lawson, *The East India Company:
A History* (London: Longmans: 1993), pp. 24–25.

[26] *CSP Col., Vol. VI, 1625–1629*, #25, pp. 16–17, Jan. 28, 1625.

[27] *CSP Col., Vol. VI, 1625–1629*, p. 46, March 30, 1625.

[28] K. N. Chaudhuri, "The East India Company and the Export of Treasure in the Early Seventeenth
Century," *The Economic History Review*, ns, 16, 1 (1963), 23–68.

to the domestic market. In the 1620s and 1630s, the price of imported pepper trended downward and the company was concerned about oversupply at home.[29] Thus, in 1626 Morewood bought sixteen bags of pepper from John Wolstenholme but in 1627 was discovered selling sixteen bags of pepper in town that were supposed to be exported. The company charged him £5 per bag. The pair of waiters from the Customs House who made the discovery received £7-15s for their pains. Nevertheless, Gilbert committed the same offense again in 1628. "Morewood having refused to attend to give satisfaction concerning his 32 bags of pepper alleged to have been sold by him in town to be charged £5 per bag in his account."[30] Throughout 1633 Morewood sued for remission of his fine of £160, "which he confessed was justly charged." He was told to go to the General Court who made the order. Although the fine was reduced to £20, Morewood sued to have the rest of the fine reduced. The General Court refused.[31]

In addition to importing pepper and other spices, Gilbert Morewood exported lead. The lead industry was growing strongly in the seventeenth century especially in Derbyshire.[32] Although exports to the East Indies constituted less than a third or even one-fifth of imports, these exports were most often made up of cloth and lead, the latter used for a variety of purposes especially building, roofing, pipes, and ammunition. In 1619 the Duke of Buckingham supported the rent-seeking project of Sir Henry Bell to search for impurities and provide a seal of approval for lead exports. The Plumbers' Company supported the Duke in this project, while the lead exporters did not. Gilbert Morewood was one of those merchants who directly challenged the Bell project. Although Bell won the project in 1619, it was revoked in 1620 before the calling of the 1621 parliament at a time when monopolies and projects came under attack.[33]

In July 1628 Gilbert Morewood, described as "of London merchant," and his brother petitioned the Privy Council to be allowed to export "two hundredth" of a "fodder" of lead from Hull to Amsterdam. Lead was measured variously in tons, fodders, and pigs. A fodder could vary from 2,100 to 2,500 pounds depending on location, whether in Derby, Hull, or

---

[29] Chaudhuri, *The English East India Company*, p. 21; Lawson, *The East India Company*, pp. 24–25.

[30] *CSP Col., Vol. VI, 1625–1629*, p. 282, Dec. 18, 1626; p. 416, Oct. 26, 1627; pp. 428, 429, Dec. 14, 1627; p. 556, Oct. 8, 1629; pp. 561–562, Oct. 22, 1628.

[31] *CSP Col., Vol. VIII, 1630–1634*, #400, p. 366, Feb. 13, 1633, p. 488, Nov. 20, 1633; p. 492, Nov. 25, 1633, 515, 586.

[32] Clay, *Economic Expansion and Social Change*, Vol. II, pp. 56–58, 164n.

[33] *Analytical Index to the Series of Records Known as the Remembrancia: 1579–1664*, ed. W. H. Overall and H. C. Overall (London: E. J. Francis, 1878), Lead project. It is possible that Gilbert Morewood senior is mentioned here, but Gilbert Morewood junior, subject of this chapter, continued in the lead trade.

London. Each hundredth traditionally weighed 112 pounds.[34] Gilbert claimed that his brother "dwelling in Derbyshire amongst the miners there has for many years together traded in lead and have furnished the said miners thereof with monies to pay the poor workmen weekly for their labor." Because the miners had delivered the "great store of lead here and at the port of Hull ... the petitioners are out of purse." They could not pay the miners without sending the lead. Morewood and his brother had contracted with the Merchants of the United Provinces before "any restraint of the exportation of lead was made to deliver two hundredth fodder of lead either at Amsterdam or Middleburgh." In response to their petition, the Privy Council authorized them to ship the lead.[35]

The petitioner's "brother" probably refers to Anthony Morewood. Prior to buying Alfreton in Derbyshire in 1629, he and his family lived in Norton, Derbyshire, four miles from Sheffield. In the late 1620s, Anthony Morewood and some other merchants shipped lead and other commodities on the River Idle in Nottinghamshire that had been rerouted in 1628 under the direction of the Dutch surveyor Cornelius Vermuyden. When their boat was confiscated for not paying tolls, the merchants sued, claiming that they were freemen of London. In the ensuing court case and appeal, they were ordered to pay the tolls.[36]

The East India Company, faced the threat of attacks from royalists and their foreign allies, the diminished funds of some of their domestic investors, and slackening demand. Still, in the 1640s Gilbert Morewood continued to supply lead to the East India Company. Thus, in November 1641 the company noted, "ten tons of lead at £10–16 per ton bought from Morewood to be shipped in the Hopewell."[37] For the voyage to Surat on November 8, 1641, they asked Morewood to supply 600 pigs of lead, a pig weighing about 300 pounds.[38]

---

[34] Clay, *Economic Expansion and Social Change*, Vol. II, pp. 56–58; Ronald E. Zupko, *A Dictionary of Weights and Measures for the British Isles* (Philadelphia: American Philosophical Society, 1985), p. 153.

[35] TNA, P.C. 2/38, 325ff., July 23, 1628. The petitioner, whose brother was in the lead business in Derbyshire, was Gilbert Morewood, son of Rowland of Bradfield. Gilbert Morewood senior had died in 1626 according to the Grocers' Company records, and Gilbert Morewood's nephew, Gilbert of Dronfield, was not baptized until August 6, 1628.

[36] Anthony Morewood's son Anthony left money to the parish of Norton, Derbyshire, where he was born. TNA, PROB11/238/74, Will of Anthony Morewood, April 22, 1654; Hunter, *Familiae Minorum Gentium*, Vol. III, pp. 1062–1065; Sheffield Archives, Crewe Muniments, CM, 1686, Nov. 13, 1629. William Lambton and Dame Katherine, his wife, Lyndley Richardson and Henry Byngley *v*. John Moseley, Anthony Morewood, Joshua Ballard and others concerning the non-payment of tolls for carrying lead and other commodities on the River Idle.

[37] *A Calendar of the Court Minutes, etc. of the East India Company, 1640–1643*, ed. Ethel Bruce Sainsbury (Oxford: Clarendon Press, 1909). p. 206.

[38] *OED*, "pig," metal.

Once war broke out, lead was needed at home. The House of Commons paid Morewood for the lead he had provided to the parliamentary army in 1642.

Ordered, That the Sum of Four hundred Thirty-two Pounds shall be paid unto *Gilbert Morewood,* Merchant, for Forty Ton of Lead bought of him, out of the Remainder of the Fifty thousand Pounds lent by the City of *London* for the Affairs of *Ireland,* in lieu of the Bullet formerly ordered by this House to be delivered unto the *Scotts* out of the *Tower.*[39]

Supplies of lead increased with parliamentary victories. Ben Coates points out that after the defeat of the royalists at Marston Moor in 1644, lead could again be shipped to London from Derbyshire and Yorkshire. Lead shipments were more than a third higher than during the previous twenty years.[40]

Gilbert Morewood did not seek office in the Grocers' Company, refusing the livery twice in the 1630s. In 1641, however, he became one of the twenty-four members or "committees," of the Court of Committees of the East India Company. This governing body of the company oversaw "setting out of ships, selling of goods, buying of provisions, victuals, stores and merchandises."[41] He first achieved this position on July 2, 1641, when he was one of six men named to the Court of Committees in place of those who routinely resigned.[42] Only those who had investments in both the Fourth Joint Stock and the particular voyage were eligible. In 1644 he oversaw the sale of company lands at Deptford and attended Lord Cottington's delinquency hearings regarding the £50,000 he owed. In 1645 he oversaw books of wages at the dockyards and in 1647 reported on the condition of the docks and suggested repairs (see Plate 4).[43] Throughout the 1640s, he continued to sell lead to the company and to invest in new joint stock ventures and individual voyages.[44]

Morewood was reelected to the Court of Committees in 1648 and 1649 as the East India Company continued to mount new ventures throughout the war years. In 1648 his brother Andrew and his son-in-law Thomas Rich were added to the Court of Committees. In a sign of the company's mounting

---

[39] *HCJ: Vol. 2, 1640–1643,* pp. 441–445, Feb. 9, 1642, www.british-history.ac.uk [accessed May 27, 2013].

[40] Ben Coates, *The Impact of the English Civil War on the Economy of London 1642–1650* (Aldershot: Ashgate, 2004), p. 58.

[41] Quoted from the Standing Orders of the East India Company, Chaudhuri, *The English East India Company,* p. 32.

[42] *Court Minutes of the East India Company, 1640–1643,* pp. 177, 331.

[43] *A Calendar of the Court Minutes, etc. of the East India Company, 1644–1649,* ed. Ethel Bruce Sainsbury (Oxford: Clarendon Press, 1912), p. 40, Aug. 16, 1644; pp. 47–48, Oct. 18, 1644; p. 121, Dec. 17, 1645; p. 206, June 11, 1647.

[44] *Court Minutes of the East India Company, 1640–1643,* p. 128, Feb. 11, 1646.

anxieties, it dispensed with the order that only those who had adventured £500 in the Fourth Joint Stock could serve. The company felt "the help of those who have formerly an insight into the Company's business will be wanted." By 1649 Andrew Morewood was dead, but Gilbert continued on the Court of Committees, as did Thomas Rich.

King Charles was executed in January 1649. The East India Company could not ignore the changed circumstances of the new Republic and called a Court of Election in August 1649 to address how trade was to be carried on amidst "the distraction of the times." Gilbert Morewood was one of those chosen to represent the joint stock investors.[45] Nevertheless, the company's problems continued. In 1650 the Governors of the East India Company and the Committee of 24, including Morewood and Rich, came under the scrutiny of the House of Commons for the trade in spices and goods. At issue was whether company members were reexporting them or selling them in town. Although the Committee of the Navy suggested that officials of the company should not be held personally liable, the Commons disagreed and ordered court cases to go forward and informers to get double their costs. Still, they added that no punishment should be meted out until they were notified. Morewood, now one of the officials at risk, must have remembered his previous fines for selling spices in town. Then he only faced impositions by the company, now it was the weight of the new Republic that sought to regulate the company.[46]

Political and Religious Views

Gilbert Morewood's service on the East India Company's Court of Committees throughout the 1640s raises the larger question of his political and religious views and those of the East India Company's leadership during the Civil War. Robert Brenner argues that Morewood was a royalist, that most of the leadership of the East India Company, including Morewood, signed important royalist petitions in 1640–1641 and that they supported Laudian and anti-Puritan ministers. Philip Lawson points out, however, that there was a political conflict within the East India Company in the 1640s and that by the end of the decade the leadership was strongly parliamentarian.[47] Morewood's service from 1641 through 1649 certainly suggests he supported parliament once their triumph became clear. He provided lead to the parliamentary army, became one of the commissioners in Cornhill Ward

---

[45] *Court Minutes of the East India Company, 1644–1649*, p. 276, July 4, 1648; p. 332, July 4, 1649; p. 342, Aug. 15, 1649.

[46] *HCJ: Vol. 6, 1648–1651*, pp. 432–433, June 27, 1650.

[47] Brenner, *Merchants and Revolution*, pp. 375–376, 376n; Lawson, *The East India Company*, p. 38.

for collecting arrears of assessments to maintain the army, and was nominated but not chosen as alderman in 1648.[48] In the late 1640s, he worked with leading puritan merchants who traded with the Americas and had close ties to parliament and the Interregnum City government.[49]

Morewood himself was an official of St. Christopher le Stocks, a notable Presbyterian parish church in the 1640s, and a supporter of its well-known Presbyterian minister, James Cranford. He became an active vestryman in the 1630s, as Arminians tried to exert their hold on the Church of England. Holding church offices throughout the 1630s and 1640s, he helped oversee apprenticeships, place children in hospitals, repair the church fabric, and refurbish the lecturer's house. The vestry minutes record, however, "at his own request . . . he was with consent of this vestry remitted, for the said place of Churchwarden, and for the place of upper church wardenship which would fall upon him the next year . . . Morewood paying for his fine Twenty pounds to be laid out for plate for the Lords Table."[50] In the 1640s Morewood served as one of the auditors of the church accounts, loaned them money, and paid for the church's lecturer.[51]

Between 1642 and 1649, religious uniformity in England broke down and different varieties of Protestant sects emerged. To gain Scottish support, Parliament adopted the Covenant agreeing to accept Presbyterianism as the official form of church government and worship in England in 1643. Gilbert Morewood and his brother Andrew lived in two of the most active Presbyterian parishes in London, St. Christopher le Stocks and St. Bartholomew by the Exchange.[52] Both wrote wills that include Calvinist statements of belief. Both supported their ministers, James Cranford and Thomas Cawton.

Anthony à Wood called Cranford "a zealous Presbyterian and a laborious preacher." In 1642 Cranford's tract entitled "The Teares of Ireland" attacked the cruelties of "blood thirsty Jesuits and the popish faction." The same year parliament appointed him to license works on divinity and to select young men for the ministry. Cranford wrote a foreward to Thomas Edwards' famous work *Gangraena* in 1643, and he delivered "Haereseo-machia: an

---

[48] C. H. Firth and R. S. Rait, *Acts and Ordinances of the Interregnum, 1642–1660*, 2 vols. (London: HMSO, Printed by Wyman and Sons, Ltd., 1911), Vol. I, p. 1131, April 24, 1648; *CSPD, 1649–1650*, p. 349.

[49] Brenner, *Merchants and Revolution*, p.192t.

[50] *Minutes of the Vestry Meetings and Other Records of the Parish of St. Christopher le Stocks*, ed. Edwin Freshfield (London: Printed by Rixon and Arnold, 1886), pp. 34, 31–39.

[51] *Minutes of the Vestry Meetings of St. Christopher le Stocks*, pp. 31, 32, 34, and passim. Guildhall Ms. 4423/1, St. Christopher le Stocks, Churchwarden Accounts, 1575 to 1660, ff. 165, 176, 180v, 182, 184, 188v.

[52] Dale, "Inhabitants of London in 1638: St. Christopher le Stocks," p. 34; Tai Liu, *Puritan London: A Study of Religion and Society in the City Parishes* (Newark: University of Delaware Press, 1986).

attack on heresy" before the Lord Mayor and the Aldermen of the City of London. Like Edwards, Cranford attacked papists and independents as heretics, poisonous to the body politic, and sought to prevent heresy's spread. Cranford did not hesitate to go on the political offensive and, in 1645, attacked members of the House of Commons for conspiring with royalists, an accusation for which he was imprisoned and fined.[53] Andrew Morewood's minister, Thomas Cawton, to whom he left £5 in his will, was active in the Presbyterian movement too. By 1648 he denounced the Army as vipers and prayed for the royal family a few months after the execution of Charles I in 1649.[54] When Gilbert Morewood made his will, James Cranford was one of his witnesses. Presumably Cranford helped shape Morewood's statement of belief on election and the "safety of all true believers."[55] Morewood's identity as a Calvinist parliamentarian not a Laudian royalist helps to explain his network of connections to other merchants who flourished under the Republic.

The Civil War, Interloping Trade, and the Dutch

Morewood engaged in interloping trading ventures outside the confines of the East India Company. Trading to the Americas, however, could be risky because of the "distraction of the times." In this atmosphere, Morewood invested in the merchant voyage of the *Concord* to Brazil along with several partners, the most important of whom was Samuel Vassall. Vassall, a cloth merchant, invested in the Levant and East India companies, and the Massachusetts Bay Colony. Vassall's voyages to Virginia, the Carolinas, and the West Indies began in the late 1620s, and he became a slave trader between Guinea and Barbados in the 1640s. At home, he was an active parliamentarian, refused to pay tonnage and poundage and ship money, and was elected to the Short and Long Parliaments. A commissioner for the navy, he was removed in Pride's Purge because his views were not radical enough for the army leaders.[56] Other partners in the *Concord* included Richard Shute, a collector of tonnage and poundage and organizer of assessments with close

---

[53] *HCJ: Vol. 4, 1644–1646*, pp. 171–173; Benjamin Brook, The *Lives of the Puritans: Containing a Biographical Account of Those Divines Who Distinguished Themselves in the Cause of Religious Liberty, from the Reformation under Queen Elizabeth, to the Act of Uniformity in 1662*, 3 vols. (London: Printed for J. Black, 1813), Vol. III, p. 268. Liu, *Puritan London*, pp. 79–81.

[54] Liu, *Puritan London*, pp. 79, 117. TNA, PROB11/206/461, Will of Andrew Morewood, Dec. 29, 1648.

[55] TNA, PROB11/212/751, Will of Gilbert Morewood, June 21, 1650.

[56] History of Parliament Online, "Samuel Vassall"; *ODNB*; Brenner, *Merchants and Revolution*, p. 135; Kenneth Andrewes, *Ships, Money and Politics: Seafaring and Naval Enterprise in the Reign of Charles I* (Cambridge: Cambridge University Press, 1991), pp. 59–61, 200–201.

ties to the New Model Army, Roger Vivian, a currants trader, and Richard
Cranley, a Levant Company member and a sea captain, sailing to Virginia
and the Caribbean.[57]

In the late 1640s, although the Dutch claimed to remain neutral, the
parliamentary navy seized Dutch ships trading with royalist ports. Royalists
seized Dutch ships although in smaller numbers. The Dutch responded in
kind. In 1647 parliament seized nine Dutch ships, seventeen in 1648, and,
by 1649, twenty-eight, almost all in European waters.[58]

In this fraught atmosphere, in June 1648 Gilbert Morewood, Samuel
Vassall, Roger Vivian, Richard Shute, and other merchants received license
from the King of Portugal to trade with Brazil. They sent off the *Concord*, a
ship of 350 tons, the size appropriate for Atlantic seafaring, laden with goods.
Approaching the Brazilian port of Bahia de Todos os Santos, the ship was
attacked by nine Dutch vessels that "made a foul depredation, and spoil of
her." Putting up a red flag, the Dutch ships fired ordnance through the
topsail, injured seventeen crew members, killed one, and claimed the *Concord* as a prize.[59] The Dutch Admiral told the English captain that he and his
crew were a "company of rogues, and rebels as well as their parliament, and
that the City of London were rogues, and rebels or used words to that effect
using … ignominious expressions against the parliament and City of
London."[60] The Dutch may have seemed far from home. But between
1630 and 1654 they had a toehold in Portuguese Brazil called New Holland
established by the Dutch West Indies Company. *Concord* had unwittingly
sailed into an area that the Dutch were fighting to continue to control.[61]

The English merchants petitioned the Council of State for redress, who
sent the case to the Admiralty Court. The judges' decision provides significant evidence about the destination of the ship, its value and contents, and
the Dutch attack. The Admiralty Court found that Bahia was commonly
reputed to be

free for any English ships to trade in with license from the King of Portugal, between
whom and the Hollanders there hath been and is by common repute peace and amity,
and that there never was any public edict or proclamation made or set forth by the
states of the United Netherland Provinces … forbidding the English to trade there.

---

[57] Brenner, *Merchants and Revolution*, pp. 135–136, 192t.
[58] Simon Groenveld, "The English Civil Wars as a Cause of the First Anglo-Dutch War,
1640–1652," *Historical Journal*, 30 (1987), 541–566, 561.
[59] TNA, SP46/101, f.1, Report by William Clerk and Thomas Exton, Admiralty Judges …
concerning the "Concord" taken by the Dutch in 1648. [November 3, 1649]; *CSPD, 1649,*
pp. 282, 287, 340.
[60] TNA, SP46/101, f. 1.
[61] See C. R. Boxer, *The Dutch in Brazil, 1624–1654* (Oxford: Clarendon Press, 1957).

The judges heard that the Dutch plundered both the cargo and the goods of the crew. When the Admiral of the Dutch ships came on board, he insisted on being shown where the "finest goods were stowed, and that thereupon the said Admiral broke open the said hold and took out what he pleased." The crew and ship were forced into a Dutch port in Brazil.

The merchants' losses amounted to £7,618 for their merchandise, which they claimed could have been sold for double that amount had they reached their markets in Brazil; £6,000 for the cost of the ship, tackle, furniture, apparel, and freight, and £3,000 for the goods of the men on the ship. "Samuel Vassall and company ... sent out upon the said ship, and voyage, for their provision, and factorage) the sum of £1523-10 shillings." In addition they had "expended in law at Pernambuco in endeavoring restitution, and wages, and other expenses there, the sum or value of £300 sterling."

Finally, the judges found that great indignities had been done to the State. The Dutch dragged the English flag in the sea under the colors of the Prince of Orange as the ship was brought into harbor "in such manner as is unused to be done unto public and open enemies and, after being told that it was against the law of arms to offer such indignity to a nation as was in amity with them, the Admiral answered that he had command from his Admiral so to do." The English captain and the lawyers retained by the vessel owners were unable to present their case. Their efforts to appeal the sentence of the local Admiralty Court failed.

As a result, the Admiralty Court judges decided in November 1649 that the supreme authority in England should demand justice from the supreme authority in Dutch Brazil and, if they could not get it, then letters of reprisal should be issued. "They have just cause to sue for letters of reprisal... But before the same be granted, they hold it necessary and fitting ... appeal be demanded from the supreme authority there in the behalf of the petitions by the supreme authority here."[62] In September 1650, Samuel Vassall and other partners petitioned the Council of State again, where they found sympathetic listeners. The Council of State once more referred the matter to the Admiralty Judges and the Collector for Prize Goods.[63]

Did the seizure of the *Concord* contribute to the First Anglo-Dutch War? At a time when the English and Dutch attacked each other's ships in Europe, Samuel Vassall, Gilbert Morewood, and their partners in the "Concord" venture provided yet another grievance against the Dutch, this one in the South Atlantic that historians have not previously noticed. The numbers of Dutch ships seized by parliament continued to climb. In 1649 parliament seized twenty-two and the royalists six; in 1650, parliament seized fifty and

[62] TNA, SP46/101, f. 1.   [63] *CSPD, 1650*, pp. 357, 362, Sept. 26, 28, 1650.

the royalists seven. But in 1651 parliament enacted a new measure, the Navigation Act, requiring all goods carried from the English colonies to be carried in English ships. That year the English seized 140 Dutch ships and declared war on the Dutch Republic. Historians have debated whether it was London merchants with connections to the East India and American trade or officials interested in state and navy building or both who pressed for both the Navigation Act and the first Anglo-Dutch War. Certainly the seizure of the *Concord* in neutral Brazilian waters and the vigorous attack by the Dutch Admiral on parliament led this group of London merchants to pursue their grievances to the Council of State and showed the reach of Civil War politics to the South American trade.[64]

Gilbert Morewood also owned shares in the ship the *Mayflower*, originally owned by Samuel Vassall, John Dethick, Alderman of London, Richard Shute, and others, some of the same partners involved in the Brazil adventure in 1648. Even as they petitioned the Council of State over the seizure of the *Concord*, they also petitioned the Council over an unspecified issue concerning the *Mayflower* in October 1649.[65] Along with the *Peter* and the *Benjamin*, the *Mayflower* took part in the Guinea-West Indies slave trade in 1647, a trade Vassall undertook in the 1640s.[66] Whether or not Morewood joined the 1647 slaving venture is not clear. After carrying merchant goods to Bristol, the *Mayflower* was "taken up for service of the State" and saw action as one of the summer fleet in 1650.[67]

Property, Moneylending, and Insurance

In addition to his ventures to the East Indies and to the Americas, Morewood diversified his assets and used his capital to make investments in real estate, moneylending, and insurance. He owned property not only in London but also in Leicestershire, Derbyshire, Staffordshire, and Oxford. His purchase of the manors of Netherseal with its Tudor manor house and Overseal in Leicestershire (now Derbyshire), for at least £2,650 in

[64] James Farnell, "The Navigation Act of 1651: The First Dutch War and the London Merchant Community, *The Economic History Review*, 2nd ser., 16, 3 (1964), 439–454; Steven C. A. Pincus, "Popery, Trade and Universal Monarchy: The Ideological Context of the Outbreak of the Second Anglo-Dutch War," *English Historical Review*, 422 (1992), 1–29.

[65] *CSPD, 1649–1650*, p. 349, Oct. 19, 1649, "The petition of John Dethick, Alderman, Richard Shute, Gilbert Morewood and other merchants and owners of the Mayflower of London referred to the Admiralty judges."

[66] Brenner, *Merchants and Revolution*, p. 192t; Andrewes, *Ship, Money and Politics*, p. 60.

[67] *CSPD, 1649–1650*, Vol. I, p. 223, July 4, 1649, Council of State to Captain Anthony Sharpe of the "Star" and Captain Phil Goose of the "Heart" frigate; *CSPD, 1649–1650*, Vol. I, p. 559, Dec, 12, 1649; *CSPD, 1649–1650*, Vol. I, p. 463, Dec.? 1649, Minute that the "Mayflower" was taken up for service of the State, beginning September 14; *CSPD, 1649–1650*, Vol. II, p. 1, Feb. 16, 1650; p. 377, Oct. 9, 1650.

1626–1627 from Sir Thomas Gresley, created another home for his family. He purchased the advowson of Netherseal for £300 in 1630, bought up further small parcels of land in the area, and leased out land in the manor. At times he was called Gilbert Morewood of Netherseal, gentleman, at other times citizen and grocer. Morewood's family lived in Netherseal for some time after he made the purchase. His daughter Grace was christened in Netherseal in 1632, his daughter Barbara was buried there in 1646, and his daughter Frances chose Netherseal when dividing her father's estate in the 1650s. All these actions spoke to the family's attachment to the land and place beyond its value as an investment.[68]

Morewood's profits from trade and real estate investments created the capital that enabled him not only to invest but also to lend money. In the 1640s the great London merchants, once the pillars of court finance as farmers of the customs duties and providers of short-term loans to the Stuart kings, were attacked and fined by the Long Parliament. Morewood was one of those to whom they turned for loans. They included Sir Paul Pindar, the great merchant and Ambassador to Turkey who had brought back treasures from Asia but by the late 1640s was deeply in debt. On one occasion Pindar borrowed £1,040 from Morewood, on another £640. The largest bonds held by Gilbert Morewood were for the Abbott family. Sir Maurice Abbott was one of the founders of the East India Company in 1600 and its long-time governor. He had five sons. One, Edward, went bankrupt in the early 1640s, leaving Sir Maurice with his debt of £3,000. Gilbert Morewood held one bond for £1,037-10-10 for Edward and George Abbott and another for £3,600 for Sir Maurice, Edward and George Abbott.[69] William Courten, son of one of the great Stuart merchants who undertook the East Asian trade to try to rival the East India Company, borrowed a total of £80,000 to unravel his father's debts. With his brother-in-law, Sir Edward Littleton, he borrowed £416 from Morewood. Morewood also loaned money to John Ferrar of Little Gidding who had returned from exile in the Netherlands by 1646. In 1648 he went to London to remove his sequestration. He owed Morewood £518–15.[70] Sir John Jacob, Lionel Cranfield's secretary and a

[68] Derbyshire Record Office, D77/1/16/5, Bundle D 21, Feoffment by Sir George Gresley of Drakelowe, 1626, Bart, and Thomas his son, Callingwood Saunders of Caldwell, Robert Radford of Lullington and Thomas Gresley of Lullington to John Bludworth of London, vintner, and Gilbert Morewood of London, grocer, of the manor of Overseal, Netherseal, and Seal Grange. Consideration, £1,000, June 27; Bundle D 22; to Morewood. Consideration £2,560, Dated Nov. 11; Bundle 23, Indenture of defeasance, Morewood–Gresley, March 7, 1626/1627. D77/1/16/6, Bargain and Sale by Zacharie Johnson of Netherseal, clerk to Gilbert Morewood, citizen and grocer of London of the advowson of Netherseal, Aug. 2, 1630.

[69] TNA, C9/22/78, Griesley *v.* Rich, Eyre and Morewood, 1654; *ODNB*, "Sir Paul Pindar," "Sir Maurice Abbott."

[70] *ODNB*, "William Courten"; History of Parliament Online, "John Ferrar."

farmer of the Great Customs, was removed by the Long Parliament as a monopolist. By 1648 he was imprisoned with debts of £100,000 and had turned to Morewood to borrow £520. At the Restoration Jacob restored his fortunes by becoming a customs farmer again.[71]

Morewood's loans were not as numerous as Simon Bennet's and usually not large. The great merchants who were his clients must have tapped many former associates for loans. Furthermore, whether or not these bonds were entirely paid back or remained outstanding remains unknown. What these debts do demonstrate is that Morewood had substantial sums to lend throughout the Civil War period and that he lent them to a network of customs farmers and international merchants with connections to the court of Charles I who had fallen on hard times.

Morewood also invested his capital in the 1640s in the insurance business. In 1642 the East India Company asked Morewood and John Massingberd "to direct Mr. Pryor to draw up two policies of assurances for the pepper shipped in the 'Mercury' and 'Victory' for which he is to be given £6-13-4d. These policies are only to be underwritten by the adventurers."[72] Marine insurance, although developed in Italy in the fourteenth century, remained unsystematic even in the middle of the seventeenth century, as the following case makes clear.[73]

Morewood was involved in a lawsuit in 1648 that began three years earlier in April 1645. A merchant named Richard Wynn claimed that he loaded goods in Hamburg aboard a ship called the "Faulken" destined for London. Wynn asked Morewood "to ensure such goods as he then pretended he had aboard the ship ... to the value of ... one hundred pounds ... for the consideration of five pounds." Having received the £5, Morewood "did subscribe a certain policy or writing ensuring the goods from Hamburg." Morewood stated that within days he had agreed with London merchant Thomas Andrewes that for £13 Andrewes would "reinsure the said wares to the value of one hundred pounds."[74] Furthermore, "upon the Exchange London" (the Royal Exchange where international merchants met to discuss business) Morewood brought Wynn and Andrewes together where it was

---

[71] TNA, C9/22/78, Griesley *v.* Rich, Eyre and Morewood, 1654; *ODNB*, "Sir John Jacob."

[72] *Court Minutes of the East India Company, 1640–1643*, p. 262, July 6, 1642.

[73] Florence Edler de Roover, "Early Examples of Marine Insurance," *Journal of Economic History*, 55, 2 (Nov. 1945), 172–200; Violet Barbour, "Marine Risks and Insurance in the Seventeenth Century," *Journal of Economic and Business History*, I (1928–29), 561–596; Christopher Ebert, "Early Modern Atlantic Trade and the Development of Maritime Insurance to 1630," *Past and Present*, 213, 1 (Nov. 2011), 87–114.

[74] See David Elliot, "Some Slight Confusion: A Note on Thomas Andrewes and Thomas Andrewes," *Huntington Library Quarterly*, 47, 2 (1984), 129–132.

agreed that, for £13, Andrewes would ensure the goods. Wynn then discharged Morewood. After making no claim for two years, Wynn turned to Andrewes who supposedly gave him satisfaction. Now, however, both were turning to Morewood for further funds.

Wynn responded to the suit saying that his wares were worth £150 and he paid Morewood £5 to insure them but that the ship was taken by a man of war and carried to Ostend in Flanders. Although Morewood had told him that Andrewes would give him £80 for his loss, when he and Morewood went to Andrewes the latter said that he had insured nothing. Wynn denied complicity with Andrewes and asked that Morewood be compelled to pay for his losses.[75] Why Wynn waited so long to make a claim and whether Morewood did reinsure his goods with Andrewes, the outcome of the case is unknown. What is clear is the informality of the reinsurance market. There appears to have been little paperwork to back up Andrewes' participation. Instead, there was the ritual of agreeing to a new contract at the Exchange. Clearly, Morewood was eager to get rid of the contract, perhaps because he was all too aware of the dangers of sea travel during the Civil War. Despite this suit, Morewood had a substantial insurance business, and at his death he still had a number of policies still outstanding.

Marriage and Mobility

By the 1640s Gilbert Morewood had married twice. With his first wife, whose identity is unknown, he had a daughter Barbara and a son who did not survive. After her death he married, as his second wife, Frances, widow of Thomas Henson. Before their marriage, Gilbert made a prenuptial agreement with her father to leave her at least £1,000 pounds in his will. She already had a daughter Joan. Gilbert and Frances then had two more daughters, Frances and Grace. Gilbert now invested in substantial marriage portions for all four girls. He did not see such an investment as a loss of capital that should have been reinvested in his business. Instead, Morewood invested in social capital, planning for the future by making financially and socially significant marriages for his four daughters with men whose prestige and wealth or significant promise was equal or greater than his own. Morewood, like Sir Thomas Bennet, embarked on a successful strategy to join the Stuart elite, through marriage.

Despite the upheaval of the first and second Civil Wars, all Morewood's daughters married well in the later 1640s. Three of the four married men who were on the rise through trade and office under the Protectorate and the

---

[75] TNA, C2/Chas I/W44/35, Wynn *v.* Morewood; C2/Chas I/M23/2, Morewood *v.* Wynn.

Restoration. The fourth married into a well-known gentry family that was among the first group of baronets. Three of the four men became sheriffs of their counties in the 1650s and 1660s. For instance, Barbara Morewood married Thomas Rich, son of a Gloucester merchant, who became a Turkey merchant, member of the Vintners Company, and East India Company investor. Although in 1640 he was probably less wealthy than Morewood, Rich rose rapidly, forging ties not only with the City elite but also with his county, the nobility, and the court.[76] Barbara had a son whom they named Gilbert who died in infancy, and she herself died probably in early 1646. In May 15, 1646, the Grocers' Company recused Gilbert from office because "he has of late sustained great loss and suffering and is grown ancient in the Company."[77]

Rich married, as his second wife, Elizabeth, daughter of Alderman William Cockayne. During the Interregnum, in 1654, he bought the manor of Sonning, Berkshire, where he built a new mansion, Holme Park. Appointed sheriff of Berkshire in 1657–1658, Rich was elected to parliament in 1660 and made a baronet in 1661 by Charles II for providing monies to Charles I.[78] His son, Sir William Rich, married Ann, daughter of Robert Bruce, 1st Earl of Ailesbury. Although remarried, Thomas Rich continued his relationship with Gilbert Morewood, who called him his son-in-law and named him one of the executors of his will in 1650. In his own will, Rich himself remembered Barbara Morewood, his first wife, leaving the large gift of £200 for bread for the poor after Sunday service to the parish of Netherseal where she was buried.[79]

Joan, Morewood's stepdaughter, married Peter Salmon, who came from a family of merchants and shipbuilders in Leigh, Essex, and was Bishop Lancelot Andrewes' nephew. Salmon became a London physician after training in Padua and other Italian cities and was physician to Charles I. Andrew Morewood, Gilbert Morewood's brother, remembered Salmon's excellence as a physician, leaving him £10 "in respect of his extra care and pains which he hath taken with me in my sickness."[80]

---

[76] *List of the Principal Inhabitants of the City of London 1640*, p. 5.

[77] Guildhall Ms., Grocers' Company, Calendar of Court Minutes, Vol. IV, Pt I, 1640–1649, f. 136, May 15, 1646; *Complete Baronetage*, ed. George E. Cockayne, 6 vols. (Exeter: W. Pollard & Co. 1900–1909), Vol. I, p. 18; John Burke and John Bernard Burke, A *Genealogical and Heraldic History of the Extinct and Dormant Baronetcies of England, Ireland, and Scotland*, 2nd edn. (London: J. R. Smith, 1844), p. 440.

[78] "Sir Thomas Rich," in *The History of Parliament: The House of Commons, 1660–1690*, ed. Basil Duke Henning, 3 vols. (London: Secker and Warburg, 1983), Vol. III, pp. 329–330.

[79] TNA, PROB11/325/394, Will of Sir Thomas Rich, Sonning Berkshire, Nov. 20, 1667. The parishioners recited his benefaction on a plaque.

[80] TNA, PROB11/206/461, Will of Andrew Morewood, Dec. 29, 1648. Andrew made "my loving brother Gilbert Morewood" one of his executors.

Salmon had strong connections to City merchants. He made his fortune by speculating in London real estate and investing in the East India Company, the New River Company, and the Merchant Adventurers of Hamburgh. While the East India Company may have been a success, Dr. Salmon had to sue the officers of the Hamburgh Company for the return on his investment. Despite winning his case, he could not get them to pay their fines.[81] He owned several properties in the City: houses on Snow Hill in St. Sepulchre parish, on Vere Street, in Stepney, on Redcross, Cripplegate, land in Seething Lane, two tenements near the Navy Office "recently burnt," as well as a house in St. Mary Oxford, and land in Lincoln and Essex. His London house in Farringdon Ward Within was described by John Strype as "a good large and handsome building, with a graceful front towards the Thames."[82] He also had a country house in Leigh, Essex.[83] Salmon named as his executors Sir John Moore, the Lord Mayor and great East India merchant, who had been Gilbert Morewood's apprentice, and Sir Leoline Jenkins, the eminent lawyer and ambassador. Salmon left £30 to free slaves, that is Christians taken in captivity, in Tunis and Algiers.[84]

Morewood's daughter Frances married Sir Thomas Gresley of Derbyshire in 1648, who succeeded his father as baronet in 1651 and became sheriff of Derbyshire in 1662.[85] The Gresleys were an old Derbyshire gentry family that traced their roots back to William the Conqueror. Sir George Gresley, Thomas's father, was one of the ten baronets who carried bannerols at Prince Henry's funeral in 1612. A Member of Parliament and, later, a supporter of parliament in the Civil War, Gresley was, however, in financial difficulties and had to sell land. As we have seen, he had sold the manors of Netherseal

[81] HLRO, L/PO/JO/10/1/340/310, Nov. 7, 1670, Salmon *v.* The Hamburgh Company; BL, Add. Mss., 41806, f. 217, Dr. Salmon's case against the Hamburgh Company, 1672. Although the House of Lords had ordered the Hamburgh Company to pay Salmon £2,895, the governor and assistants claimed they had not been in office when the decree was issued.
[82] John Strype, *A Survey of the Cities of London and Westminster ... By John Stow, citizen and native of London ... Now lastly, corrected, improved, and very much enlarged ... by John Strype ... In six books.* 2 vols. (London: Printed for A. Churchill, J. Knapton, R. Knaplock, J. Walthoe, E. Horne, [and 5 others], 1720), Vol. I, Book 3, chap. 8, p. 194, Farringdon Ward Within; TNA, PROB11/349/164, Will of Peter Salmon of Saint Martin in the Fields, Middlesex, Nov. 18, 1675.
[83] Margaret Pelling and Frances White, *Physicians and Irregular Medical Practitioners in London, 1550–1640 Database* (London, 2004), *British History Online*: www.british-history.ac.uk/no-series/london-physicians/1550-1640 [accessed Oct. 31, 2016]; BL, Sloane Ms. 3203, ff. 103–108v, contains "Dr. Salmon's receipts," but there is no indication that these are Dr. Peter Salmon's prescriptions.
[84] TNA, PROB11/349/164, Will of Peter Salmon of Saint Martin in the Fields, Middlesex, Nov. 18, 1675.
[85] *Complete Baronetage*, ed. Cockayne, Vol. I, p. 40.

and Overseal in Leicestershire to Gilbert Morewood for £2,650 in 1624.[86] Morewood presented these lands back to the Gresleys twenty-five years later when Frances married Sir Thomas. Frances's prominent role in Gresley family life is discussed in Chapter 4.

Morewood's youngest daughter Grace married Simon Bennet in 1649. As we saw in Chapter 1, Simon was the son of the City merchant Richard Bennet and Elizabeth Cradock, who had married as her second husband Sir Heneage Finch. His grandfather, Sir Thomas Bennet, had bought the Buckinghamshire manors of Beachampton and Calverton with the adjacent market town of Stony Stratford for his eldest son Sir Simon Bennet, the philanthropist, who was created a baronet by James I. When Sir Simon died without children, his nephew Simon inherited his estate. Simon Bennet thus combined a City fortune based on trade with a seat in Buckinghamshire. With widespread property holdings in several counties, he settled Beachampton, Calverton, and Stony Stratford on Grace as part of their marriage settlement.[87] Their wedding in 1649, festooned with ribbons, had been celebrated at Kensington House. Simon and Grace and their daughters who became wealthy heiresses figure largely in later chapters.

Religon and Family: Morewood's Will

Gilbert Morewood's will of June 1650, written in the opening days of the English Republic, provides us with our greatest insight into his personal and religious beliefs, his love and trust in his wife, his generosity toward his extended family, and continuing connections between city and country. We saw earlier that he had close ties to his Presbyterian parish church. In his will Morewood presented himself as a grateful and prosperous merchant, sure that he was one of God's elect. His good fortune, he wrote, came from God, drawing attention to "my personal estate which God of his infinite goodness hath lent me." With his fortune made and all his daughters well married off, Gilbert Morewood noted that God had favored him. He had promised his wife's father that he would provide her with £1,000:

---

[86] Falconer Madan, *The Gresleys of Drakelowe* (Oxford: Printed for subscribers by [H. Hart], 1899), p. 83.

[87] Hull History Centre (Hull University Archives), Papers of the Forbes Adam/Thompson/Lawley (Barons Wenlock) Family of Escrick, U DDFA2/24/1, Marriage Settlement: Symon Benet of Beachampton, co. Bucks. esq. (son and heir of Richard B. of London dec'd) to Gilbert Morewood of London esq.: Prior to marriage of Symon Benet and Grace Morewood, daughter of Gilbert, Oct. 9, 1649, "Manor, mansion house and advowson of Beachampton ... Manor and advowson of Calverton alias Calveston with Stony Stratford, co. Bucks, with fairs and markets and fishing in the River Owse."

Now in as much as God hath blessed me and my poor labours with a more plentiful estate of his mere and free mercies ... she shall have and enjoy that parte and share of my estate which I hereby give and leave unto her and which by Gods blessing will amount to a greater proportion than the said sum promised before marriage.[88]

Morewood made his wife the chief heir of his personal estate after other legacies. He also left her a tenement in St. Albans in Hertfordshire and ordered that his Cornhill property should go to his nephew and apprentice, Benjamin Morewood, after the death of his wife.[89] Having settled half of his lands and tenements in Leicester, Derby, and Strafford on his daughter Grace and Simon Bennet at their marriage, he now gave the other half to his daughter Frances and Sir Thomas Gresley. To Thomas Rich, his son-in-law who had now remarried, he left £100 as well as £100 to Rich's new wife Elizabeth Cockayne. To Dr. Peter Salmon, who had married his stepdaughter, he left £20 and his best cloak as well as £20 to Joan and £10 each to their daughters to buy black clothing for mourning.

Morewood did not simply focus on his nuclear family. Like Sir Thomas Bennet, Morewood remembered with affection his extended family to whom he left legacies. Among others he provided £30 to his sister-in law Sarah to buy "blacks," black clothing for mourning, and £5 more for her daughter. He provided monetary bequests to his brothers and sisters and to his recently deceased brother John's many children, both boys and girls, leaving them not only blacks for their mourning but £20 each for the boys and £20 for plate for the girls at their marriages or when they were twenty-one. He left a long-term lease to his godson Gilbert Morewood of Dronfield, Yorkshire. He also left his Derbyshire brother Anthony Morewood and his wife a £40 bequest. He remembered the poor in all those places that meant most to him: his place of birth in Yorkshire, the City neighborhood where he did his apprenticeship, and the London parish where he now lived.

Morewood made his son-in-law Thomas Rich his executor for his estate in London and Reginald Eyre, his sister's son, who had also been his apprentice, executor for his property in the country. Morewood's daughter Frances claimed that his estate was worth at least £30,000. Whether wishful thinking or, if true, collectable, such an amount would have placed him among the richer merchants in London. In 1624 only 24 of 140 aldermen of London

---

[88] TNA, PROB11/212/751, Will of Gilbert Morewood, June 21, 1650.

[89] TNA, PROB11/212/751, Will of Gilbert Morewood, June 21, 1650. Morewood left property in Oxfordshire to "Old Mr. Lawrence Lee" and after him to his son Ralph Lee who maintained close connections to Gilbert's family.

had estates of £20,000 or more.[90] Certainly, Morewood had been able to gain a position of influence in the East India Company in the early 1640s that he maintained until his death in 1650. Morewood was buried in the parish church of St. Christopher le Stocks on May 23, 1650. Unexpectedly, his wife Frances died just days later on May 31, 1650. They joined a Morewood child who was buried twenty-two years before.[91] Gilbert left £12 for the poor and £8 to the parish. Christopher Wren rebuilt the medieval church on Threadneedle Street damaged in the Fire of London, but the church was torn down in 1732, its tombs lost.

Gilbert Morewood's Will and Women's Property Rights

Because Frances Morewood died a few days after Gilbert, their estates became tangled in lawsuits. These lawsuits cast light not only on Morewood's wealth but also on the relationship of women and property in the seventeenth century. The first question to be decided was who inherited; the second, what did they inherit? Most married women did not make wills and Frances did not have time to make a will after Gilbert died. Because she died intestate, her estate was divided according to the custom of London.

By his will, Gilbert Morewood had divided his real estate between his biological daughters. Under the common law doctrine of coverture, while they were married, Frances's and Grace's husbands handled their property. Sir Thomas and Lady Frances Gresley took the manor of Netherseal with its manor house worth £1,692 at 18 years purchase and its advowson, that is the right to present a clergyman to its living. The manor house contained a new parlor with a drawing table that extended with leaves, a livery cupboard for food and drink, nine leather chairs, three joined chairs, and three "twigger" chairs. Reginald Eyre reported that between January 10, 1652, and May 5, 1653, he received £136-14-9 in rents from Netherseal.[92] Simon and Grace Bennet took Overseal, its manor house, court leet and court baron, gardens and orchards, as well as New Hay and Elford in Staffordshire and Duransthorpe, Derbyshire.[93]

---

[90] Robert G. Lang, "The Greater Merchants of London in the Early Seventeenth Century" (unpublished D.Phil. thesis, Oxford University, 1963).

[91] *The Register Book of the Parish of St. Christopher le Stocks in the City of London*, Vol. I, ed. Edwin Freshfield (London: Printed by Rixon and Arnold, 1882), pp. 45, 41; Guildhall Ms. 4423/1, ff. 186v, 188v.

[92] Derbyshire Record Office, D77/2/1/374, Netherseal Estate rental.

[93] Derbyshire Record Office, D77/1/16/7, Particular of Mr. Gresley's manor house of Netherseal with the demesne and realty there unto belonging, *c.* 1650s. D77/1/16/7, Schedule of Morewood's goods around Seale. The Hall contained, in addition to the new parlor, the great parlor, great chamber, chamber over the hall; mill; Total £441-00-7; Debts desperate £282-03. D77, 1/16/7, Bundle F2, Division of Property between the Gresleys and the Bennets.

But, as we saw, Gilbert Morewood had left his wife Frances Morewood his movable property. Under the custom of the City of London, all *three* of Frances's daughters, Frances, Grace, and Joan, were due the Child's portion, which was one-third of Gilbert Morewood's personal property. Therefore, in June 1650, Simon Bennet, Thomas Gresley, and Peter Salmon agreed to divide Frances's estate in equal thirds because her daughter Joan was entitled to a third of her estate.[94]

As they sorted out how to divide the movable property, the question arose of how much there was to divide. Sir Thomas and Lady Frances Gresley sued Thomas Rich and their cousins, Reginald Eyre and Benjamin Morewood, for failing to collect the outstanding debts of the estate in 1654. The size of Gilbert Morewood's estate came under scrutiny when the high hopes of the Gresleys clashed with the hardheaded realism of their former brother-in-law, Thomas Rich. The Gresleys claimed that Morewood had had an estate of £20,000 in the City, and £10,000 in the country, and much more in debts due him yet they had not seen their share of the estate. Rich answered that Morewood had had a "good personal estate but of what certain value this defendant knoweth not."[95] Benjamin Morewood had initially been in charge of collecting debts, making an inventory of Gilbert Morewood's goods, submitting it to the Ecclesiastical Court, and providing updated accounts, including the debts received and paid out, to the husbands of the three daughters. Rich claimed that Benjamin had made errors in the account, that many of the outstanding debts were impossible to collect, and that Morewood himself had debts too. Rich had not been hesitant, however, to collect his own legacy from the estate. Reginald Eyre, too, had collected his riding charges and money.[96]

To settle their quarrel, Sir Thomas Gresley and Thomas Rich drew up a deed stating that Gilbert Morewood at his death possessed a "good personal estate" in and about London and elsewhere. They agreed that Frances Morewood's three daughters inherited after her death and therefore her three sons-in-law had a right to one-third of the personal estate Frances inherited from Gilbert, according to the custom of London, because he was a citizen and freeman. The three sons-in-law, therefore, agreed that after debts and funeral expenses were paid, the Gresleys would get the first £100 of all rents, and all residue equally shared and divided into nine equal parts, four-ninths to the Gresleys and five-ninths divided between the Bennets and Salmons.[97]

[94] Derbyshire Record Office, D77/1/16/7, June 20, 1650.
[95] TNA, C9/22/78, Pt. II, Griesley *v.* Rich, Eyre, and Morewood, 1654.
[96] TNA, C9/22/78, Pt. II, Griesley *v.* Rich, Eyre, and Morewood, 1654. *Court Minutes of the East India Company, 1650–1654*, p. 170, May 14, 1652.
[97] Derbyshire Record Office, D77/1/23/11–17, Deeds relating to Seal, Overseal, Netherseal and Overseal.

This odd and unequal arrangement didn't work either. Sir Thomas Gresley complained that his £100 had not been paid and the four-ninths had not been received. Finally, in exchange for Rich paying them £1,600, Sir Thomas Gresley acquitted him of all claims he and Frances had to the goods and chattels of the Morewoods' estate. The acquittal did not include bonds and bills in the hands of Reynold Eyre for money due to Gilbert Morewood from rents and goods in Leicester, Derby, Stafford, and Warwick and monies remaining in Eyre's hands that he had acknowledged in Chancery.[98]

Final Accounts

Thomas Rich's answer to the Gresleys' suit provides evidence about the variety of ways in which Morewood made his wealth even as it suggests that there were no systematic accounts. Rich stated out that "in his lifetime [Gilbert] had received some great sums of money" which Rich could not find. Morewood had had £3,400 in the second general voyage of the East India Company but had received £2,234 from the company during his lifetime according to their accounts. Rich explained that when he took over the administration of the estate he had received £500 from Benjamin More-wood and then a further £700.

Rich recovered assets from Morewood's moneylending activities, including loan repayments from Sir John Wolstenholme, a leading East India Company investor, customs collector, and supporter of exploration and Sir John Nulls, who was an East India Company man, Virginia Company member, and customs farmer in the 1640s. In addition, the East India Company paid a dividend, a mortgage yielded £647-2-6, and the St. Albans property paid a small amount.

Rich described Morewood's insurance business as extensive. Sir Nathaniel Barnardiston, Member of Parliament from Suffolk, who was a strong parliamentarian and Presbyterian, paid him for "assurance."[99] The scale and uncertainty of the business, however, Rich argued, was preventing him from winding up Morewood's estate. "Being a Merchant and using to ensure great sums of money for diverse and sundry Marchants, divers sums of money have bin required of this defendant for losses for moneys assured by the said Gilbert Morewood and divers other sums may hereafter come in and be charged upon this defendant in such that this defendant cannot yet discover." Rich said he could not pay out monies remaining in his hands without indemnity. For

[98] TNA, C9/22/78, Pt. II, Griesley *v.* Rich, Eyre, and Morewood, 1654.
[99] TNA, C9/22/78, Pt. II, Griesley *v.* Rich, Eyre, and Morewood, 1654; History of Parliament: Sir John Wolstenholme; Sir Nathanial Barnardiston. Sir John Nulls.

example, the creditors of Edward Abbott were demanding £900 or £1,000. Rich also listed several people who claimed the loss of £100 and £200 each.

Rich summed up the state of Morewood's overseas imports and ventures. Still in the East India Company warehouse lay Morewood's pepper, cardamom, and cinnamon worth £300 or £400 not yet sold. As to the fate of the *Concord* that had been seized in Brazil, although "the State of England having made peace with the State of Holland and with the King of Portugal some moneys which the said Gilbert Morewood lost" might yet appear. Rich had not received any word. Gilbert also had small shares, a 1/32 and 1/64 part, of the *Jeremy* costing £32-6, a ship that was lost. Rich had had to pay out for losses for two other ships, the *Patrick* and the *Prosperous*.[100]

Gilbert Morewood's career and the dispute over his will display the adaptability of entrepreneurs and the varieties of new enterprises available to them in the early seventeenth century. While moneylending and rental property were not new, trading to the East Indies and the Americas did provide new opportunities. Morewood began as a Grocer specializing in pepper and at the end of his life still had hundreds of pounds in spices in the East India warehouse. He also had money in East India Company ventures, shares in ships in interloping trades, and a thriving insurance business before the Civil War. During his lifetime he did well. Nevertheless, in the mid seventeenth century these were risky businesses, large sums could and did disappear, and merchants waited anxiously, like Antonio, in *The Merchant for Venice*, for the return of their ships. Neither the *Concord* nor the *Prosperous* did. Morewood did not leave as much money as his family expected. Perhaps that was why the prosperous Sir Thomas Rich, Morewood's son-in-law and executor, who had become wealthy and was made a baronet by Charles II in 1661, left his sisters in law, Frances Gresley, Grace Bennet, and Joan Salmon, the large sums of £500 each in his own will in 1667.[101] Belated payment rather than affection appears to have been the motive, since he only referred to Joan in loving terms.

In a final accounting, Morewood's no-nonsense son-in-law Simon Bennet sought payment of the income from the Morewood country properties. On April 10, 1669, Reginald Eyre, Morewood's nephew, apprentice and executor, was summoned to reply at Newport Pagnall, Buckinghamshire, for rent of £2,000. They drew up a document stating that Eyre owed Bennet £1,565 for rent and monies. If he did not pay by September 29, 1671, Eyre would be liable to pay the full £2,000.[102]

[100] TNA, C9/22/78, Pt. II, Greisley *v.* Rich, Eyre, and Morewood, 1654.
[101] TNA, PROB11/325/394, Will of Sir Thomas Rich, Sonning Berkshire, Nov. 20, 1667.
[102] Hatfield House Archives, Legal 11/13, 1669, papers re a judgment for debt.

Conclusion

Sir Thomas Bennet and Gilbert Morewood, both younger sons from minor gentry families, became wealthy London merchants in the late sixteenth and early seventeenth centuries. Morewood was part of a new wave of gentlemen apprentices from an extended family in Yorkshire and Derbyshire who became apprenticed to the Grocers' Company, while Bennet and his older brother became Mercers. Bennet and Morewood demonstrate how new commercial fortunes could be made in seventeenth-century London through the luxury European cloth trade, trade to Asia and the Americas, and the use of state authority. They both diversified their wealth into property holdings and other ventures. Sir Thomas Bennet and his son, Sir Simon, supported the established church and the Crown. Gilbert Morewood was a committed Presbyterian and supporter of parliament in the 1640s. Simon Bennet held office under the Protectorate during the 1650s, but there is no evidence for his religious beliefs.

Marriage alliances, too, proved profitable types of investments connecting the Bennet and Morewood families to upwardly mobile lawyers, new baronets, Members of Parliament, and, later, members of the aristocracy and nobility. Both Bennet and Morewood, while identifying themselves as merchants and citizens of London, bought country property linking their families again to the land and to the gentry and the Stuart elite. Their wealth and the forms it took helped shape the lives of their families for three generations. For most it offered important opportunities for social mobility. At the same time, the attraction of London continued through the generations. Bennet and Morewood heiresses proved irresistible to suitors even if their fortunes were made in trade. The next chapters examine the second and third generations of Morewood and Bennet women as they fought for, strengthened, hoarded, spent, and added to the commercial fortune made in the late sixteenth, seventeenth, and early eighteenth centuries by their grandfathers and themselves.

PART II

Marriage

CHAPTER 3

"The £30,000 Widow" and Kensington House
The Finches, the Conways, and the Cliftons

At the heart of Kensington Palace nestles a Jacobean mansion once owned by a City widow who inherited a fortune made in international trade. The year 1628 was a tumultuous one. Britain was at war with France. Responding to Charles I's war measures, the House of Commons passed the Petition of Right calling on the king to end arbitrary taxation, arbitrary imprisonment, and the billeting of troops. The Duke of Buckingham was assassinated by a disgruntled soldier. In April of that year Elizabeth Bennet inherited £20,000 on the death of her husband, Richard, son of Sir Thomas Bennet whose funeral procession she followed in Chapter 1. Despite pressing military and political issues, Elizabeth Bennet and her fortune immediately became the locus of desire for several Members of Parliament and peers of the realm.

Elizabeth's lively courtship resembled a city comedy, filled with characters like the ridiculous doctor, the narcissistic gentleman, and the newly made viscount, all of whom competed for her hand. Secretly, she decided to marry the canny lawyer. Her marriage was discussed publicly by contemporary news writers in letters that circulated widely and privately by friends of the participants. It even found its way into the courts. Elizabeth Bennet not only had to fend off unwanted suitors who went to the extremes of trespass and bribery to try to gain her consent, but also had to gain the wardship of her son from a conniving courtier.

Elizabeth ultimately chose Sir Heneage Finch, Speaker of the House of Commons, as her second husband (see Plate 5). She made a prenuptial agreement with Heneage to protect her own inheritance and her son's, and her fortune provided additional funds to maintain their suburban villa which they renamed Kensington House. They barely had time to enjoy it together before Finch died in 1631. But Elizabeth lived in Kensington House for thirty years making it a center of Finch family life. Her stepson Heneage, who later became Earl of Nottingham, bought the house from the estate, and his son Daniel, 2nd Earl of Nottingham, sold it to William III in 1689 as a new royal palace in the healthier air of the suburbs. William and Mary had Christopher Wren make additions to Kensington House and George I transformed it into a palace, turning its Jacobean core into his new state rooms: the Privy Chamber, the Cupola Room and the Withdrawing Room.[1]

The role of Elizabeth Finch in the history of Kensington Palace is hardly known. And yet the Finches might never have enjoyed Kensington House and its gardens without the money the Bennets made in the cloth trade, East and West Indian ventures, and court finance. Conventional Jacobean and Caroline city comedies such as Thomas Middleton's *The City Madam*, seek to divide rich City merchants and their wives from the aristocracy, both in status and in culture. They fail to capture the life of Elizabeth Finch whose natal and marital families spanned merchant, legal, and courtly elites.[2]

This chapter and the following chapter turn to women in the second generation of the Bennet and Morewood families: Elizabeth Bennet, now Lady Finch, and her daughters Frances and Anne Finch, and Lady Frances Gresley, daughter of Gilbert Morewood. They enable us to see how the wealth made in trade affected their lives and the kind of power and independence they were able to exercise within their families and the larger society. Lady Finch, her daughter Frances, and Lady Gresley managed their own property, cemented city, court, and country relations, promoted their children's education and upwardly mobile marriages, and, especially in the case of Lady Frances Gresley, managed their family's economy. At times, their actions caused conflict with their husbands, brothers, and sons over their property and led to accusations about their lack of transparency, foolishness, and greed. Simon Bennet demanded an accounting of his inheritance from Lady Finch. His stepsister, Frances Finch, once she became Lady Clifton, went to court to preserve her property after the death of her husband, Sir Clifford Clifton, who left her with great debts. Lady Gresley, Simon's sister-in-law, arranged her sons' apprenticeships in business, sought to influence their choice of trade, and struggled to keep them from going overseas. Her son sued her for illegally holding onto parts of his father's estate. All of these women used the law and their social connections to protect the value of their property for themselves, their families, and their female heirs. While many aristocratic women had the same aims, Lady Finch's and Lady Gresley's money and property came directly or indirectly from trade. As a result, Lady Finch' and Lady Gresley's experience of the world of business helped shape their attitudes and practices.

---

[1] Edward Impey, *Kensington Palace: The Official Illustrated History* (London: Merell, 2003), pp. 11–22.
[2] Linda Levy Peck, "A Consuming Culture," Program for Philip Massinger's *The City Madam* (Stratford on Avon: Royal Shakespeare Company, 2011).

Wealth in early seventeenth-century England took many forms including land, houses, and gardens, ships and merchandise, movable goods such as gold and silver plate, linen, clothing, furniture, jewelry, and coaches. By the late seventeenth century, new financial instruments such as bank accounts, stocks, and bonds appeared. Even as wealth took new forms in the seventeenth century and women's access to property expanded, traditional forms such as gold and jewels continued to be valued along with luxury goods in new forms such as silver coffee and chocolate pots, and silver sugar boxes that reflected Britain's triangular trade.

English women, especially widows, could hold property in their own name, bring suit in the courts, dispose of their property, and make contracts. Under the common law doctrine of coverture, however, fathers or husbands represented daughters or married women in common law courts and they were unable to hold land in their own names. In marriage, their husbands received the portions women brought to the marriage and controlled their property during marriage. As a result, few wives in England made wills. But these limits on women's rights to property were increasingly breached in the seventeenth century. Jointure, a specific contract, had usually replaced dower, spelling out the inheritance of the wife after the death of her husband. Parents could also establish trusts to provide for daughters. In Bennet *v.* Davis, a court decision in 1725, a wife could hold property separately if her father left it to her even without a trust.[3] Over the course of the seventeenth century, judges also expanded the doctrine of necessaries by which women could make contracts to buy goods that upheld the status of their husbands. Women below the level of the gentry who had their own businesses often could control their property even when married.[4]

As we will see, the elite women in this book were under coverture for part of their lives. Nevertheless, few of them were willing to leave the oversight of their property rights to others. By 1700 the third generation of Bennet and Morewood heiresses were investing in the Bank of England, and the East India and South Sea Companies.[5] Thus even before the Married Women's Property Act of 1882, women's ability to hold property had expanded significantly.

[3] On women and property, see Amy Louise Erickson, *Women and Property in Early Modern England* (London and New York: Routledge, 1993); Susan Staves, *Married Women's Separate Property in England 1660–1833* (Cambridge, MA: Harvard University Press, 1990); *Baron and Feme: A Treatise of the Common Law Concerning Husbands and Wives* (London: Printed by the assigns of Richard and Edward Attykns, Esqs. for Jon Walthroe, 1700).

[4] Christine Churches, "Women and Property in Early Modern England: A Case Study," *Social History*, 23 (May 1998), 165–180.

[5] Anne Laurence, "The Emergence of a Private Clientele for Banks in the Eighteenth Century: Hoare's Bank and Some Women Customers," *The Economic History Review*, ns 61 (2008), 565–586.

Elizabeth Cradock

Elizabeth Bennet not only had to fend off unwanted suitors who went to the extremes of trespass and bribery to try to gain her consent, but she also had to gain the wardship of her son from a conniving courtier.

Elizabeth Cradock was a smart and attractive woman of great foresight who grew up in a well-to-do merchant family at the beginning of the seventeenth century. Her father, William Cradock, came from a prominent Staffordshire family of wool merchants who sat in Elizabethan parliaments for the town of Stafford. He himself was a cloth and linen merchant and served as a factor in Hamburg. Cradock established important ties to Alderman William Cockayne and served as Deputy of Cockayne's New Company of Merchant Adventurers from 1616 to 1618.[6] Elizabeth's first cousin, Matthew Cradock, who was apprenticed to Cockayne, became an extraordinarily successful international merchant. By the late 1620s, along with his memberships in the Merchant Adventurers, the Eastland Company, the Russia Company, and his stock in the East India Company, Matthew Cradock became a founding member and first governor of Massachusetts.[7] He later sat in the Short (1640) and Long (1640–1660) Parliaments.

Elizabeth Cradock thus united two successful merchant families when she married Richard Bennet. A member of the Mercers' Company and a cloth merchant like his father, Richard expanded his trading interests in the 1620s to the East Indies and Virginia.[8] He became a tobacco importer, some of which remained in his warehouse at his death in 1628.[9] Elizabeth and Richard lived in Sir Thomas Bennet's house near Mercer's Hall, in the parish of St. Olave's Old Jewry off Cheapside. They also had a house in Pebworth, Gloucestershire, bought for Richard by Sir Thomas. Elizabeth had jewelry that resembled the ropes and rings of elaborately worked pearls, gold, and diamonds found in the famous Cheapside Hoard of Elizabethan and Jacobean jewelry now at the Museum of London.[10]

Judging from Richard Bennet's will, he and Elizabeth had a strong and affectionate marriage. In his will Richard expressed his attachment to

[6] Wolf-Rudiger Baumann, *The Merchant Adventurers and the Continental Cloth Trade, 1560s–1620s* (Berlin: Walter de Gruyer, 1990), pp. 340–341.

[7] *ODNB*, "Matthew Cradock"; Robert Brenner, *Merchants and Revolution: Commercial Change, Political Conflict, and Overseas Traders, 1550–1653* (Princeton, NJ: Princeton University Press) pp. 137–138.

[8] Hatfield House Archives, Legal 12/12, E. Scott's bill of complaint against Richard Bennet about an East Indian Adventure.

[9] TNA, E199/28/40, London and Middlesex, Schedule of Goods of Richard Bennet, 22 James I.

[10] Hazel Forsyth, *London's Lost Jewels: The Cheapside Hoard* (London: Museum of London, 2013).

Elizabeth and his belief in the soundness of her judgment. Dividing his estate in three parts according to the custom of the City of London, Richard left one-third of his estate to his wife and one-third to Simon, their only surviving child, who was then almost four years old.[11] He left Elizabeth "all her jewels and chains of pearls and gold with diamond rings and other rings which I have at any time bestowed upon her. Also I do give to my said wife my coach and my four gray coach mares and geldings with all things thereunto belonging." Richard then went further. From the remaining third he made a series of small bequests to relations and the rectors and officers of the churches where he worshipped. He left the remainder of the estate to Elizabeth. He made her sole executor of his will and ordered that Elizabeth "have the education and bringing up of my son Symon Bennet" until he was twenty-one.[12] In all, Elizabeth may have inherited between £20,000 and £30,000 from Richard Bennet including control of Simon's inheritance until he came of age.

Elizabeth now had the power of a wealthy widow. She asserted her own choice about her remarriage, the wardship of her son, the control of her inheritance, and the dispersal of her goods. She made a prenuptial contract with her second husband and, widowed once more, when leaving bequests to her daughters in her will, insisted that their husbands have nothing to do with their inheritances.

Courtship

Elizabeth Bennet's courtship came to public notice when, in November 1628, John Raven, a member of the College of Physicians, decided to risk all, including Elizabeth Bennet's reputation, by bribing her servant and gaining access to her bedroom at midnight when she was asleep. The 46-year-old Doctor of Physic of Christchurch, Southwark, City of London, physician to Anne of Denmark and Charles I, Raven had apparently already buried three wives.[13] Reverend Joseph Mead described the scene:

Dr Raven, the physician, having been long suitor to Mrs. Bennet, the £20,000 widow, and being held in suspense, thought, by a more compendious way to achieve

---

[11] Hatfield House Archives, Legal 64/6, 1627. A man named Cole sued Bennet for non-payment of wages for Mrs. Cole who had served as "milch nurse to his son."

[12] TNA, PROB11/153/479, Will of Richard Bennet, May 7, 1628.

[13] Margaret Pelling and Frances White, *Physicians and Irregular Medical Practitioners in London 1550–1640 Database* (London, 2004), *British History Online*: www.british-history.ac.uk/no-series/london-physicians/1550-1640 [accessed Oct. 31, 2016]. J. Milton French, "George Wither's Verses to Dr. John Raven," *Publications of the Modern Language Assocaition*, 63 (1948), 749–751.

his end, so on Wednesday night (her maid, as it is thought, being of the conspiracy and now in prison), he hid himself in her chamber, and about two of the clock in the morning came, unready to her bedside, awaked her, and proffered some service that was not fit; for she, out of a virtuous disposition, refused, cries "Thieves, thieves! murder, murder!" Up comes her man, apprehends the Raven, whom they carried the next day before the recorder [Sir Heneage Finch] sometimes his counsel in his love, who committed him to prison.[14]

Reverend John Rous in Sussex, eager for London news, recorded specifically in his diary that Raven had put his leg into Elizabeth's bed.[15] Touching legs was a symbol of consummation in arranged marriages, but Dr. Raven may have meant something less symbolic. Whether Dr. Raven thought that Elizabeth would succumb to his charms or would allow herself to be raped because no one would believe her story, it is hard to say. As it turned out, Dr. Raven was arrested and brought up on charges before the Recorder of London, Sir Heneage Finch, one of Elizabeth's suitors. Mr. Pory reported Dr. Raven's fate to Reverend Mead two weeks later. "Dr. Raven (he that offered at midnight to steal to bed to the widow Bennet) was on Wednesday arraigned of burglary; and had not Judge Richardson most nobly jeered him out of his frantic humor, he would have persisted in pleading himself guilty, and so would have condemned himself of a deadly crime, whereof he was quite innocent." Given time to change his plea overnight, Raven ultimately pleaded guilty only to "ill demeanor."[16]

Elizabeth's many suitors included widowers with debts and widowers with children and sometimes men with both. Parliament had adjourned at the end of June 1628 after voting for the Petition of Right. Between sessions, several members of the House of Commons and the House of Lords pursued Elizabeth Bennet. Sir John Eliot, the staunch opponent of Charles I, Sir Sackville Crowe, Treasurer of the Navy, and Sir Peter Temple, the Buckinghamshire MP, were just a few of the succession of suitors who courted the well-to-do widow.[17] Sir Henry Waller, MP, suggested to Sir John Eliot that

---

[14] Rev. Joseph Mead to Sir Martin Stuteville, Christ Church, Nov. 22, 1628, Thomas Birch, ed., *Court and Times of Charles the First*, 2 vols. (London: Henry Colburn, 1848), Vol. I, pp. 436–437.

[15] Mary Anne Everett Green, ed., *Diary of John Rous: Incumbent of Stanton Downham, Suffolk, from 1625 to 1642*, Camden Society, Series 1, no. 66 (London: Printed for the Camden Society, 1856), p. 34.

[16] Mr. Pory to Rev. Joseph Mead, Dec. 5, 1628, Birch, ed., *Court and Times of Charles the First*, Vol. I, pp. 441–443.

[17] *Proceedings, Principally in the County of Kent, in connection with the Parliaments called in 1640, and especially with the Committee of Religion appointed in that year. Ed. the Rev. Lambert B. Larking, M. A., from the collections of Sir Edward Dering, Bart., 1627–1644, with a preface by John Bruce* ([Westminster]: Printed for the Camden Society, 1862), pp. xivff.

he pursue Elizabeth. He argued that, because Eliot had recently lost his wife, now was the time to find another one. Waller described Elizabeth Bennet's attractions, her newly inherited wealth, and her status: "The gentlewoman I mentioned is a merchant's widow. Her husband was an Alderman's son." Furthermore, he stressed that she was already being "solicited by men of great birth and wealth."

She is neere above 30 years of age and for person and parts fit for a gentleman of worth. She hath but one child which is a son and her ward. Her husband left to her and her child an estate of £30,000 or neere upon and one half at the least to her self. She hath two kinsmen (the one a merchant in London, the other a gentleman in Staffordshire a member of our house) upon whose advice she doth rely. I have spoken with him [in] London & he doth well approve of the motion and wished it were in his power to further it. He tells me she is so solicited here in London she is gone into Gloucestershire & is to go shortly into Staffordshire to her kinsman, one Mr. Mathew Cradock, to free herself from suitors ... Among others our worthy Recorder is a very earnest suitor.[18]

Waller reported that Elizabeth said that she did not want to marry anyone with children. He later remarked, however, that women were not always constant and that few women "have that power over themselves" in the case of a man "against whom no exception could be made." Although Eliot expressed interest to Waller, his failure to come to London to pursue his cause meant that he lost ground to competitors.

Just after Dr. Raven's misadventure in November 1628, Sir Edward Dering, MP, Baronet and antiquary, who had recently lost his wife, began his courtship.[19] His autobiographical narrative vividly portrays him and his society as rich, materialist, and striving.[20] Between November 20, 1628 and February 25, 1629, he documented his pursuit of Elizabeth Bennet, tracing the time and money he spent sending her letters, waiting on her at her house, gazing upon her at church, bribing her servants, and entreating friends to sing his praises to the widow. He even tried to ingratiate himself with little Simon. Elizabeth turned to her relatives for protection. These included Matthew Cradock as well as her brothers–in–law George Lowe and Sir George Croke, Justice of the King's Bench, who was married to Richard Bennet's sister Mary. Dering tried to use them as intermediaries without

---

[18] Reverend Alexander B. Grosart, ed., *De Jure Maiestatis, or Political Treatise on Government (1628–1630) and The Letterbook of Sir John Eliot (1625–1632)*, 2 vols. (London: Printed for Earl St. Germans, 1882), Vol. II, pp. 15, 18–20, 22.

[19] *Proceedings, Principally in the County of Kent*, p. xvii. Marjorie Hope Nicholson, ed., *Conway Letters: The Correspondence of Anne Viscountess Conway, Henry More and Their Friends, 1642–1684* (New Haven, CT: Yale University Press, 1930), p. 3.

[20] *Proceedings, Principally in the County of Kent*, pp. xivff.

much success. Elizabeth often put off her suitors by saying she needed to
wait for the return of "cousin Cradock." Even as she was pestered by suitors,
she was also engaged in negotiations with Walter Steward, a member of
Charles I's Privy Chamber, for the wardship of her four-year-old son Simon.

Thus, courting Elizabeth was a complicated matter. On December 4,
1628, for example, Dering, having waited for her at her house the previous
day only to find her out because she was at Dr. Raven's trial, returned once
more. There he met George Lowe who brought him Elizabeth's answer:
"That Steward was so testy that she durst not give admittance unto any until
he and she were fully concluded for the wardship."

> That she had a good opinion of me.
> That he [i.e. Loe [*sic*]] had heard nobly of me.
> That he would inform me when Steward was off.
> That he was engaged for another.
> That I need not refrain from going to the church where she was,
>   unless I thought it to disparage myself.[21]

When Elizabeth finally agreed to see Dering on December 11, she told him
that she did not intend to marry. On January 1, Dering asked for all of his
letters back, the sign that his courtship was over. But he quickly regretted
that moment of pique when he heard more about Elizabeth's wealth. He
noted in his manuscript journal "George Newman says she hath two suits of
silver plate, one in the country and the one here, and that she hath beds of
100 l the bed!"[22] On January 12, Dering met her at the door of Sir George
Croke's house where she was about to pay a visit, helped her out of her
coach, and escorted her into the house. There he renewed his suit. "She told
me that she had denied me, and I had denied myself … So in hope of
another sight, then I kissed her and took my leave."

Dering now hoped that Mr. Cradock's arrival would support his suit, but
Sir George Croke told him he saw "no likelihood." Dering left no stone
unturned. Paying off Lady Elizabeth's servants, two days later Dering met
Simon Bennet's nursemaid Susan Newman and George Newman in Finsbury Fields. "I entertained the child with cake, and gave him an amber box,
and to them wine. Susan professed that she and all the house prayed for me,
and told me the child called me 'father.' I gave her 5s."[23] Still Dering
persevered. He asked Izaak Walton, who later wrote *The Compleat Angler*,
to use his connections to the Cradocks to influence Elizabeth Bennet.

---

[21] Quoted in *Proceedings, Principally in the County of Kent*, pp. xviii–xvix.
[22] Quoted in *Proceedings, Principally in the County of Kent*, p. xxiii.
[23] Quoted in *Proceedings, Principally in the County of Kent*, pp. xxiv–xxv.

Dering took note of his rivals. In addition to the parliamentarians, these included Richard, Viscount Lumley of Waterford. Lumley had only recently been raised to the Irish peerage in 1628 but used his court allies to influence Elizabeth. Lumley's first wife had been a widow. When his pursuit of Elizabeth failed, he married still another widow, Elizabeth Cornwallis, in 1630. Their marriage was so unhappy that the House of Lords heard their grievances and, in her will, his wife warned Lumley not to "meddle with anything in my possession."[24] Throughout *his* courtship Dering consulted with Sir Heneage Finch who assured him that although he himself had been interested in the widow he had withdrawn from the contest.

Even as her courtship became a topic of public conversation, Elizabeth fought to recover Simon Bennet's wardship from Walter Steward. As we saw in Chapter 1, although Simon's father was a City merchant and his inheritance included wealth from business, Simon also inherited land from his uncle, Sir Simon Bennet, which was held by knight service directly from the king. Bennet's wardship was therefore administered through the Court of Wards.[25] In the late sixteenth and seventeenth centuries, wardships became rewards for courtiers who negotiated with family members to regain control over their own children. Walter Steward, commendator of Blantyre, who was brought up with James VI at the Scottish court, became Keeper of the Privy Seal, Gentleman of the Bedchamber to King James, and Lord Treasurer of Scotland. His younger son and daughter received favor from Charles I. Walter, a member of Charles's Privy Chamber, was awarded Simon Bennet's wardship. He kept increasing the price for selling it to Elizabeth and may have been as interested in the widow as in the wardship.[26] Beginning with an asking price of £1,500, he ultimately reached £4,000.[27] Elizabeth regained Simon Bennet's wardship before she remarried.

Elizabeth Bennet made her choice known publicly when, on April 16, 1629, she married Sir Heneage Finch, Recorder of London and Speaker of the House of Commons. Finch, who had provided a sympathetic ear to the other suitors, including Dr. Raven and Sir Edward Dering, was not her most high-ranking suitor: Viscount Lumley was a nobleman and Sir Edward Dering was a baronet. Dering had connections to the court and to the Duke

---

[24] *ODNB*, "Elizabeth, Viscountess Lumley of Waterford (*c.* 1578–1658)."
[25] TNA, Court of Wards, WARD 7/81/208, IPM Sir Simon Bennet: Buckingham, 7 Charles I (c. 1632); Court of Wards, WARD 7/77/75, IPM Richard Bennet: Gloucester, 4 Charles I.
[26] *Proceedings, Principally in the County of Kent*, pp. xivff. On Walter Steward, see Keith Brown, *Noble Society in Scotland* (Edinburgh: Edinburgh University Press, 2004), p. 183; TNA, SP17/H/ 12, Grant to Anne Stewart, Lady Saltoun, June 17, 1630, to search for rents in arrears in the Exchequer and Duchy of Lancaster.
[27] *Proceedings, Principally in the County of Kent*, p. xxx.

of Buckingham, although that connection was no longer useful with the Duke's assassination. Elizabeth had said that she did not want to marry a man with children, and Finch's children were aged ten and under. Nevertheless, Finch was a very well regarded common lawyer; he had first been selected for parliament in 1610, and had been chosen by the City of London as Recorder in 1621. He represented the City in the final parliaments of James I in 1621 and 1624 and Charles I's parliaments of 1625 and 1626. Perhaps Elizabeth was attracted by his religious views. Finch was a Calvinist.[28] Even more important may have been his age, stability, and family connections. He was forty-eight and his first marriage had lasted twenty years while Dering, aged thirty, had buried two wives after three or four years each. Finch was also the younger son of one of the first baronets, Sir Moyle Finch, and Elizabeth Heneage, who was created a peeress for life by James I as Viscountesss Maidstone and later Viscountess Winchelsea. In any case, Elizabeth chose Sir Heneage Finch leaving her other suitors to find other wealthy brides. Elizabeth and Heneage were married in St. Dunstan's in the West in London on the same day and in the same place that her niece Mary, daughter of Mary Bennet and Sir George Croke, married Harbottle Grimston, another parliamentarian and lawyer.[29]

Marriage and Widowhood

Prior to her marriage, Elizabeth had secured her property and wealth through an agreement with Heneage that provided her with a substantial income in case of his death and protected the financial interests of children that they might have together. She had also made sure to guarantee the large inheritance of her young son Simon Bennet. Finally, she maintained her legal roles as executor for her first husband, her father-in-law, and her father.

Elizabeth Cradock, once the City widow Elizabeth Bennet, was now Lady Finch, and had a new home, a villa in Kensington (see Plate 6). Designed by John Thorpe for Sir George Coppin, sometime between 1616 and 1618, it joined two other Jacobean mansions, Camden House, owned by the great City merchant, Sir Baptist Hicks, and Holland House, built originally for Sir Walter Cope and owned by his son-in-law, Henry Rich, Earl of Holland. The Coppin House, called Kensington House by the Finches, while the smallest of the three, became the Finch home. When the Finches bought the Coppin mansion is unclear. It has usually been thought that Sir Heneage Finch and Elizabeth Finch, both of whom lived in the City, bought the

[28] *ODNB*, "Finch, Sir Heneage (1580–1631)."
[29] *Proceedings, Principally in the County of Kent*, p. xxxiii, note a.

Kensington mansion with her fortune after their marriage in 1629. Olivia Fryman suggests, however, based on her research in the overseers' records for St. Margaret's, Westminster, that Sir Heneage Finch may have rented the Coppin House or even bought it a few years earlier in 1625 and lived there with his family and first wife Frances Bell, who died in 1627.[30] Tax records for 1628 and 1629, however, state that Heneage was no longer liable for taxes in Westminster because he was living in London. These tax records raise questions about Finch's continuous ownership or rental of the Coppin House from 1625 on.[31] Moreover, in his will of 1631, Heneage, who describes himself as of St. Bartholomew the Great, London, refers to the Coppin mansion that he "lately bought," which suggests that the purchase coincided with his marriage to the wealthy Elizabeth Bennet in 1629. Sir Heneage Finch died in 1631. Although most accounts suggest that Kensington House was left to his son John Finch, his will left the house and all its furnishings to Elizabeth for life and required his executors to sell the house on her death unless his brother Frances wished to live there.

Heneage requested burial in Eastwell, Kent, in the vault where "my dearly beloved wife [Frances] together with the first pledge of our love, our first son lye all interred, and where a poor monument in remembrance of myself is already erected."[32] Indeed, a funeral bust was commissioned from Nicholas Stone for the Eastwell church. But Finch's brother Francis and his brother-in-law Thomas Twisden decided to create a longer memorial inscription that also honored Elizabeth, the Cradocks from whom she was descended, and their two-year-old marriage. The inscription, translated from Latin, reads in part:

To Heneage Finch, the radiant knight who served London as Recorder for decades, Member of Parliament, and under King Charles Speaker of the House of Commons ... To the best son, husband, employer and friend, from Elizabeth his second wife. Who came from the ancient family of Cradock. One of two daughters, having survived her husband by two years, two months and seven days. He most serenely gave up his soul into the hands of his Saviour when he was taken away by the dropsy on the 5 September 1631.[33]

---

[30] Olivia Fryman, ed., with contributions by Sebastian Edwards, Joanna Marschner, Deirdre Murphy, and Lee Prosser. *Kensington Palace* (New Haven, CT: Yale University Press, in association with the Paul Mellon Centre for Studies in British Art, forthcoming).

[31] TNA, E115/151/171, Certificate of Residence showing Sir Heneage Finch to be liable for taxation in London and not in (county unknown), the previous area of tax liability 1628; TNA, E115/143/54, Certificate of Residence showing Sir Heneage Finch to be liable for taxation in London, and not in the city of Westminster, etc., Middlesex, the previous area of tax, 1629.

[32] TNA, PROB11/160/764, Sentence of Heneage Finch, Recorder of London, of Saint Bartholomew the Great, City of London, Dec. 7, 1631.

[33] Philip Parsons, *The Monuments and Painted Glass of Upwards of One Hundred Churches Chiefly in the Eastern Part of Kent* (Canterbury: Simmons, Kirkby and Jones, 1794), p. 22.

Perhaps because of the brevity of their marriage, Sir Heneage, while attentive, was not as generous to Elizabeth as her first husband had been. Elizabeth had made sure, however, that her property rights and those of her children were protected before her marriage. Her prenuptial agreement now came into effect, the inheritance of her son Simon was protected, and the movable goods, those she had inherited and those Heneage had given her, became hers outright. Thus, Sir Heneage ordered his executors to "lay out £10,000 in land to be conveyed and assured according to the true meaning of the agreement made by me upon my marriage, so as my wife may enjoy them during her life without power to sell them and that the lands may after come to her children by me." Until the lands were purchased, he ordered that Elizabeth was to be paid £600 a year. As we saw in Chapter 1, Heneage and Elizabeth had posted a bond with the Court of Orphans that they would provide sureties for Simon Bennet's inheritance from Richard Bennet within a month after they married.[34] They had also sued Sir Simon Bennet in 1630 to make sure that he shared with Elizabeth any remaining debts and legacies from Sir Thomas Bennet's estate.[35] Most important, Sir Heneage Finch provided for Simon's rights in his will and Elizabeth's role as executor.

And my Executors must also secure (if I shall not do it in my life) to the Chamber of London for the use of Symon Bennet her sonne such money as shalbe due unto him for his child part of his father's estate, and must likewise pay all such things for the performance of her husband Richard Bennet's will or Sir Thomas Bennet's will as my wife should have done if she had continued a widow . . .

In addition to the £10,000 in land, Heneage also left Elizabeth the rich material goods, jewelry, coaches, silver, and household furnishings that he and her first husband, Richard, had given her. These luxury goods included the "necklace of diamonds and the diamond ring that I gave her. And all such other rings, jewels, and pearls as were her own before." He gave her £200 immediately and all the household furnishings at Broad Marston, which she had inherited from Richard Bennet, for her own use. "And all my coaches and coach horses and horse or gelding as at the time of my decease she shall use for her own saddle, together with the saddle and furniture for horse which I gave her and 500 ounces of silver plate as she shall choose out of the rest." If Elizabeth wanted silver above the 500 ounces Heneage had given her, he wanted her to have it "at the rate that the silver shalbe worth without paying anything for the fashion of it." Heneage also

---

[34] LMA, Orphans Deeds, 33 CLA/002/04/033.
[35] TNA, C3/402/53, 1630, Sir Heneage Finch and Dame Elizabeth Finch *v.* Sir Simon Bennet re personal estate of deceased Sir Thomas Bennet knight in London, 1631 or before.

gave Elizabeth the use of all the hangings, carpets, and household stuff and furniture at either the house in St. Bartholomew in the City or "my house at Kensington," as long as she remained unmarried and called for an inventory to preserve it.

And after her decease I would have my dwelling house at Kensington with the gardens and grounds thereunto adjoyning, and other lands which I lately bought of Mr. Muchampe or Coppin (all which I have freely given to my wife for her life) to be sold ... saving that if my dear brother Mr. Francis Finch shall like to live in it I would have him to enjoy the said house and lands and the rents thereof wholely to his own use during his life and after to be sold by those that shall remain trusted.

Francis Finch was living at Kensington House as part of the family when he made his will in December 1657.

Heneage provided £1,500 for their year-old daughter, Frances, when she became eighteen or when she married, assuming she was at least sixteen and had her mother's permission. What Heneage didn't know was that Elizabeth was pregnant with another little girl, Anne, born after his death.[36]

Lady Finch was thirty-two years old. She now had six children under ten, including her stepsons, Heneage, Francis, and John Finch, and her own son Simon Bennet. Elizabeth had married Heneage in April 1629 and they had two children together: Frances was a year old, and a new baby, Anne, was born posthumously in December 1631.[37] Kensington House became the family home. Lady Finch stayed there throughout the Civil War in the 1640s with Frances and Anne. In the 1650s Anne often visited when Elizabeth was plagued by the gout and other illnesses. "My mother continues extreamly ill and much worse then she useth to be, and therefore you may imagine she will not discourse of removing from here this summer, which I very impatiently wish she may do quickly, if it pleaseth God." Lady Finch continued to live in Kensington House until her death in 1661.[38]

When Sir Heneage Finch bought the house at Kensington, it had probably already been extended to include "barns, stables ... gardens, and orchards." Elizabeth bought more property, and by the 1660s the garden had a grotto. Samuel Pepys, who visited it in the 1660s, commented on the

---

[36] TNA, PROB11/160/764, Sentence of Sir Heneage Finch, Dec. 7, 1631. To fulfill his will, goods at both houses were to be sold including all his dishes, "gilt and plate," and furniture, and the lease of the house at St. Bartholomew's, but not his books.

[37] *ODNB*, "Sir Heneage Finch," drawing on genealogical evidence mentions another surviving daughter named Elizabeth, but there is no mention of her in the correspondence.

[38] Nicholson, ed., *The Conway Letters*, pp. 148–149; Anne Conway to Edward Conway at Ragley, April 30, 1658. Various taxation certificates show Elizabeth Finch's residence in Middlesex rather than in Gloucestershire, TNA, E115/142/57.

gardens and the fountains: "a mighty fine cool place it is, with a great laver of water in the middle, and the bravest place for music I ever heard."[39] The 1664 inventory of Finch houses, made two years after Elizabeth's death, shows that that the Finches owned richly upholstered furniture, tapestry, including a series on the story of Augustus Caesar, the story of Solomon, and Troy, ebony and Indian cabinets, and masses of silver.[40]

Education at Kensington House

With six young children, Kensington House might have provided its own kindergarten, but we know little about early education in general and the Finch children's early education in particular. While the Finch boys went to Oxford and Cambridge and Simon Bennet enrolled at Lincoln's Inn, the girls, Frances and Anne, were educated at home. Reading was generally encouraged across status groups as the key to understanding the scripture, but much of what we know about early modern education draws on the experience of the nobility and monarchy. Some mothers, like Sir Thomas More's daughter Margaret or Lady Anne Clifford, taught their young children to read.[41] In the sixteenth century, several outstanding women such as Lady Jane Grey were famous for their learning and writing, as well as their piety. Sixteenth-century female monarchs, such as Mary Tudor and especially Queen Elizabeth had humanist educations that included ancient and modern languages and classical texts.[42] The Sidney circle, the Countess of Pembroke, her niece, Mary Wroth, and Lucy, Countess of Bedford, were all highly educated. John Florio, the distinguished Italian translator, was tutor to Queen Anne and other Jacobean women such as the Countess of Kent to whom he dedicated his English–Italian dictionary and translation of Montaigne. In the 1650s Anna Maria Van Schurman, whose works were widely translated including into English, argued that women should be educated but should not take up professions. By the late seventeenth century, however, writers like Bethsua Makin and Mary Astell agreed that women's education should be equal to men's because their merit was equal and should include philosophy and poetry.[43] In 1673 Makin lauded sixteenth- and

[39] Impey, *Kensington Palace*, p. 16.
[40] Impey, *Kensington Palace*, p 17; Fryman, ed., *Kensington Palace*.
[41] Kenneth Charlton, *Women, Religion, and Education in Early Modern England* (London and New York: Routledge, 1999), pp. 204–206, 217–218.
[42] Aysha Polnitz, *Princely Education in Early Modern Britain*, Cambridge Studies in Early Modern British History (Cambridge: Cambridge University Press, 2015).
[43] Frances Teague, *Bethsua Makin, Woman of Learning* (Lewisburg, PA: Bucknell University Press, 1998). My thanks to Georgianna Ziegler for advice on seventeenth-century women's education.

seventeenth-century aristocratic women whose education and piety she held up as exemplars from Lady Jane Grey to Margaret Cavendish, Duchess of Newcastle, and several of her own students: the Dowager Countess of Huntingdon, Princess Elizabeth, daughter to Charles I, and Princess Elizabeth, eldest daughter to the Queen of Bohemia.[44]

The Finch daughters were not royal, noble, or at court, but they were from a well-known legal and parliamentary family. As their brothers were educated for university, their sisters too had tutors. Both Frances and Anne were encouraged to learn languages. Heneage Finch, who went to Oxford in 1635 and to the Inner Temple in 1638, traveled on the continent during the Civil War. While in Rouen he wrote to twelve-year-old Frances in French to allow his sister to show off her comprehension and express concern that his absence was a burden to her.[45]

Anne Finch's interest in philosophy was encouraged by her brother John's tutor, Henry More, a Cambridge Platonist. John Finch attended Oxford followed by Cambridge in the late 1640s, where his brother Francis joined him. More began writing to Anne Finch in 1650 when she was in her late teens, and they maintained their well-known correspondence on philosophy throughout her life.[46] Anne eventually became More's friend and equal. A brilliant analyst, she also corresponded with Gottfried Wilhelm Leibnitz (1646–1716), Franciscus Van Helmont (1614–1698), and others.

Anne's work addressed the nature of God, the world, and matter. A vitalist, she argued that God infused all things with his spirit. In the 1670s Anne composed a study on ancient and modern philosophers that critically analyzed the work of her contemporaries, including Hobbes, Spinoza, Descartes, and Henry More. She criticized materialists like Hobbes and Spinoza and argued that More himself went only halfway to accepting the vitalist position. Published in Latin after her death in 1690, Anne's treatise was translated and published in English in 1692. Leibnitz owned a copy of her work.[47] Anne's correspondence was published in 1930, and since 1979 scholars have written extensively on her philosophical writings

---

[44] Bethsua Makin, *An Essay to Revive the Antient Education of Gentlewomen, in Religion, Manners, Arts & Tongues. With an Answer to the Objections against this Way of Education* (London: Printed by J. D. to be sold by Tho. Parkhurst, at the Bible and Crown at the lower end of Cheapside, 1673).

[45] University of Nottingham Mss., Clifton Papers, Cl C 177, 178, 179, Heneage Finch to Frances Clifton, from Rouen, Oct. and Nov., 1643. *ODNB*, "Heneage Finch, Earl of Nottingham."

[46] Nicholson, ed., *Conway Letters*, passim. Sarah Hutton, *Anne Conway: A Woman Philosopher* (Cambridge: Cambridge University Press, 2004), pp. 36–52.

[47] Hutton, *Anne Conway*, pp. 233–235.

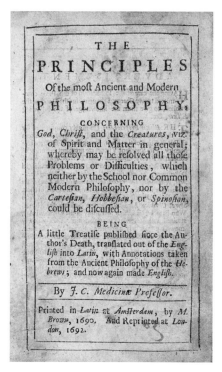

Figure 3.1 Anne Conway, *The Principles of the most Ancient and Modern Philosophy*
Concerning God, Christ, and the Creatures (London, 1692), 2nd edn., title page.
The Folger Shakespeare Library, 153–318q. The book was published after her death.

and her network of correspondence. More recently, studies have analyzed
her philosophical writings alongside contemporaries such as Margaret
Cavendish.[48]

Most scholars suggest that Anne's childhood at Kensington House was
solitary, omitting the presence of her sister Frances entirely and underesti-
mating the emotional importance of her mother. Anne's sister Frances, just a
year older, was also well educated although she was not a prodigy like Anne.
Henry More maintained a correspondence with Frances too, assured her that
she was "sufficiently complete in the Art of Rhetorik," and sent Frances the
work of Descartes adding that should she need help "she had so good

[48] Sarah Hutton, "Anne Conway, Margaret Cavendish and Seventeenth Century Scientific
Thought," in *Women, Science and Medicine 1500–1700: Mothers and Sisters of the Royal Society*, ed.
Lynette Hunter and Sarah Hutton (Stroud: Sutton Publishing, 1997), pp. 218–234; Stephen
Clucas, "The Duchess and the Viscountess: Negotiations between Mechanism and Vitalism in the
Natural Philosophies of Margaret Cavendish and Anne Conway," *In-Between: Essays & Studies in
Literary Criticism*, 9, 1–2 (2000), 125–136.

assistants ... Mr. Clifford Clifton and my dear pupil Mr. Francis Finch."[49] On another occasion More sent Frances three books, unidentified, one for Mr. Clifton, one for herself, and one for Anne.[50] More continued to send copies of his works to Frances as well as to Anne and sought to visit her in London throughout his decades-long friendship with the Finch family.[51] Henry More assumed that Frances as well as Anne might be interested in the leading philosophical treatises of the time.[52]

Civil War Marriages

During the Civil War the Kensington family had divided loyalties. The Finches remained neutral despite their royalist leanings. Lady Finch's brother-in-law, Francis, arranged for a pass on August 10, 1643 to take Lady Finch and her daughters into exile in France, but it was apparently never used.[53] Heneage Finch returned from the continent to set up his law practice in London in the 1640s. In contrast, Simon Bennet held office under the Republic in the 1650s, serving as Sheriff of Buckinghamshire in 1651. Elizabeth Finch's children married or found their partners during the 1640s and 1650s. The Finch daughters married at twenty and appear to have had some choice in their husbands. Anne married Edward Viscount Conway, a peer who supported her intellectual interests, in 1651. They spent the early years of their marriage in Kensington House. Frances married Sir Clifford Clifton, a friend of her brother's and the son of Sir Gervase Clifton, a Nottinghamshire baronet who had loaned money to King Charles.

We saw in Chapter 1 that Lady Finch's son by her first marriage, Simon Bennet, spent hundreds of pounds on ribbons when he married Grace Morewood, the daughter of the Presbyterian East India merchant Gilbert Morewood in 1649. Perhaps because the Interregnum frowned on frivolity or money was short, Lady Finch opted for a simpler wedding for her daughter Frances, Simon's stepsister. She and her brother-in law Francis Finch wrote to Sir Gervase Clifton that "there is only wanting a common prayer book and a ring with the benediction (for we will abate you nothing of these Holy Rites in a thing (as holy, if not a sacrament) ... For other festival, ribbons (rybers), as empty foyles, vanity bestowed in other times, my

---

[49] University of Nottingham Mss., Clifton Papers, Cl C 333, Henry More to Frances Finch, Aug. 5 (1645–1650).

[50] University of Nottingham Mss., Clifton Papers, Cl C 334, Henry More to Frances Finch (1645–1650).

[51] Nicholson, ed., *Conway Letters*, pp. 69, 70, 155, 334.

[52] Hutton, *Anne Conway*, pp. 233–235.   [53] History of Parliament Online, "Francis Finch."

sister (with your leave) in these seeks to avoid them or at least return them to your disposing."[54]

The younger son, Francis Finch, kept track of the family romances and the newlyweds in a series of letters in 1650. In April he referred to his sister Frances's marriage, although Sir Clifford Clifton had not yet made his proposal. "You have so many ways of enchantment that no person that sees or hears you is capable of freedom." He told Frances that he could not obtain leave to visit her except to be present at her wedding, and then could not attend. In October he inquired about his sister Anne's marriage prospects. "You will tell me when I am in election of a new brother and who may be the man ... How does the Recluse Gratiana? And the Gentlemen her husband. My service to them and to my brother Clifton wheresover he be." In November 1650, after Simon Bennet was appointed Sheriff of Buckinghamshire at the young age of twenty-six, Finch wrote to his sister: "Present my most faithful service to Gratiana and Mr. Sheriffe with all the contentment he can desire."[55]

As for the Finch sons, Heneage married Elizabeth Harvey, the daughter of Daniel Harvey, a Levant Company merchant in 1646. Francis Finch married the widowed Elizabeth Parkhurst in the late 1650s, daughter of Sir Robert Parkhurst, a strong supporter of parliament during the Civil War.[56] Sir John Finch formed a lifelong relationship with Dr. Thomas Baines who became his constant companion from the time they met while studying with Henry More at Cambridge in the late 1640s. Together they went to Padua to study medicine. Once John became a diplomat, Charles II enabled Dr. Baines to accompany him on all his diplomatic postings. They lived together throughout their lives. Together even in death, Finch arranged for their burial together in Christ Church, Cambridge. Their memorial inscription testifies to their "beautiful and unbroken marriage of souls, a companionship undivided during 36 complete years."[57]

Elizabeth Finch made her will in 1657. But she had one more task to do. Her longtime guest, her brother-in-law Francis Finch, made a nuncupative (oral) will on December 14, 1657, naming her his executrix and on January 18, 1658, when the will was proved, it fell to her to deal with his goods,

[54] University of Nottingham Mss., Clifton Papers, Cl C 167, Elizabeth and Francis Finch to Sir Gervase Clifton, June 1650.

[55] University of Nottingham Mss., Clifton Papers, Cl C 170, Francis Finch to Frances Finch, April 8, 1650; Cl C 171, April 15, 1650, Francis Finch to Frances Finch; C173, Francis Finch to Frances Finch, 1650, C 174, Francis Finch to Lady Frances Clifton, Oct. 11, 1650.

[56] "The Huguenot Family in England: III, The Vandeputs," *The Ancestor*, 4 (1903), 32–43.

[57] *ODNB*, "Sir John Finch;" Royal College of Physicians, Lives of the Fellows, "Sir John Finch."

chattels, and debts. It was a function she had carried out several times. What he left and whom he left it to is not known.

When Elizabeth died in 1662, her own will named as her executors Orlando Bridgeman, Chief Justice of the Court of Common Pleas, her eldest stepson Heneage Finch, now Solicitor General, and her cousin the lawyer Thomas Russell. She bequeathed her "great diamond ring" to her son Simon Bennet, and £1,000 to her grandchild and godchild Elizabeth Clifton, Frances's daughter, "to be paid on the day of her marriage." Until that time, she ordered her executors to invest the £1,000 and pay Elizabeth the interest along with the principal, and not deduct any money for her maintenance. She remembered her sister and her cousins. She left her sister and cousin, Nicholas Barnes's sister, who was beyond seas, each £50. The land she had purchased in Kensington she left to her cousin Nicholas Barnes's eldest son, as well as £50 each to his daughter and younger sons, and another £50 each to her cousin Thomas Russell's children. There is no mention of Grace Bennet, Symon Bennet's wife; perhaps the diamond ring was ultimately meant for her or one of her children.

Throughout her married life, Lady Elizabeth Finch had sought to protect and enhance her property whether it took the form of jewelry, coaches, money, land, or houses. She invested the trading fortune that she inherited from Richard Bennet in Kensington House and other real estate. Using prenuptial agreements, wills, and litigation, she ensured the transmission of her property to her children and preserved Simon Bennet's inheritance. In particular she planned for her daughters' financial independence.

Elizabeth Finch divided the rest of her estate between her two daughters. She made clear that she did not want any of the money to go to her daughters' husbands, but her effort to circumvent coverture required complex directions.

Whereas they are both now married, and my desire and intent is that their husbands should have nothing to do in the dispersal therof, my will therefore is that my executors shall from tyme to tyme during their husband's lives dispose of the same with the consent of my said daughters and the proceed thereof from time to time shall pay into the proper hands of my daughters equally but if either of my daughter's husbands shall die before their wives, then I will that my daughter so surviving her husband shall have her half of the estate made over to her to be at her own disposal.[58]

Should the daughter die before her husband, then her share would go to her children equally. If she had no children, then her share was to go to her sister.

[58] TNA, PROB11/307/365, Will of Elizabeth Bennet, Feb. 27, 1662.

If neither sister survived or had children, then the inheritance went to Simon Bennet's children, "which he hath or shall hath." As it turned out, Anne Conway predeceased her husband, but her only child, Heneage, died of smallpox as a small child. Lady Frances Clifton did outlive her husband. But as we shall see, Lady Finch's plan that their husbands would not share in her estate failed to be completely realized.

By the doctrine of coverture, Frances and Anne could not inherit Lady Finch's estate outright while they were married. But Lady Finch had instructed her executors to allow her daughters to direct the use of their inheritances even while married. The monies therefore could be paid out at the direction of each sister. In April 1662, John Finch reported to Viscount Conway that Sir Orlando Bridgman had relieved Thomas Russell of his duties as executor and given the "writings" to Lady Clifton. Bridgman had "called in all the money and let it out to the Duchess of Somerset and the Earl of Bridgewater, they being exact at their days of payment of interest and excellent security." Each sister was currently owed £272 of interest. Mr. Finch of Groveshurst would soon be paying another £1,500 and the money would then be available.[59] Nevertheless, Anne's letter in December 1662 illustrates how complicated it was to have money dispersed on her behalf. She wrote to her husband while he was in Dublin and she was in the north of Ireland to ask her brother-in-law to pay for a muff and cambric and to send a pacquet to Frances (or the Duchess of Somerset). "I have writ to her to hasten the sending me an account of what money she will have of mine in her hands (of that she expects to receive) after Mr. Taylor is paid, for I told her I should have occasion for the payment of some in London." Anne wondered that she had not heard from her brother Heneage. "My brother John having referred me to him for an account of my business." She asked her husband to raise the issue with Heneage if he wrote to him from Dublin.[60] Even with an inheritance, a married woman found it difficult to spend it without male support. The issue of their mother's estate came up again when Anne died.

After Lady Elizabeth Finch died in 1662, her stepson Heneage Finch became Earl of Nottingham and Lord Chancellor and lived at Kensington House. Sir John Finch, physician and connoisseur, held several diplomatic posts and ultimately became Ambassador to the Ottoman Empire. Simon and Grace Bennet lived in Calverton Manor in Buckinghamshire. Anne, Viscountess Conway, continued to write to Henry More and Leibnitz while her husband Edward, Viscount Conway served in the House of Lords, lived

---

[59] Nicholson, ed., *Conway Letters*, p. 201, John Finch to Viscount Conway.

[60] Nicholson, ed., *Conway Letters*, p. 210, Anne Conway to Viscount Conway, Dec. 9, 1662.

at Ragley Hall in Worcestershire, looked after his estates in Ireland, and forged ties with major political figures such as the Duke of Ormond and the Earl of Arlington. Frances, Lady Clifton lived at Clifton Hall while Sir Clifford Clifton, now a baronet, sat in the House of Commons for East Retford. Lady Clifton could not anticipate that when her husband died ten years later he would leave her in debt and faced with fighting for her property in court and in parliament.

Frances Clifton and Anne Conway

The Cliftons were a major country gentry family in Nottinghamshire. They lived at Clifton Hall in the village of Clifton, near Nottingham, served as justices of the peace, deputy lieutenants of the militia, and, in the seventeenth century, exerted influence over the East Retford borough seat in the House of Commons. The baronet Sir Gervase Clifton was known for his hospitality and concern for his tenants but most of all for his seven wives. When his eldest son by his first wife, also named Gervase, proved to he a spendthrift and unable to produce an heir, his father arranged for his estate to go to Clifford, his son by his second wife, and descend to his heirs. The Civil War had greatly affected Clifton finances. Sir Gervase, a royalist, had been fined in the late 1640s and had accumulated great debts. Clifford Clifton agreed to take on his father's debts of £10,526 in 1649 and to pay him £500 a year. While elite families frequently sought large dowries, Peter Seddon suggests that Clifford Clifton particularly needed to make a rich marriage.[61]

Born in 1626, Clifford was admitted to Grey's Inn in 1647 and in 1650 proposed to Frances Finch, the year after he had assumed the role of heir apparent. Clifford already knew the younger Finches. As he courted Frances, Clifford's letters to his father promised reform, in particular avoiding bad company and taverns. Meanwhile, Frances and the Finches received him warmly at Kensington House. "I have been most kindly received there since my last coming . . . [I] have gotten her favor which now I wear."[62] By the end of May, Clifford and Frances had become engaged and he visited Kensington everyday. To his father he described his "new moulding of myself." He now had "a stricter lye upon me when I look to the future happiness which I may,

---

[61] P. R. Seddon, "Marriage and Inheritance in the Clifton Family during the Seventeenth Century," *Transactions of the Thoroton Society*, 84 (1980), 33–43. "Sir Clifford Clifton," in *The History of Parliament: The House of Commons, 1660–1690*, ed. Basil Duke Henning, 3 vols. (London: Secker and Warburg, 1983), Vol. II, pp. 94–95.

[62] University of Nottingham Mss., Clifton Papers, Cl C 555, Clifford Clifton to Sir Gervase Clifton, May 11, 1650.

with God's grace enjoy, not lonely but jointly with the party, my Lady, and the family which I may justly stile her the flower of."[63]

On June 11 they signed the marriage settlement. Clifford once again sounded the theme of moral renewal along with the notice that Clifton money was short: "But a few days remaining before the nuptials ceremony be executed, I am (as I have theretofore promised) to perform a reformation which will be a great content to all parties." Expressing regrets for the year's expenses, he asked for another £40, which he would repay.[64] Clifford's efforts at reform won Lady Finch and her daughter. Elizabeth Finch and her brother-in-law Francis Finch expressed their pleasure about the alliance of the Finches and the Cliftons to Sir Gervase. Claiming that it cemented an old alliance, they wrote, "the work already is done in their hearts ... My cousin hath written himself in such a noble character of sobriety and discretion on her breast that he hath not gained much less upon the Mother."[65] The wedding took place in London in July 1650.

Knighted in 1661 by Charles II, Sir Clifford Clifton took up his role as a leading member of the country gentry in Nottinghamshire, serving as justice of the peace, deputy lieutenant, and Member of Parliament for East Retford in Richard Cromwell's Parliament in 1659 and again from 1661 to 1670. Clifton inherited his father's baronetcy in 1666 and the rest of his debts. Meanwhile, Frances had several pregnancies; three children survived to adulthood, William, Katherine, and Arabella.[66] Shortly before his death in 1670, Sir Clifford thanked one Mr. Hodgson for promising to give money to Frances while he was away in London. "I perceive by a late letter from my wife that Mr. Clayton [probably Robert Clayton, the banker] failing her of £200 or £300, you have promised her a supply in the case which is kindly done to the Female and Feme covert."[67] Sir Clifford's letter points to the limits the common law placed on married women, including their ability to borrow money as well as to his own lack of funds.

---

[63] University of Nottingham Mss., Clifton Papers, Cl C 556, Clifford Clifton to Sir Gervase Clifton, May 28, 1650.

[64] University of Nottingham Mss., Clifton Papers, Cl C 557, Clifford Clifton to Sir Gervase Clifton, June 11, 1650.

[65] University of Nottingham Mss., Clifton Papers, Cl C 167, Elizabeth and Francis Finch to Sir Gervase Clifton June 1650.

[66] Frances was prescribed medication against miscarriage. University of Nottingham Mss., Clifton Papers, Cl C 371, Francis Pruitan to Mrs. Clifton September 24, 1661.

[67] University of Nottingham Mss., Clifton Papers, Cl C 96, Sir Clifford Clifton to Mr. Hodgson, Feb. 7, 1669/1670. Clayton was not knighted until 1671.

Heneage's Legal Advice

Sir Clifford's death in 1670 at the age of forty-four brought both great sorrow and legal difficulties. While Frances reacted with understandable grief, her brother, Heneage, who had once supported her French studies, advised her to overcome her tears and take systematic steps to protect her financial interests. Sensible of "the loss of so good a brother and a friend," he feared, having heard that Frances herself was overcome, that it would keep her from looking after her children.

The best cure of grief for the present will be to apply your self in such business as require your personal diligence. Inform your self as soon as you can what will your husband hath made, what debts he owed, who are his executors, and obey the pleasure of your dead husband to the uttermost of your powers. Then look into the writings that concern your own estate, your jointure, and the money lent to your husband by your trustees, send for Mr. Sacheverell your worthy friend and mine and take his advice and Mr. Holland in such things as require present dispatch. Entreat Mr. Holland to assist you in your affairs and use him with all kindness that he may be willing to help you. Do not engage yourself in any matter of consequence touching your estate without taking some time to deliberate that so the business may be full understood. And write to me as often as you can.[68]

Gervase Holland, a Nottinghamshire gentleman, had longtime ties to the Clifton family. William Sacheverell was a Member of Parliament for Nottinghamshire in 1670 who later became a leading Whig politician. He took an active role in the Exclusion Crisis between 1679 and 1681.

The Clifton estate also offered Heneage Finch political advantages. In the same letter Heneage asked Frances to use her influence over the East Retford borough to support Sir Edward Dering (son of the Sir Edward Dering who had courted his stepmother). Heneage had gained the support of Henry Bennet, Earl of Arlington, Lord Ogle, son of the Duke of Newcastle, and other court supporters for Dering and Heneage had pledged the Clifton interest on Frances's behalf for Dering.[69] Dering won the seat.

Lady Clifton now took up the challenge of managing the family finances. Sir Clifford's will of 1669 made clear that his estate was still encumbered with his father's Civil War debts.[70] Frances drew on her political capital to

[68] University of Nottingham Mss., Clifton Papers, Cl C 180, Heneage Finch to Frances Lady Clifton, June 23, 1670.
[69] University of Nottingham Mss., Clifton Papers, Cl C 180, Heneage Finch to Frances Lady Clifton, June 23, 1670.
[70] Seddon, "Marriage and Inheritance," p. 37. University of Nottingham Mss., Clifton Papers, Cl D 1504, Copy of will of Sir Clifford Clifton of Clifton, 1669.

put through a private bill in parliament allowing her to make leases on the Clifton property to raise marriage portions for her daughters while her son William was under age.[71] Private acts of parliament were not unusual. In fact they were often the central legislative business of parliament in the seventeenth century.

Frances also went to law to enforce her property rights. Her correspondence with Gervase Holland and the letters of Ralph Edge, her attorney, to Holland reveal searches in the records for Clifton leases and plans to go to court on her behalf. Yet, Frances's relations with her men of business were testy. Instead of relying on Gervase Holland and William Sacheverell, as her brother advised, Frances told Holland that she had reviewed the accounts herself and had a pocket book in which she kept track of them. She instructed him on how to handle the will, complained that she had received "naught yet but my jointure," claimed he ignored her orders, and told him that she did not like how her affairs were being managed. She concluded one letter by saying: "But if I should chance to want any counsel . . . I shall think myself as capable to chuse it as you or most others for me."[72]

Sir Clifford Clifton's will appointed Lady Frances and Gervase Holland as executors of the estate and Gervase Holland and William Sacheverell as guardians of her son William and therefore in charge of the funds of one-third of the estate.[73] After Holland died, Lady Frances sued William Sacheverell in Chancery for a full accounting of the estate. Frances's petition was formally addressed to the Lord Chancellor – her brother Heneage! Sacheverell provided accounts of rents from the various holdings of the Clifton estate. He answered Frances's case through a series of interrogatories that sought to discover from her tenants and neighbors whether or not Frances herself had begun to collect some of the estate's rents after Holland's death. If so, Sacheverell argued he could not be held liable for any shortfall.

Despite the entanglements of the Clifton estate, its problems could not keep Lady Frances from the lure of London society and culture. She reminded Gervase Holland that she had told him and everyone else "I should always equally divide my time between London and Country."[74] Lady

---

[71] HLRO, HL/PO/JO/10/1/34/320, "Amended Draft of an Act for the better payment of the debts of Sir Clifford Clifton, knight deceased, and raising portions for his daughters, Nov. 18, 1670." See Chapter 5.

[72] University of Nottingham Mss., Clifton Papers, Cl C 97, Lady Frances Clifton to Gervase Holland, July 1, 1673; Cl C 98, Lady Frances Clifton to Gervase Holland, n.d.

[73] HLRO, HL/PO/JO/10/1/34/320, "Amended Draft of an Act for the better payment of the debts of Sir Clifford Clifton, knight deceased, and raising portions for his daughters, Nov. 18, 1670."

[74] University of Nottingham Mss., Clifton Papers, Cl C 716, Lady Frances Clifton to Gervase Holland, Saturday, 13 May.

Frances's decision to spend six months a year in Southampton Square, Bloomsbury, is not really surprising. Elite men and women spent more and more time in the capital in the seventeenth century in a pattern that had begun even earlier with attendance at parliament and the law courts during term times. From the late sixteenth century on, the possibility of shopping at retail boutiques such as the Royal Exchange and the New Exchange increased the attraction of the City and Westminster. By the late seventeenth century, the cultural season, the marriage market, and the development of aristocratic housing in the aftermath of the Great Fire in 1666 encouraged the nobility and gentry to stay even longer in town.[75]

Because Sir Clifford Clifton represented East Retford in parliament from 1661 to 1670, the Cliftons' year always included time in London. Lady Frances Clifton's house in Bloomsbury was furnished with luxurious silver accessories including silver plates, silver candle sconces, and silver tankards, as well as the products of Britain's triangular trade, a silver coffee pot and a silver sugar box. When she died, she left them to her son William along with the lease of her house in Bloomsbury that was to be let until he reached his majority.[76]

Frances and Anne: Last Days

Elizabeth, Lady Finch had divided the bulk of her estate between Lady Clifton and Lady Conway. Shortly before her death, she gave each one some table linen, and to Anne, Lady Conway, whom she probably saw most and was closest to, a handsome carpet that her first husband Richard Bennet had paid £60 for as well as £20 or £30 of plate.[77] After their mother's death, Frances and Anne remained in touch but rarely saw each other. Suffering from debilitating headaches from her youth, which only got worse with age, Anne traveled to Paris to investigate the procedure called trepanning, the opening of the scull to relieve the pressure that was thought to be causing the headaches. But the procedure was thought too dangerous. The sisters appear to have been on good terms. In 1665 Frances and her children visited Anne at Ragley Hall. Anne wrote to her husband "My sister Clifton with her children came hither upon Thursday last, 'tis so long since we had a meeting that I think we shall not now agree to part till you are ready to return."

---

[75] Linda Levy Peck, *Consuming Splendor: Society and Culture in Seventeenth-Century England* (Cambridge: Cambridge University Press, 2005), pp. 45–61.

[76] TNA, PROB11/364/424, Will of Lady Frances Clifton, Nov. 29, 1680. She also left him a diamond knot and pendant, a topaz and ruby ring, and an agate cup and cover.

[77] Nicholson, ed., *Conway Letters*, p. 161, Conway to Major Rawdon, July 5, 1659, p. 161.

In 1673 Henry More encouraged another visit, hoping "my Lady Clifton will make some stay with your Ladyship, she will be good chearful company for you when your pains will permit you to enjoy it."[78]

In her last few years, Lady Clifton suffered from breast cancer and Lady Conway became a Quaker. She urged Frances to turn to religion for her pain and counseled patience. Frances replied "Good and wholesome counsel is always seasonable but especially in such a condition as your letter and paper found me ... I shall endeavour to observe and practise all those Christian rules and precepts therein contained and which I wish I had been so happy as to have received from your mouth rather than from your hand." She vowed to "submit to God's holy will." Then at the bottom she wrote, "turn the leaf." Now the tone of the letter took a decidedly darker and more desperate tone as she revealed her real physical condition.

I groan continually, and am ready to give up the ghost for breath and have so great an oppression, that I can hardly gasp, or move, or stir my self the least in my bed, or from one chair to another though but a yard's space without excessive torment. My stomach and legs are very much swelled, in so much that what my distemper was and will be, I can scarce give you an account. It began with a kind of pleurisy and then turned to an ague and fever, and at last to lethargy: which I doe all I can to remove.[79]

When she wrote again to Anne two weeks later, her feet and legs had swollen "like mill posts" and she was unable to walk "half a chamber-length."[80] Yet early in November 1678, Frances wrote again to her "dearest sister" with relief and something bordering on happiness that she had arrived in London and was feeling better.[81] But happy discussions of improved health and wine were only temporary and quickly turned grim for both sisters.

At the end of her life, as Anne's spiritual interests turned to the Jewish Kabbalah and Quakerism, her husband, Viscount Conway, had little sympathy for the direction and people his wife had taken up. Asked where his niece might be placed in England, he rejected both his own home and Lady Clifton's. "In my family all the women about my wife and most of the rest are Quakers, and Mons. Van Helmont is governor of that flock, an

---

[78] Nicholson, ed., *Conway Letters*, p. 263, Anne Viscountess Conway to Lord Conway, Oct. 22, 1665; p. 393, Henry More to Ann Conway, Sept. 17, 1674.

[79] TNA, SP29/406/227, Conway Papers, Dame Frances Clifton to Anne, Vicountess Conway, Oct. 3, 1678.

[80] TNA, SP29/407/41, Conway Papers, Dame Frances Clifton to Anne, Vicountess Conway, Oct. 17, 1678.

[81] TNA, SP29/407/132, Conway Papers, Dame Frances Clifton to Anne, Viscountess Conway, Nov. 2 [1678]. She discussed why the six dozen bottles her sister had expected had turned into five because Mr. Sacheverell could spare only eighteen gallons of wine

unpleasing sort of people, silent, sullen, and of a removed conversation." As for his sister-in-law Lady Clifton, Conway said: "my sister Clifton lives so sluttishly and foolishly, that it would not be of any advantage to my niece."[82] Simon Bennet, her stepbrother, thought more highly of Frances and made her one of the executors of his will.

Anne, Viscountess Conway died in 1679. Viscount Conway went into mourning as did members of the Finch family and Lady Frances Clifton. Heneage Finch, Earl of Nottingham, took charge of embalming Anne's body to remove it from the Quakers who surrounded her and whom, he feared, might prevent a traditional burial. After his wife's death, Viscount Conway inquired about her will and goods. Christopher Cratford, one of his men of business, provided answers not only about the will but also about the current value of her jewelry and her furs. He also sent information about Lady Clifton's health.

As to my Lady's will, you may please to open it and by the contents may better judge what is to be done. The estate that came by my Lady Finch's will is to go according to my Lady Conway's will but nothing more, unless your lordship yet pleases. Pearls that are round and white, bear a good value, and are always in esteem. Other jewels alter both in fashion and value and are of late much lower in esteem. Sables are newly come again into fashion and are (if not decayed), of good value . . . My Lady Clifton has a sore breast and not been out of her chamber for a good space and she fears it grows worse.[83]

As we saw, in leaving her estate to Anne and Frances or the survivor, Elizabeth, Lady Finch clearly stated that should one daughter predecease her husband and have no surviving heirs, her share was to go to her sister. It was unusual for a wife to make a will, but Anne, Viscountess Conway made her will on June 30, 1673 leaving the estate she inherited from her mother, both property and goods, to her husband Viscount Conway except for legacies left by her will. These bequests were in the following amounts: £500 to her sister Frances, £500 to her brother Sir John Finch, £400 to Henry More, and £300 to Baron Helmont.[84] Christopher Cratford claimed that Anne's will was controlling. He also left nothing to chance. He urged Conway to open Anne's will before the funeral as a means or pretext of consulting Anne's preferences about burial and then prove the will

---

[82] Nicholson, ed., *Conway Letters*, pp. 439–440, Viscount Conway to George Rawdon, Dec. 28, 1677.

[83] TNA, SP29/411/f. 293, Conway Papers, Christopher Cratford to Viscount Conway, April [8?], 1679.

[84] TNA, PROB11/359/541, Will of Anne, Viscountess Conway, 1679.

immediately before the payment of any legacies, thus supporting his inheritance of Anne's half of Lady Finch's estate.

As to the will, most persons have in their wills something relating to their funerals, in which respect it may not seem amiss to take a right information of things betimes, and after the funeral the will maybe more solemnly opened, and then if your Lordship pleases to prove the will, that gives your Lordship a legal and just right to all your bonds and puts a final end to that affair, shutting the door to all pretences, which may else hereafter arise, and it is certain a prudent and safe way to effect this before payment of the legacies.[85]

Frances demanded the legacy from her mother's estate even as her breast cancer continued to advance, but in her last year she met resistance from Conway and Cratford. After her death, Cratford informed Conway "I did formerly intimate to your Lordship that I could not be in quiet without lending her Ladyship money. The way I did it was to let her have 300 l. residue of her legacy and take a full discharge to you for the same."[86]

Frances also sought another medical opinion in 1679, settling on Dr. John Troutbeck whom Dr. Rugeley of York had recommended to her as an able man.[87] Troutbeck had been surgeon to Cromwell's forces in the north in the 1650s and served as surgeon general to Charles II in 1660. Frances thought highly enough of his help to leave Dr. Troutbeck £100 and his brother Joseph £50 in her will in 1680 and request that they wrap her body in cerecloth, a kind of oilcloth used for wrapping the dead.[88]

Lady Clifton and Heneage Finch had encouraged Viscount Conway to remarry within weeks of Anne's death. Frances thanked him for the plaster he had sent for her sores. Then she went on:

I had not seen the Lord Chancellor but once in all my great sickness of nine months until the last Sunday, when he charged me to assure you that he will not excuse [your honor], unless that he may be assured that you will be married next week, or at the furthest the week after, for else he protested he would send out a commission of enquiry for your understanding.[89]

---

[85] TNA, SP29/411, f. 301, Conway Papers, Christopher Cratford to Viscount Conway, London, April 15, 1679.

[86] TNA, SP29/413/f. 65, Conway Papers, Christopher Cratford to Viscount Conway, London, March 2, 1680.

[87] University of Nottingham Mss., Clifton Papers, Cl C 391, L. Rugeley to Lady Frances Clifton, May 15, 1679.

[88] University of Nottinghamshire Mss., Portland Papers, DD/4P/36/7, Will of Dame Frances, Feb. 6, 1679/1680, codicil, Feb. 23, 1679/1680; *CSPD, 1666–1667*, Troutbeck to Arlington, Dec. 16–27. Troutbeck had a pension of £200.

[89] *CSPD, 1679–1680*, p. 126, Dame Frances Clifton to Viscount Conway, April 22, 1679.

Created an Earl in 1679, Conway's lack of a male heir moved him to marry again the next year. Christopher Cratford proposed that Conway marry a relative of Lord Townshend's in 1680. "Her portion will be 10,000l down and another 10,000l after her father and mother if her brother, who is a weak youth . . . miscarry."[90] Conway did not take up that offer, but he did marry twice in the years before he died in 1683. Elizabeth Booth, daughter of the first Baron Delamere, became his second wife bringing him a dowry of £13,000. She died in 1681. One month later he married Ursala Stawell who had a dowry of £30,000. Conway died in 1683 quite rich but without any heirs.[91]

Conclusion

Because of her own financial and legal acumen and network of connections through natal and marital families, Elizabeth, Lady Finch achieved wealth not only for herself but also high status for all her children. Her daughters married into the nobility and landed gentry, and her son Simon, who continued in business, married the daughter of an East Indies merchant. Her Finch stepsons, two of whom were appointed to court office, married respectively, a rich merchant heiress and the daughter of a country gentleman. Lady Finch and her family blur the status and cultural distinctions between the City and the landed assumed to exist in the early seventeenth century. The marriage of this City widow to Sir Heneage Finch, the City official and Speaker of the House of Commons, brought merchant wealth to an old landed and legal family just at the time the Finches climbed the ladder to important court position.

Her daughter Anne, Viscountess Conway, became an important philosopher who corresponded with an international network of writers despite terrible physical pain. She carved out both time and space within her marriage to carry on her work. Frances, Lady Clifton asserted control over her own property and her husband's estates. She spent several months of the year in London even as she tried to make some sense out of the debt-ridden Clifton properties. Heneage Finch, Gervase Holland, and William Sacheverell wished her to leave all matters to them, but Lady Clifton insisted on making her own decisions. As we shall see in the next chapter, Frances and Anne's sister-in law, Lady Frances Greslcy, proved even more capable of taking care of her own interests, asserting her property rights, and managing her family's economy.

---

[90] *CSPD, 1679–1680*, p. 566, Christopher Cratford to Viscount Conway, July 22, 1680.
[91] *ODNB*, "Edward Conway, Earl Conway."

CHAPTER 4

"I Was Never Any of Fortune's Darlings:"
City and Country
The Gresleys

Lady Frances Gresley was strong willed, outspoken, determined, and affectionate to a man who was not her husband. Born in 1630, Lady Frances Gresley was almost the same age as Lady Frances Clifton. Both had married baronets and were connected through extended kinship ties. They adopted different strategies, however, to protect their own property and promote their family's interests. While Lady Clifton turned to her brother Heneage Finch, Earl of Nottingham and Lord Chancellor, and other members of the aristocracy to help her, Lady Frances Gresley turned to her City connections. She and her husband Sir Thomas Gresley stressed the importance of business education for their younger sons and placed them as gentlemen apprentices in the City. Even at times of political crisis in the late seventeenth century, their letters demonstrate the continuing links between the country gentry and City merchants. Lady Gresley also showed how a wife still under coverture could effectively fight for her property rights against her husband and later, as a widow, against her son.

Frances, the daughter of Gilbert Morewood, had married Sir Thomas Gresley of Derbyshire at the age of eighteen in 1648. The Gresleys were an old Derbyshire gentry family whose home, Drakelowe, was located in Church Gresley in southern Derbyshire. Sir Thomas's father, Sir George Gresley, a Member of Parliament, was in financial difficulties, selling the manors of Netherseal and Overseal to Gilbert Morewood in 1624. Morewood returned these manors to the Gresleys twenty-five years later when his daughter Frances married Sir Thomas. Indeed, when we last saw the Gresleys in Chapter 2, they were suing their brother-in-law, Sir Thomas Rich, in the 1650s for more of Gilbert Morewood's estate. Sir Thomas Gresley succeeded his grandfather as baronet in 1651 and became sheriff of Derbyshire in 1662.[1]

---

[1] Falconer Madan, *The Gresleys of Drakelowe* (Oxford: Printed for subscribers by [H. Hart], 1899), pp. 83, 93–94; *Complete Baronetage*, ed., George E. Cockayne, 6 vols. (Exeter: W. Pollard & Co., 1900–1909), Vol. I, p. 40.

The Gresleys had fourteen children between 1649 and 1673, eleven girls and three boys. All three boys and five girls married, five girls remained single, and one girl died in infancy.[2] Lady Frances's goal was to place her two younger sons with London merchants in the City and to find husbands for her daughters. Sir John Moore (1620–1702), Lord Mayor of London and the second largest investor in the East India Company, came to the Gresleys' aid (see Plate 7).

Sir John Moore had been Gilbert Morewood's apprentice in the Grocers' Company, and Lady Frances had known him since she was a teenager and he was in his 20s. Her letters to him, whom she calls "Deaire Frind," are characterized by remarkable warmth. The surviving letters begin in 1672 when she was forty and Sir John was fifty-two.[3] Moore, an Alderman of London, Master of the Grocers' Company, one of the Committees of the East India Company, and Sheriff of London, had just been knighted. By the time the letters end in the late 1690s, he had served as Lord Mayor in 1682, was a gentleman of William III's Privy Chamber, and was in his seventies.[4]

The themes of the Gresley–Moore letters range from gift giving, to luxury purchases in London, placing the younger Gresley sons as apprentices with London merchants, and hopes that Sir John would marry one of the Gresley daughters. Sir John Moore was a nonconformist, taking communion in the Church of England only when he took office in 1671.[5] Brought up in a Presbyterian household in the 1640s, Lady Gresley herself uses Calvinist language in some of her letters. Thus, in her first surviving letter to Moore she wrote, "I unfainedly desire as it hath pleased God to give you a healthful body, a full purse, reputation, and esteem amongst men which are dangerous engines to intangle, I hope that God will inable you to walk in the way which he hath set before his Chosen that you may tread in that narrow path which is hardly found and not easily kept."[6]

Both Lady Gresley and her husband Sir Thomas had relatives in the City. Their connections underline the continuing interweaving of merchant and landed families who sent younger sons to make their fortunes in London. Frances made this point to Sir John Moore: "it is but a littill while a goe since we heard my Uncle Burdett died and now we hear my cossen Hopegood is dead: so that Mr. Gresley's relations are almost extinct in the City."[7] "Uncle Burdett" was Robert Burdett, younger son of Sir Thomas Burdett, first

---

[2] Madan, *The Gresleys of Drakelowe*, pp. 93–94.

[3] Folger, V.b. 25, Gresley Mss. Twenty-four autograph letters from Frances Gresley and Sir Thomas Gresley to Sir John Moore between 1672 and 1696.

[4] *ODNB*, "Sir John Moore."   [5] *ODNB*, "Sir John Moore."

[6] Folger, V.b. 25, Gresley Mss., Letter 1.

[7] Folger, V.b. 25, Gresley Mss., Letter 4, Oct. 6, 1679.

baronet (created 1618), and his wife, the literary patron, Jane Francis, of Foremark, Derbyshire. A member of the Skinners' Company engaged in trade to Spain, Robert made his stepbrother, Leicester, his apprentice in 1653 and his younger four sons became his apprentices between 1670 and 1678. Nominated an Alderman of London in 1656, Robert Burdett's will was proved sometime in October 1679.[8]

Edward Hopegood was also a London merchant. His father was a citizen and cloth worker. He married Jane Burdett and was buried at Margaret's Lothbury on October 3, 1679.[9] Hopegood, who was interested in curiosities, provided the Royal Society with samples of ash from a recent eruption of Mount Aetna.[10] As we will see, younger generations of the Hopegoods and Burdetts remained in touch with the Gresley family at Drakelowe.

Between 1678 and 1681, the Popish Plot and the Exclusion Crisis gripped London, parliament, and the country. False accusations of a Roman Catholic plot to assassinate Charles II, built on the king's lack of a legitimate heir. Parliament debated whether the king's brother James, Duke of York, could be excluded from the throne because he was a Roman Catholic. Charles II dissolved parliament twice and three elections ensued in which Tories and Whigs campaigned over the issue. Angry Whigs accused Sir John Moore, a Tory, who had been elected Mayor of London in 1681, of manipulating the London election for sheriff in favor of the Tory candidates.[11]

Yet between 1679 and 1681, the Gresley letters refer only glancingly, if at all, to national politics. Instead, Lady Frances Gresley sent butter, cheese, and venison from the country and told Sir John how to preserve it. "I have sent you a pot of butter, a pot of venison, a large cheese; the pot of butter hath but little salt in it is for present use. The cheese will not be ready to cut this month or six weeks . . . The maid should put a little salt and water to the butter." In return Sir John Moore sent nutmegs in syrup and two boxes of goods that Lady Gresley shared with her daughter Frances and son-in-law William Inge at Thorpe Hall, Staffordshire.[12]

---

[8] *ODNB*, "Jane, Lady Burdett"; TNA, PROB4 17737, Engrossed Inventories, Oct. 30, 1679. Derbyshire Record Office, D5054/12/3, Letter book of merchants trading to Alicante, Spain, 1648–1652. Robert Burdett was a partner. *Miscellanea Genealogia et Heraldica*, ed. Joseph Jackson Howard, Vol. I, 3rd ser. (London: Mitchell Hughes, and Clarke, 1896), "Burdett."

[9] Pedigree of Hopegood, in Frederic Cass, *Monken Hadley* (Westminster: J. B. Nichols and Son, 1850).

[10] Thomas Birch, *The History of the Royal Society*, 4 vols. (London: A. Millar, 1756–1757), Vol. II, p. 597, Oct. 21, 1669.

[11] *ODNB*, "Sir John Moore."

[12] Folger, V.b. 25, Gresley Mss., Letter 2, Lady Gresley to Sir John Moore, Oct. 14, 1678; Letter 3, April 14, 1679.

The news that Frances wanted was not political but word of family and old friends. Moore, who continued to be in touch with some of them – especially Joan Salmon, her stepsister, who was now living in Chelsea – obliged her. In October 1679, Frances wrote to him that she had not heard from him recently.

It being a great while since I heard of you or from you, it forceth me to send this carector of my love. I very well know that time and times are true triers of realty: but thay are as nothing to my conserne: I bless God we are here and tharpe [her daughter's home] in health but it is a very sickly time in the country . . . pray when you have opportunity to rite a word let me know how my cossen Lee and my cossen Joseph Morewood doe.[13]

While London was caught up in the frenzy of fear and popular unrest in November 1679,[14] Sir Thomas Gresley asked Sir John Moore to commission a new watch for him from London's greatest clock and watchmaker, Thomas Tompion. Tompion had been recommended by his country neighbor and cousin Sir Frances Burdett. "I know your judgment to be good in choosing the watch is for my one youse and would have it a good handsome size, a small sized one can never go true, a studed case, no chain, no minutes, on those terms I desire it may go 30 hours more then otherwise."[15] Tompion worked almost exclusively for members of the royal family, the aristocracy, and the merchant elite. While it may seem odd that Sir Thomas was ordering a watch with no minute hand, the introduction of the balance spring to pocket watches had only recently provided greater accuracy. The addition of the minute hand did not occur until about 1680. Tompion, however, was, in fact, beginning to produce watches that added seconds dials as well.[16] Sir Thomas Gresley does not seem to have been concerned that Sir John Moore, then a London alderman, might have been too engaged in policing the City at this time of popular political demonstrations to concern himself with Gresley's watch. In later letters Sir Thomas apologized for the effort he put Sir John to in having the watch made.[17]

---

[13] Folger, V.b. 25, Gresley Mss., Letter 4, Lady Gresley to Sir John Moore, Oct. 6, 1679.
[14] Mark Knights, *Politics and Opinion in Crisis, 1678–1681* (Cambridge: Cambridge University Press, 1994), p. 4.
[15] Folger, V.b. 25, Gresley Mss., Letter 5, Sir Thomas Gresley to Sir John Moore, Nov. 14, 1679.
[16] British Museum, "Thomas Tompion."
[17] Folger, V.b. 25, Gresley Mss., Letter 6, Sir Thomas Gresley to Sir John Moore, Jan. 22, 1679/80, "am sorry I have given you so much trouble about the watch. In my last I left it to you to be speak it where you pleased . . . I return my harty thanks for your care and pains about it." Also, in Letter 7, Sir Thomas Gresley thanked Sir John Moore for the watch which he had received, February 14, 1679/80.

Gentlemen Apprentices

Historians have suggested that gentlemen apprentices were dying out in the second half of the seventeenth century. Yet in 1686 and 1687 the Gresleys were determined to place their younger sons, Thomas and Charles, as apprentices with London merchants. International trade had grown dramatically in the seventeenth century, incorporating more and more areas of the globe after the Restoration. Now, in addition to the well-established trade to the East Indies, sugar plantations in the Caribbean Islands made the West Indian trade even more profitable. The restructuring of the Royal African Company in 1672 raised hopes of further expanding trade to another continent. The Gresleys, however, especially Frances, wanted their sons placed in a domestic trade, not sent abroad. They feared for their son's safety even as they may have feared for their finances. Sir John Moore had found a master in London for Thomas Gresley, and his father, Sir Thomas, paid £500 for his apprenticeship. Frances sent Sir John her thanks, "I am glad that my sister, [Joan Salmon] and all are well at Fulham: and I am pleased to here that Mr. Broking and my son like one another so well which is a great content to me and I give you many thanks for being so great an instrument in that bisnis."[18] According to Falconer Madan, Thomas Gresley had been apprenticed to John Broking, an oil merchant, as early as 1684, when Thomas was sixteen, with the intention of placing him in Livorno.[19]

Having successfully placed Thomas, in March 1687 Sir Thomas wrote to Sir John Moore to arrange a position for his youngest son Charles, now seventeen. He made clear that the family's claim on Moore was through Frances.

I must once more take the boldness upon my wifes interest in you and favor you have formerly been pleased to doe us upon my son Thomas account: makes us desire that you will be pleased to grant us this second request and that is you will be pleased to think of some inland trade in London for our third son Charles: we desire your opinion what trade you think will bee most advantageous to him, and that you and Cozen Lee will bee pleased to advise together and to provide us a master for him with what convenient speed may bee.[20]

Sir Thomas argued that country education did not prepare gentry boys for work in the City that required good writing and accounting skills. Sir

---

[18] Folger, V.b. 25, Gresley Mss., Letter 9, Frances Gresley to Sir John Moore, Oct. 1686.
[19] Madan, *The Gresleys of Drakelowe*, p. 103. Lincolnshire Archives, 2 THOR HAR 3/8/33, Aug. 5, 1685. John Broking of London, merchant, With Charles Thorold of London, esq: sale of 95 tuns of oil, and the repayment of £2,060 and interest.
[20] Folger, V.b. 25, Gresley Mss., Letter 10, Sir Thomas Gresley to Sir John Moore, March 30, 1687.

Thomas sent Moore a sample of Charles's writing adding, "for arethmatick and accounts he hath not lerned as yet. I think it will be better for him to lerne that when he come to town for there is none in Country understands the way so well as in London: I know I must and am willing to pay for his lerninge to cast accounts when he come up."

Young men were eager to gain the skills needed to be merchants. In 1678 Thomas Finch wrote to Sir John Moore asking that he enroll him in a "writing school in London" in order to be "fit in writing and casting accounts to undertake a merchant." He thought he was spending his money in vain learning rhetoric since his intention was to become a merchant, even though his school had "the best teaching of Latin in England." Sir John, who was apparently overseeing his education, does not seem to have responded to this plea because a year later he was sending Thomas black cloth for his gowns.[21] Margaret Hunt suggests that interest in accounting characterized the middling sort.[22] Yet both Sir Thomas Gresley and Lady Gresley were firmly committed to their sons gaining the educational skills to become merchants. In particular, Lady Gresley, who grew up in a merchant family, took a keen interest in the education and trades her son would take up in London.

Lady Frances did not want her sons to go beyond the seas or become grocers – or linen drapers, but she never says why. She did, however, insist that they have the liberty to choose something they liked. She told Sir John,

> My son [Charles] you think may be a grocer: but truly I did never like that trade; you were pleased to say in your other letter that you would have my son to have sum liking of the trade: which his father tould him of, but he said he knew not what to chuse ... I tell his father all have that liberty ... he may see something of trades when he learneth to write and cast account, he is mighty desirous to com up ... I thank God he is a very ingenious briske boy.[23]

Sir John Moore and Cousin Lee arranged an apprenticeship for Charles with a member of the Grocers' Company but Frances would not hear of it. In May 1687, Sir Thomas wrote Moore: "I received your two last letters and one from my Cozen Lee, wherein I find you have been very careful and had provided a Master for my son according to your liking and I have agreed with you ... but my wife is so averse to the trade of a grocer that she will not any

---

[21] Guildhall Ms. 29445/1, f. 25 a, Thomas Finch to Sir John Moore, April 6, [1678]; Ms. 29445/1 f. 44, Thomas Finch to Sir John Moore, March 4, 1678–1679.

[22] Margaret Hunt, *The Middling Sort: Commerce, Gender and the Family in England 1680–1780* (Berkeley and Los Angeles: University of California Press, 1996).

[23] Folger, V.b. 25, Gresley Mss., Letter 12, Lady Frances Gresley to Sir John Moore, April 12, 1687.

ways be persuaded to it by me nor any other: so that I must beg the favor of you both to think of some other beneficial trade for him."[24]

Having made her views clear as to Charles's apprenticeship, Frances next wanted to replace Thomas's master Mr. Broking. But within ten days the issue of masters and apprentices had changed to graver matters of life and death. Thomas Gresley fell ill with smallpox. In the same month, Frances's sister, Joan Salmon, died. Now the letters about Tom's condition flew back and forth between Drakelowe and Mincing Lane, Sir John Moore's house in London. The Gresleys sent great thanks to Mr. Broking and his household for nursing the young man back to health.[25] Still, Lady Gresley did not want Tom to continue with Mr. Broking "because he was so very much under a cloud," although she did not say why. Reiterating that she did not want him to go abroad, Frances offered Tom a way to pay back the £500 paid to Mr. Broking for his apprenticeship.

The letters from my cousin Lee and Sir John speake that they would have you continue with your master, which I believe will be no great matter of advantage to you, they are over fearful of venturing again of another having given £500 already ... For my part I do not licke of it. I am not very willing you should go beyond see, for your father I beleeve will not be willing to furnish you with money as you may expect, my Cousin Hopgood and her brother, think that your going to Mr. Broking will do you no good."

Instead, Frances offered to give Thomas the manor of Seal when he was twenty-one, which was worth more than £200 a year, while reserving the timber rights for herself if she should survive his father. The rents from Seal would enable Tom to repay the £500. Although Sir Thomas proved reluctant, he finally agreed. Lady Frances urged her son to "take advice from somebody that you may trust what is best to be done about this bisnis of Mr. Broking ... but say nothing of this to Sir John Moore or my Cousin Lee," and to come into the country before anything was concluded with Mr. Broking. She added, "They think of putting your brother [Charles] to two masters that are linen drapers which I do not like because I think one is better neither do I like that trade."[26] Lady Gresley's many letters about her

[24] Folger, V.b. 25, Gresley Mss., Letter 13, Sir Thomas Gresley to Sir John Moore, Drakelowe, May 11, 1687.
[25] Folger, V.b. 25, Gresley Mss., Letter 15, Sir Thomas Gresley to Sir John Moore, July 18, 1687; Letter 16, Frances Gresley to Sir John Moore; Letter 17, Frances Gresley to Sir John Moore, July 24, 1687; Letter 18, Thomas Gresley to Sir John Moore, July 30, 1687; Letter 19, Thomas Gresley to Sir John Moore, Aug. 8, 1687.
[26] Derbyshire Record Office, D77/4/5/2, Dame Frances Gresley to Thomas Gresley, "For Mr. Thomas Gresley at Mr. John Nuberry's house at Blackfriars," n.d.

sons' apprenticeships demonstrate her eager involvement in their education and strong opinions about their choice of occupation, a desire for them to be educated for business, but a fear of their going abroad. Now she urged Thomas to leave the City and return home. Sir Thomas and Lady Gresley gave Seal to Thomas on September 24, 1690. Out of the rents he was to reimburse his father £500 over four years. His mother retained the right to cut down timber.

After Sir John Moore's wife died in 1690, Lady Gresley sought to cement their ties by proposing a match between her unmarried daughter Anne, now in her thirties, with Sir John, a widower in his seventies. She reported that Sir Thomas Gresley was in favor of the match, although he feared he could not provide a portion equal to Sir John's expectations. Frances was sanguine that Sir John would not "stand much upon fortune." But Sir John raised the issue of the difference in their age. In her frank reply, Frances reeled off a series of her male acquaintances who had not only married in their seventies and eighties but also had children.

As to that of age you desired me to consider of, I have taken notes of some of our neighbors 3 or 4 miles off, have done on the like occasion, as namely Sir Samuel Sligh married a daughter of my brother Harpers 7 or 8 years since he was fourscore when he married her. He had only one daughter which is a good fortune. Mr. Lucas, our minister, married when he was 3 score and 8 and had six children. Sir Gilbert Clark married a third wife about half a year ago and ten children by his two first and hath five living 2 sons and 3 daughters, his age I do not know, but his hair put it into 4 parts two is white. We have a servant that hath bin at Drakelowe this 3 score years married a second wife 3 years since when he was 3 score and here hath one child and his wife be breeding again ... I do believe my daughter can like you as well as a younger man and do believe [her to] be very affectionate unto you and now it may be I have said too much for which I beg your pardon ... it shall not lessen the love and affection I bare to you whilst I live.[27]

Despite Lady Gresley's best efforts, Sir John remained a widower.

From the beginning of their correspondence, the Gresleys had marked their relationship with Sir John Moore with gifts. Yet Frances claimed to eschew material goods. In one letter she contrasted herself to her stepsister Joan Salmon, and sister Grace Bennet. "The other day my sister Salmon's maid told me her Mrs. was well but very fraid to lose her estate and that my sister Bennet was in much trouble about her daughters and her estate. For my part, I was never any of fortune's darlings: to have very much of the fading perishing treasures of this life: and it is my desire that I may not be too

---

[27] Guildhall Ms. 00507, ff. 96–98, Frances Lady Gresley to Sir John Moore, Feb. 28, 1692/1693.

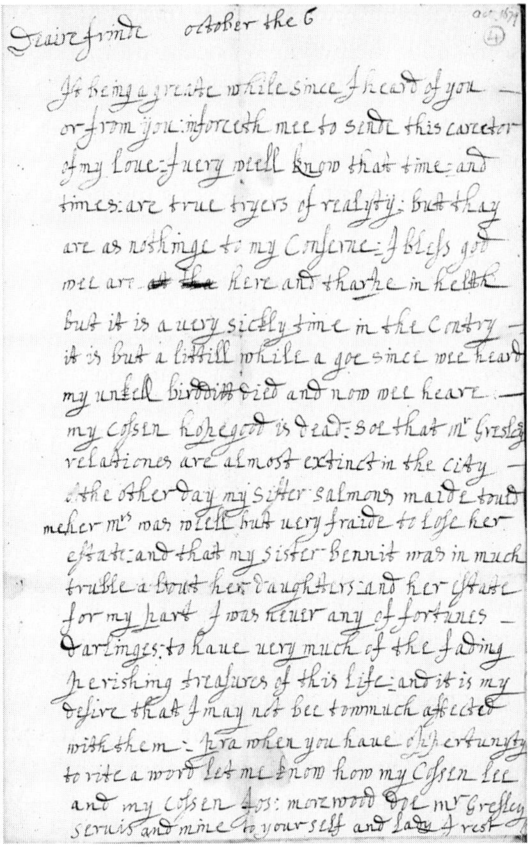

Figure 4.1 Manuscript letter from Frances Lady Gresley to Sir John Moore,
October 6, 1679. The Folger Shakespeare Library, V.b. 25, Letter 4. Lady Gresley
describes her sisters' worries about their estates and claims in contrast that she
eschewed "the perishing treasures of this life."

much affected with them."[28] Despite such sentiments, Lady Gresley did not
reject worldly goods.

In 1686, as they placed their son Thomas with Mr Broking, Lady Frances
wrote to Sir John that she understood that he wished to give her a ring.

I received a letter from daughter Anne about five or six months since wherein she
told me that you had a desire to give me a ring and also that I must send word
whether I would have one stone: or 3 but I being loth that you should bee at that
charge said nothing of it but my son said that he did hear you speak of it – to my
daughter and he thought you had the stone by you: now that you desire to bestow a
ring of me I like the black water [presumably pearl] better then the white and one

[28] Folger, V.b. 25, Gresley Mss., Letter 4, Frances Gresley to Sir John Moore, Oct. 6, 1679.

stone better then 3 and set in gold rather then silver. Pray excuse this freedom it being desired by you.[29]

Five years later, in June 1691, Lady Gresley returned to the subject of Sir John Moore's gift, apparently never having received it. She said that she never doubted his kindness and now requested instead of the black water pearl ring, silver plate with just the two initials of his name. Her sister Salmon had given her plate with JS on it so that she could remember her. As to coming to London, "I think I shall see it no more." Sir John wrote back quickly to ask exactly what kind of plate she wanted.

There is some plate in the house but Mr. Gresley hath given all within and without to my son William, giving his brother Charles and 5 sisters seven hundred pounds apiece so that if I survive I shall have a house and nothing to put in it. There is no plate either made or sold in the country that ever I knew of. I do not want a dressing box nor silver boxes but anything what you please.[30]

Whether or not Sir John Moore's plate arrived, we don't know. In 1696 Sir John Moore's new school at Appleby, Derbyshire, which was designed by Christopher Wren, offered Lady Gresley one last opportunity to press the interests of her family to her old friend. Her gossipy letter about the school's leading competitor, Ripon School and its head master, led her to the issue of the matter of the trustees. First, she commended Moore for making the tenure of the headmaster on good behavior rather than life. "Reppon[Ripon] scule is utterly ruined by having the head school master setiled for his life he being not fit for it the master before him had betwixt seven and 8 score scollors now the head scule master hath but 2 and the second but 5 you may inquire of any Darbyshire gentilmen of it." Assuming that Appleby School would require trustees, Lady Frances put forward her claim: "I desire that the eldest sons of this family may be as well as other families."[31]

The Family Economy: Backwoods Squires, Wills, and Women's Property

The affection of Lady Gresley's letters to Sir John Moore stood in contrast to the conflicts within her own family. Frances's disagreements with her husband and sons became vitriolic by the end of the decade. If she had played a

---

[29] Folger, V.b. 25, Gresley Mss., Letter 9, Lady Frances Gresley to Sir John Moore, Oct. 1686.
[30] Folger, V.b. 25, Gresley Mss., Letter 21, Frances Lady Gresley to Sir John Moore, June 15, 1691.
[31] HMC, *Tenth Report of the Royal Commision on Historical Manuscripts*, Part IV, Captain Stewart's Mss., p. 132 (1906, Reissue of 1885 edition); Folger, V.b. 25, Gresley Mss., Letter 24, Frances Gresley to Sir John Moore, Feb. 24, 1695/1696.

central role in promoting her children's advancement, she had also vigorously protected her own property rights. Formally, women's rights to property were circumscribed. While widows could hold property freely, under the common law husbands and wives were one unit; married women had no separate standing in common law courts and ostensibly could not make contracts.

Lady Gresley's husband and sons challenged her power over marriage and the estate, accusing her of greed and withholding money and goods that she was not entitled to under coverture. First, the Gresley's eldest son William – who sounds rather like Squire Booby in Henry Fielding's *Shamela* – looked for a bride in 1696. His courting was the satirical subject of his Derbyshire cousins and neighbors and disapproved of by his mother. Although William had enrolled at Oxford, books and polite language appear not to have made much impact on him. Born in 1661 and now thirty-five, William admired a young woman in Shropshire. Francis Hopegood, son of "cousin" Hopegood, who, like his father, was a merchant in the City, told the story to Thomas Coke who was traveling on the continent. Coke, from a leading Derbyshire family at Melbourne Hall, and Hopegood were cousins with the Burdetts, as were the Gresleys. Hopegood gossiped:

Esquire Bill [Gresley] of Drakelowe went a wooing into a far country, but his mistress was not much smitten with either his phiz (face) or beau meene; however he made shift to captivate the heart of a widow. I know not who this venturesome woman is, but they say she has 250 l. p. a. jointure, and 2,000l. stock, and seven children, but all provided for. The knight and his lady [the Gresleys] are much against it.

Hopegood returned to the story, which he had just heard from another informant.

Uncle R.B. [Robert Burdett] is going with him to see his mistress; vizt. the gentleman with the handwhip begad was motioned to a virgin lady in Shropshire: he went and liked her, but she did not like him; so an elder sister of hers, a widow, told her if she would not have him, she would, to which the Squire agreed. But not to the liking of his parents, which gave him much disturbance, and in his language said "Kill mother begad, zuns shoot her"; which so terrified his mother that she was fain to get away to Burton with her daughters; but the knight errant is resolved and says – "Zuns will have her and that quickly too, for hunting is coming in and then cannot awhile."[32]

---

[32] Quoted in Madan, *The Gresleys of Drakelowe*, pp. 101–102; HMC, *Cowper*, Vol. II, pp. 361–362. Francis Hopegood, London, to Thomas Coke, Anvers.

In September 1696, Hopegood informed Coke that the match had been consummated. "Squire Bill of Drakelowe is married to the Shropshire widow. Lord have mercy upon her! Sure men are very scarce, for they say she is a comely woman, has wherewith to keep her clean and her children provided for."[33] The story did not end there. Elizabeth Coke, recovering from illness at the Burdetts' house at Foremark Hall in Derbyshire in 1698, wrote to her brother who had returned from the continent and was staying at Mrs. Hopegood's in Lothbury in London. While discussing friends and prominent Derbyshire families, she again turned to William Gresley. "Esquire Bill and his lady are in Derbyshire, and are daily expected here. He swears he has got 'best best wife world [sic]. I took her down in her wedding shews (shoes?) and the best in the world.'"[34] Gresley's relatives and neighbors satirized him as a backwoods squire, ignorant, swearing oaths, whip in hand, and threatening to kill his mother in the bargain. As the eldest son, William did what he wanted including marrying without parental approval.

Sir Thomas Gresley's conflict over money with Lady Gresley spilled over into his will. He noted that his eldest son had married and his property was spelled out in his marriage settlement. Asking Frances to make a lease with Sir Robert Burdett to raise money for their children's portions and settlements, he left money to his daughters to bring their portions up to £1,000 each. These portions were small, but it must be remembered that five Gresley daughters had already married and five more were still to be wed. In particular, Sir Thomas left money to his daughter Ward, who had eloped with a Drakelowe servant, as "a separate maintenance for her wherewith her husband shall have no power to intermeddle."

Sir Thomas claimed that Lady Gresley pretended that he had settled a small property on her, but he did not remember doing so. He gave her £100 of his household goods to be valued by two assessors, one chosen by her, one by him, £50 in money, a coach and two coach horses, the furniture of her choosing, her wearing apparel, jewels and rings. Timber was a central issue between the Gresleys. Sir Thomas required that "the lumbering goods in my house at Drakelowe that are fixed to the freehold shall go along with my house as heirlooms and be from time to time enjoyed by those to whom the house shall come."

Although he and Frances had settled Netherseal on Thomas, Sir Thomas claimed that Frances threatened to void the settlement after his death. He

---

[33] Madan, *The Gresleys of Drakelowe*, pp. 101–102.
[34] Madan, *The Gresleys of Drakelowe*, pp. 101–102, Elizabeth Coke to Thomas Coke at Mrs. Hopegoods in Lothbury, April 6 1698.

reaffirmed the settlement and provided Thomas with other land. Once again linking country and city, Sir Thomas asked his son "to set my daughter Ward's children forth apprentices to some handicraft trades in London as they shall be capable there in case I shall not do the same in my lifetime." Sir Thomas made Thomas the executor of his will, dated May 13, 1698, and Sir Robert Burdett and Walter Burdett, esq. the overseers. The next year, on April 21, 1699, he added a more generous codicil that gave his wife Frances all the other household goods in the house at Drakelowe, the heirloom lumber and goods affixed to the freehold excepted.[35] Although the codicil was more generous than the original will, it did not compare in liberality to Richard Bennet's will, which left Elizabeth Finch more that two-thirds of his estate and made her his executor seventy years earlier.

After Sir Thomas's death in 1699, Thomas Gresley sued his mother in Chancery as his father's executor. Thomas accused his mother of keeping large amounts of gold and silver that his father had hidden as he became mentally unstable in his last years and suffered from what we would call dementia. Thomas claimed that these valuables did not belong to Frances because as a wife she was under coverture. The suit states that Sir Thomas possessed "a great personal estate" made up of ready money, securities, commodities, and rents due entered in almanacs and pocket books. Because Sir Thomas had been very infirm and unable to look after his affairs, "Dame Frances had heaped up great riches which she kept to her own use, or otherwise concealed the same from the said Sir Thomas." Lady Gresley

did ... possess herself of great quantities of gold, silver and other rich things, which he, the said Sir Thomas, had hid and laid up, and particularly she, the said Dame Frances, either by herself, or some other person or persons by her imployed, took up a floor or some boards in a floor, under which the said Sir Thomas Gresley had hid great quantities of gold, silver and other rich things, all which she took and carried the same forth of the said room in her apron, or otherwise ... And the house where the said Testator dyed being in jointure to the said Dame Frances for her life, she refuseth to permit your Oratour to make a full and effectual search in the same.

In addition, Thomas asserted that during his father's lifetime his mother saved money which she concealed and said was not part of his estate "when as she well knows, she was capable of taking no money to her own use during the coverture, but that whatsoever was saved by her was for the benefit of her husband and ought to be accounted part of his personal estate."[36]

---

[35] TNA, PROB11/458/22, Feb. 1700; PROB11/458/42, Will of Sir Thomas Gresley, May 11, 1700.
[36] TNA, C9/172/27, Gresley *v.* Gresley, 1700; C9/473/73 Gresley *v.* Gresley, 1702.

Claiming that "the household goods were given to her, Lady Gresley possessed herself of all the plate which was not in use in the house," as well as all of Sir Thomas Gresley's books and pictures. Furthermore, after she asked for the almanacs and notebooks listing the rents, she returned them with pages cut out and refused to provide the legal documents showing the ownership of Netherseal. Finally, pretending that Sir Thomas Gresley was not *compos mentis* when he made his will, Lady Gresley rejected offers of reconciliation and had threatened to ruin him. Thomas requested a subpoena for his mother and his brother William and anyone else who had helped her.[37]

The extraordinary charges made in the case and its continuation into 1702 were finally resolved in 1703 when Thomas and his mother reached a reconciliation agreement. Lady Gresley agreed to pay Thomas £140, to give back all of Sir Thomas Gresley's books except those in her own closet, and all the "sawed boards and planks" in Drakelowe. In exchange, Thomas recognized on his own behalf and his heirs, "such part of the personal estate of the said Sir Thomas Gresley as is now in her custody . . . (the said books and planks . . . only excepted)" as well as the rents that she had collected on a farm whose lease was in dispute. It was agreed that William would collect the rents going forward.[38] Thomas's claims of hidden gold served to shake loose cash, books, and lumber from his mother.

When it came time to make her own testament, Dame Frances, who it will be remembered had had fourteen children, followed the rules of primogeniture. She overwhelmingly favored her grandson Thomas, son of her eldest son Sir William. She left him the profits from the sale of her timber, the furniture of Drakelowe Hall, and "my necklace of pearls which cost £200 and was given me by my Cozen Morewood," probably Rowland Morewood (d. 1647), to whom she had once been engaged. To his father, Sir William, she left £100. Her son Thomas, who had sued her, got £5 while his brother Charles got £20. To her surviving six daughters, Frances left £20 each. She gave her gold watch to her daughter Grace. Should her grandson Thomas die before age twenty-one and should there be no male heirs of Sir William, then all Frances's children would share in the money from the timber sales and the sale of her goods, except Dorothy Ward. She was to get nothing but £20 because she had married the Gresley steward.[39]

---

[37] Madan, *The Gresleys of Drakelowe*, pp. 95–98.

[38] Derbyshire Record Office, D77/1/23/27–28, Two copies of agreements between Dame Frances Gresley, widow of Sir Thomas Gresley and Thomas Gresley, second son and sole executor of Sir Thomas's will, 1703.

[39] TNA, PROB11/523/198, Will of Dame Frances Gresley, Oct. 1, 1711.

Wealth for Frances Gresley took several forms. Materially it ranged from the pearl necklace she had treasured from her first fiancé to the pearl ring she wanted but never received from Sir John Moore, to the gold her husband had hidden, which she supposedly discovered, and the household goods she had carried away. Just as important, perhaps, was the timber. Her father Gilbert Morewood and his family had lived in Netherseal before giving it back to the Gresleys, and Frances was determined to reap the benefits of the place where she was born. Even while married, she had secured timber rights as part of her jointure, and she was determined to uphold them.[40]

The 1690 concord in which Sir Thomas and Dame Frances bestowed Netherseal on their son Thomas included a provision reinforcing his mother's right to fell timber: "With liberty for Frances, wife of Sir Thomas, to cut down and carry away timber during her life and for her assigns for seven years after her death."[41] That "liberty" for which she fought had a substantial value. In 1710 Frances struck another agreement "whereby Dame Frances bargains and sells to Thomas Gresley Spittle Wood and Short Wood in Netherseal and all other timber, trees, woods, and underwoods within the manor and lordships of Netherseal and Thomas pays to Dame Frances £2000, Thomas to leave standing sufficient timber for the repair of Drake-lowe House."[42]

Conclusion

Chapters 3 and 4 have followed the lives of the second generation of Bennet and Morewood heiresses and their fortunes, Elizabeth Finch, her daughters Frances Clifton and Anne Conway, and Gilbert Morewood's daughter, Frances Gresley. Several themes link the stories of the second generation of Morewood and Bennet women: the continuing relationship of City and country, of land and trade, the placement of younger sons as City apprentices, and the yearning for London. These women defended their own property rights as wives or widows, through prenuptial agreements, litigation, family settlements, suits, and wills. They became strong advocates for

[40] Derbyshire Record Office, D77/1/23/10, "Review of landed estate and income of Sir Thomas Gresley prior to marriage." Pre 1650.

[41] Derbyshire Record Office, D77/1/16/9 Bundle H3, Frances Gresley's timber rights, 1690–1698. Some time after 1712 or 1713, Grace Bennet the younger and Sarah Frowde, wife of Ashburnham Frowde, struck an agreement with Thomas Gresley and Richard Moor and various freeholders concerning disputes over Mill Green in Netherseal. Grace must have inherited property rights in Netherseal from her grandfather, Gilbert Morewood. Derbyshire Record Office, D77/1/16/11, Bundle K, August 16 (after 1713, death of Frances Countess of Salisbury).

[42] Derbyshire Record Office, D77/1/16/10, Bundle J7, Oct. 11, 1710. Lady Gresley sells woods and timber to her son Thomas for £2,000.

themselves and their property, whether it took the form of land, money, timber, jewelry, household goods, or gold. At the same time, they all developed a strong sense of independence. Anne, Viscountess Conway studied ancient and contemporary philosophy, Jewish Kabbalah and Quakerism despite the disapproval of those around her; Frances, Lady Clifton, refused to follow the advice of her brother the Lord Chancellor and sued his chosen advisor; and Frances, Lady Gresley, as a married woman supposedly hemmed in by coverture, insisted on her rights against her husband and her son.

Lady Finch sorted through the many suitors for her hand when she became a rich widow in 1628, making sure that her prenuptial agreement protected her son, her children to come, and herself. She created an environment at Kensington House that supported the aspirations of a future lord chancellor, a future ambassador to the Ottoman Empire, a major banker, and an important philosopher. As a widow for a second time, Lady Finch made Kensington House the center of family life for the children of her blended family, who ranged in age from ten down to infancy. She supported them through education and litigation, buying Simon's wardship, suing his uncle, arranging her daughters' marriages, and leaving them her estate.

The next chapter takes up the issue of marriage in the third generation of the Bennet families. While the marriage of Elizabeth Finch's children seemed to have posed no problems to her, Sir William Gresley, the backwoods squire, threatened metaphorically to kill Frances Gresley if she thwarted his courtship, and one of her daughters married the Gresley steward. We will see how much liberty Lady Finch's granddaughters enjoyed in their choice of husbands fifty years after she married Sir Heneage Finch.

CHAPTER 5

"One of the Greatest Fortunes in England:"
Money, Marriage, and Mobility
The Bennet Heiresses

William Hogarth's series of paintings, *Marriage A-la-Mode*, opens with the exchange of merchant wealth for noble title (see Plate 8). The father of the bride, a London alderman, examines the marriage settlement through his spectacles while the gouty father of the groom, Earl Squander, points to his family tree. The girl weeps, her suitor remains disinterested, and a new country house, paid for by the bridal portion, rises in the background. Hogarth unfolds this tale of aristocratic marriage in a series of vignettes that present luxury, sin, and disease as its product. What begins as a satirical attack on marriage for money ends with Hogarth's dark moral judgment on the consequences for family, society, and even the body that can be passed down the generations.[1]

Historians have not ignored the role of heiresses in the economic life of the early modern aristocracy so starkly painted by Hogarth.[2] Their focus, however, has been the property these women brought to indebted noble families, not the life, aims, and values of the heiresses themselves. In the previous chapters, however, we found smart, active, and independent heiresses who, whether married or widowed, managed their own property, shaped their children's educations, and in the case of Lady Conway, pursued her own scholarship.

This chapter turns to the three Bennet sisters, the daughters of Grace Morewood and Simon Bennet, who inherited a substantial part of the Morewood–Bennet fortune in the late seventeenth century. Two of them married noblemen when they were young teenagers. Their life stories have remained untold and their own voices are rarely heard. Yet, the Bennet sisters provide important contemporary evidence about arranged marriages, fears of

---

[1] Ronald Paulson, *Hogarth: His Life, Art and Times,* 2 vols. (New Haven, CT: Yale University Press, 1991).

[2] See H. K. Habakkuk, *Marriage, Debt, and the Estates System* (Oxford: Clarendon Press, Oxford University Press, 1994); P. G. M. Dickens and J. V. Beckett, "The Finances of the Dukes of Chandos: Aristocratic Inheritance, Marriage, and Debt in Eighteenth Century England," *Huntington Library Quarterly*, 64, 3/4 (2001), 309–355.

clandestine alliances, the permeability of the English elite, and the extent of female agency within and after marriage.[3] This chapter analyzes how the Bennet sisters' marriages were decided by their parents, relatives, leading courtiers, and Charles II himself.

Alongside the Bennet sisters, two other sets of elite sisters were on the marriage market at the same time. The Clifton sisters were the Bennet sisters' first cousins, while the Newcastle sisters, daughters of the Duke of Newcastle, shared suitors with the Bennets. All these elite young women were expected to make "good" marriages, i.e., honorable, prosperous, and politically helpful alliances for their families and, perhaps they hoped, for themselves.[4] Marriage portions in the form of land and money that these sisters brought to their marriages helped to shape their marital choices. In the marriage market in the 1670s and 1680s, the Bennet sisters had portions of £10,000 and £20,000, as much as five times the amount their Clifton cousins had.

Of course, Simon Bennet and his stepsister Lady Clifton both had important political connections through their Finch relatives. One step-brother, Heneage Finch, was Solicitor General and about to become Lord Chancellor. Sir John Finch, doctor and diplomat, was serving in prestigious diplomatic posts in Italy and the Levant. Just as important, through the Bennets, Simon was second cousin to Henry Bennet, Earl of Arlington, Secretary of State, and later Lord Chamberlain. Arlington took part in an extended correspondence about the marriages of Simon and Grace's daughters.

Money, however, proved to be just as important as political connections. By the 1670s, the Bennet and Morewood fortune, originally made in the cloth and East India trades, and Jacobean court finance, had been multiplied by Simon Bennet's moneylending and property business. In hopes of upwardly mobile marriages, Simon invested in large portions for his daughters. Gossiped about since at least the fifteenth century, the cash value of the money and land a bride brought to her marriage was increasing in amount in

---

[3] On early modern marriage, see Lawrence Stone, *Broken Lives: Separation and Divorce in England, 1660–1857* (Oxford: Oxford University Press, 1993), pp. 27–28; also *Uncertain Unions: Marriage in England, 1660–1753* (Oxford: Oxford University Press, 1992), pp. 12–13, 31–32; Joanna Bailey, *Unquiet Lives: Marriage and Marriage Breakdown in England, 1660–1800* (Cambridge: Cambridge University Press, 2003); Elizabeth Foyster, *An English Family History, 1660–1857* (Cambridge: Cambridge University Press, 2005); Lawrence Stone and Jeanne C. Fawtier Stone, *An Open Elite? England 1540–1880* (Oxford: Oxford University Press, 1981); T. H. Hollingsworth, *The Demography of the British Peerage*, Supplement to *Population Studies*, 18, 2 (London: London School of Economics, 1964); J. V. Beckett, *The Aristocracy in England, 1660–1914* (Oxford: Blackwell, 1986).

[4] Barbara J. Harris, *English Aristocratic Women, 1450–1550: Marriage and Family, Property and Careers* (Oxford: Oxford University Press, 2002).

the early modern period.[5] The need for the infusion of cash in an increasingly indebted agricultural society made large portions very attractive. As a result commercial and landed wealth intertwined in practice in seventeenth-century England, creating a Stuart elite in which status distinctions became increasingly blurred. Nevertheless, for some the Bennet sisters raised the question of whether or not a nobleman should marry the daughter of someone connected to trade, a question familiar to later readers of Jane Austen's *Pride and Prejudice*.

Birth and status did matter in the late seventeenth century. As we will see, the Duke of Ormond in the 1680s made explicit what it would cost to make a match with those who had what he called a "defect of quality." Such a defect, an image conjuring up blood and bodily imperfection, could only be overcome by a large sum of money as a dowry that, if made from trade, caused the defect in Ormond's view in the first place.

Although Grace Bennet had seven children, only three girls, Elizabeth, Grace, and Frances, survived to the age of twelve. Contemporaries avidly discussed their marriage negotiations, revealing how their husbands were chosen, their ages at marriage, the money or land they brought to their husbands, and whether their family's links to commerce were in any way a problem to their marrying well. This evidence suggests that in at least two cases the Bennet sisters had no choice in the selection of their husbands. Yet religious ideas of companionate marriage had informed the English Book of Common Prayer and circulated throughout the sixteenth and seventeenth centuries. Many young people were able to choose their marriage partners. But this was not the case in two of the Bennet sisters' courtships.[6] Lawrence Stone claims the period between 1680 to 1710 displays "abnormally cynical, mercenary and predatory ruthlessness about human relationships."[7] Nevertheless, marriage was a family not an individual strategy. By marrying the

---

[5] Harris, *English Aristocratic Women*, passim; "Marriage as Business: Opinions on the Rise in Aristocratic Bridal Portions in Early Modern England," *Business Life and Public Policy, Essays in Honour of D. C. Coleman*, ed., Neil McKendrick and R. B. Outhwaite (Cambridge: Cambridge University Press, 1985), pp. 21–37; Amy Louise Erickson, "Common Law versus Common Practice: The Use of Marriage Settlements in Early Modern England," *The Economic History Review*, ns, 43, 1 (1990), 21–39. The terms *dowry* and *portion* are at times used interchangeably: dowry includes the money or property the bride brings her husband; more technically, the marriage portion the wife brings may be part of an estate given or passing by law to her heirs. See the *OED*.

[6] David C. Cressy, *Birth, Marriage, and Death: Ritual, Religion, and the Life-Cycle in Tudor and Stuart England* (Oxford: Oxford University Press, 1997), p. 297. Ingrid H. Tague points to the spread of ideas of companionate marriage in the eighteenth century in *Women of Quality: Accepting and Contesting Ideals of Femininity in England, 1690–1760* (Woodbridge: Boydell and Brewer, 2002), pp. 39–41, 44.

[7] Stone, *Broken Lives*, pp. 27–28.

young men their parents had chosen for them, the Bennet daughters shared their aspirational values as well as demonstrating their obedience.

Age of Marriage and Fear of Abduction

By the 1670s Elizabeth, Grace the younger, and Frances Bennet attracted a variety of suitors who ranged in status from great noblemen to knights to country gentry relations. In the seventeenth century, most women married in their early twenties while the mean age of marriage for peers born between 1650 and 1674 was 23 years and 7 months.[8] During the Restoration, however, a group of young heiresses married before the age of 17. Between 1674 and 1682, Elizabeth Bennet married the son of Thomas Osborne, Earl of Danby, at 15; Grace Bennet the younger married John Bennet at 16 or 17; and Frances Bennet married the 4th Earl of Salisbury at 13. Nor were the Bennets unique. In 1677 Mary Davies, aged 12, married Sir Thomas Grosvenor, bringing the Mayfair estates to the Grosvenors, later Dukes of Westminster.[9] Thomas Tufton, Earl of Thanet, had five daughters, all of whom married at 15 and 16. And the Earl of Arlington, Simon Bennet's cousin, arranged his own daughter's wedding contract when she was 5 years old.

Why did they marry so young? Settling large properties before the death of parents and building alliances were undoubtedly important. Fear of clandestine marriage and even of abduction may have played a role too. Canon law required a license and marriage in church before a clergyman according to the ceremonies of the Church of England. Minors required parental permission. Marriages that did not meet all these requirements were called clandestine. Historians think that most marriages in sixteenth- and early seventeenth-century England took place before a minister.[10] Few think abduction was important. Yet the Bennet sisters' mother Grace worried

[8] Hollingsworth, *The Demography of the British Peerage*; Susan Whyman, *Sociability and Power in Late-Stuart England: The Cultural Worlds of the Verneys, 1660–1720* (Oxford and New York: Oxford University Press, 1999), p. 123. For the Verneys, another Buckinghamshire gentry family, the age of marriage was rising.

[9] John Cannon, *Aristocratic Century: The Peerage of the Eighteenth Century* (Cambridge: Cambridge University Press, 1984), p. 72. "The Acquisition of the Estate," in *Survey of London: Volume 39, The Grosvenor Estate in Mayfair, Part 1 (General History)*, ed. F. H. W. Sheppard (London, 1977), pp. 1–5, *British History Online*: www.british-history.ac.uk/survey-london/vol39/pt1/pp1-5 [accessed Oct. 3, 2009].

[10] See Cressy, *Birth, Marriage, and Death*, pp. 316–335; Rebecca Probert, *Marriage Law and Practice in the Long Eighteenth Century: A Reassessment* (Cambridge: Cambridge University Press, 2010), pp. 1–10. Compare R. B. Outhwaite, *Clandestine Marriage in England, 1500–1800* (London and Rio Grande: Hambledon, 1995).

aloud that her daughters would be carried off. She agreed to the marriage of her daughter Frances at the age of thirteen because she was "afraid her daughter would be stole and married meanly."[11] In 1679 the girl's aunt Frances Gresley wrote to Sir John Moore that "my sister Bennet was in much trouble about her daughters and her estate."[12]

But was abduction really a major issue in the 1670s and 1680s? There was a statute of 1487 in Henry VII's reign, "Against the Taking Away of Women." Examples from Wales and Ireland, and Star Chamber cases from the Jacobean period documented young women and young men who, it was claimed, were abducted and married to those of lesser status or were otherwise unacceptable to the parents.[13] Yet it is unlikely that Grace Bennet had these in mind. One immediate example stood out. In 1665 the Earl of Rochester, a well-known figure at Charles II's court, abducted the wealthy heiress Elizabeth Malet. Sent to prison by the king, he later married Elizabeth. The emergence of the figure of the rake, especially in the literature of the Restoration, was perhaps an added reason to safeguard heiresses by marrying them as soon after 12, the age of consent, as possible.

Moreover, in the 1660s, 1670s, and 1680s, as clandestine marriages increased, the House of Lords repeatedly tried to pass a Clandestine Marriages Bill that sought to control marriages and prevent young people from making marriages on their own.[14] The bill appeared to focus on the issue of parental control rather than on criminal abduction. But the language of the debate and part of the bill mirrored Grace Bennet's own anxieties. Thus, the preamble to the 1685 Bill read: "Minors, having or expecting considerable estates real or personal, are daily subject to be inveighed or forced away from their fathers or guardians."[15] The House of Lords suggested that the danger of abduction or seduction was a constant threat. The culture mirrored this concern with plays in which the rake, in some cases based on Rochester, became the hero.[16] Indeed, perhaps a third of plays in the Restoration had clandestine marriages in the plot.[17] While heiresses had always tended to marry at a younger age than non-inheriting women, one result of this cultural anxiety in the Restoration

---

[11] Hatfield House Archives, Legal 184/6.

[12] Folger, V.b. 25, Gresley Mss., Letter 4, Oct. 6, 1679.

[13] Chris Durston, "'Unhallowed Wedlocks': The Regulation of Marriage during the English Revolution," *Historical Journal*, 31 (1988), 45–99. Liam Meyer, "'To Rise and Not to Fall': Representing Social Mobility in Early Modern Comedy and Star Chamber Litigation" (Ph.D. thesis, Boston University, 2014).

[14] Cressy, *Birth, Marriage, and Death*, pp. 332–335.   [15] Outhwaite, *Clandestine Marriage*, p. 70.

[16] I am grateful to Nigel Smith and the Princeton British history seminar for discussion of the rake in Restoration literature.

[17] Gilbert Alleman, *Matrimonial Law and the Materials of Restoration Comedy* (Wallingford, PA: Published privately, 1942), p. 80, cited by Paulson, *Hogarth*, p. 423, n. 19.

was to force some young heiresses into particularly early marriages and to redouble parental control over their daughters as property. For property was what these young marriages were about: it was usually understood that the couples would not live together until the bride was sixteen. Grace Bennet's anxiety was not completely misplaced. One of her daughters married against her parents' wishes and so did one of her Clifton cousins.

The Bennets' Marriage Negotiations

The marriage network operated alongside and was indeed part of the political and economic networks of early modern England. In the Restoration, elite negotiations took place against the backdrop of court and parliamentary politics, the Popish Plot, and the Exclusion Crisis. Marriage politics crossed factional and party lines. As we shall see, at least eight major political figures found themselves linked in the marriage negotiations for the Bennet sisters and their cousin, Sir William Clifton. Henry Bennet, Earl of Arlington, like Simon Bennet, was descended from the Bennets of Calcot (see Plate 9). A diplomat and connoisseur as well as a government minister, Arlington was a member of the Cabal, the five peers who were the leaders of Charles II's government between 1667 and 1672. Arlington then took up the position of Lord Chamberlain. His rival at court, Thomas Osborne, became Lord Treasurer in 1673 and was made Earl of Danby and later, Duke of Leeds. Both achieved their peerages through office. In contrast, James Butler, Duke of Ormond, who came from a distinguished Irish noble family, became Lord Lieutenant of Ireland and was a longtime supporter of the Stuarts (see Plate 10). Henry Cavendish, 2nd Duke of Newcastle, was the royalist son of William Cavendish, 1st Duke. William Chiffinch, Keeper of the King's Closet, was widely thought to pander to Charles II's sexual desires. Sir John Finch was, as we have already seen, a leading Restoration diplomat. In contrast to these high-ranking Tories, Francis Charlton was a Shropshire gentleman who became sheriff of the county and went on to be a radical Whig supporter of the Earl of Shaftesbury and the Duke of Monmouth. William Sacheverell, Lady Clifton's sometime advisor, was a strong Whig, deeply engaged in the Exclusion parliament. Whether as principals or brokers, all of these men took active roles in the marriage negotiations of the 1670s and 1680s.

Elizabeth Bennet and Viscount Latimer

Brokers helped make the marriage market in Restoration England. Sir John Finch, the Earl of Arlington, and Francis Charlton connected the rich

Bennets to the greatest officials in the land. The Bennets' Finch relations helped to make an important political match between Edward Osborne, Viscount Latimer, eldest son of the Earl of Danby, and Elizabeth, their eldest daughter. As early as 1672 when Elizabeth was only thirteen, Sir John Finch, Simon Bennet's stepbrother, wrote to their brother-in-law Edward, Viscount Conway, about a possible match. He had met Sir Thomas Osborne twice. "He was pleas'd to mention to me a concern in which if all the interests I leave in England can do anything he shall be serv'd, I could wish the young lady so well plac'd. But I intend to wait upon him before I leave England, though I am under a hurry of business."[18] For Finch, making the match with Osborne who was about to become Lord Treasurer in 1673 was more important than his niece whose name and family he does not mention.

After two years of negotiations, Elizabeth Bennet married Edward Osborne in May 1674. She was fifteen and he was twenty. A month later, in June 1674, Charles II granted the Lord Treasurer the title of Earl of Danby and his son Edward became Viscount Latimer. Andrew Browning, biographer of the Earl of Danby, points out that the marriage had "political significance" because Simon Bennet was half-brother to Anne, Vicountess Conway, and connected to the Finches. In October, Latimer was appointed a member of the Bedchamber of Charles II with a salary of £1,000 per annum.[19] Elizabeth's £10,000 portion was to be used to purchase lands to settle on her and Lord Latimer during her life. After her death the land would be in trust for their heirs. But "in default of such issue," from the marriage, the portion money would be returned to her father, Simon Bennet.[20]

Danby had two sons and five daughters. The Lord Treasurer later bragged that he had successfully married off five daughters in the 1670s without giving them very large portions.[21] While his political influence was no doubt important, presumably, the Bennet portion of £10,000 was helpful. Three Danby daughters married noblemen as either their first or their second husbands.[22]

[18] Marjorie Nicholson and Sarah Hutton, eds., *The Conway Letters: The Correspondence of Anne, Viscountess Conway, Henry More and their Friends, 1642–1684* (Oxford: Clarendon Press, 1930, 1992), p. 364 and note. Sir John Finch to Lord Conway, Nov. 2, 1672.

[19] George E. Cockayne, *The Complete Peerage of England, Scotland, Ireland, Great Britain and the United Kingdom: Extant, Extinct or Dormant*, revised, V. Gibb, 13 vols. (London: St. Catherine Press, Ltd., 1910–1959); Andrew Browning, *Thomas, Earl of Danby and Duke of Leeds, 1632–1712*, 3 vols. (Oxford: Blackwell, 1913), Vol. I, pp. 136–137.

[20] BL, Egerton 3352, ff. 72, 74, Symon Bennet, declaration in regard to marriage settlement of Elizabeth Bennet and Edward Viscount Latimer

[21] Habakkuk, *Marriage, Debt, and the Estates System*, p. 152.

[22] Habakkuk, *Marriage, Debt, and the Estates System*, p. 152.

Marriages based on money and political power may not at first lead to affection. In Latimer's voluminous correspondence, only a single letter survives that may be to his wife Elizabeth later in their marriage. Rather, Danby chastised his son for leaving Elizabeth when she was about to give birth two years after their marriage in 1676.

I know not whither to blame your carelessness, your ill manners, or your ill nature, but there is such a mixture of them all in staying from [your] wife till her labour and at a time when I believe you scarse know what else to do with yourself, that I am truly ashamed of you... I now find I have not educated you to that common civility which scarse anybody wants. I suppose this will bring you to town, by which time your wife may either bee a dead woman, or not beholding to you if she be not; and women of less kindness to an husband then she has to you does not use to want that satisfaction.[23]

Elizabeth lost the baby son, named Thomas, shortly after his birth.

While Danby as a peer sat in the House of Lords, his son could stand for election to the House of Commons. Viscount Latimer was MP for Corfe Castle in 1677 and Buckingham in 1677 and 1679. In parliament Latimer was a strong if inactive supporter of the court party.[24] The 1679 Buckingham election was fought in the midst of the Popish Plot, the false accusation that there was a secret plan to put James, Duke of York, on the throne. Latimer had support from his father-in-law, Simon Bennet, who had twice served as sheriff of Buckinghamshire. Latimer wrote to Danby, "My father Bennet has been very kind to me and went to Buckingham himself with me."[25] Rebuilding the town hall that had burnt down was a continuing issue in Buckingham elections. Latimer had a commitment from King Charles, helped no doubt by Simon Bennet, to rebuild it. On February 8, 1679, Latimer wrote a loving letter from Simon Bennet's house in Beachampton to "My dearest deare," presumably his wife Elizabeth, describing the local factions at the elections.

I cannot express how kindly I take it that you, who are in a place of so much divertisment, do so often think of me who am in a place of so much trouble and give me so full accounts of all your passages there and I do assure you the reading of your letters is all [the] pleasure I have for since the Duke of Buckingham is come I fear it will go hard with Sir Richard Temple for we have had swords drawn between Sir Henry Andrews and Charles Terrell and I believe we must have more before we have done but on Monday we shall end it and if you will send the coach to meet me at

[23] Browning, *Danby*, Vol. II, pp. 39–40.
[24] History of Parliament Online, "Edward Osborne, Viscount Latimer," 1660–1690.
[25] BL, Add. Mss. 28087, ff. 1–1v, Edward Osborne, Viscount Latimer, to his father the Earl of Danby, n.d.

Aylesbury that night I will endeavor to kiss your hands on Tuesday night ... I am dearest thine for ever.[26]

Reelected unanimously by all thirteen electors, Latimer and Temple were, nevertheless, attacked in Charles Blount's *The Sale of Esau's Birthright or the New Buckingham Ballad*. Arguing that the electors of Buckingham had "led the way to popery" and sold out the Crown and country for a new town hall, Blount focused on Latimer as a court candidate and attacked Danby.

> The Father is a Reprobate
> And yet the Son's elected
> The Gawdy Youth comes down in State
> And must not be Rejected
>
> . . .
>
> These men do to their choosing trudge
> With all the speed that can be
> And make the son the Father's judge
> To save great Tom of D_____[27]

It was no wonder that Latimer was eager for his coach and to return home! Relations between Edward and Elizabeth had obviously improved, but Danby fell from office in 1679.[28] Elizabeth died on April 29, 1680, just days after giving birth to a daughter Grace, named after her mother. Elizabeth and her daughter were buried in Westminster Abbey.[29] Because her marriage produced no living children and she predeceased her father, Viscount Latimer could not keep Elizabeth's marriage portion. Yet hope sprang eternal. In 1682 Danby, who was now in the Tower, notified his son of Simon Bennet's death. "Your father Bennet is dead ... Nor do I know whither you have any expectations upon his death. I hear he has made a will."[30]

   Although Latimer had the reversion of the Mastership of the Rolls, worth £10,000, when the post fell vacant in 1685 it went to Sir John Churchill.[31] Latimer continued to feel Elizabeth's death. His letters to his sister in the 1680s complained that his parents had not provided him with a settlement

---

[26] BL, Add. Ms. 28050, f. 7, Edward, Viscount Latimer to unknown, presumably his wife, Elizabeth Bennet, Feb. 8, 1679.
[27] Charles Blount, *The Sale of Esau's Birthright or the New Buckingham Ballad* (1679), EEBO.
[28] *ODNB*.
[29] Joseph Lemuel Chester, ed., *Marriage, Baptismal and Burial Register of the Collegiate Church of St. Peter Westminster* (London: Mitchell and Hughes, 1876), p. 199; Burial of their son in the Abbey on December 29, 1676, p. 190.
[30] Browning, *Danby*, Vol. II, pp. 39–40.
[31] History of Parliament Online, "Edward Osborne, Viscount Latimer."

to make an offer, for instance, to Lady Mary Compton, after the loss of the
£10,000 portion of his "late dear wife."[32] Indeed, lack of funds appears to
have made it difficult for him to remarry. He was one of a group of suitors
for a daughter of the Duke of Newcastle. He and his father Danby discussed
how to get around marrying Newcastle's daughter Frances because Latimer
was interested in her sister Margaret. Danby was concerned that Frances
might be too ill to bear children. After visiting the Duke of Newcastle in
1687, where the talk was of a match between the Duke's youngest daughter
and the son of the Duke of Devonshire, Latimer wrote to his father that he
was going to Lincoln where he hoped to see the daughter of Sir Richard
Rothwell, an MP, and make "some trial on the father."[33] Latimer never did
remarry and died of syphilis in 1689.

The Ormond Courtship

The death of the young Elizabeth and her baby no doubt brought grief to both
families and not least to Latimer who had to relinquish her portion. On the
brighter side, the death of the Bennets' eldest daughter opened up opportunities for those seeking to marry her surviving sisters. Within a mere two weeks
of Elizabeth's interment in Westminster Abbey, Thomas Butler, Earl of
Ossory, son of James Butler, Duke of Ormond, brother-in-law of the Earl
of Arlington, and a very popular figure at the court of Charles II, wrote to his
father about the two remaining Bennet heiresses. "That Mr. Bennet I did
mention relating to a match for my son has two daughters; the fortune is so
great, though divided between them, as I hear not of so considerable a one in
the kingdom. I shall so govern myself in the matter as I hope you will not
disapprove what I shall do."[34] Between 1680 and 1682, an extended correspondence developed between the Duke of Ormond and the Earl of Arlington
about the marital prospects of Grace and Frances Bennet and the money the
latter could bring to the Duke's family.

With Elizabeth dead, Simon Bennet now provided his two younger
daughters with portions of £20,000 each, to be paid to them at the age of
twenty-five or on the day of their marriage if they were at least sixteen. In his
will, he sought to control their marriages even after his death, requiring the
consent of his wife, "my cousin Mr. Ralph Lee of London merchant and my
sister the Lady Frances Clifton or one of them." Should either daughter
marry under the age of sixteen or without consent, she would receive only

[32] BL, Add. Mss. 28050, f. 73, Edward, Viscount Latimer to his sister.
[33] University of Nottingham Mss., Cavendish Papers, Pw1/662, Latimer to Danby, Oct. 4, 1687.
[34] HMC, *Ormonde*, Vol. V, p. 321.

half, that is, £10,000 pounds.[35] Such control was not unusual. Lady Clifton threatened to cut her daughters out of her will should either marry a Scot, a Welshman, or an Irishman.[36]

Ossory's sudden death shortly after he recommended the Bennet match made the marriage of his son, still a teenager, even more pressing. Ormond was not idle. Not only a high-ranking nobleman with an impressive Irish lineage and a long and illustrious career on behalf of the Stuarts, Ormond also had great debts.[37]

A clear-eyed picture of young Ossory emerges from his uncle Arlington's letters (see Plate 11). While Ossory stayed with Arlington after his father's death, the Earl thought he would benefit from Faubert's academy because he was proving a poor student at Oxford. Established with support from Charles II, the academy taught its elite students riding, shooting, and swordsmanship.[38] Arlington wrote enthusiastically to Ormond, "The discipline of Faubert's academy would have turned more to account with him than that of the college and the exercise have done him more good, for his taille (figure) wants it as well as the strength of his constitution."[39] Arlington was also frank that the young man needed a tutor. "For the teacher he must have a plain preceptor who may teach him the Latin tongue under the authority of the Governor, and in a plainer method than he was put into in the University, the want of which perhaps is the principal cause of his backwardness therein."[40]

But Ormond ordered Ossory back to Oxford and then, in September, back home to Ireland. Young Ossory himself was not focused on his studies or a wife, but on his desire for another horse. The Duke promised Ossory a new horse in the spring and sought a more important purchase, a rich bride.

A Defect of Quality

Looking back after two years of frustrating marriage negotiations, the Duke of Ormond concluded that if he wanted a large portion immediately – which

---

[35] TNA, PROB 11/371/283, Will of Symon Bennet of Calverton, Buckinghamshire.

[36] TNA, PROB 11/364/424, Will of Dame Frances Clifton, Nov. 29, 1680.

[37] Toby Barnard and Jane Fenlon, *The Dukes of Ormonde, 1610–1745* (Woodbridge: Boydell and Brewer, 2000), Introduction.

[38] *The Diary of John Evelyn*, ed. E. S. de Beer, 6 vols. (Oxford: Clarendon Press, 1955), Vol. IV, Sept. 17, 1681, Aug. 9, 1682, Dec. 18, 1684; *London Past and Present: Its History, Associations, and Traditions*, ed. Henry Benjamin Wheatley and Peter Cunningham (Cambridge: Cambridge University Press, 2011), p. 70. John Evelyn witnessed some of the exercises performed on horseback by the students in 1684.

[39] HMC, *Ormonde*, Vol. V, p. 385, Arlington to Ormond, Arlington House, Aug. 17, 1680.

[40] HMC, *Ormonde*, V, p. 416, Arlington to Ormond, Audley End, Sept. 4, 1680.

he did – he would have to sacrifice status. He candidly and ruefully analyzed the bridal market in 1682 this way:

Where there is birth and an unblemished family there is but little money to be had: £10,000 is the most that can be expected in such cases. Where money is to be had, there is neither birth nor alliance to be expected and none of those that I can hear of have such sums as to countervaile the defect of quality, £20,000 or £25,000 being the most that I can find anywhere to be had … Some that pretend to know Mr. Bennet and his wife would make us believe a treaty may be renewed, but beside the uncertainty of that couple, the girl will not be of age to make the agreement irrevocable till October. And then if they shall have no mind to it, they may easily make her disapprove of it … the wench is too young to cohabit with a husband.[41]

Frances Bennet was too young because she was only twelve years old at the time of Ormond's letter.

But hopes were high at the beginning of negotiations. In 1680 Arlington sought to arrange marriages for the remaining two Bennet heiresses. The parallel correspondence between Arlington and Ormond and Ormond and his family at once displays Arlington's eagerness to play the broker and Ormond's desire to marry off Ossory quickly for as large a portion as possible. Their negotiations bring to life Hogarth's *Marriage A-la-Mode*. To his son, Ormond makes clear his disdain for Simon Bennet and his relations. His only interest in the Bennets is their money. And yet he hesitates: should he trade his bloodline for their wealth?

In October 1680, Arlington tried to juggle two Bennet marriages at once, using Frances Charlton, whom he claimed to have met through Ormond's daughter Lady Mary Cavendish, as a go-between. According to Arlington, during the summer Charlton discussed alliances "with my cousin, Simon Bennet, the rich man of Buckinghamshire." Arlington had for "some years past" promoted "the marrying of the eldest daughter to my cousin Bennet [John Bennet] who is in remainder the heir to the estate, which is above £6,000 per annum, with at least £100,000 pounds in ready money." Having learned of Arlington's proposal for Ossory and young Frances, Charlton told him that Grace Bennet, "who rules the roost in the house likes it very well … The land she seems to wish may go with the eldest daughter, and the money with the youngest, who is much the handsomer." Arlington urged Ormond to authorize him to "treat" further in the matter in a letter he could produce and suggested that "a little kind mention of Mr. Charlton therein may be of good use."[42]

---

[41] Bodleian, MS Carte 70, ff. 552–552v, Duke of Ormond to Matthew, June 10, 1682.
[42] HMC, *Ormonde*, Vol. V, pp. 465–466, Arlington to Ormond, Westminster, Oct. 30, 1680.

Arlington promoted the marriage of Frances Bennet and Ossory to secure a handsome portion for his nephew Ossory whose father had been his brother-in-law and close friend. Simon Bennet was his rich cousin, and that sufficed for him but not for the haughty Ormond who emphasized lineage and loyalty to the Crown as principal virtues.[43] Within three months, Ormond wrote to Arlington that he had given over the Bennet match. Instead, he wrote to his son, the Earl of Arran, on January 6, 1681, to suggest that they turn to one of the daughters of the Duke of Newcastle. Ormond's wife had been told by a friend that Newcastle's eldest daughter Elizabeth thought "that an address in behalf of my grandson for a younger sister of hers would not be displeasing." Admitting he knew nothing about the young woman, Ormond said he was "abundantly satisfied of the advantage of the alliance in reference to birth and the honour and constant loyalty of the family."[44]

Ormond's emphasis on birth, honor, and constant loyalty suggests that Simon Bennet's support for the Interregnum regime as well as his money-lending made him unsuitable despite his Finch connections. Ormond also suggested that an even greater figure had intervened in the matter. The Duke of York was said to have written to Arlington stating his wish that "any prosecution of the overture for marriage of the Earl of Ossory be laid aside."[45] Arlington, however, had already arranged for Ossory's mother (his sister-in-law) to meet Simon Bennet and his daughter Frances. Ossory's mother still approved the match after her visit to Simon and Frances in Buckinghamshire on January 11, 1681. Arran, however, attributed her views to the influence of her sister, Arlington's wife.[46]

As for the Bennets, they were in no rush to seize on Ormond's interest. Throughout 1680 and 1681, Arlington kept Ormond apprised of the progress of the negotiations, the problems with Mrs Bennet in particular, and the crucial importance of Ormond buying an English estate for the couple. In early 1681 the negotiations remained in abeyance. As Lord Chamberlain, Arlington was attendant on the king on progress and did not respond to Ormond until February saying that he had nothing of satisfaction to say. "My cousin Bennet was in town this last term, but came not at me, neither would he let Mr. Charlton know where he lay, which is a sign he is yet under correction at home." Ormond reported to his son

[43] *ODNB*, "James Butler, Earl of Ormond."
[44] HMC, *Ormonde*, Vol. V, p. 546, Ormond to Earl of Arran, Jan. 6, 1680/1681.
[45] Bodleian, MS Carte 219, f. 198, No. II, Ormond to Arran, Jan. 6, 1681.
[46] HMC, *Ormonde*, Vol. V, pp. 525, 529, Earl of Longford to Ormond, Dec. 14, 1680, Dec. 18, 1680; p. 550, Arran to Ormond, Jan. 11, 1680–1681.

"I suppose the negotiation managed by Mr. Charlton with Mr. Bennet is wholly mortified, having heard nothing of it.[47]

Grace Bennet and John Bennet

In the meantime, the long-running negotiations for Grace Bennet's marriage continued. Even as he negotiated for Frances, Arlington claimed to have arranged the marriage of John Bennet, their Buckinghamshire cousin, to Grace Bennet. John was the great grandson of Sir Thomas Bennet, the Lord Mayor. His grandfather John had been a successful London merchant; his father had bought Great and Little Abington, Cambridgeshire, and married Elizabeth, daughter of Sir Thomas Whitmore, first baronet of Apsley Park, Shropshire. Born in 1656, John Bennet attended Trinity College, Cambridge, and in 1663, when his father died, he inherited his Cambridgeshire estates.

Another high-ranking cousin lobbied for the marriage too. On December 7, 1679, Henry Capel, brother of Arthur, Earl of Essex, who had married Dorothy Bennet, wrote to Simon, his second cousin by marriage, to claim kinship.

Loving Cousin. I give you many thanks for your kind receiving of my cousin Benet and myself the other day. I do hope that your kindness will still increase towards us and that by your goodness and worthiness to your own family you will let Jack Bennet, your nearest relation, have the benefit in due time of both our labors. And because I take Jack Bennet to be a youth that is very likely to prove a sober man, and one that is like to look after his estate well, I do hope that by your preferring of him to your alliance you yourself may in time reap some benefit by it, relieving you when you shall grow in years, with his care in the management of your concerns, which so nearly related to you already as he is, and his quality, will be better able to do than those of greater quality.[48]

Capel hoped that his appeal to kinship would override the Bennets' aspirations to a superior marriage. Of course, his statement assumes that the Bennet daughters could not look after the family estate themselves.

Unlike twelve-year-old Frances, Grace was at least sixteen, old enough to have an opinion of the match. John Bennet's enthusiastic courtship of Grace was opposed by both mother and daughter, as Simon Bennet wrote ruefully to Arlington who was taking such an active interest in the match.

[47] HMC, *Ormonde*, Vol. V, pp. 591, 593, Arlington to Ormond, Whitehall, Feb. 26, 1680/1681; Ormond to Arran, Dublin, March 1, 1680/1681.

[48] Hatfield House Archives, General 72/27, Henry Capel to Simon Bennet from Kew, Dec. 7, 1679. Capel claimed to be "performing a duty in memory and in kindness to my dear friend that is dead," possibly John Bennet's father or his father-in law Richard Bennet of Kew.

As concerning my cousin John Bennet's business, it stands thus: My daughter Grace is more violent against him than her mother, and after she had given him five or six denials she hath ever since locked herself up whenever he came to the house, both mother and daughter keep themselves very close from him, insomuch that he is forced to get a ladder to climb up to the window to them, but cannot see them when he hath done. Sometimes they fling out a pail of water upon his head and wet him to the skin, the difference being so high among them; yet for all this he is not at all dismayed, but is fully resolved to stick by it and pursue his design, although it should last yet these seven years.[49]

Nevertheless, despite the supposed violent opposition of mother and daughter, the 25-year-old John Bennet married Grace Bennet three months later, on August 20, 1681. In fact they eloped to the continent. How and why Grace changed her mind is unclear. A desire to establish her own household and John Bennet's persuasion may have made elopement attractive. A gossipy newsletter writer wrote that both mother and father tried to trace the couple all the way to Geneva.[50] The Earl of Arlington, however, claimed the couple married through his brokerage. As he had told Ormond, Bennet was "the heir in remainder" to Bennet's very large estate.[51] No wonder John Bennet was said to be willing to wait seven years for Grace.

Grace and John Bennet returned to London after traveling to Europe in October 1681. Arlington informed Ormond because Grace's marriage had implications for Ossory. "At our return to London I suppose we shall meet my young cousin Bennet returned from France, his young wife and his old father and mother-in-law, from whom I shall be able to learn I hope quickly how worthy the younger daughter may be of your Grace's acceptance for my Lord of Ossory."[52] But Grace Bennet remained unreconciled to young Grace and John's match, which she believed was clandestine and her daughter stolen. Indeed, even after the marriage, the legal settlement was not signed.

My cousins Bennets came over some days since from their long peregrination. The father and the mother accompanied the young man to his house, near Bourne-bridge in the way to Newmarket, but when they came thither the father and mother, by her ill humoured persuasion, went and lodged in a little ale house near the young man's dwelling house and from thence went onward on their way the next day

---

[49] HMC, *Ormonde*, Vol. VI, pp. 54–55, Simon Bennet to Arlington, May 2, 1681. "When I came home from Gloucestershire I received your lordship's letter by my cousin John Bennet. I am sorry I had the ill fortune to be away when your lordship passed through Stony Stratford to Euston . . . When I see your lordship at London I shall tell you more of it."

[50] *The Entring Book of Roger Morrice*, ed. Mark Goldie et al., 6 vols. (London: Boydell and Brewer, 2009), Vol. II, p. 293, Thursday, Nov. 17, 1681.

[51] HMC, *Ormonde*, Vol. VI, pp. 465–466.

[52] HMC, *Ormonde*, Vol. VI, p. 191. Arlington to Ormond, Euston, Oct. 15, 1681.

towards their own in Buckinghamshire. I am obliged to tell your Grace this, otherwise unnecessary story, thus distinctly, that you may see, though the marriage be completed and allowed of, that the mother is not yet so appeased as to be quiet upon it, neither have they yet declared what portion the young man shall have with his wife whom I have seen to-day in his own mother's house.[53]

According to later documents no marriage settlement or jointure was ever drawn up for Grace. John, however, claimed her £20,000 marriage portion.

Frances Bennet and the Earl of Ossory

John Bennet and Grace Bennet had married, but the issue of the marital prospects of Simon Bennet's youngest daughter Frances remained open. Arlington continued in his role as marriage broker, promising to keep Ormond informed.[54] By December 1681, Arlington was putting pressure on Ormond, telling him of rivals for Frances's hand, the need to reward those helping Ormond's suit, and, again, the necessity of an English estate for the couple. Ormond replied on December 24, "I will not stint you in the gratifications you shall think fit to make to those that shall effectually help us in the pursuit we are upon, since it is probable the rivals your lordship mentions will bid largely and since Mr. Charlton will not hear of gratification at least for the present ... as for a purchase to be made for a jointure in England I shall be content that two parts of three of the portion, whatever it shalbe, should be so employed."[55] As for Ossory, he, too, had his defects for which a wife was the solution. Ormond was candid.

I am off from all thoughts of trusting my grandson to travel under the conduct of any governor ... the youth is hard to govern and the prosperity or ruin of my family depending so much upon him. Here under my care he behaves himself to my satisfaction and visibly improves in his person and parts, for which he is beholding to nature which we cannot get him to take any pains to cultivate, so that a good wife is what must be sought for him, and the search must be by such friends as your lordship. When therefore the affair of your kinswoman shall be desperate, I hope you have your eye elsewhere.[56]

In February 1682, the match seemed close to a conclusion. Arlington met with Simon Bennet, and together they signed a preliminary agreement for

[53] HMC, *Ormonde*, Vol. VI, pp. 242–243, Arlington to Ormond, Whitehall, Nov. 29, 1681; *The History of Parliament: The House of Commons, 1660–1690*, ed., Basil Duke Henning, 3 vols. (London: Secker and Warburg, 1983), Vol. I, pp. 172–173.
[54] HMC, *Ormonde*, Vol. VI, pp. 242–243, Arlington to Ormond, Whitehall, Nov. 29, 1681.
[55] HMC, *Ormonde*, Vol. VI, p. 275, Ormond to Arlington, Dec 24, 1681.
[56] HMC, *Ormonde*, Vol. VI, p. 550, Ormond to Arlington, Dec. 3, 1681.

Frances's marriage to the Earl of Ossory on the following three conditions: Simon's offering an appropriate portion, Ormond's providing a jointure based on an English estate, and the two young people liking each other.[57] This last provision suggested that Frances might have a choice in her husband. The participants, however, never got to the third condition.

Based on the agreement, Arlington urged Ormond to come to England from Ireland to cement the agreement. Ormond agreed. He replied on February 18, 1682, that he had a copy of the paper signed by Arlington and Simon Bennet, which Ormond called "as fair an introduction to a further treaty as could be expected." Despite his letter of withdrawal over a year earlier, he now planned to come himself "with the greater confidence of success in the matter of marriage, because I know I can fully satisfy Mr. Bennet in the point of settling an estate, and that any objection to the country it is in may be removed by my consenting that such a part of the portion as shall be thought fit or even desired may be laid out upon the purchase of land in England."[58] The same day, however, Ormond wrote to his son, the Earl of Arran, stating his true feelings. The portion was everything. "I would be glad to have some knowledge of the portion before the affair be far engaged in, for besides the portion there are few other inducements to make it desirable; my Lord Chamberlain is not to be told that neither the quality or qualifications of the father and mother are great attractives."[59]

By February 20th, Ormond made plans to travel from Ireland to London to seal the bargain with Simon Bennet. He made clear to Arlington that he had only two months to complete arrangements and that his wife might travel with him "because she must join in any deeds or assurances and that all parties may be pleased. He urged Arlington to bring Bennet "to a certainty." Otherwise "I must find some other match."[60]

Ormond's son, the Earl of Arran, consistently opposed the match based on the Bennets' defect of quality. Now he advised his father to say that his

---

[57] HMC, *Ormonde*, Vol. VI, pp. 308–309, Feb. 9, 1681–1682. "Several discourses being passed betwixt the Right Honorable Henry Earl of Arlington, Lord Chamberlain of this Majesty's Household, and Simon Bennet, esqre., concerning a marriage to be made betwixt the Right Honorable James Earl of Ossory, grandchild to His Grace James Duke of Ormond and Frances Bennet youngest daughter of the said Simon Bennet ... that in case, his Grace the Duke of Ormond shall settle upon his above named grandchild such an estate as shall be to the liking and satisfaction of Mr. Simon Bennet, and he the said Mr Bennet shall give such a portion in moneys to the liking of the said duke, and that the parties to be married shall like each other, and in the usual form at the age required in law declare the same, then the said marriage shall be consummated." Witnesses, Robert Chapman, Michael Bebington. Feb. 9, 1681–1682.
[58] HMC, *Ormonde*, Vol. VI, pp. 316.   [59] HMC, *Ormonde*, Vol. VI, pp. 310, 316.
[60] HMC, *Ormonde,* Vol. VI, p. 318.

travel to London was to see the king and not to marry Bennet's daughter but "I dare not say so much to Lord Arlington for he is so concerned in the matter, and does really believe he does you great service in it ... Besides by what he told me ... I have reason to believe Bennet ... will marry his daughter to the Duke of Richmond if this match should break off as I hope it will. There is a daughter of the Duke of Newcastle's, who is very pretty and will be a very great fortune and the relations your grandchild will have by that match will not make him or your Grace ashamed to own them."[61] Arran's hope for Newcastle's daughter's fortune proved illusory.

Differences in status were acute in early modern England. Despite the fact that Simon Bennet was stepbrother to Lord Chancellor Finch and Ambassador Finch and brother in-law to Viscount Conway as well as cousin to the Lord Chamberlain of the Household, these connections did not appear to have carried much weight with Ormond. Grace was the offspring of a merchant in international trade and so was Simon. Moreover, Simon was not even a banker; he was a moneylender although an extremely rich one, as his contemporaries emphasized. Furthermore, Ormond seemed to be commenting on the Bennets' erratic behavior, as described in Arlington's letters.

Ormond also drew attention to the strange political bedfellows drawn together by Bennet matchmaking. After Arlington's detailed description of Simon Bennet's wavering, Ormond wrote, "The account you are pleased to give of the conduct of your two cousins in the case of their elder daughter looks as if they did not so perfectly know their own minds. Yet in our condition as little time would be lost as might be. It is no less extraordinary that Mr. Charlton should at the same time be bail for my Lord of Shaftesbury [a radical Whig] and give himself the trouble of soliciting such an affair for me. Your lordship in your own time will say when it is to be given over."[62]

Finally, to overcome all of Ormond's doubts and reinforce his own position as marriage broker, Arlington revealed the origins of the matchmaking by turning to Charles II himself. Showing the king Ormond's request for leave to come to London, he went on,

if His Majesty, had any thoughts of having the child disposed otherwise of, I durst boldly answer that you [Ormond] who had so frankly hazarded your life and your fortune for him, and were ready to do it again, would not dispute this point one moment with him. He seemed to understand me though not without some unwillingness, for I named no persons, but protested withal he had no thought of it, and

[61] HMC, *Ormonde*, Vol. VI, p. 327, Arran to Ormond, Feb. 28, 1681/1682. Richmond was the illegitimate son of Charles II and the Duchess of Portsmouth and two years younger than Frances. He married Anne Brudenell, daughter of Lord Brudenell, in 1692.
[62] HMC, *Ormonde*, Vol. VI, pp. 256–257, Ormond to Arlington, Dublin, Dec. 12, 1681.

should be loath any body could think he would do so unkind a thing to my Lord of Ormond, especially having with his own mouth recommended the affair to the father [i.e. the late Earl of Ossory].[63]

It was King Charles himself then who had suggested the Bennet match to Ossory's father and proved the greatest marriage broker of all.

The Duke of Ormond made a grand entry into London in May 1682 with 27 coaches and 300 horsemen.[64] By June 1682, however, Ormond had given up. One observer claimed he had asked Simon Bennet for a £50,000 portion.[65] Concerned with "what to do with James two or three [of] the most dangerous years of his youth," Ormond approached the Duke of Newcastle. "But his resolution is not to part with any money at all ... And he will assure but £20,000 to his daughter on his death which puts an end to that matter."[66] Having tried the Bennets and the Duke of Newcastle, Ormond turned to James, Duke of York, who stepped in to make a match for Ossory with Ann Hyde, daughter of the Earl of Rochester. They married in July 1682. Ormond had claimed that Ossory's marriage would help repair the family finances. He himself was made an English duke in November 1682, purchased the largest townhouse in St. James Square for £9,000, and died at least £100,000 in debt in 1688.[67]

Frances Bennet and James, 4th Earl of Salisbury

With Grace married, young Frances was a great prize made even more so after her father's death in 1682. Narcissus Luttrell recorded in his diary, "The great Mr. Bennet of Buckinghamshire is lately dead, and is said to have left a most prodigious estate."[68] Another observer noted, "Mr. Bennet is dead since you left us, and has made his youngest daughter one of the greatest fortunes in England being worth at least in lands and money £150,000."[69] Even as Ormond's two-month stay in London was coming to an end, one of his rivals proved successful in making the match with the Bennets. Instead of marrying Ormond's grandson, Frances Bennet married James Cecil, 4th Earl of Salisbury.

---

[63] HMC, *Ormonde*, Vol. VI, p. 334, Arlington to Ormond, March 4, 1682.

[64] Bodleian, MS Carte 216, f. 49, Longford to Arran, May 13, 1682.

[65] HMC, *Ormonde*, Vol, VI, p. 379.

[66] Bodleian, MS Carte 70, ff. 552–552v, Ormond to Arran, June 10, 1682; f. 75, Fitzpatrick to Arran, June 9, 1682.

[67] *ODNB*, "James Butler, Earl of Ormond."

[68] Narcissus Luttrell, *A Brief Historical Relation of State Affairs from September 1678 to April 1714*, 6 vols. (Oxford: At the University Press, 1857, Vol. I, p. 216. Aug. 30–Sept. 1, 1682.

[69] Quoted in Hatfield House Archives, FP 9, 1678 to 1689.

Figure 5.1 Portrait of James Cecil, 4th Earl of Salisbury, *c.* 1687, by Willem
Wissing (1656–1687), Hatfield House, Hertfordshire. Reproduction by courtesy of
the Marquess of Salisbury. The portrait was later found to have been painted
over a portrait of the Duke of Monmouth, illegitimate son of Charles II.

On May 29, 1682, in the same month that Ormond made his grand entry
into London, Margaret, Countess of Salisbury wrote urgently to a Hatfield
servant that the 3rd Earl had "something to acquaint him with in relation to
'Mr. Bennet's business.'" His journey absolutely had to be taken this week;
"the sooner the better (as we all judge) for delays may ruin or at least hazard
the thing since the opportunity seems so faire and proper."[70] By February
1683, the Salisbury men of business were still trying to complete the
marriage settlement. Samuel Percivall wrote to his nephew William Dobyns
at Lincolns Inn that they were down to the issue of annuities of servants and
how to assign land to pay for Frances's jointure. He urged Dobyns to look
quickly over the document and return it, "driving on all other parts of this
business as fast as you can lest anything should stick with him."

[70] Hatfield House Archives, General 21/13, Margaret, Countess of Salisbury, to John Fisher re Mr.
Bennet's business, May 29, 1682.

Dobyns then brought up the crucial and difficult issue of Frances's portion. Simon Bennet had left Frances £20,000 if she married with the consent of her guardians at the age of sixteen, but only £10,000 if she did not. She had her guardian's consent but she was underage. The Salisbury side needed Grace Bennet senior to testify that before his death Simon had been willing for Frances to be married before she was sixteen. Thus Dobyns wrote to Percivall: "And also bring the great question of £10,000 or £20,000 to a decision at my Lord Keeper's. To this end ... let you step to Mr. Best and tell him we must not fail of Madame Bennet's answer then, and that he will be ready when petitioned for a quick hearing. And ... press him to a dispatch in this business because I know it will give great countenance to this other great affair of the decree."[71] Grace Bennet did agree to the marriage of Frances and James, 4th Earl of Salisbury, with a £20,000 portion. Nevertheless, from 1683 to 1691 John Bennet sued his brother-in-law Salisbury to prevent his receiving it.

At the same time, in February, 1683, when the 3rd Earl of Salisbury drew up the papers for Frances Bennet, he also arranged a match for his daughter Katherine with Sir George Downing. The rush to complete the settlement was twofold. First, the Earl of Salisbury was ill. Second, the promised Bennet portion of £20,000 helped underwrite a portion of £8,000 for Katherine Cecil. Katherine's portion was smaller than Frances Bennet's and so was her jointure. Downing's father offered £1,200 while Salisbury insisted on £1,500. When Downing urged Salisbury to meet his son, Salisbury responded, "My seeing his son will not alter the case at all nor make the £1200 jointure he offers seem more considerable to me than it does at present ... there shall be no interview between my daughter and his son till this of the jointure be settled."[72] Both marriages were agreed by the time the 3rd Earl of Salisbury died in June 1683. Katherine married Sir George Downing on July 12, 1683, aged twenty, and Frances Bennet married James, now 4th Earl of Salisbury, on July 13, aged thirteen.

All agreed that the 4th Earl of Salisbury would not consummate his marriage with Frances Bennet until she was at least sixteen.[73] Lady Chaworth wrote to her brother, the Earl of Rutland, "Lord Inchiqueen was with Lord S[alisbury], his Lady only with us women. They are too young to live together; but she to breed her, and he to travell two or three years."[74]

---

[71] Hatfield House Archives, General 19/19, Percivall to Dobyns about Grace Bennet's answer, Feb. 8, 1683.

[72] Hatfield House Archives, General 20/23.   [73] Hatfield House Archives, Legal 184/6.

[74] HMC, *Rutland*, Vol. II, p. 80, July 21, 1683.

Luttrell's Diary noted that "The young Earl of Salisbury hath lately married the daughter of great Bennet who is about 13 years old; and his lordship hath waited on His Majesty and kissed his hand and begged his pardon for his father's being concerned in any party against His Majesty's interest."[75] Salisbury, who was seventeen and had attended St. John's College, Cambridge, went off to Italy and France where it was said he lost thousands of livres gambling at the French court.[76] He and Frances did not live together until 1688. Painted as a beautiful child by John Michael Wright, Salisbury grew into a corpulent, self-indulgent young man. A supporter of James II, Salisbury converted to Roman Catholicism in 1687, a year before the Glorious Revolution, and was appointed to James II's Bedchamber in 1688. Salisbury was accused of treason as a Roman Catholic and a Jacobite, and was in and out of the Tower for political offences between 1689 and 1690 and again in 1692.[77] Nevertheless, he and Frances "lovingly" cohabited in the Tower and had a son named James in June 1691.[78] Although his brother Robert Cecil had sought to take over the estate for his Protestant relatives, the effort failed when Frances had a male heir in 1691. When Salisbury died unexpectedly in 1694 at the age of twenty-eight, their son James became the fifth Earl of Salisbury and Frances became the Dowager Countess of Salisbury at the age of twenty-four.

The Cliftons

If the Bennet marriage negotiations revolved around large portions, their Clifton cousins faced the opposite issue. How could they marry without any? The Clifton property was deeply in arrears because of the debts that Lady Clifton's father-in-law had amassed during the Civil War. Because the Clifton property had, by primogeniture, been inherited by Lady Clifton's underage son William, she sought a private act of parliament so that she and Gervase Holland, joint trustees of the estate, could make leases on the Clifton property to raise £4,000 portions for her daughters. Private acts of parliament were not unusual. Sir Clifford Clifton had himself sat on

---

[75] Narcissus Luttrell, *A Brief Historical Relation of State Affairs from September 1678 to April 1714*, 6 vols. (Oxford: At the University Press, 1857), Vol. I, p. 269, July 1683.

[76] *ODNB*, "James, 4th Earl of Salisbury."

[77] History of Parliament, draft biography of James Cecil, 4th Earl of Salisbury. I am most grateful for the opportunity to read the biography of the Earl in draft form.

[78] Hatfield House Archives, General, Samuel Percivall to George Stillingfleet, Feb. 10, 1689/1690. In 1690 Salisbury petitioned for release. Danby, Elizabeth Bennet's father in-law, and Thomas Tufton, Earl of Thanet, were among his sureties.

committees in the House of Commons considering bills for raising portions
for other indebted landed gentlemen.[79]

The Clifton act stated that the estate had become indebted "by reason of
the late unhappy War" among other reasons. Although Sir Clifford had
meant to renew several leases, he had been "surprised by Death." By his will,
Sir Clifford gave Lady Clifton and Gervase Holland, his executors, two-
thirds of the "Premises" until William reached twenty-one. He bequeathed
his daughters, Katherine and Arabella, £4,000 portions with the proviso that
if one died the survivor received £6,000. Because Sir Clifford had been
unable to conclude his leases and "his personal Estate being but small, his
debts and daughters' portions cannot be satisfied unless such leases be
made ... during the minority of the said William." Sir Orlando Bridgeman,
Lord Keeper of the Great Seal, and Heneage Finch, Attorney General, as
executors and administrators, decided that each girl would receive £50 per
annum until they were twelve and thereafter £120 until they married.[80]

After assuring her daughters' portions and maintenance in 1670, a decade
later Lady Clifton attempted to control both her children's educations and
their marriages through her will. She asked Henry, Duke of Newcastle, to
become guardian of Sir William Clifton. Sir William's education, however,
was not to include "sending him beyond seas." The growing development of
international trading companies made parents particularly sensitive to this
issue. As we saw in Chapter 4, Lady Frances Gresley did not want her son
sent abroad as an overseas merchant. Lady Clifton may have had the same
concern or worried that Sir William might be sent to the East or West Indies
or the North American colonies. Lady Clifton also asked Diana Bruce,
Countess of Ailesbury (1626–1685), to oversee the upbringing of her daughters Arabella and Catherine. She asked that they be educated "in her family
or at any such place where her Ladyship is or her daughters shalbe educated if
her Ladyship shall so please." Requesting that their current servants continue
to look after the children, at the least she wanted to make sure that the girls'
companion was at least "near forty." The Countess, widow of Robert Bruce,
2nd Earl of Elgin and 1st Earl of Ailesbury (1625–1689), had as many as
seventeen children, thirteen of whom survived.

Lady Clifton may have hoped to engage the help of the Duke of Newcastle and the Countess of Ailesbury in raising her children through her court

[79] *HCJ: Vol. 9, 1667–1687*, pp. 25–26, Nov. 26, 1667, www.british-history.ac.uk [accessed May 27, 2013].
[80] HLRO, HL/PO/JO/10/1/341/320, "Amended Draft of an Act for the better payment of the debts of Sir Clifford Clifton, Knight, deceased, and raising portions for his daughter, 18 Nov. 1670"; University of Nottingham Mss., Clifton Papers, CL L261/8, Printed case of Dame Frances Clifton and William Clifton and Catherine and Arabella Clifton.

Plate 1 Portrait of Elizabeth Ingram, Lady Bennet, daughter of Sir Arthur Ingram and wife of Sir Simon Bennet, circle of George Jameson, on loan to Temple Newsam House, Leeds, West Yorkshire, Leeds Gallery and Museum, © The Halifax Collection. Elizabeth served as Sir Simon's executor, oversaw his donation to University College, Oxford, and left a substantial sum to his heir, Simon Bennet.

Plate 2 Portrait of Mary Taylor, Lady Bennet, daughter of Robert Taylor and wife of Sir Thomas Bennet, *c.* 1590, by Hieronymus Custodis (fl.1589–93), Leeds Museums and Art Galleries (Temple Newsam House), UK/Bridgeman Images. She wears a vest embroidered with the kind of silks imported by Sir Thomas Bennet.

Plate 3 Abraham Ortelius, *Theatrum Orbis Terrarum* (London, printed by John Norton, printer to the King's Most Excellent Majesty, 1606), The Folger Shakespeare Library, STC 18855. Plate 108, map of Indiae Orientalis, India and the Maluku Islands where the English were challenging the Dutch East Asian trade.

Plate 4 East India Company Ships at Deptford, English school, seventeenth century, National Maritime Museum, Greenwich, London, BHC 1873. Gilbert Morewood invested in East India Company ventures and oversaw the dockyards in the 1640s.

Plate 5 Sir Heneage Finch, unknown artist, © National Portrait Gallery, London. NPG 4552. Heneage Finch was a lawyer, Recorder of London, Speaker of the House of Commons, and second husband of Elizabeth Bennet.

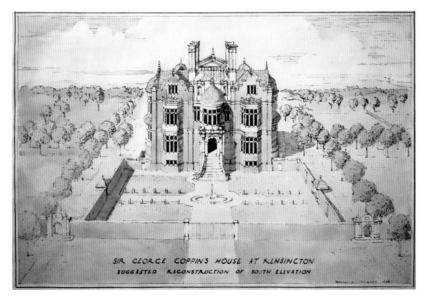

SIR GEORGE COPPIN'S HOUSE AT KENSINGTON
SUGGESTED RECONSTRUCTION OF SOUTH ELEVATION

Plate 6 Sir George Coppin's House, Kensington, South elevation, 1948, later Kensington House, The National Archives, Work 38/42. Elizabeth, Lady Finch lived in Kensington House for thirty years after the death of her husband Heneage in 1631. It later became part of Kensington Palace.

Plate 7 Sir John Moore, President of Christ's Hospital 1686–1702, Lord Mayor of London 1682–1683, attributed to John Riley (1646–1691), Oil on canvas 122.2 cm × 99.7 cm. By kind permission of Christ's Hospital, © Image courtesy of Richard Valencia. Sir John Moore, Gilbert Morewood's apprentice, later Lord Mayor and philanthropist, was a long-time friend of Morewood's daughter Frances.

Plate 8 William Hogarth, *The Marriage Settlement*, National Gallery, London/Art Resources, New York. From *Marriage A-la-Mode*, a series of six paintings satirizing aristocratic marriage, particularly marriage for money.

Plate 9 Portrait of Henry Bennet, Earl of Arlington, after Peter Lely based on a work of 1665–1670, © National Portrait Gallery, London, NPG 1853. Arlington, part of Charles II's CABAL and later Lord Chamberlain, was Simon Bennet's cousin.

Plate 10 Portrait of James Butler, 1st Duke of Ormond, *c.* 1680–1685 by Willem Wissing (1656-1687), © National Portrait Gallery, London, NPG 5559. Ormond, a large landowner and major political figure in Ireland, was a strong supporter of the Stuarts.

Plate 11 Portrait of James Butler, 2nd Duke of Ormond when Lord Ossory, *c.* 1686, by William Gandy (1660–1729), National Maritime Museum, Greenwich, London, Caird Collection, BHC2923. Painted a few years after his courtship with Frances Bennet and after his marriage to Ann Hyde.

Plate 12 Portrait of Frances, Countess of Salisbury, 1695, by Godfrey Kneller (1646–1723), Hatfield House, Hertfordshire. Reproduction by courtesy of the Marquess of Salisbury. Painted after the death of her husband and the murder of her mother.

Plate 13 *The Battle of Vigo Bay, Oct. 12, 1702*, by Ludolf Backhuysen (1630–1708),
National Maritime Museum, Greenwich, London, Caird Collection, BHC 2216.
The 2nd Duke of Ormond and George Jocelyn took part in this battle.

Plate 14 William Hogarth (1697–1764), painting of *The Western Family*, c. 1738,
The National Gallery of Ireland, bequeathed by Sir Hugh Lane, 1918. A conversation
piece from the 1730s showing the family in a domestic setting taking tea.

Plate 15 Portrait of Lady Anne (Tufton), Countess of Salisbury, in her coronation robes before Westminster Hall, *c.* 1714, by Charles Jervas (1675–1739), Hatfield House, Hertfordshire, UK/Bridgeman Images, Ref. HTF739823.

Plate 16 William Hogarth (1697–1764), painting of *The Strode Family*, *c.* 1738, Tate, London, bequeathed by Rev. William Finch, 1880, No. 1153. Anne Cecil, wife of William Strode and sister of the 6th Earl of Salisbury, who inherited £1,000 from Grace Bennet.

connections. Her stepbrother, Heneage Finch, became a member of Charles II's Privy Council in 1679, the same year as the Duke of Newcastle, joined by Finch's son Daniel in 1680, and his brother-in-law, Edward Viscount Conway and the Earl of Ailesbury in 1681. In her will, Lady Clifton also expressed her hope that her son William would marry Katherine, daughter of the Duke of Newcastle.

And that there may be no objection in my most desired marriage between my said son and the Lady Katherine Cavendish, one of the daughters of the said Duke of Newcastle, I desire my said Executors to secure to the said Lady Katherine the sum of two thousand pounds in case my said son shall happen to die before he attains the age of One and Twenty years. But so soon as he attains that age then this condition to be paid and he to receive her portion and she to receive her fifteen hundred pounds year jointure.[81]

Assuming that the average jointure, the estate the widow would receive on the death of her husband, might be 10 percent of the portion, Frances's provision for her future daughter-in law suggests that she expected a marriage portion in the range of up to £15,000.[82] As we saw earlier, Newcastle was not willing to pay a marriage portion upfront to the Duke of Ormond. It is not probable that Newcastle would want to pay such a portion to Sir William Clifton.

Frances left a substantial part of her estate to her daughters, but nothing at all should they marry without the consent of their uncle, Edward, Viscount Conway or, as we saw, if they married a Scotchman, an Irishman, or a Welshman. In 1685 her daughter Arabella married Francis Wheler or Wheeler, a younger son of a baronet, who had a very successful naval career. Knighted in 1687, he became Governor of Deal Castle in 1690 and a Rear Admiral in 1693. Wheler led a major expedition to the Caribbean and North America in 1693 that had few results. He had orders, not implemented, to take Canada. The next year, on February 19, 1694, while commanding ships in the Mediterranean, he drowned off of Gibraltar. His estate was worth about £600 in cash and household goods in addition to his property.[83]

---

[81] Nottinghamshire Archives, DD4P, Portland of Welbeck (4th deposit), Deeds and Estate Papers, DD4P/36/7, Copy of will of Dame Frances, widow of Sir Clifford Clifton of Clifton, Feb. 6, 1679/1680; TNA, PROB11/364/424, Will of Dame Frances Clifton, Nov. 29, 1680.

[82] Habakkuk, *Marriage, Debt, and the Estates System*, argues that by the end of the seventeenth century the portion was ten times the jointure so that £1,000 of portion equaled £100 of jointure, pp. 147–148.

[83] *ODNB*, "Sir Francis Wheler"; *Complete Baronetage*; K. A. J. McLay, "Sir Francis Wheler's Caribbean and North American Expedition, 1693: A Case Study in Combined Operational Command during the Reign of William III," *War in History*, 14 (2007), 383–407.

In 1680 Lady Clifton's daughter Katherine married Sir John Parsons, an Anglo-Irish baronet of Langley, Buckinghamshire, against her mother's wishes. Called "penniless" by a contemporary, Parsons may have had the help of Katherine's brother, Sir William Clifton. According to her uncle, Heneage Finch, Earl of Nottingham, she was "stolen away,"[84] unknowingly echoing the fears of Grace Bennet about the marriage of her daughter Grace to John Bennet. Lady Clifton therefore added a codicil to her will. Because Katherine had married Parsons since the making the will, the monies there granted her, £200 per annum, would now be given to Sir William Clifton and Sir William Finch in trust for Katherine's children.

Sir William Clifton

Sir William Clifton disappointed his mother's hopes too. William Chiffinch (1602–1691), Keeper of the King's Cabinet Closet, was very close to Charles II. His roles included overseeing backstairs politics and fostering the king's many affairs. Chiffinch's daughter Barbara was of marriageable age and became the focus of Sir William Clifton's attentions. According to Daniel Finch, who heard it from Sir John Parsons, Clifton's brother-in-law, Chiffinch offered a portion of £8,000, and "the reversion of Philbutts, which is £500 a year, after his death and all his personal estate. Mrs. Nun gives her £5000 at her death and it may be some part of it presently, and Mr. Chiffinch promises she shall turn Protestant. Sir William settles in jointure £1,200 a year."[85] Despite Barbara's handsome portion, young Sir William's Finch relatives were aghast. In the midst of the Exclusion Crisis, William Sacheverell, one of the leading Whigs and one of Clifton's guardians, wrote to his uncle, Lord Chancellor Heneage Finch that such a match with a Roman Catholic would ruin Clifton's political career and cast Finch in a bad light too.

Sir William is in treaty with one bred a Papist, some say with your Lordship's privity, but this none here believe, since your great experience cannot but have shown you the many inconveniences that follow when husband and wife are of different churches. One thing will certainly follow if Sir William marry with a Papist or reputed Papist; "he will infallibly lose both his interest and friends in these parts."[86]

Replying that he had not seen Clifton in ten weeks, Nottingham described Clifton's earlier fraught marriage negotiations with the Duke of Newcastle.

[84] HMC, *Finch,* Vol. II, pp. 83–85.
[85] HMC, *Finch,* Vol. II, p. 81, Daniel Finch to his wife, Lady Essex Finch, July 19, 1680.
[86] HMC, *Finch,* Vol. II, p. 83, William Sacheverell to Heneage Finch, Earl of Nottingham, Aug. 17, 1680.

Clifton had wooed Newcastle's daughter Katherine but then sent anonymous letters accusing himself of debauchery in order to end the romance. His mother, Lady Clifton, wrote to Newcastle too begging him to continue the negotiations, and Nottingham added his voice. Newcastle agreed. But when a sticking point over the marriage articles arose, Clifton used that as a way to end the courtship entirely. Confronted by his uncle over the Chiffinch match, Clifton proved "uncounselable."[87]

In the end Clifton did not marry Barbara Chiffinch, who married Edward Villiers, Earl of Jersey, instead.[88] Sir William Clifton recovered from his marital antics, gained court favour, and sat in parliament; he died unmarried in 1686 at the age of twenty-three. Lady Frances Clifton's plans went unfulfilled.

The Duke of Newcastle's Daughters

In the 1680s, even as the Bennet sisters were being courted and the Clifton sisters were finding their own beaux, the daughters of Henry Cavendish, Duke of Newcastle, were mentioned in the Duke of Ormond's correspondence, in Lady Clifton's will, and Nottingham's correspondence. Given their high status and their father's connections at court, it might be thought that the Newcastle daughters would outshine the Bennet sisters as they did the Clifton sisters. But the difference was money. Ormond considered a Newcastle match for Ossory, but the Duke of Newcastle was not offering a portion at the time of the marriage. The widowed Latimer too paid a visit to the Duke of Newcastle. Sir William Clifton, heir to the Clifton estate, who was under his mother's orders to marry one of the Newcastle sisters, initially courted Katherine but turned instead to the daughter of William Chiffinch. Although the Duke of Newcastle was concerned about the marriage of his daughters, Elizabeth, Frances, Margaret, Katherine, and Arabella, he refused or was unable to provide large portions for them, perhaps because there were five of them. Moreover, he insisted that the older ones marry before the younger.

In 1684 Newcastle wrote a letter to his son-in-law the 2nd Duke of Albemarle, who had married his eldest daughter Elizabeth, about the marriage of his second daughter Frances with the son of the Earl of Breadalbane. Claiming that Frances had been undutiful and "refused to marry the man he proposed," he questioned whether he had any reason to give Frances a good

---

[87] HMC, *Finch*, Vol. II, pp. 83–84, Heneage Finch to William Sacheverell, Aug. 21, 1680.
[88] *ODNB*; D. Allen, "The Political Function of Charles II's Chiffinch," *Huntington Library Quarterly*, 39 (1975–1976), 277–290.

portion or propose any marriage to her. He asked Albemarle what portion he would be expected to give. In a second letter within a month, he reiterated that he would not give Frances a great portion but would submit himself to Albemarle's judgment.[89] In 1685 Lady Frances Cavendish married John Campbell, 1st Earl of Breadalbane, with a portion of £5,000, a quarter of the portion that Frances Bennet brought to the Earl of Salisbury two years earlier in 1683.[90] Although, in 1686, Jean Beaumont proposed the marriage of Newcastle's third daughter Margaret to the Earl of Shrewsbury, Shrewsbury decided not to marry on the financial terms offered by Newcastle. When Frances, Duchess of Newcastle, wanted to go to London, the Duke wrote that parting from him would be a prejudice to herself, their two unmarried daughters, and to him. If she was determined to go, he wanted her promise not to spend more than £1,000 a year.[91]

Conclusion

We might well conclude that the Bennets with their connections to trade and finance were more successful in their marriage negotiations than the Duke of Newcastle, the Duke of Ormond, and their Clifton cousins. Despite Ormond's focus on "a defect of quality," the Bennets appear not to have had much difficulty marrying their daughters into the nobility. The marriage negotiations of the Bennets shared several similarities with those of the fifteenth- and early sixteenth-century English elite. Yet the age of their daughters was younger both because they were heiresses, and because the chronic concern over clandestine marriage was culturally heightened in the Restoration. The size of the Bennet marriage portions was much larger because of the expansion of the economy in which the Bennets and the Morewoods had participated. Ideas of companionate marriage, even if circulating in the early modern period, had no impact on the choice of marriage partners for two of the Bennet sisters, and its role in the marriage of Grace and John Bennet remains unclear.

For Simon and Grace Bennet, Lady Clifton, and the Duke of Newcastle believed strongly in parental control over children's marriage both in the present and from beyond the grave. When it failed, the resulting marriages were labeled clandestine, and the daughters, as in the cases of Grace Bennet

[89] University of Nottingham Mss., Cavendish Papers, Pw1/635, Duke of Newcastle to the Duke of Albemarle, Dec. 21, 1684; Pw1/636, Jan. 22, 1685.

[90] University of Nottingham Mss., Cavendish Papers, Pw1/335–337, 1685.

[91] University of Nottingham Mss., Cavendish Papers, Pw1/548, Newcastle to Frances, Oct. 26, 1687; Pw1/550, Jean Beaumont to Henry, 2nd Duke of Newcastle, Oct. 9, 1686.

and Katherine Parsons, were described as "stolen away." Money was central to the marriages of all those whose alliances we have considered, whether they had a lot of it, as in the case of the Bennets, whether they had to turn to parliament, like the Cliftons, or whether, as in the case of the Newcastle daughters, they had to depend on the whim of their father. Furthermore, even in the midst of the Popish Plot and the Exclusion Crisis, leading political figures like Arlington and Ormond and Chiffinch became brokers in the marital politics of the Bennet and Clifton families because these alliances were important politically and financially too.

After Simon Bennet's death, his widow Grace continued to live in their Calverton home. His two daughters Grace and Frances were co-heiresses of his large fortune. Young Grace, married to John Bennet, was living at Great Abington, Cambridgeshire. Frances, who had married the Earl of Salisbury in 1683, was, by 1688, settled at Hatfield House. "Great Bennet" could not have imagined how abruptly their comfortable lives would be overturned and why.

PART III

Murder

CHAPTER 6

"The Most Sordid Person That Ever Lived"
The Murder of Grace Bennet

Simon and Grace Bennet had renovated their Tudor mansion at Calverton, Buckinghamshire, in 1659. Now, in 1694, the house along with its large orchard and acres of arable fields lay neglected. Grace, an elderly widow, was reclusive and rich. For years, people had gossiped about the gold she had amassed in the house. According to a contemporary pamphlet, "she had the reputation of having by her (for many years last past) at least threescore thousand pounds [£60,000] in gold and silver, which was piled up in her bed chamber in loose parcels." With an estimated income of £4,000 a year, she was rumored to have hardly spent £100 and lived poorly. But her penury existed in the midst of greed. She not only surrounded herself with gold and silver, "like corn in a granary," but also was said to actually have "vast quantities of corn worth thousands . . . which she kept by her to sell to advantage in the time of scarcity." The tract's accusations against Grace Bennet compounded the vice of greed with the crime of engrossing. At one time, the pamphlet claimed, she had reached her bedroom by ladder, pulling it up afterward "to secure her pecuniary paradise from the attempts of robbers." Her efforts, however, proved unsuccessful.

At 9 am on Wednesday, September 19, 1694, a butcher named Barnes from Stony Stratford, Buckinghamshire, walked three miles to the old manor house in nearby Calverton. Barnes found Grace Bennet alone in the servants' hall and broke her neck so viciously that "her face turned behind her." Accused of violating contemporary norms and denying others' rights, Grace Bennet died a violent death. Other stories claimed that she was hit on the head or had her throat cut. The murderer was quickly caught. At 11 am one of Grace Bennet's threshers saw the butcher climbing over the garden wall at the back of the house. "He cried out: How Now Friend! What have you been robbing my lady's house?" The butcher denied it but gave him half a crown to remain silent. Found later drinking in the alehouse, the thresher identified Barnes. Quickly caught, the butcher of Stony Stratford was supposedly arrested with 300 guineas, while the murder pamphlet claimed

Figure 6.1 Calverton Manor, Photograph, *Inventory of Historical Monuments in Buckinghamshire* (London, 1913), Vol. II, Plate 21. The Folger Shakespeare Library. Calverton Manor was the home of Simon and Grace Bennet. Grace Bennet was murdered at Calverton in 1694.

that the victim left altogether £80,000 in gold.[1] Barnes was committed to St. Alban's gaol.

Grace Bennet's murder was extraordinary. She was not simply an isolated and rich widow. She had two daughters of important political and social rank: one, Frances, was the Countess of Salisbury, wife of James Cecil, the 4th Earl, the other, Grace the younger, was wife of John Bennet, a Member of Parliament. Both because of her status and because homicide rates in general were declining in the late seventeenth century, Grace's murder impels us to inquire further.[2] Grace Bennet may have been the only female relative of a peer to be murdered in the seventeenth century.

Grace's funeral was lavish as befit the mother of the Countess of Salisbury. At Hatfield House her body lay in state in a double coffin covered with

---

[1] Anon., *The Unfortunate Lady: A brief Narrative of the Life, and Unhappy Death of the Lady Bennet, Late of Buckinghamshire; Who was Most Barbarously and Inhumanly Murthered at her own House, on Wednesday the 19th of September, 1694, by a Butcher of Stony-Stratford* ... (London: Printed for H. Maston in Warwick-Lane, 1694).

[2] Randolph Roth, "Homicide in Early Modern England, 1549–1800: The Need for a Quantitative Synthesis," *Crime, History & Societies*, 5, 2 (2001), 33–67.

velvet. The rooms were elaborately hung with black cloth and forty rings were given to each of the male and female mourners. Her hearse, drawn by six horses, moved at a stately pace over five days, carrying her corpse to the Beachampton church in Buckinghamshire where she was interred. The parish church register recorded: "Madam Grace Bennet was buried the seven and twentieth day of September." She joined her dead children as well as her husband Simon Bennet and his uncle Sir Simon Bennet.[3] Small flags were placed on Simon's funeral monument for her interment.[4]

As for the murderer, the Earl and the Countess of Salisbury took a close interest in Barnes's trial, paying for both the judicial proceedings and the materials for his execution. Their accounts record the financial details of Barnes's trial as it moved from St. Albans, Hertfordshire, near Hatfield, to Ailesbury, the country town of Buckinghamshire. Their careful record began with the "money that was found upon Barnes, £140-0-0" (not £300). Mr. Sadler, the Hatfield man of business, provided another £20. With that capital sum, drawn from the robbery itself, the account then proceeded to expenditures. Because Barnes was held at the gaol at St. Albans: his gaol keeper received £10-12-0. Judicial proceedings took place in Ailesbury: there, the inn called "The George" was paid £33-5-6. For the trial itself, the Earl of Salisbury paid twenty-six witnesses £1 a piece for their testimony. Justice was swift: Barnes was found guilty of Grace Bennet's murder. At the conclusion of the trial, John Billington received £2 for "making the bodies and ironwork to the gallows" and John Gray was paid £2-12 for making the gallows and finding timber. Afterwards, John Clarke earned £1-10 for fetching the body from Ailesbury.[5] Although the purpose of moving Barnes's body after execution might suggest burial, the reason was grimmer. Behind Grace Bennet's Calverton Manor ran Gib Lane where the butcher entered her property. Here, it was said, the body of the hanged murderer was left to rot in chains.

Celia Fiennes recalled later that in 1697, on her journey from Coventry to London, she had passed "by the rich Mrs. Bennet's house, remarkable for covetousness which was the cause of her death – her treasures tempted a butcher to cut her throat who hangs in chains just against her house. She had

---

[3] Centre for Buckinghamshire Studies, BP13/1/1, Parish register, Beachampton, p. 143.

[4] Hatfield House Archives, Bills 360, Grace Bennet's funeral. Browne Willis, *The History and Antiquities of the Town, Hundred, and Deanry of Buckingham* (London: Printed for the author, 1755).

[5] Hatfield House Archives, Accounts 115/24, Trial of Barnes. Mr. Sadler himself attended the trial and received £2-5-0; Mr. Lawley was paid £9-11; Mr. Cooper received £2-17-6. The Cork in Stony Stratford was paid £16-11 and the Constable at Dunstable, 5 shillings.

3 daughters, the two youngest are living, one married to a Benet, the other the Earl of Salisbury, and are great fortunes by their mother's penuriousness."[6]

Analyzing the Evidence

Unfortunately, almost all our knowledge of Grace Bennet comes from other people's comments in letters, lawsuits, memoirs, and histories. They paint a picture of a strong-minded woman of independent views, anxious when young, angry in middle age, and vindictive, as she grew older. She herself has left only one letter, no documents, no portrait, and no will. Because of the absence of her immediate family correspondence, there is little direct evidence of family affection for one another.

While the story of Grace Bennet's murder is initially straightforward, it raises questions beyond who murdered her, how she was murdered, and why. To contemporaries, the why seemed excessively simple. Grace Bennet was rich, she was old, and she was alone: in short, she was a ripe target. And yet, as the mother of the Countess of Salisbury, she should have enjoyed the protection provided by family and servants expected in late seventeenth-century England's hierarchical society. Therefore, we begin with somewhat different questions: who was Grace Bennet? What were the reasons that she was seen in such a negative light and why was she without protection? How did she differ from other Bennet and Morewood women, who also sought to enlarge and protect their property and promote their families? Who benefitted from her murder? The answers to these questions shed light not only on Grace Bennet's life and death but also on changing attitudes toward money and property in the late seventeenth century.

If Grace Bennet's funeral ritual marked her daughter's status as much as her own, contemporary observers did not mourn her. On the contrary, Thomas Bruce, 2nd Earl of Ailesbury, who knew her daughter Frances and whose sister married into the family, called Grace Bennet "the most sordid person that ever lived."[7] A later eighteenth-century writer repeated these views, describing her as "a miserable, covetous, and wretched person, she lived by herself in the old house at Calverton; and, being supposed to have great store of money by her, tempted a butcher of Stony-Stratford to get

---

[6] Celia Fiennes, *Through England on a Side Saddle in the Time of William and Mary* (London: Field and Tuer, The Leadenhall Press, 1888).

[7] *Memoirs of Thomas, Earl of Ailesbury*, ed. W. E. Buckley, 2 vols., Roxburghe Club Publications (Westminster [London]: Nichols and Sons, 1890), Vol. II, p. 481. Ailesbury's sister married Sir William Rich, the son of Thomas Rich, whose first wife was Grace's sister, Barbara.

artfully into the house; and there being no body to assist her, or call for help, barbarously murdered her."[8]

The Earl of Ailesbury's extraordinary characterization of Grace Bennet gives us pause. Sordid, according to the *Oxford English Dictionary*, can mean variously dirty, mean, low, and greedy. Ailesbury claimed Grace Bennet was sordid because she buried gold on her property. Such hoarding was identified with avarice and greed, and he suggested that she was later murdered because of it. Did contemporaries also think Grace sordid because she had strong views on her daughters' marriage negotiations? Or because she enclosed land and refused to pay tithes? Or because she fell out with her neighbors?[9] Or was she sordid because her family failed to look after her? Or were all of these possibilities true?

The lurid murder pamphlet, that lucrative genre for seventeenth-century London printers, provides the most extensive if factually inaccurate representation of Grace Bennet at the time of her death. Entitled *The Unfortunate Lady*, it attacked Grace more than it did the murderer. The tract's enumeration of Grace's fatal defects reflects its uneasiness about women and property, money and mobility, and the role of wives and widows within the family and society at large. The late seventeenth century offered new opportunities for social mobility and female independence that caused anxiety about old and new forms of material culture and behavior. The attack on Grace Bennet as "sordid" mobilized traditional tropes of "the moral economy" of the community against the disorder of self-interest, private property, and female agency.[10] At the same time, Grace was attacked for hoarding instead of upholding her status through conspicuous consumption.

In general, murder pamphlets claimed to be morally uplifting as they titillated with tales of violence. In particular, they specialized in remorseful prisoners who found religion on the verge of their executions. This conversion narrative was especially characteristic of the puritan murder pamphlets of the early and middle part of the seventeenth century. Even

---

[8] Quoted in George Lipscomb, *The History and Antiquities of the County of Buckinghamshire*, 4 vols. (London: J. and W. Robins, 1847), Vol. IV, p. 25, where it is ascribed to William Cole, the Cambridge antiquary who held the living at Bletchely, Buckinghamshire, to which he was appointed by Browne Willis. It is possible that that Cole echoed Browne Willis's *The History and Antiquities of the Town, Hundred, and Deanry of Buckingham*.

[9] Nina Taunton, *Fictions of Old Age in Early Modern Literature and Culture* (New York and London: Routledge, 2007), pp. 95, 112, 113. On old age, also see Lynn Botelho and Pat Thane, eds., *Women and Aging in British Society since 1500* (Harlow: Longman, 2000).

[10] See E. P. Thompson, "The Moral Economy of the English Crowd in the Eighteenth Century," *Past and Present*, 50 (1971), 76–131; Sara Mendelson and Patricia Crawford, *Women in Early Modern England, 1550–1720* (Oxford: Clarendon Press: 1998); Hilda Smith, *Reason's Disciples: Seventeenth-Century English Feminists* (Champaign-Urbana: University of Illinois Press, 1982).

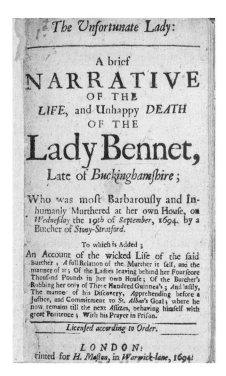

Figure 6.2 *The Unfortunate Lady*, by anonymous (London, 1694), title page.
© The British Library Board, 1076.l.15 (1). The pamphlet told the story of
Grace Bennet's murder.

The Unfortunate Lady included the accidental discovery of her murderer and
his prayer for forgiveness while he was in prison.[11] But in an era of satirical
attacks on banks and the monied interest, "The Unfortunate Lady" focused
on money and gold, its attention more on Simon and Grace Bennet than on
the murderer and the murder.

According to the pamphlet, Simon Bennet came from "rich and noble
stock." Grace was wealthy but Simon was richer. Living together happily,
Simon found that he had been too "generous in his housekeeping, and acts
of hospitality." Realizing his error, he began to manage his estate more
prudently. He also inherited another estate, and, as a result, he had provided
large dowries for his three daughters, who made important marriages. (In
reality, Simon inherited both his father's and uncle's estates while under age.)
In contrast, after Simon's death Grace Bennet dismissed her servants, kept

---

[11] Peter Lake, "Popular Form, Puritan Content? Two Puritan Appropriations of the Murder
Pamphlet from Mid-Seventeenth-Century London," in *Religion, Culture, and Society in Early
Modern Britain, Essays in Honour of Patrick Collinson*, ed. Anthony Fletcher and Peter Roberts
(Cambridge: Cambridge University Press, 1994), pp. 313– 334.

her corn off the market, hoarded large amounts of gold, and chose "never to keep up that port of grandeur answerable either to her riches or her quality."[12] If Grace had the misfortune to be murdered, the pamphlet implied, it was really her own fault for transgressing cultural norms, Tudor statutes against engrossing, and the Bible itself. "He that withholdeth corn, the people shall curse him," read the King James translation of Proverbs 11:26. Three themes in particular characterized contemporary comment about Grace Bennet: her negotiation of her daughters' marriages, her hoarding of gold, and her relationship to her local community.

Wife and Mother

Although the picture that rises from the pages of the murder pamphlet is of Grace Bennet as an elderly widow, in fact, most of her life was spent in marriage and motherhood. Born in Netherseal, Leicestershire, in 1632, Grace Bennet was the youngest daughter of Gilbert Morewood, the East India Company merchant. Morewood had purchased Netherseal and Overseal in the 1620s from Sir Thomas Gresley. Even as Gilbert made his fortune in the City, his family lived in the country in Netherseal. While *The Unfortunate Lady* states that Grace was well educated and witty, nothing is known about her education. The pamphlet, often liable to error, also claims that she was eighty when she died, when she was only sixty-two.

In 1649, at seventeen, Grace married Simon Bennet, who was twenty-five, at St. Bartholomew the Less in London. She brought him a £6,000 marriage portion. Their wedding followed by a banquet was festive, and Simon settled the manors of Beachampton and Calverton with Stony Stratford and its market on her.[13] Her brother-in-law Francis Finch called her Graziana and commented on her beauty and her reclusiveness.[14] Although still a teenager, Grace soon found herself very much on her own as a young married woman. Her father and mother died in 1650. Her oldest sister Barbara, who had married Sir Thomas Rich, had died in 1646; her sister Frances had married Sir Thomas Gresley and lived in Derbyshire; and her stepsister Joan Salmon

---

[12] *The Unfortunate Lady*, pp. 3–5.
[13] Hull University Archives, Brynmor Jones Library, Papers of the Forbes Adam/Thompson/Lawley (Barons Wenlock) Family of Escrick, U DDFA2/24/1, "Marriage Settlement: Symon Benet of Beachampton, co Bucks, esq (son and heir of Richard B. of London dec'd) to Gilbert Morewood of London esq, prior to marriage of Symon Benet and Grace Morewood, daughter of Gilbert, Manor, mansion house and advowson of Beachampton . . . Manor and advowson of Calverton . . . with Stony Stratford, co Bucks, with fairs and markets and fishing in the River Owse," Oct. 9, 1649.
[14] See Chapter 3.

lived in London. Simon, whose business was located at Lincoln's Inn in London, was already living in Beachampton, Buckinghamshire, and they soon moved to Calverton. In 1651, Simon became sheriff of the county. Grace at nineteen now settled down to two decades of running a household and to motherhood.

Grace and Simon had seven children between 1652 and 1670; a period marked by birth and repeated loss. Although three daughters lived to adulthood, three others, two girls and a boy, lived to eight and ten, and one died in infancy. In a traditional manner, Simon and Grace named their children after their close relatives. Thus when Grace's first child Marie was born in July 1652, she was probably named after Mary Taylor, Simon's grandmother. Thomas, named after Sir Thomas, the Lord Mayor, was born just nine months later in April 1653 but died the next month in May. A significant space of seven years then occurred between their children. Whether Grace had miscarriages, an illness, or withdrew from marital relations in this period is not clear. In October 1655, she consulted John Metford of Northampton, a well-known physician who treated several high-ranking women including the Countess of Banbury, the Countess of Northampton, Dorothy Spencer, daughter of the Countess of Southerland, Anne Sidney, daughter of the Earl of Leicester, and Anne Haslewood, daughter of Sir Anthony Haslewood, Baronet.[15]

Grace's childbearing now continued but not without difficulty. Grace had her next child, Elizabeth, named for Simon's mother, Lady Finch, in February 1659. In 1663 Marie died at the age of ten. Grace the younger, named for Grace herself, was born the following year, in September 1664. Two years later, on April 28, 1666, the Bennets had another child, and they again hopefully named the new baby Marie. She lived until the age of eight in November 1674. Simon, named after his father, was born in June 1668 and died in August 1674. Finally, Frances was born in 1670, probably named after Simon's half-sister, Lady Frances Clifton, or perhaps Grace's sister, Lady Frances Gresley.[16]

While the death of children in this period was not unusual, with many not surviving past infancy or the age of five, the loss of two daughters both named Marie who lived to ten and eight and a son named Simon after her husband who lived to the age of six, as well as the death of Thomas, must have been heartbreaking to both parents. By 1670 only three children

---

[15] BL, Sloane Ms. 2812, f. 50, John Metford, MD, of Northampton, Medical case book, medical prescription for Grace Bennet, wife of Simon Bennet of Beachampton of Buckinghamshire, 1655.

[16] Willis, *The History and Antiquities of the Town, Hundred, and Deanry of Buckingham*, "Simon Bennet's Monument."

survived, Elizabeth, Grace, and Frances. The lack of letters deprives us of any insight into Grace's immediate feelings, but they can be imagined from other contemporary comment on similar losses. Her long-term response to the loss of both newborns and young children may have aggravated the anxiety she demonstrated in worrying that her teenage daughters would be stolen away.[17]

Still these years saw happier times. Simon and Grace expanded the manor house at Calverton, which had sixteenth-century features, adding several rooms and a large porch decorated with shields. Completed in 1659, the year their daughter Elizabeth was born, Simon Bennet proudly placed the date on the new columned porch along with his initials. Grace Bennet also had an eye for luxury goods.[18] She admired, for instance, a piece of silver that Lady Finch had at Kensington House. In a letter to Simon in London in May 1662, Grace expressed her pleasure that he had reached London safely and found their daughter in good health. She then added: "I want a thing; such a one as your mother had to put sugar in: tha are to be bought at the gold smiths; tha are made of silver and tha youst to call them sugar chests. If you buy one let it be of the biggest sis as youshally is made."[19] Such a purchase initially suggests hospitality rather than hoarding.

Making her Daughters' Marriages

Marriage negotiations for the Bennet heiresses began by the time they were twelve and thirteen. As we saw in Chapter 5, the dowries Simon Bennet offered with his three daughters as well as his connections to the Finch family and Henry Bennet, Earl of Arlington, made up for his own lack of title. The Bennets wanted to marry their daughters to English noblemen while they were teenagers. Arranged marriages, a traditional English practice among the landed, were changing in the sixteenth and seventeenth century as companionate marriage appeared in prescriptive literature and children of elite families claimed the right to make their own decisions in marriage.[20] There is little evidence, however, that either Bennet parent

---

[17] See Chapter 5. On contemporaries' varying grief over the loss of infants and young children, see Alan MacFarlane, ed., *The Diary of Ralph Josselin, 1616–1683*, Records of Social and Economic History, New Series (Oxford University Press for the British Academy, 1976) and Ralph A. Houlbrooke, *The English Family, 1450–1700* (New York and London: Longman, 1984), pp. 134–140.
[18] VCH, *Buckingham*, Vol. IV, pp. 308–311, "Calverton Parish."
[19] Hatfield House Archives, General 72/35, Grace Bennet to Simon Bennet, May 5, 1662. The daughter was presumably Marie who was almost ten; Elizabeth was only three.
[20] Houlbrooke, *The English Family*, pp. 68–78.

concerned themselves much with their daughters' preferences, unless it coincided with their own.

Grace had decided views of her own on her daughters' suitors and their marriages. She supported Elizabeth's marriage to Viscount Latimer even though Elizabeth was only twelve or thirteen in 1672 when Sir Thomas Osborne, soon to be Earl of Danby, first raised the issue of a marriage alliance with Sir John Finch, Simon Bennet's stepbrother. The couple married in 1674 when Elizabeth was fifteen. Cool to the marriage of Frances to the grandson of the Duke of Ormond, Grace supported instead Frances's marriage to the Earl of Salisbury when she was thirteen.

Grace Bennet's emotions and behavior emerge in contemporary comments by her sister, her husband, and the Earl of Arlington at the time of the marriage negotiations for her daughters Grace and Frances. In 1679 Grace's sister Frances Gresley commented "my sister Bennet was in much trouble about her daughters and her estate."[21] Simon Bennet himself vividly portrayed Grace's opposition to the marriage of Grace the younger to her cousin John Bennet. Despite the backing of Henry Bennet, Earl of Arlington, and other members of the Bennet family, neither Simon nor Grace liked the match. When her daughter eloped with her cousin John, Grace believed it was actually abduction. She refused to meet John and put off the financial settlements even after the marriage. The Earl of Arlington represented this to the Duke of Ormond as the cantankerousness of the Bennets, especially Grace. Although the marriage was completed, the Bennets would not say what portion John was to have with young Grace.[22] In a later lawsuit, Grace Bennet the younger stated that that she had never had a marriage settlement or jointure and claimed dower from John Bennet's estate.[23] The history of the relationship of Grace Bennet and John Bennet suggests that her mother may indeed have had her best interests at heart in opposing the match.

Frances Bennet was a much sought after heiress. Although Arlington tried to make the match with the Duke of Ormond's grandson, he painted a picture throughout the negotiations of the difficulty of dealing with the Bennets, especially with Grace. It seems clear that the title and Stuart loyalties that Ormond offered could not overcome his Irish roots. The Bennets' demand for an English estate for their daughter must have come from both mother and father. Frances was thirteen when she married the 4th

[21] Folger, V.b. 25, Gresley Mss., Letter 4, Frances Gresley to Sir John Moore, Oct. 6, 1679.
[22] HMC, *Ormonde*, Vol. VI, pp. 242–243. "John Bennet, 1656–1712," in *The History of Parliament: The House of Commons, 1690–1715*, ed. D. Hayton, Evelyn Cruickshanks, and S. Handley (Cambridge: Cambridge University Press, 2002).
[23] TNA, C110/175, Morrett *v.* Paske, Particular of John Bennet's estate, 1726–1733.

Earl of Salisbury after the death of her father.[24] John Bennet challenged the Earl of Salisbury's right to the full marriage portion of £20,000 that Simon left Frances in his will because they had married before Frances was sixteen. Grace Bennet testified, however, on behalf of Salisbury that Simon supported the marriage and that negotiations between the parties had already begun even before his death.

Simon and Grace Bennet are presented as unusually difficult in the Ormond–Arlington correspondence, because of their unwillingness to come to terms with the Duke of Ormond, their continuing negotiations with several parties, and their rejection of their cousin John Bennet. They appear, however, little different from other wealthy contemporaries who sought the best matches for their daughters and placed just as much emphasis on rank and marriage settlement. Nevertheless, the negotiations do underline Grace's continuing anxiety about abduction and her long-lasting anger at John Bennet's courtship of Grace.

Grace's Estate

In 1679 Simon placed all of his landed property in a trust for himself, his male heirs, which he did not have, and his daughters. In his will, Simon made Grace co-executor of his will along with Ralph Lee, a merchant of London, and co-guardian of his daughters along with Lee and his sister Lady Clifton. He left her £1,000 as well as lands and tenements in Sinnington and Marton in Yorkshire while she remained a widow. Their marriage settlement had already settled Beachampton, Calverton, and Stony Stratford on her.[25]

But Simon Bennet was very rich and Grace wanted more. In a lawsuit in 1682, Roger Chapman, Bennet's man of business, testified that Grace Bennet wanted property worth £5,000 or £6,000 for "pin money." The annual income from the land, which would be £200–£240 a year, was not an unusual sum for pin money. Well-to-do fathers or husbands often granted women an annual sum of money for their own use called pin money, usually at the time of their marriage.[26] Grace Bennet, however, asked for pin money when she was almost fifty. Roger Chapman described Grace Bennet as very angry with him when he would not help her:

---

[24] Hatfield House Archives, General 22/35, Ebenezer Sadler to William Dobyns, July 29, 1686.

[25] TNA, PROB11/371/283, Will of Symon Bennet of Calverton, Buckinghamshire, 1682.

[26] *OED*, "Pin money." William Blackstone, *Commentaries on the Laws of England in Four Books*, 12th edn. (London: A. Strahan and W. Woodfall, 1793–1795), Book II, pp. 498–499: "If she has any pin money or separate maintenance, it is said she may dispose of her savings thereout by testament, without the control of her husband."

the said defendant Grace several times in the lifetime of the testator [Simon Bennet] spoke to him . . . and believes she did the like to others to help her to the purchase of lands and tenements to the value of five or six thousand pounds or more which she said was to be settled upon her and at her dispose and so said that such a sum was either raised by her or due to her for pin money by agreement as she said between the testator and her but this defendant neither did or knows any that any other did purchase any such or other lands by reason whereof she was very angry with this defendant, that he had not [provided] such lands for her.[27]

Before Simon died in 1682, Grace Bennet felt aggrieved that her father and Simon had not granted her lands for pin money. She already had land and goods and was certainly not poor, but she devised a different remedy to soothe her anxiety and anger.

Hoarding Gold

Gold and silver were a major basis of wealth in medieval Europe. Burying gold, silver, and jewelry was an ancient and even modern practice in times of war and disorder. It could also have a religious and ritualistic aspect.[28] Hoards of coins and jewelry have been found at Anglo-Saxon sites and across the routes traveled by the Vikings. London's Cheapside Hoard contained over 500 pieces of jewelry hidden sometime after 1640 in the midst of Civil War. In the absence of banks, families kept their liquid capital in precious metals. Because circulating coins were often in short supply, these metals often took the form of silver plate and family jewels which could be sold or pawned for ready cash.

In the sixteenth and early seventeenth centuries it was just as likely for country gentry to borrow money from each other as it was for them to have large stashes of gold on hand. Thomas Gresley, however, claimed that his father, Sir Thomas Gresley, had hidden gold in the walls or floors of one of his houses. Simon Bennet's extensive rental income meant that he did have cash on hand that he then transferred to London. After bills were paid, he put out the remainder, "upon the Exchange," that is, lent it at interest.

Hoards did not often belong to women, but Grace Bennet certainly had gold. She received fine and very valuable gold coins from Simon's business. Between 1675 and 1678, for instance, she received over 393 fine gold pieces

---

[27] TNA, C6/275/19, Bennitt (Bennet) *v*. Bennett, 1682, John Bennett, Grace Bennett, his wife and Frances Bennett *v*. Grace Bennett, Ralph Lee, Galathiel Lovell, Roger Chapman and Sir Robert Clayton, Personal estate of the deceased Simon Bennett, of London, Buckinghamshire, Gloucestershire, Leicestershire, and Staffordshire.

[28] Wade Tarzia, "The Hoarding Ritual in Germanic Epic Tradition," *Journal of Folklore Research*, 26, 2 (1989), 99–121.

worth over £460.[29] Roger Chapman himself testified in 1682 that Grace Bennet had received "considerable sums of money" during the lifetime of Simon Bennet, "and this defendant saith that he doth not know what became of the monies after the same was so delivered to her."[30]

Evidence of what became of the money comes from the Earl of Ailesbury's *Memoirs*. During the Glorious Revolution in 1688–1689, Captain John Meers commanded a troop of soldiers in Buckinghamshire on behalf of James II. Ailesbury recalled that

Captain Meers had his quarters at Madam Bennet's, mother to the late Countess of Salisbury, the most sordid person that ever lived, and she [Grace Bennet] hid her bags of money underground in her garden, and was some years after knocked on the head by a workman in the village. Captain Meers' Grenadiers had found out where the bags were and offered their Captain to go shares with them. He in indignation and like a man of honour, threatened them that if they took one shilling they should be hanged without mercy; which so terrified the men that they put into the ground again what they had taken out.[31]

Ailesbury's story of the soldiers finding gold buried in Grace's garden while the regiment was encamped in the neighborhood appears to have been believed by Grace's daughter Frances. In 1696, two years after Grace's murder, the Hatfield accounts show payment of five shillings to "several men for digging up some part of Stratford churchyard upon an information that money was hid there by a soldier concerned with several others in a robbery some years since at Madam Bennet's at Calverton, but nothing found."[32]

Keeping her gold in the house or burying it in the ground brought opprobrium on Grace Bennet from contemporary sources such as the Earl of Ailesbury and *The Unfortunate Lady*. Widowed and alone, at a time of upheaval such as the Glorious Revolution and perhaps even before, Grace Bennet turned, as did Sir Thomas Gresley, to the traditional practice of the hoard. Her behavior may have been augmented by feelings of anger and anxiety that she had displayed throughout her life. In the period of growing trade and consumption, banking, investment, and bills of exchange, however, such behavior reinforced her reputation for eccentricity and greed.

---

[29] Hatfield House Archives, Accounts 142/12A, pp. 22, 24: "Paid Mrs Bennet in gold broad pieces: March 17, 1675, Mrs Bennet 70 broad pieces of gold at 23s 10d, £83-8-04; June 25, 1676, Paid Mrs Bennet in gold 100 broad pieces at 23 6d, £117-0-0; more 20 pieces at 23s 8d, £23-13-04 ... Feb 28, 1678 to Mrs Bennet 200 broad pieces at 23-3d; £232-10."
[30] TNA, C6/275/19, Bennitt v. Bennett, 1682.
[31] *Memoirs of Thomas, Earl of Ailesbury*, Vol. II, p. 481.
[32] Hatfield House Archives, SFP 3/300. Hatfield House Archives, Accounts 125/24.

What appeared to her as safety appeared to others as sordid. Here was money that could be put to use and invested. Instead it was buried and unproductive. Her contemporary Nicholas Barbon argued as much in his tract, *A Discourse of Trade*, in 1690:

The Covetous Man thinks he grows rich, he grows poor; for by not consuming the Goods that are provided for Man's Use, there ariseth a dead Stock, called Plenty, and the Value of those goods fall, and the Covetous Man's Estates, whether in Land, or Mony, become less worth: And a Conspiracy of the Rich Men to be Covetous, and not spend, would be as dangerous to a Trading State, as a Forreign War; for though they themselves get nothing by their Covetousness, nor grow the Richer, yet they would make the Nation poor."[33]

Changing Attitudes Toward Money

Attitudes toward investment and gold were changing in the seventeenth century. The growth of domestic and international trade to the East Indies and the Atlantic offered new investment opportunities alongside land and property. As we saw earlier, in the late 1640s, early banking grew out of the businesses of goldsmiths and scriveners, and it became possible to both deposit and draw out money from individual accounts. The Crown and major merchants usually turned to goldsmiths, while individuals tended to use scriveners. Bills of Exchange allowed the well-to-do to use their wealth while abroad, underwriting travel and spending. The Great Fire of London created possibilities to invest in speculative rebuilding. When the Bank of England was founded in 1694, it offered a way for individuals to invest in the national debt. People could purchase shares in the Bank and the East India Company and, later, the South Sea Company.

By the 1690s, English men and women were investing in domestic and international trade, banking, real estate, and luxury consumption. They were also beginning to speculate on the stock market. In that economic and social environment, hoarding and burying gold in the ground could be seen not only as avarice but as a deprivation of the family and the larger economy of funds that could be put to good use. Moreover, Grace Bennet's behavior differed from that of other members of her family. The Bennets and Morewoods invested in trade, Crown finance, mortgages, private banking, and property. This was true of the women of the family as well as the men. Lady Finch provided money for the support of Kensington House, while her

---

[33] Nicholas Barbon, *A Discourse of Trade* (London: Thomas Milbourn for the author, 1690), p. 63.

daughter Lady Clifton defended her property rights in the country and established a home in Bloomsbury. Lady Gresley insisted on retaining independent wealth while married, including exploiting her timber rights. Later, the Countess of Salisbury spent expansively on European travel and her sister Grace invested in shares in the Bank of England and the South Sea Company. All of them took the opportunity to invest or spend some of their wealth. In contrast, by burying gold in the garden, Grace Bennet under-mined a commodity that fostered trade, growth, and consumption according to later seventeenth-century theorists like Nicholas Barbon and Edward Mandeville.[34]

In the early seventeenth century, precious metals were thought to have fundamental value in what Joyce Appleby described as the bullionist pos-ition. The 1620s debates over the East India trade among Gerard Malynes, Edward Misselden, and Thomas Mun, focused on the question of whether or not the trade led to the loss of specie needed to pay for East Indian imports. The balance of trade debates put more emphasis on the develop-ment of commerce than the intrinsic value of gold and silver. In the 1690s, before Grace Bennet's death, there was a shortage of coin in England. The accompanying debate included works by John Locke who argued the pos-ition for the intrinsic worth of silver and gold as a measure of all other commodities.[35] In contrast, Nicholas Barbon argued that gold and silver did not have any intrinsic value at all.

Gold and Silver are Commodities as well as Lead or Iron; and according to their Plenty or Scarcity will make those things that are made of them Dearer or Cheaper; to wit, Gold and Silver-Plate, Lace, &c. but they cannot make Corn, Cloth, Lead, or Iron Dearer or Cheaper, because they cannot supply the uses of those Commodities. There is no difference or distinction in things of equal Value: That is, one Commodity is as good as another that's of the same Value. An Hundred Pounds worth of Lead or Iron, is of as great a value as an Hundred Pounds worth of Silver or Gold ... The Man is as Rich that has an Hundred Pounds worth of Corn or Cattel, as he that has an Hundred Pounds in Money by him, for his Corn and his Cattel may be soon turn'd into so much Money: And the Merchant and Trader are always changing their Money for Commodities, because they can get more by them than by

[34] See Joyce Oldham Appleby, "Locke, Liberalism, and the Natural Law of Money," *Past and Present*, 71 (May 1976), 43–69; Joyce Oldham Appleby, *Economic Thought and Ideology in Seventeenth-Century England* (Princeton, NJ: Princeton University Press, 1978), pp. 221–230; Linda Levy Peck, *Consuming Splendor: Society and Culture in Seventeenth Century England* (Cambridge: Cambridge University Press, 2005).
[35] *Locke on Money*, ed. Patrick Hyde Kelly 2 vols. (Oxford: Oxford University Press, 1991), Vol. I; Appleby, *Economic Thought and Ideology*, pp. 236–241.

Money; either by Transporting of them where such Commodities are most scarce, or else by changing the shape of them by which they are made more useful, and therefore of more value.[36]

For Barbon, burying gold or silver in the ground took it out of the commercial circulation that gave it value.

In 1720, Grace Bennet the younger who held shares in the South Sea Company might have thought her mother wise in holding on to her gold. In the third of *Cato's Letters*, Thomas Gordon and John Trenchard attacked the government and the South Sea Company as stockjobbers and monsters that should be hanged. "This nation has formerly been bought and sold: but arts were used to blind the people's eyes... we have felt our pockets picked, and we know who have done it: vengeance abides them."[37] The crash of the heady speculation of the 1720s might have made Grace's hoarding of gold in the 1680s look rather prudent. Yet Grace's shares ultimately held their value.

Relations with her Neighbors

After Simon Bennet's death in 1682, negative descriptions of Grace multiplied. She refused to pay her poor rates to Calverton parish. In Easter session 1687, she appealed a justice's order to pay the poor rates of 19s-8d to the overseers of Calverton and lost her appeal.[38] Further, her goods were ordered distrained for not paying her rates in Easter session 1688 and the Chief Constable of Newport was ordered to give the money raised from the distraint on her goods to the overseers of Calverton. At the Epiphany Session in 1688, the justices ordered that "Mrs. Grace Bennet shall at once give up to the overseers of Calverton, "several notes duly made and allowed ... and several other books, papers and Memorandums" belonging to the parish, which she has in her custody and has refused to give up." The overseers were then ordered to hand these papers over to the justices "to settle all matters in dispute."[39] In addition, in the late 1680s and early 1690s, Grace Bennet was fined for not contributing to the repair of the highways and not scouring watercourses.

---

[36] Nicholas Barbon, *A discourse concerning coining the new money lighter in answer to Mr. Lock's Considerations about raising the value of money* (London: Printed for Richard Chiswell, 1696), pp. 7–8; *A Discourse of Trade*, pp. 24–26.

[37] Thomas Gordon and John Trenchard, *Cato's Letters or Essays on Liberty, Civil and Religious, and Other Important Subjects*, ed. and annotated, Ronald Hamowy, 2 vols. (Indianapolis: Liberty Fund, 1995), Vol. I, Letter no. 3, Nov. 19, 1720.

[38] *Calendar of Buckinghamshire Quarter Sessions*, ed. William Le Hardy, Buckinghamshire Record Society (Aylesbury: Buckinghamshire County Council, 1933), Vol. I, pp. 224, 260, 126, 479.

[39] *Buckinghamshire Quarter Sessions*, Vol. I, p. 270.

At the same time, Grace Bennet became embroiled in several legal disputes over firing her steward and refusing to pay her minister's tithes. The lawsuits paint a picture of Calverton Manor as a working farm in the early 1680s that had dramatically changed by the 1690s. Simon Bennet began to enclose the land he owned on the manors of Beachampton and Calverton. In late August and early September 1682, for instance, eight to thirteen people were engaged in mowing and haymaking on Bennet's property. The wages for men ranged from 4s–2d for four days to 5s–6d for six days labor. These wages compared favorably with those paid by his contemporary Sir Richard Newdigate.[40] Grace continued his policy of enclosure, but in the 1692 suit with her minister, depositions stated that the land that Grace held in her own hands went untilled. "The fields look like a wilderness, little being mowed and that which was generally so late and kept so long till it was spoiled." As a result, witnesses claimed that the parish was becoming depopulated.[41] Grace Bennet herself said "she had lost £10,000 by her management of the Lordship of Calverton."[42]

Grace discharged her steward Leonard Thomson, claiming that he had held back money from her, loaned her money to others, and grazed his animals on her land. In response, Thomson argued that he had worked satisfactorily for several years for her husband before working for her and had given her money without obtaining receipts. He denied he had ever "delivered up her securities for money" and claimed he had only loaned her money out on one occasion. Indeed, he stated that she was withholding accounts that would support his case. Grace had in her custody

several accompts of cattle sold and bought and wood sold and corne and several other commodities bought and sold and several other papers of accompts which the said defendent will not be so faire as to shewe your Orator or let him have copies of neither will she admit the payment of the said moneys but most unduly endeavors whilst she has those papers by her to charge your Orator again with the payment.

He asked for back wages of £50 a year as well as expenses.[43]

[40] VCH, *Buckingham*, Vol. IV, pp. 308–311; Hatfield House Archives, Legal 177, Answer of Leonard Thomson in Grace Bennet *v.* Leonard Thomson for the use of the complainant, 1691; Steve Hindle, "Work, Reward and Labour Discipline in Late Seventeenth-Century England," in *Remaking English Society: Social Relations and Social Change in Early Modern England*, ed. Steve Hindle, Alexandra Shepard, and John Walter (Woodbridge: Boydell and Brewer, 2013), pp. 255–280.
[41] VCH, *Buckingham*, Vol. IV, pp. 308–311.
[42] TNA, E134/4W&M/Mich9, William Carpender, clerk v Grace Bennett, widow, 1692.
[43] Hatfield House Archives, Legal 184/7, Bill, Thomson *v.* Bennet. Feb. 26, 1691.

Tithes

In addition to her steward Thomson, Grace Bennet was at odds in the late 1680s and early 1690s with the longtime Calverton minster, William Carpender, MA. Simon Bennet had appointed Carpender minister in 1661. He was a pluralist, holding another living and serving at that time as the chaplain for Richard Rich, then Earl of Holland and later, Earl of Warwick.[44] Carpender had been paid £25 for his tithes by Simon Bennet as well as £200 for the two years 1677 and 1678, possibly composition for the tithes of the whole parish.

According to William Blackstone, "tithes are to be paid for everything that yield an annual increase as corn, hay, fruit, cattle, poultry, and the like." Scripturally based exactions, by the late seventeenth century they extended beyond the great tithes of corn, hay, and wood, and the small tithes of livestock, wool, and other crops, to new vegetables like turnips, grasses like clover, and all kinds of fruit to support the local rector or vicar. In many places, the tithe was being replaced by composition. Tithes could be bought and sold and leased out by the clergyman. Resistance to the payment of tithes for religious and other reasons sprang up throughout the century over the size of the composition and the tithes themselves.[45] Joan Thirsk points out that litigation grew when land usage changed, when the size of composition grew, and when new crops were included. These included "tithes of gardens & orchards & fruit trees & shrubs in fields and elsewhere." A woman refused to play tithes on clover in 1711 because she was "unwilling to begin a custom for paying tithe for that particularly sort of grass."[46] Grace Bennet tried to make a similar case.

Carpender sued Grace twice in 1686 and 1692. In the first case the interrogatories posed to witnesses on behalf of Carpender began with his right as rector to receive "all manner of . . . tithes" in the parish. Carpender sought to show that Simon and Grace Bennet had enclosed arable common land, which formerly had paid tithes, and converted it to pasture. They had also turned some of their own land into an expansive orchard. "And do you know the large orchard inclosed with a stately wall in Calverton . . . how many acres doth the same contain?" He asked its value before it was

[44] CCED, Clergy of the Church of England Database, "William Carpender," "Calverton."

[45] On tithes see Sir William Blackstone, *The Commentaries of Sir William Blackstone, Knight, on the Laws and Constitutions of England* (Chicago: American Bar Association, 2009), p. 83; Christopher Hill, *The Economic Problems of the Church* (Oxford: Clarendon Press, 1956), chap. 6; Joan Thirsk, ed., *Agrarian History of England and Wales*, Vol. V, *1640–1750* (Cambridge: Cambridge University Press, 1984), pp. 390–402.

[46] Quoted in Thirsk, *Agrarian History of England*, Vol. V, p. 400.

converted into an orchard, the tithes then and now, and what quantity of fruit was now being grown.[47]

In response, in her interrogatories, Grace Bennet claimed that Simon Bennet had paid tithes only on hay and grain, not on animals and fruit. "Do you know whether the said Symon Bennet in his life time did pay either for the orchard gardens, yards, homestead, or little close adjoining to his house at any time to the said William Carpender or whether he did not enjoy the same tithe free."

Testimony in the two cases mainly supported Carpender, but some supported Grace Bennet. Frances Dabb, a laborer aged sixty, said that both Simon and Grace had enclosed land in the parish, although Nicholas Mead-flower, a husbandman, said that Simon had enclosed 200 acres and Grace only 8. Dabb testified that Simon did pay tithes on the orchard with apples and pears. On Grace Bennet's behalf, however, Roger Chapman denied that Simon Bennet ever paid tithes on the orchard. Instead he pointed out that Carpender had contracted to have Simon Bennet collect his tithes from the parish.

He doth not know that ever the said Symon Bennet paid any tithes in kind for the Orchards, gardens, yard, or homestead or place in the Interrogatory mentioned to the plaintiff but believes that for many yeares (but cannot saye how many) he paid a composition ... And this Deponent says that he believes the plaintiff did let great part of the Tythes of Calverton to the said Symon Bennet by lease in writtinge to which this deponent refers.[48]

Was the Carpender case really about collecting composition for tithes rather than his share of apples and pears?

In the 1692 case between William Carpender and Grace Bennet, property management and the orchard were once again great issues. Although the interrogatories asked about improvement in land usage, sheep, and cattle, the most vivid testimony appeared on these two issues. In bearing witness in the two suits, her neighbors testified not only on the question of whether Grace Bennet had paid her tithes but also on the larger questions of how she used her land and whether or not she was a good neighbor. Some of the depositions claimed that she was vindictive and was letting her fields lie fallow out of ill will toward the minister. William Wolton of Calverton, aged thirty eight, made this claim most pointedly and in doing so painted an extraordinary picture of Grace Bennet.

[47] TNA, E134/2Jas2/Mich.23, Carpender *v*. Bennet.
[48] TNA, E134/2Jas2/Mich.23, Carpender *v*. Bennet.

Hath heard the Defendant [Grace Bennet] say with a great deal of spite and malice
that if she might but have her will of the complainant [Carpender] she did not care if
she spent both the Lordship of Beachampton and Calverton and that if she could
but wrong the minister of his right she did not care if she lost her own ... the
Defendent hath a very fair large orchard conteyning about six acres and the same is
planted with all sorts of choice fruits (to wit) Apricocks, peaches, pears, and many
good apples, and that this deponent hath heard the Defendent say that there hath
been thirty or forty quarter of fruit in the said orchard in a year but the Defendent
did not suffer them to pull the same because the parson should not have his Tythes
and that she had rather they fell down and rotted under the trees than he should
have his dues. And this deponent further sayeth that the Defendent doth yearly let
her hay lie and rot upon the ground on purpose to defraud the complainant of his
dues and that he hath heard her say she had rather lose all her crop than he should
have his tythe.[49]

Thus, the accusations against Grace were that, first, she enclosed common
land and then let it lie fallow, thereby not allowing others to use it. Secondly,
her beautiful six-acre orchard, presented as a veritable Garden of Eden,
which implicitly could have fed many in a large and hospitable household
and neighborhood, was left to rot, because of deliberate malice. Grace
Bennet's decision not to gather all the fruit once she lived on her own or,
as the lawsuit argued, to spite the minister, posed individual right against
traditional communal values and the church's right to collect tithes on newly
made gardens. William Carpender and those who testified for him invoked
what E. P. Thompson called "the moral economy," the values and statutes of
the Tudor era, in order to get his tithes.

Francis Dabb testified "he hath heard the defendant declare that she hath
lost ten thousand pounds by her management of her lordship of
Calverton ... and that her lordship would last as long as the complainant's
parsonage." William Hutchins, a laborer, provided a similar tale but with a
different outcome. He "believes there was about 20 quart in the said
orchard that year." He heard Grace Bennet say that the minister would
not get any of fruit "because he would not have his due, whereupon this
defendant gave them to the poor." Finally, testifying on Grace's behalf, her
bailiff presented a completely different story. John Holloway was bailiff to
Grace Bennet in 1687:

in which time she did always give a strict command to this deponent to be very
careful to pay all manner of tithes due out of her estate to the complainant and
particularly in the yeare aforesaid the [respondent] had fifty four bushels of apples

[49] TNA, E 134/4W&M/Mich9, William Carpender, clerk *v.* Grace Bennett, widow, 1692.

and peaches two quarts of grapes and seven quinces the tithe of which was tendered to the complainant. But he refused to take the same although the same was measured in the orchard at the roots of the trees.[50]

The testimony in the 1692 case suggests that minister Carpender may not have wanted the fruit as much as he wanted the money and sought to use the "moral economy" argument to force Grace Bennet to pay composition on all of her property. Grace's feud with her steward and minister had a larger significance. Together with her resistance to paying poor rates, repairing the highways, and letting her land lie fallow, it robbed her of significant local support.

Who Benefitted from Grace Bennet's Murder?

Grace Bennet died intestate in 1694, which was unusual for a rich widow and very different from her mother-in-law Lady Finch and her sister Lady Gresley. She thus left no legacies at all. She did favor her son-in-law, Salisbury, who from the 1680s struggled to claim his wife Frances's full marriage portion against the suits of John Bennet even as he was imprisoned in the Tower as a Jacobite. Mr. Fuller, one of the Hatfield men of business, wrote to Mr. Sadler that on occasion he had discussed matters with Madame Bennet and proposed "to help Madam in her trial with Carpender, in order to gain her good will."[51] The Hatfield family worried about Grace as she grew older. Samuel Percivall wrote to George Stillingfleet from London in 1690 that he had been summoned to town to "consult about old Madam's posture at Calverton. She is grown sickly and our interest persuades we set some kind of guard about her to observe and keep fair play if she should die."[52] Presumably the Earl and Countess wished to safeguard Grace's wealth from John Bennet and others as well as look after the aging widow. The letter also suggests that Grace was frail when she was murdered. It is hard to believe, however, that the Earl and Countess of Salisbury and their officials would have left Grace surrounded with a hoard of £60,000 or £80,000 in gold. Salisbury did nevertheless expect to profit from Grace's death.

A contemporary candidly said as much. William Gifford wrote to the Earl of Salisbury at his house in Gerrard Street on October 23, 1694, a month after Grace's murder.

---

[50] TNA, E134/4W&M/Mich9, William Carpender, clerk *v.* Grace Bennett, widow, Feb. 13, 1692.
[51] Hatfield House Archives, General 25/31, April 15, 1687. See also Samuel Percivall to William Dobyns as to Madam Bennet's "answer." Hatfield House Archives, General 19/19, Feb. 8, 1684.
[52] Hatfield House Archives, FP10/118a.

The first thing is to congratulate your honor's happy fortunes of late from your mother's death, tho an unfortunate one, I rejoice not at the cause but the effect, not at her death, but at your honor's advantage by it. The next thing is to lament your present illness, which I heard of accidentally very lately. No one my Lord is sorrier than I am.

He prayed for Salisbury's recovery and suggested that if the Earl bestowed anything on him, "it will be great charity."[53] Unfortunately for the favor-seeking Gifford, the Earl died the next day. Thus it was Grace's daughter Frances, now Dowager Countess of Salisbury, who came into her half of Simon Bennet's estate in her own right with remainder to her young son the 5th Earl in October 1694, a month after her mother's death.

John Bennet hoped to benefit too because his wife Grace inherited her half of her father's estate, which he now controlled during their marriage. He had initiated a series of lawsuits as soon as Simon Bennet died in 1682, claiming that Grace Bennet and Ralph Lee, the executors, were not carrying out Simon's will and that Roger Chapman, Simon Bennet's man of business, was not providing the accounts.[54] But John Bennet's hopes of a great windfall were ultimately stymied. In 1679 Simon Bennet had created a trust in which he placed all his real estate, first for his own benefit and then for his daughters and their heirs. If they were unmarried or widowed, they could spend the money themselves; if married, the procedure was more complicated, but their husbands were not to have the use of the money.[55] The result ultimately complicated John Bennet's access to Grace's inheritance. Although he was able to spend a large amount of her marriage portion and use her real estate as collateral, as we will see in later chapters, by 1698 John Bennet had been arrested and removed to the Fleet.

"The Most Sordid Person that Ever Lived?"

Grace's own voice remains missing throughout this story. While as a landowner she may have been seen as grasping and neglectful, the epitaph on the monument to Simon Bennet placed in Beachampton church celebrates them both, drawing attention to her ancestry as well as his. It commemorates the

[53] Hatfield House Archives, General 93/26, William Gifford to the Earl of Salisbury at his house in Gerrard Street, Oct. 23, 1694.
[54] TNA, C6/275/19, Bennitt *v.* Bennett, 1682; TNA, C6/275/25, Bennet *v.* Bennett, 1683.
[55] TNA, C6/275/19, Bennitt *v.* Bennett, 1682, Roger Chapman's answer: "after their respective marriages in trust to pay the respective share and proportion of her or them so married from time to time yearly to such person or persons and in such manner as they respectively by writing under their respective hands and attested by two or more credible witnesses a part and without their respective husbands from year to year shall direct . . . and not otherwise."

Morewoods' old Yorkshire connections, the Bennet's ties to commerce and to the Lord Mayor of London, and their merchant kin. The memorial lists each of her seven children and the marriages that the three heiresses had made, dramatizing their movement to nobility in two generations.[56]

While wives often commissioned funeral monuments for their deceased husbands, Simon Bennet's cannot be ascribed to Grace.[57] For five years after his death in 1682, Simon had no monument. Ironically, his monument resulted from a bad debt. John Brograve had borrowed money from Simon Bennet. Although he owed much more, Samuel Percivall on behalf of the Earl of Salisbury and Ralph Lee, executor of Bennet's will, accepted £82 to settle the claim. The judge in the case decided the £82 should be given to Roger Chapman, Simon Bennet's agent, "and do also think fit that a monument be made for the said Simon Bennet as the said Mr Percivall

---

[56] Browne Willis's *The History and Antiquities of the Town, Hundred, and Deanry of Buckingham* described the monument this way:

> Inclosed by Iron rails a curious White Marble Monument supported by two round Pillars; at the Top the Arms and Crest of **Benet** viz. Gules, three Demi Lions Rampant Or; in Fess point a Besant. Underneath the Bust of a Man and below it this Inscription on a Tablet,
> S.
> M. S.
> *Symonis Benet Armigeri*
> *Filii et hæredis* **Ricardi Benet** *Armigeri, Nepotis Avi sui* **Thomæ Benet**,
> *Eq. Aurati, necnon Urbis London. dignissimi quondam Prætoris.*
> *In unicam duxit Uxorem,*
> **Graciam**, *filiam Cohæredem* **Gilberti Moorwood**, *ex antiquiss. Moorwoodorum Prosapia, de Shireoaks, Agro Eborancensi, Arm.*
> *Per quam vii Liberorum Pater evasit;*
> **Mariæ**, *natæ 10 Julii, 1652, et 20 Julii, 1663, denatæ;*
> **Thomæ**, *nati 28 Aprilis, et 2° die Maii, 1653, denati;*
> **Elizabethæ**, *natæ 27 Februarii 1659, Nuptæ Honoratiss.* **Edwardo Vice-comiti Latimer**, *Fil hæredi Nobilissimi* **Thomae Comitis de Danby**, *quæ primo die Maii, 1680, denata est;*
> **Graciæ**, *natæ 27 Sept. 1664, præsentis Uxoris ornatissimi* **Johannis Benet**, *de Abington in Agro Cantabr. Arm. descendentis ab Honorabili* **Thomæ Benet** *de Lond. Eq. Aurati;*
> **Mariæ**, *natæ 28 Aprilis, 1666. Nov. 26, 1674, denatæ;*
> **Simonis**, *nati 27 Junii 1668. Augusti 23, 1674, denatæ;*
> **Franciscæ**, *natæ 20 Octob. 1670, præsentis Uxoris Nobilissimi Domini* **Jacobi, Comitis Sarisburiensis**.
> *Vir erat probus, prudens, et frugi;*
> *Christiane providus, temporaie liberalis;*
> *Ecclesiæ, Regi, Reipublicæ, cordate devotus;*
> *Maritus Charus, Indulgens Pater, Herus misericors, qui postquam se Deo resignasset, 20 Augusti, Æræ, Christianæ 1682,*
> *Ætatis Anno circiter Sexagesimo Vivis excessit,*
> *Et heic in Fide Christiana sui Servatoris expectat adventum.*

[57] Barbara J. Harris, *English Aristocratic Women's Religious Patronage, 1450–1550: The Fabric of Piety* (Amsterdam: Amsterdam University Press, 2018).

and Complainants have or shall direct. And the said Mr. Chapman pay for the same."[58] The question then of who commissioned and wrote the Latin epitaph on Simon Bennet's monument remains unknown, but may well have originated with Hatfield House, the Countess of Salisbury, and her chaplain, Benjamin Conway.

Had we the evidence of correspondence and diaries, we might build an alternative story about Grace Bennet, one told from her point of view. It might include warm relations with her husband, her children, and grand-children. It would allow us to see the visits to London that we know took place. Perhaps she stayed at a Bennet property, or with the Countess of Salisbury, or even Grace Bennet the younger. Perhaps not.

Certainly Grace Bennet resembled many seventeenth-century elite women who sought to expand their property while promoting their family interests. Like her sister Lady Gresley, Grace was a strong figure in her family, helping to shape her daughters' marriage choices and her husband's decisions. Like other women we have discussed previously, Lady Finch, Lady Clifton, and Lady Gresley, Grace Bennet was eager to improve her family's status. Both she and Lady Gresley had large families and lost children. While Grace focused on her daughters' marriages, Lady Gresley focused on her son's apprenticeships. After Simon Bennet died in 1682, Grace Bennet had diffi-culty managing Calverton manor. Like Lady Clifton, who had conflicts with Gervase Holland and sued William Sacheverell, Grace fired her steward and tangled with her minister. Like Lady Gresley, she looked out for her own economic interests. Yet while she shared many qualities with other strong Bennet and Morewood women, Grace Bennet appears especially fearful and angry. Grace was fearful for her young daughters and angry with Simon and Roger Chapman for not providing her with "pin money," angry with her minister for demanding tithes on everything including her beautiful orchard, and so fearful about her money that she buried it in the ground. She had an intense desire for money but was unwilling to spend it. A judge ordered her husband's funeral monument because no one in the family had yet paid for it.

Still, Grace Bennet was not merely a weak elderly widow. Rather, used to having a strong voice in her household, she now faced problems beyond her abilities in running the Calverton and Beachampton estates. Like many others, including Lady Clifton, Grace feared she was being cheated. Her desire for independence was not at all unusual, but she lacked a network of support. When Lady Finch became frail, Anne, Viscountess Conway, came to stay. In contrast, in Grace's last years, her sons-in-law were in trouble: the Earl of Salisbury was in the Tower off and on for Jacobitism, where his wife

[58] Hatfield House Archives, Legal 169, May 10, 1687.

Frances joined him, and John Bennet, although an MP, was deeply in debt and his mother-in-law was one of those he sued. Grace's disputes with her steward, her minister, and the local authorities revealed her lack of support from her neighbors and apparently her children.

Conclusion

The murder of Grace Bennet was not only a robbery gone bad; it was a more general attack on what was perceived as a misuse of capital. Grace Bennet was a rich woman who hoarded gold at a time of scarcity when it was thought she could have invested it more productively. She refused to pay the taxes necessary to support church and locality. She was accused of misusing her property through enclosure, letting land lie fallow, and depopulating the neighborhood, setting the interest of her private property against the "moral economy" of her neighbors. Furthermore, her tenants testified that that she wasted her hay and the fruit in her orchard out of malice.

Had Grace Bennet argued in a more modern idiom that she was allowing her fields to lie fallow to renew them or that she had a religious objection to tithes, perhaps she would have earned less opprobrium. Evidence in the lawsuits, however, created a picture of an angry, even eccentric old woman determined to deny the minister his tithes on her beautiful orchard. By choosing to hoard and waste assets against community interests, she became vulnerable. Grace Bennet's unhappy relationship with her tenants, minister, and neighbors as well as her distance from her family cost her the protection that her wealth and status might have been expected to provide. Despite the plans of the Hatfield men of business, no guard was there to protect her when Barnes arrived. She faced the butcher alone.

The next generation of Bennets was exactly the opposite. In the next chapter, we shall see how Frances Bennet, Countess of Salisbury, who lost her mother and her husband within a month, responded to these losses. She did not follow her mother's example by hoarding her wealth. Quite the contrary. The Countess of Salisbury lived up to the status, culture, and grandeur of her rank and set off on the longest journey of any aristocratic woman in the seventeenth century.

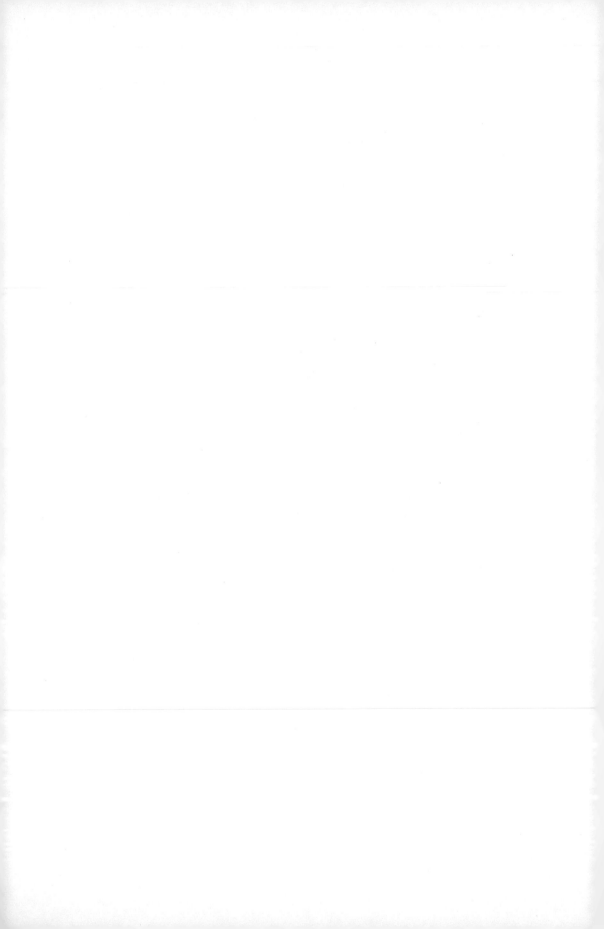

PART IV

Metropolis

CHAPTER 7

"The Countess of Salisbury Who Loved Travelling:"
From Hatfield House to the Grand Tour
The Earl and Countess of Salisbury

The Lady Vanishes

Early one April morning in 1699, a hired coach with four horses waited to take the Countess of Salisbury from London to Dover. Her small company traveled rapidly, changing horses twice in order to get to the coast by evening. Then they disappeared. On April 19, 1699, a London newsletter breathlessly announced, "One of the richest matches in England is gone for France without any servants to wait on her." In May, it reported, "a great search has been made for the Countess of Salisbury." It had just been discovered that she "was gone to Flanders . . . some say to marry the Earl of Ailesbury."[1] The Secretary of State, James Vernon, more soberly informed the English ambassador to the Hague that "The Countess dowager of Salisbury is lately gone for France in a very private manner; neither communicating it to her relations or servants, except those very few she took with her."[2] The Countess dismissed sixteen servants "at the time of her Honor's going to travel," taking only five people with her in the coach to Dover.[3] There appears to be no evidence that she bothered to get a license to travel.

The mystery of the countess's disappearance did not evoke fears of foul play, as in the case of her mother, but a social felony of a different sort, that she had made a secret engagement or eloped. For Frances, dowager Countess of Salisbury, continued to be identified as a prospective bride although she

---

[1] Oxford University, Bodleian, E. Edwards, "Calendar of the Carte Manuscripts," vol. 66, f. 402, April 19, 1699, f. 409, [May 1699], Newsletters to Theophilus Hastings, Earl of Huntingdon.
[2] *CSPD, 1699–1700*, pp. 150–151, April 28, 1699; TNA, SP32/15, f. 346, James Vernon to Lord Ambassador Williamson.
[3] Hatfield House Archives, Accounts 75/11, Account of Hugh Hawker, Steward of Household from Michelmas 1698 to May 2, 1699. SFP3/59, April 2, 1699, "Hire of a good coach and three sets of fresh horses 4 at each time to carry 6 persons from London to Dover on Tuesday next between 4 in the morning and 8 at night for 6 persons to Dover and 5/ for carrying my Lady from Dover House to the coach."

179

had been a widow for five years. As a child of twelve she had been on the marriage market, an heiress whose property had been much sought after. Still in her twenties, pursuit resumed. Now, however, Frances made her own choice and, rejecting her commodification as "one of the richest matches in England," she decided to leave the country. But she did not elope. Drawn by the attractions of the continent, the countess traveled extensively in France, Italy, and the Netherlands for four years between 1699 and 1703 despite the outbreak of the War of the Spanish Succession and her own serious illness. She left behind her son James, 5th Earl of Salisbury, who was only eight years old.[4] Through her long journey, the countess created an identity that conflicted with established British politics and religion, the pull of family, and contemporary gender roles. At the same time, she took part in one of the great pleasures of the Stuart elite, continental travel.

Contemporaries defined the Countess of Salisbury simply in terms of her wealth, rank, and marital status. The countess struggled against these limitations. Like her husband, she leant toward Jacobitism and Roman Catholicism, but she was more prudent politically, never breaking openly with the regime of William III. Culturally, she adopted the manners and language of European and especially French aristocrats. Socially, she challenged the prescriptive role of women as wives and mothers by leaving her son and, after contemplating remarriage, rejecting it. Financially, like many wealthy widows she wielded economic power and independence.

Not surprisingly, the Countess of Salisbury was the richest of the Bennet and Morewood women, drawing her income from both her dower and her inheritance from her father. In contrast to her mother, Grace Bennet, she did not hoard her wealth but spent it on her cosmopolitan life at home and abroad. In particular Frances used her considerable financial resources to live a life on the continent marked by intrepid travel, curiosity, luxury consumption, self-improvement, and cosmopolitan taste. Some contemporaries criticized the Countess of Salisbury and her travels. A wealthy noblewoman on the Grand Tour evoked satire and envy among Samuel Pepys and his friends. Frances, however, had the last laugh, using her wealth to experience the world in ways usually open only to elite men.

Travel, its history, literature, and mentality, has generated much work on the Grand Tour. Scholars have focused on the emergence of continental travel to France and Italy as part of elite male education in the sixteenth, seventeenth, and eighteenth centuries. Contemporary travel writers such as

---

[4] Hatfield House Archives, SFP "notes from the bills" (particularly SFP 3/69–70). This refers to bills while the Countess of Salisbury was in Europe and Grace Bennet, her son, and their cousin Mrs. Gresley dined with the young 5th Earl while she was away.

Richard Lassels and later writers define the Grand Tour as masculine.[5] Italy itself was viewed as feminizing and the subject of the masculine gaze.[6] Less has been written on the experience of women travelers in the seventeenth century.[7] Thus, Antoni Maczak suggests, "tourism was not the domain of ladies."[8] Brian Dolan's *Ladies of the Grand Tour* focuses on the second half of the eighteenth century. In her work on Italian guidebooks in the eighteenth century, Rachel Sweet notes one source as saying in 1733 that more women than before were traveling in Italy.[9]

But English women did travel in Europe, indeed globally, in the seventeenth century and earlier. Although James I had issued stringent regulations in 1606, these were later relaxed. Often licenses could be issued at the port itself. Women received licenses to travel in the 1620s and 1630s. While many traveled with their husbands, some did not. Their destination was often Spa in Liège, where they stayed for the season. Alatheia Talbot, Countess of Arundel, who was Roman Catholic, created a new pattern, living in Venice in the 1620s near her sons, who were studying at the university in Padua.[10] Sir Robert and Lady Shirley were in Rome in the 1620s. Later, royalist women went into exile during the Civil War. Lady Catherine Whetenhall traveled to Rome in 1650 with her husband and Richard Lassels while pregnant and died in Italy.[11] Quaker women traveled from Constantinople to Boston. At home, Celia Fiennes explored Britain at the end of the century.[12]

---

[5] See Chloe Chard, *Pleasure and Guilt on the Grand Tour: Travel Writing and Imaginative Geography 1600–1830* (Manchester: Manchester University Press, 1999), pp. 36 and 91n. Edward Chaney, *The Grand Tour and the Great Rebellion: Richard Lassels and "Voyage of Italy" in the Seventeenth Century* (Geneva: Saltine, 1985).

[6] Chard, *Pleasure and Guilt on the Grand Tour*, p. 36.

[7] See Chloe Chard and Helen Langdon, eds., *Transports: Travel Pleasure and Imaginative Geography, 1600–1830* (New Haven, CT: Yale University Press, 1996); *Women's Studies*, 26 (1997), special issue on women and travel; Kay Dian Kriz et al. "Grand Tour Forum," *Eighteenth Century Studies*, 31 (1997), 87–114.

[8] Antoni Maczak, *Travel in Early Modern Europe*, trans. Ursula Phillips (Cambridge: Polity Press, 1995), p. 140. Jeremy Black, *The British Abroad: The Grand Tour in the Eighteenth Century* (Stroud: Sutton Publishing, 1992); Brian Dolan, *Ladies of the Grand Tour: British Women in Pursuit of Enlightenment and Adventure in Eighteenth-Century Europe* (New York: Harper Collins, 2001); Bruce Redford, *Venice and the Grand Tour* (New Haven, CT: Yale University Press, 1996); Edward Chaney, *Evolution of the Grand Tour* (London: Frank Cass, 1998).

[9] Rosemary Sweet, "British Perceptions of Italian Cities in the Long Eighteenth Century," in *British History, 1600–2000: Expansion in Perspective*, ed. Kazuhiko Kondo and Miles Taylor (London: IHR, 2010), pp. 153–176.

[10] Linda Levy Peck, *Consuming Splendor: Society and Culture in the Seventeenth Century* (Cambridge: Cambridge University Press, 2005), pp. 135–139.

[11] Chaney, *The Grand Tour and the Great Rebellion*, pp. 235–236.

[12] I am grateful to Georgiana Ziegler for the reference to Quaker women. On Celia Fiennes, see Christopher Morris, ed., *The Journeys of Celia Fiennes* (London: Cresset Press, 1949) and later editions.

The travels of Frances, Countess of Salisbury, who embarked on perhaps the longest trip undertaken by any English noble woman in the seventeenth century, remain virtually unknown. Although none of her own correspondence has survived, her detailed financial accounts and the correspondence of others document her sightseeing, language study, and visits to antiquities, galleries, gardens, opera, theatre, concerts, and music making. These accounts also show the countess's entry into international Roman Catholic and Jacobite networks including gift exchange with political contacts. The letters further reveal a love affair in which her suitor spent an extraordinary fifteen months wooing her. Indeed, as the countess toured the continent, she herself became a sight of interest. This chapter and the next look at Frances, Countess of Salisbury, from her child marriage to James Cecil, 4th Earl of Salisbury, to her travels on the continent and the cultural life she enjoyed there on the cusp of the War of the Spanish Succession.

Marriage to the Earl of Salisbury

In 1683 the thirteen-year-old Frances Bennet married the seventeen-year-old Earl of Salisbury. As we have seen, Frances was the daughter and co-heir of Simon Bennet, whose father, uncle, and grandfather were well-to-to London merchants; she and her sisters were wealthy heiresses. They also had connections at the court of Charles II through their cousin Henry Bennet, Earl of Arlington, one of the Cabal, and through their father's stepbrothers, Heneage Finch, Earl of Nottingham, and Sir John Finch. Frances became a widely sought prize that Arlington dangled before the Irish nobleman the Duke of Ormond who was in search of a bride for his grandson. But Frances's parents chose James Cecil, son of the 3rd Earl of Salisbury. After their wedding Frances went off to a decaying Hatfield House to live and to take music, dancing, and French lessons, while James, now the 4th Earl of Salisbury, left immediately for his own Grand Tour, spending time and a fortune gambling in Paris.[13] The earl and countess did not begin their married life together until early 1688 when Frances was almost eighteen and the earl was twenty-two.

From the time of William Cecil, Lord Burghley, Elizabeth I's chief minister, the Cecils had been part of the Protestant and political establishment. In the late seventeenth century, however, the 4th Earl of Salisbury rejected the political legacy of his father, who had voted to exclude James, Duke of York, from the throne because he was a Roman Catholic. In

---

[13] David Cecil, *The Cecils of Hatfield House* (London: Constable and Company, 1973), pp. 175–178. Hatfield House Archives, SFP 3/237, Expenses at Calverton: payments for teaching Countess dancing £24, music £18.

1684 Aphra Behn, the well-known playwright, dedicated *Poems upon Several Occasions and Voyage to the Island of Love*, to young Salisbury who, at the time, was enjoying the pleasures of continental travel. Writing in the aftermath of the Exclusion Crisis, Behn called him a "true Tory." The politically conservative author lauded the Earl's youth and loyalty to Charles II and assured him of a bright future.

Who should one celebrate with Verse and Song, but the Great, the Noble and the Brave? Where dedicate an *Isle of Love*, but to the Gay, the Soft and Young? The violent storms of Sedition and Rebellion are hush'd and calm'd; black Treason is retir'd to its old abode, the dark Abyss of Hell ... you have nothing before you but a ravishing prospect of eternal Ioys, and everlasting inviting Pleasures ... Your Lordship amongst Your other Vertues is Loyal too, a true Tory! (a word of Honour now).[14]

Behn's ecstatic prognosis of Salisbury's future happiness was to be proved wrong by the end of the decade.

In contrast to Behn's apotheosis of Salisbury, a satirical broadside appeared entitled "Newes from Hertfordshire" while James was on the continent and Frances was at Hatfield. Declaring that the gentlewoman who looked after Frances had been fired, it asserted, "My Ladies allowance must be taken away and she must be sent home again to live upon curds and whey." Sensationally, the tract claimed variously that James had lost 40,000 livres gambling with the King of France, had turned Roman Catholic, and had been captured by pirates.

The broadside was not unique: stories were circulating in London too. A worried Hatfield official drafted a letter to the Earl urging him to return because the story was damaging his reputation.

Convince the world of the falseness of a report, which has of late generally prevailed, viz. That your Lordship is taken prisoner by a pirate of Tunis, and £40,000 ransom to be paid. There is scarce a person in London but has the report in his mouth ... Nor is this the only story; there are some who have moralized the fable and metamorphosed the Turkish pirate into French gamesters and the £40,000 demanded in ransom in a composition for that sum lost at play. My Lady's going to Calverton is strongly represented and your Lordship is wrongly censured for that which was done without your privity, if not against your order.[15]

Some months later Ebenezer Sadler confirmed the story that Frances had gone home to her mother. "My Lady Salisbury has gone to Calverton and

---

[14] Aphra Behn, *Poems upon Several Occasions: With a Voyage to the Island of Love* (London: Printed for R. Tonson and I. Tonson, at Gray's-Inn-Gate Next Gray's-Inn Lane, and at The Judges-Head at Chancery Lane End Near *Fleetstreet*, 1684).

[15] Hatfield House Archives, General 74/8, [the letter is not dated] Aug.– Nov., 1685.

Mrs. Stumpe [Frances's gentlewoman] to London and the family at Hatfield is dissolved. Very strange stories go about the town concerning my Lord and his affairs."[16]

Although Frances did go to Calverton, she went back to Hatfield in late 1687 to prepare for Salisbury's return. Ralph Lee, Simon Bennet's executor, revealed his views of Salisbury to Frances's mother Grace Bennet. "This night expect Sarah from Hatfield, for my Lady Salisbury is prudent, and will give no offence on her part to the great fat man. I believe it will be a month before she will see him in England ... he is making great preparations to come in splendidly. I shall for my good Lady's sake endear him to me, and acquaint you how far the temper is refined."[17] Lee's description of the Earl as the "great fat man" is confirmed in his portraits.

Salisbury got his wish to be splendid, but only briefly. His loyalty to the Stuarts was now rewarded. He had converted to Roman Catholicism in France and was appointed to James II's Bedchamber late in 1688. But the arrival of William of Orange with his Dutch army, James II's flight to France, and the Glorious Revolution, which placed William and Mary on the throne, made Salisbury's religion and politics a serious liability. Loyal to the exiled James II and to other Jacobites, Salisbury was accused of treason and imprisoned in the Tower in late 1688 both for his religion and for having his armed troops ride through the streets.[18] Frances visited him and other Jacobite prisoners there and later joined him. Samuel Percivall, the Earl's steward, wrote of Salisbury in February 1689/1690, "his spouse and he now very lovingly cohabit. An unhappy self-willed man, has put fair to undo himself, his relations, friends, all that had to do with him or for him."[19] Percivall's analysis was prescient. Although Salisbury was released in October 1690, in 1691 he encouraged his younger brothers, William and Charles, to leave Eton and study abroad. While in Rome they quarreled in the middle of the night and in the dark, Charles killed William.[20]

---

[16] Hatfield House Archives, General 22/35, Ebenezer Sadler to William Dobyns, July 29, 1686.

[17] Hatfield House Archives, General 92/38, Ralph Lee to Madam Grace Bennet at Calverton, Dec. 20, 1687, p. 77. "The other fat gentleman [John Bennet?] is possessed of the gout of late, and confined to the square of Bloomsbury, which hinders his journey into France, that he might make his complaint to the great person. I find that Old Nick has spun a fine thread for him, making rods for his own back. He pretends he will not go to law, for that he will regain his beloved by kindness and patience." Sarah was probably Sarah Lee, Frances's cousin and companion.

[18] *ODNB*, "James, 4th Earl of Salisbury." History of Parliament, draft biography of James Cecil, 4th Earl of Salisbury.

[19] Hatfield House Archives, General 131/121. Although as a Jacobite, Salisbury was always under a cloud, John Dryden, himself a Tory, dedicated a late work, *Love Triumphant* (1694), to Salisbury, thanking him for his previous patronage and claiming kinship.

[20] History of Parliament, draft biography of James, 4th Earl of Salisbury.

By Michelmas 1690, Frances had become pregnant.[21] In 1691 she gave birth to a boy whom they named James. This was not merely social news as it also meant that the Earl's Protestant brother, Robert Cecil, would not be able to claim the estate. Frances was quickly pregnant again with another child in August 1692. In preparation, a velvet bed costing £100 was ordered along with feathers costing £5-8-6, presumably for the urns at the top of the bed. One Mrs. Dod attended the countess. But the baby, a girl, was stillborn. In the midst of this sad loss, Ebenezer Sadler, Hatfield's Receiver General, tried to charge Frances with the cost of the midwife.

1692 August 20 Then delivered to Mrs. Dodd 20 guineas for attending the Countess of Salisbury when she lay in for a daughter still born, which sum I placed to the said Countess her account of pin money, but she refused to allow the same nor indeed did it belong to her to pay it, therefore it remains to be charged to the Earl's account.[22]

As we have seen, pin money, granted by a father or husband, was allocated to a woman to use as she wished. This financial dispute shows that the Countess of Salisbury paid close attention to her accounts. She refused to be charged for her dead child. Sadler probably reconsidered because by December 1694, the 4th Earl was dead of a fever and Frances, now dowager countess, was guardian of the 5th Earl who was only three years old. In short, she was now Sadler's only employer.

Frances inherited nothing outright under Salisbury's will, unlike his sisters, except the guardianship of her son. In the 1692 version of his will, Salisbury left Frances all the jewels that he had given her and those she had in her custody. This was not at all unusual. Both of Lady Finch's husbands and Lady Gresley's husband left them their jewelry in their wills. What was unusual was Salisbury's codicil executed two years later. Frances now received the jewelry only for her lifetime and in the meantime had to make a covenant with the executor to deliver the jewelry upon her death.[23] Salisbury's motive appears to have been to keep the jewelry in the Cecil family in the same way that he decided in the same codicil to keep the household furnishings.

Misfortune reached its pinnacle in autumn 1694 when the premature death of Salisbury in October followed the murder of Frances's mother a month earlier. In mourning for both, Frances commissioned Sir Godfrey Kneller to paint her as a widow, a sentimental image that became a popular

---

[21] Hatfield House Archives, Estate and Private Mss., p. 204, Percivall wrote to Stillingfleet that the Countess was "certainly with child now," Michaelmas, 1690.

[22] Hatfield House Archives, SFP 3/2; 3/299, Dec. 18, 1694, Ebenezer Sadler, "Death of abortive child and churching of my Lady."

[23] TNA, PROB11/423/102, Will of James, 4th Earl of Salisbury.

engraving (see Plate 12). Samuel Pepys himself owned a copy in his extensive print collection.[24] But Frances did not sink into melancholy for long.

After Salisbury died, Frances sued her young son for her income as dowager countess because her husband had been too young to make a contract for her jointure when they married in 1683 and did not do so thereafter. As a young bride, she had brought the Earl a portion of £10,000 in cash and another £10,000 that was the source of years of litigation; £1,800 annual income in real estate and £1,100 in reversion. Frances claimed that she expected a jointure of £4,000. But when the Earl died, his estate was so encumbered with debts that Frances said she was satisfied to accept dower, which was a third of the income of her late husband's property. Frances brought suit in the Court of Common Pleas to claim her dower, the court appointed Robert Cecil, her brother-in-law, to act as the young Earl of Salisbury's guardian in the case and awarded her £2,614 as her dower.[25] The Salisbury estate paid her thirds from rents on its holdings in the country, the City of London, and on the Strand, including the New Exchange, Sir Robert Cecil's' innovative shopping mall. Her son confirmed her dower by indenture when he reached the age of twenty-one in 1712.[26] In addition to her dower, she inherited half of her father's trust upon her mother's death. Because she was a widow, she controlled both herself.

Now Dowager Countess of Salisbury in her twenties, Frances had to decide what to do next. To begin with she took up her duties at Hatfield. She undertook Hatfield's clerical patronage and sought to secure the Bennet estate. Only one of her letters survives. Addressed to her brother-in-law, Robert Cecil, she refused his request for the patronage of a Hatfield living, telling him that the post had already been filled.[27] Her tone was firm and

---

[24] Earlier, the earl had commissioned a double portrait of the couple now at Hatfield, "Paid to Willem Wissing for 2 original pictures of the Earl and Countess and for 2 copies of the Earl's £60. Paid for 2 frames for the Earl and Countess's pictures £7-10." Hatfield House Archives, Accounts 108/405, 1687. She also commissioned a portrait of her little boy, the 5th Earl of Salisbury, in classical dress, National Portrait Gallery.

[25] TNA, C5/266/4, Earl of Salisbury *v.* Countess of Salisbury, 1698.

[26] Hatfield House Archives, FP10/124, 1694, Case of the Countess of Salisbury's dower; Deeds, 94/10, Nov. 21, 1712. Schedule containing names and rents of all messuages, fairs, farms, lands, shops, tenements and hereditaments which are set out in dower to the right honorable Frances Countess of Salisbury for her dower or thirds of her late husband Earl of Salisbury or son current Earl. These included rents at Hatfield and in London, on Cecil Street, St Martins Lane, Cranborne Street, Salisbury Street and Britain's Burse. Salisbury's will named Mary Cecil, not Robert, as alternative guardian. Other documents (i.e. S. Percivall to G. Stillingfleet) mention £3,000 per annum as jointure. Cranborne Papers Supp. 6/13, Jan. 5, 1685.

[27] BL, Add. Mss. 33572, f. 376, Frances Cecil to Robert Cecil. My thanks to Robin Harcourt Williams for this reference. Because the letter is undated, it is possible that it was written while the 4th Earl was in the Tower.

confident, and while polite not diffident, indicating that she was exercising the independence and authority that her widowhood provided.

I should be extremely glad of an occasion to oblige my brother Cecil in anything he should desire of me; but as for this . . . I am sorry to tell you, that tis already deposed of to Mr. Percivall that had it before or else should not in the least doubt of any person you should recommend to it and since tis not now in my power to do this I shall impatiently wait for some other opportunity to show myself Your affectionate sister and humble servant. Fr. Salisbury.

Since Robert Cecil had brought suit against her husband, one wonders just how impatiently Frances was waiting for some other opportunity to hand over Cecil patronage to him. In the 1690s, she brought suits to gather debts owed to her father's estate, continued the lawsuits her husband initiated against her father's man of business, Roger Chapman, to require an accounting from him, as well as suits against her brother in-law, John Bennet, over her father's will.[28]

London

Restoration London attracted the Stuart nobility and gentry for longer and longer periods of the year, not only during term time and parliamentary sessions, but also for an elaborate social season. New building increased in the aftermath of the Great Fire with speculators like Nicholas Barbon putting up townhouses for the well-to-do. Arlington Street, along with Albemarle and Bond Streets, had recently been built on Piccadilly on the site of Clarendon House that had been torn down. Frances decided to live part of the year in London like other members of the Stuart elite. She rented a London house of her own rather than staying in any of the existing Cecil properties. Frances's accounts show that in 1695 she viewed and then rented Dover House off Piccadilly Street from Henry Jermyn, Lord Dover. (A Caroline courtier and Jacobite, Lord Dover had joined James II in exile and later returned to England.) Soon Frances was buying pictures and goods for the house worth £467-4-7 including a new clock, looking glasses, and glass lanterns for the door as well as two blunderbusses and gunpowder. She also bought flowers, crocuses, double roses, and hyacinths, for the garden and a harpsical (or harpsichord) spinet.[29] As we shall see, Frances's interest in

[28] See TNA, C5/218/46, Countess of Salisbury *v.* Chapman, 1695, regarding personal estate of Simon Bennet; C5/186/183, Earl of Salisbury *v.* Chapman, 1693; Earl of Salisbury and Frances Countess of Salisbury *v.* John Bennet and Grace Bennet, C5/71/86, 1690, and HLRO, 1691.

[29] Hatfield House Archives, FP10/230a; SFP 3/29–30, SFP 3/40. In TNA, C5/266/4, Earl of Salisbury *v.* Countess of Salisbury, 1698, Frances claimed that that she lived in the great house at

gardens and music was constant on her European travels. Trinity Chapel, a small Anglican chapel at the top of the new streets, was built for well-to-do City worshippers, including John Evelyn.[30] In 1696 Frances paid its rent of £2-2.

Overall, Hugh Hawker her steward reported a total expenditure of £2,529-1-6, in the year 1695/1696. The countess's household staff numbered twenty-one including two cooks, all of whose wages amounted to £215-7-6.[31] She had a new coach covered with leather with 10,000 brass nails. That year she and her family spent thirty-two weeks in London, according to Hawkers' account, and Dover House remained Frances's London residence for the rest of her life. Her expenditures were primarily on luxury goods for her household, supporting her status as a dowager countess, and travel to see family and friends.

Frances's accounts document the round of family visits in the country and in London and attendance at public events that characterized aristocratic women's lives in town.[32] Thus in the 1690s, Frances visited her close relations who were near to her own age. She stayed with her sister Grace at Abington, Cambridge, for five days and Grace stayed with her at Hatfield. Frances also spent time with her sister-in law Margaret Cecil, widow of the 2nd Lord Stawell who died in 1692. Margaret, twenty-three, was two years younger than Frances, and she married Viscount Raneleigh as her second husband in 1696. Frances also visited her cousin Sarah Lee in London. Lady Mary Howard, wife of Sir James Fenton, the Jacobite plotter, and Lady Cholmondeley, wife of Thomas Cholmondeley, executor of Lord Salisbury's will, also visited her at Hatfield.[33] At various times she saw Thomas Cholmondeley, Sir William Forester, her brother-in-law, who was married to Mary Cecil, and Sir Thomas Gresley, her uncle. Frances dined with Sir John Moore at Mincing Lane in London, the former Lord Mayor who had been her grandfather's apprentice and close friend of her aunt, Lady Gresley. She watched the launching of a ship and attended one of the trials of Lord Mohun, the well-known duelist who was on trial before the House of Lords

Hatfield most of the time, spending only a few days in London. She insisted that she had a tutor and servants for her son, the 5th Earl and claimed the £600 for being guardian of her son as specified in her husband's will.

[30] *The Diary of John Evelyn*, ed. E. S. de Beer, 6 vols. (Oxford: Clarendon Press, 1955), Vol. V, p. 445, n. 1.

[31] Hatfield House Archives, Accounts 73/5, 1696, Household Account of the Dowager Countess of Salisbury.

[32] Susan Whyman, *Sociability and Power in Late-Stuart England: The Cultural Worlds of the Verneys, 1660–1720* (Oxford and New York: Oxford University Press, 1999).

[33] Hatfield House Archives, Bills 369; SFP 3/26, 1695. Others whom she visited were Sir Edward Mansell and Lord Rutland, SFP 3/48.

for murder in 1693 and again in 1699. Yet this record of London entertainment fails to include the suitors, often unwanted, who pursued Frances. Frances's grandmother, Lady Finch, had left London to escape her admirers in the 1620s; Frances left for the continent in 1699.

Grand Tour

Frances's decision to leave for France took place against the backdrop of continental war. The progress of war and peace between England and France and their allies helped shape the travels of the late seventeenth-century elite, including those of the Countess of Salisbury. William of Orange's purpose in bringing a Dutch Army to England in 1688 had been to gain English support for his war with France. Once on the throne with Mary, William had benefitted from English resources. In 1697 William III and Louis XIV signed The Treaty of Ryswick, bringing the Nine Years' War to an end, and most of the English army was demobilized by 1699.[34] Nevertheless, the question of the Spanish succession loomed over European diplomacy. Charles II of Spain was childless, and Louis XIV wished to place his grandson on the Spanish throne when Charles died, creating Bourbon hegemony stretching from Spain and France to the Spanish Netherlands and parts of Italy.

In this interval of peace between the end of the Nine Years' War in 1699 and the outbreak of the War of the Spanish Succession, the Dowager Countess of Salisbury, now twenty-nine, left Dover House and went abroad. Some contemporaries attributed such travel to Roman Catholicism and Jacobitism. Thus one diplomat wrote, "It's said the Countess of Salisbury and Earl of Exeter with a numerous trayne are arrived in Milan but I believe it is the countess only. Some say devotion, others that disgusts to our present government is the occasion of their traveling."[35] Indeed, Frances had close connections to four peers who were nonjurors, that is, those who refused to swear allegiance to William III as king: the Earl of Salisbury, Frances's deceased husband, the Earls of Exeter and Winchelsea, her cousins by marriage, and the Earl of Thanet, whose daughter was to marry her son.[36]

As we have seen, one newsletter writer attributed her travels to a clandestine marriage to the Jacobite Lord Ailesbury. Thomas Bruce, Earl of

---

[34] Shirley Kenny, *The Works of George Farquhar*, 2 vols. (Oxford: Clarendon Press, 1988), p. 135.
[35] BL, Add. Mss. 28904, f. 191v, George Broughton to John Ellis, Nov. 13, 1699.
[36] Paul Monod, *Jacobitism and the English People, 1688–1788* (Cambridge: Cambridge University Press, 1993), p. 142. Monod suggests that the "least explored area of Jacobite political culture is that which encompasses the behaviour of the landed elite," p. 269.

Ailesbury, served in both Charles II's and James II's Bedchambers. He continued to support the exiled king and participated in Jacobite plots to gain the support of Louis XIV against William III. Allowed to leave England in 1698, he was now living in Brussels. Ailesbury was just a few years older than Frances and a recent widower. Contemporaries thought it possible that she had left London to join him. Ailesbury, however, had another romantic interest, a Flemish noblewoman whom he married in 1700. There is no evidence that Frances met Ailesbury at the beginning of her trip.

Why the countess left England abruptly in April 1699 remains unclear. Three motives, religion, politics, and romance, may have helped shape the countess's journey to the continent. But, equally, a fourth motive must be stressed, the independence and opportunity that her widow's wealth afforded her. Frances began with only a retinue of five, which probably included her cousin Sarah Lee, her lady's maid and three other people, members of her household. The earliest extant bill for her journey shows that she stayed at an inn in Paris before she rented a house.[37] By May 7, 1699, four weeks later, she had settled down in Paris. She was now accompanied by at least nine people, including her chaplain Benjamin Conway, Sarah Lee, and her husband's younger brother, Charles Cecil. The countess was now accompanied by a retinue more appropriate to her status, one that could protect her and ward off the unwanted or unsuitable. Her retinue grew larger as the journey continued.

Sarah Lee provides one of only two comments from the travelers themselves; the many letters that they sent have not been found. In her letter to the countess's Receiver General, Ebenezer Sadler, Sarah emphasized the countess's freedom of action.

I give you thanks for your letter and should be very glad you would sometimes repeat the favor, for it was very diverting to us: and the discourses of people no ways surprising, but expected it in such a case where many was disappointed and others angry for not being consulted. But I hope it will end well and to my Lady['s] satisfaction and then tis no matter and as yet she is very well and hope will continue so for the weather is pretty moderate and the place very diverting, and Versalis much finer then we could imagine the water works are so extream fine. Mr. [Charles] Cecil is now with us, and now we begin to be a little settled . . . she would have you send her the newsletters once a week. I am very glad to hear my pretty Lord continues so well and that Mrs Sadler will be so kind to be near him, which I believe, will be a great means to keep him so.

---

[37] Hatfield House Accounts, Bills 387. "Disbursements after my Lady came to Paris before she went to housekeeping, Account of James Lowen." In these early days she gave money to Capuchins.

Figure 7.1 "Versailles Waterworks," [*Grandes pieces de la Potre*], by Jean Le Pautre, engraving, Art Flat a 17. The Folger Shakespeare Library. One of several Versailles waterworks which Frances, Countess of Salisbury, and her entourage saw on their European trip.

The Countess's surprise departure had disappointed suitors and angered family. In particular, the countess was running away from one potential husband, Thomas Neale, who had "found out a way to write to my Lady and

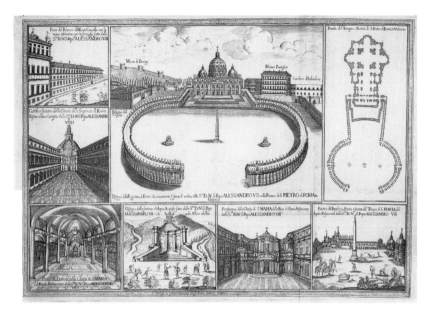

Figure 7.2 "Perspectives of 8 Buildings and Monuments commissioned by
Alexander VII during his Pontificate," engraving by Giovanni Batista de Rossi, Rome,
c. 1665. The Folger Shakespeare Library, Art BOX R763 no. 1. Sites that
Frances, Countess of Salisbury saw during the year she spent in Rome.

tells her he is coming into France and with such circumstances that I am
afraid he is in earnest."[38]

While the grandeur of Versailles was a great attraction, the centerpiece of
Frances's trip was Rome. Rome had drawn pilgrims throughout the Middle
Ages. Beginning in the fifteenth century, the collection of antiquities on
display in private collections had burgeoned and, in the sixteenth century,
Roman clergy and princes displayed these collections in the gardens and
courtyards of new villas and palaces.[39] Sixteenth- and seventeenth-century
Rome saw not only the building of Counter-Reformation churches and new
palaces and villas but also the rebuilding and extension of the city itself with
a new cityscape. Created especially through the vision of its greatest artist and
architect Giovanni Bernini, this was the Rome whose theatrical spectacle
many on the Grand Tour came to witness. Baroque Rome celebrated the

---

[38] Hatfield House Archives, General 127/12, June 7, 1699, Fr stile [May 28, 1699], Mrs. Sarah Lee
to Mr. Sadler. She added "My Lady would have you Mr. Sadler go to Mr. Griffin the dancing
master and persuade him to go to Hatfield to my Lord as soon as he can and stay as long at a time
with him as he can."

[39] William Stenhouse, "Visitors, Display, and Reception in the Antiquity Collections of Late-
Renaissance Rome," *Renaissance Quarterly*, 58 (2005), 435–465.

power and authority of the Roman Catholic Church and its elites against the backdrop of the ancient ruins of the Roman Empire and the new city architecture built in the sixteenth and seventeenth centuries.

Pope Innocent III declared a Jubilee year in June 1699 for 1700.[40] The ritual of the church and the grandeur of the Baroque city became especially visible in Jubilee years, which attracted not only pilgrims from all over Europe but also travelers on the Grand Tour. Jubilee brought "the happy effects" of forgiveness. The Pope's declaration stated that those who hoped to "reap the fruits of plenary indulgence, must qualify themselves for it by many acts of charity, a true penitence, and other good works." These included pilgrimage: "confession, communion and visits to the four basilicas in Rome, St. Peter, St. Paul, St. John de Lateran, and St. Maria Majori" for fifteen days.[41] While many English travelers who attended the elaborate ceremonial of the opening of the holy door of St. Peter's on Christmas Eve did so out of curiosity or critique, others attended out of respect and belief. The Roman Catholic Church and Roman nobility drew the foreign elite who participated in the Jubilee's ritual into the networks through which the city's elite social life operated.

In England, however, contemporaries commented negatively on such pilgrimages. George Farquhar's popular comedy, *The Constant Couple or a Trip to the Jubilee*, was performed in November 1699.[42] Its characters, the wealthy and beautiful Lady Lurewell who had many suitors, Sir Henry Wildair, a well-known rake, and Colonel Standard, a demobilized soldier much in love with Lady Lurewell, provided models that could in some ways be applied to the Countess of Salisbury and her entourage. Another work, *A Pilgrimage to the Grand Jubilee in Rome, in the Year 1700*, went through four editions by 1718. Despite his satire on ritual, the author observed, "It cannot be denied but there is something in these representations that does extremely take the eye."[43]

Many of the English who traveled to Rome for the Jubilee were not Roman Catholic. Among those visitors was John Cecil, 5th Earl of Exeter, the

[40] *A True and Exact Account of all the ceremonies observed by the Church of Rome, at the opening, during the progress, and at the conclusion of the next approaching Jubilee* (London: Printed by D. Edwards in Fetter-Lane, 1699).

[41] *A True and Exact Account; Catholic Encyclopedia*, "Jubilee."

[42] For print culture on the Jubilee, see Richard Morton and William Peterson, "The Jubilee of 1700 and Farquhar's *The Constant Couple*," *Notes and Queries*, 200 (1955), 521–525; Kenny, *The Works of George Farquhar*. Jubilee was announced in June 1699, although it was well known before, p. 135.

[43] A. F., *The travels of an English gentleman from London to Rome: on foot. Containing a comical description of what he met with remarkable in every city, town, and religious house in his whole journey*, 4th edn. (London: Printed for A. Bettesworth, 1718), p. 120.

Countess of Salisbury's cousin by marriage, a frequent traveler to Europe. Leaving London on September 25, 1699, with a company of twenty-four, five months after Frances, Exeter arrived in Rome on December 23, where he took a house in Piazza di St. Marco.[44] Richard Creed who traveled with the Earl's large entourage documented his journey.[45] The Countess of Salisbury remained in Paris until October when she joined Exeter on the way to Rome.

The Countess followed one of the popular routes to Italy, which was laid out in Richard Lassels's 1670 guidebook *Voyage of Italy*, crossing the Alps at Mount Cenis.[46] As thousands of pilgrims clogged the road from Paris to Lyons, it was not perhaps surprising that the countess bought carbines and pistols for the week-long trip. The Countess's smaller entourage outpaced Exeter's.[47] Purchasing new coaches and litters for the difficult traversing of the Alps, she and Sarah Lee were carried in chairs, along with two maids, over Mount Cenis, the crossing point to Susa, Italy.[48] Nine mules carried her servants. Traveling to Turin, the countess added two horse-litters hung on poles carried between two horses,[49] another coach with five saddled horses and an additional pair of pistols and holsters.

Most of the countess's routes and destinations in Europe were not unusual. Whether by coach, boat, or chair, she followed in the path of English tourists who had visited the continent before her. More unusual was the length of her journey of over four years, including the year she spent in Rome, her stay in Venice, her summer in the south of France, almost a year all told in Paris and visit to the Low Countries. The Countess spent handsomely, much more than a young gentleman with his tutor.[50] In one year between October 1699 and November 1700, as she and her entourage traveled through France and Italy, she spent £3,326, more than the annual income from her dower. Frances must have drawn as well on Hatfield funds or on her inheritance. The whole trip cost over £11,161.[51] Travelers paid for

---

[44] Richard Creed, *Richard Creed's Journal of the Grand Tour, 1699–1700 to Rome with the 5th Earl of Exeter*, ed. Alice Thomas (Oundle, Peterborough: Oundle Museum, 2002).

[45] *Creed's Journal of the Grand Tour, 1699–1700*, p. 23.

[46] Richard Lassels, *The Voyage of Italy, or a Compleat Journey through Italy: In two parts. With the characters of the people, and the description of the chief towns, churches, monasteries, tombs, libraries, pallaces, villas, gardens, pictures, statues, and antiquities. As also of the interest, government, riches, force, &c. of all the Princes. With instructions concerning travel* (Newly printed at Paris, and are to be sold in London, by John Starkey, 1670), pp. 70–71.

[47] *Creed's Journal of the Grand Tour, 1699–1700* for Exeter's itinerary.

[48] Hatfield House Archives, Accounts 173, Expenses while the Countess of Salisbury was in Europe.

[49] *OED*, "horse litters."

[50] J. Walter Stoye, *English Travellers Abroad, 1604–1667* (London: Jonathan Cape, 1952), p. 54, estimates that Lord Roos and Lord Clifford and their tutors spent £1,000 in a year on the Grand Tour in the first decade of the seventeenth century.

[51] Hatfield House Archives, Accounts 173; 76/2.

their journeys in advance with letters of credit or with bills of exchange drawn on local merchants. The Countess of Salisbury received funds from home everywhere she traveled in Europe.[52] She also had scales on which to weigh gold and may have brought some with her.

The countess's account books document the difficulty of travel and the prevalence of disease as well as the pleasures, politics, and cost of travel. The Countess contracted smallpox in Rome and her chaplain Benjamin Conway died there. Her brother-in-law, Charles Cecil, fell seriously ill and later died. Her cousin, John Cecil, 5th Earl of Exeter, died in 1700 returning from Rome, while Charles Ellis, an acquaintance, died in Venice. She and her companions summoned doctors and were bled in several different countries.

Nevertheless, the countess was an indefatigable traveler. Everywhere she went throughout her four-year journey, she visited antiquities, Renaissance palazzi, and art collections, walked in famous gardens, listened to music, attended the opera, hired harpsicals, read French and learned Italian, bought books, and entertained continental aristocrats and Roman Catholic clerics. She does not seem to have bought important works of art. Rather, she made the most of her opportunity to enjoy the culture of France and Italy and later the Low Countries. In short, she used her resources to create a cultivated European life and identity for herself and her retinue.

How did the Countess of Salisbury and other seventeenth-century travelers know what to learn and to see? English travelers of the sixteenth and seventeenth centuries had an extensive didactic literature to aid them. Francis Bacon had urged gentlemen to keep travel diaries and encouraged attention to country, customs, politics, and people. In addition, Bacon and others focused on the importance of learning other languages as the mark of the cultivated traveler, both for royal service and personal enrichment.[53] James Howell, writing in 1642 as many royalists went into exile, focused not only on language and politics, but also on the "preeminence of the eye."[54] Through their gaze, travelers saw, evaluated, and appropriated the foreign, whether art, manners, or material culture.

Even as they embraced travel and the revelation of the new, these didactic works expressed fear of the seduction of the foreign and succumbing to the luxurious desires they created. Thomas Coryat said that Mantua "did . . . ravish his senses" but added that the inhabitants were idolaters.[55] By the late

---

[52] Hatfield House Archives, Accounts 173.

[53] Francis Bacon, *The Essayes or Counsels, Civill and Morall*, ed. Michael Kiernan (Oxford: Clarendon Press, 2000), pp. 56–58, 208–212.

[54] James Howell, *Instruction for Forreine Travel* (London, 1642). A second edition was published in 1650.

[55] Thomas Coryat, *Coryat's Crudities* (London, 1611), pp. 117–123.

seventeenth century, however, such criticism had been jettisoned. The most popular guidebook to Italy was by Richard Lassels, a Roman Catholic priest who served as tutor to English aristocrats. His *Voyage of Italy*, first published in 1670, was republished in 1698 just before the countess began her travels.[56]

In Turin, for instance, the Countess of Salisbury visited the Duke of Savoy's handsome palace that Lassels described in enthusiastic detail. He drew particular attention to

the curious invention for the Duchess to convey herself up from the bedchamber to that bathing room by a Pulley and a Swing, with great ease and safety, the great Hall painted curiously, the Noble staircase, the old Long Gallery 100 paces long with the pictures in it of the princes and princesses of the House of Savoy with the statues of the ancient emperors and philosophers in marble, with a rare library locked up in great cupboards.

Not content to see the Duke's palace, the countess and the Earl of Exeter went into the country to see La Venerie Royale, which was described by Lassels as filled with paintings of the Duke and his family on horseback as if they were going hunting.[57] In Savoy, the countess attended the Duke of Savoy's music, stayed in the house of a count for three days, and bought maps of Italy.[58]

Antiquities, churches, the visual arts, music, and gardens took pride of place in Frances's itinerary as she traveled through Italy. In Milan and Bologna, the countess paid "my lady's antiquary," presumably her guide. In Florence, she visited the Uffizi Gallery, San Lorenzo, Villa del Poggio Imperiale, the ruling family's country retreat, and paid for "seeing several things in churches."[59] Having arrived in Rome about November 29, 1699, before the Earl of Exeter, the countess immediately set off for Naples! While this might appear surprising, it was actually recommended by Lassels for the nobleman on the Giro d'Italia.

Being thus come to Rome about the middle of November . . . while yet the weather is good, and while some friend furnish you a house and whiles your Tayler is making you clothes suitable to that Court, your Lordship may go to Naples, a journey which will cost you only fifteen days that is, five in going, five in coming, and five in staying there.[60]

---

[56] Lassels's *The Voyage of Italy* continued to be republished into the eighteenth century. On Lassels see Chaney, *The Grand Tour and the Great Rebellion*. For other guidebooks, see Tony Claydon, *Europe and the Making of England* (Cambridge: Cambridge University Press, 2007); Sweet, "British Perceptions of Italian Cities."

[57] Lassels, *Voyage of Italy*, pp. 76–78.   [58] Hatfield House Archives, Accounts 173, f. 154.

[59] Hatfield House Archives, Accounts 173, ff. 153–154.

[60] Lassels, "Description of Italy," in Chaney, *The Grand Tour and the Great Rebellion*, p. 172.

Once in Naples, the Countess of Salisbury saw the Church of the Annunciation, Santa Maria del Carmine, and visited the catacombs.[61] The accounts show that she paid special attention to ancient sites. Even before Herculaneum and Pompeii were uncovered in the 1730s, the Grand Tourist visited Roman ruins above ground in and around the Bay of Naples, which Lassels described in detail. Thus, sixteen boatmen rowed the countess to Pozzuoli, the old Roman port outside of Naples, and to the surrounding areas on the bay. Once there, the countess paid an antiquary to show her the sights. These included Virgil's tomb, which, according to Lassels, was covered with bay trees, and the Dog's Grotto at Pozzuoli. There dogs placed in the grotto were shown to die from its sulphurous vapors and then miraculously spring back to life once released. Finally, eight chair men carried the countess and Mrs. Lee to see Mount Vesuvius.[62]

Rome

The Countess of Salisbury's accounts underline her eagerness to participate in cultural life wherever she traveled even if they do not by themselves capture all of her life abroad. When she returned to Rome in early December 1699, the countess began to establish herself in Roman society. Her travels drew critical comment from her countrymen on her spending, her religious and political leanings, and even her sexuality. What a shock it must have been, then, when on the verge of the opening of the holy door at St. Peters, the symbol of the beginning of the Jubilee year, Frances came down with smallpox. Richard Creed noted in his travel diary: "this day my Lady Salisbury fell ill of the smallpox, so she could not come to see the holy door opened, nor any of the ceremonies."[63] The accounts record her being bled and her consultations with Italian doctors. Her journey seemed in jeopardy. Still she did not return home.

The countess had intended to go to Venice for Carnival in the spring of 1700. Instead she settled in Rome for the whole year during her lengthy recovery. At first she took up residence on the Strada Paolina, a street that had been home to leading artists in the sixteenth and seventeenth centuries.[64] She then moved to the house that the Earl of Exeter had taken in the Piazza di San Marco that accommodated twenty-four people. Following Lassel's advice, Exeter had put off his entrance into Roman society until

---

[61] Lassels, "Description of Italy," p. 176. [62] Lassels, "Description of Italy," pp. 176–178.
[63] *Creed's Journal of the Grand Tour, 1699–1700*, p. 27.
[64] John Ingamells, *A Dictionary of British and Irish Travellers in Italy, 1701–1800* (New Haven, CT, and London: Yale University Press, 1997), p. 838.

new liveries were made, in grey, trimmed with silver buttons, for his entourage.[65] After the earl departed from Rome in June 1700, the countess took over the palazzo for the rest of the year.[66] Putting her own stamp on it, she paid "Signor Abraham the Jew" for green silk furniture to fit out the room of state for the summer.

The countess's accounts chart her year in Rome after she recovered, her meetings with Roman nobility, cardinals, and members of the English College. At the same time, they document her many visits to churches, palazzi, and gardens where she actively participated in the musical and cultural life of Rome throughout Jubilee year. As the countess immersed herself in Roman society, she established connections with Marie-Anne de Tremoille, Princess Bracciano, also known as Princesse des Ursins, one of Louis XIV's most important agents in Rome. In close contact with Madame de Maintenon, the princess held a famous salon in Rome that Frances attended. The Prince of Bracciano's man brought gifts to Frances that ranged from a couch to citrons and partridges.[67]

Rome was a center of European music and opera whose chief patron in the 1690s was Cardinal Pietro Ottoboni, nephew of the previous pope. Cardinal Ottoboni had become patron to Angel Corelli and Alessandro Scarlatti and Roman opera generally in the 1690s and composed libretti for operas himself. Corelli continued to be part of his household at the Palazzo della Cancellaria in 1700.[68] Richard Creed described one of Ottoboni's concerts in his travel diary. "Cardinal Ottabone invited the Queen of Poland and her three sons, and all the Cardinals to a fine music. There were 26 Cardinals there, and a great many strangers, and a sermon in the middle of the music. Cardinal Ottabone is a rich and great Cardinal and keeps in his house Corelli the famousest man in the world for the violin."[69] Corelli was famous not only as a violinist but as a composer and conductor of his own and others' compositions.

Music particularly interested the Countess of Salisbury. She attended concerts in churches throughout her year in Rome among them the French

[65] *Private Correspondence and Miscellaneous Papers of Samuel Pepys 1679–1703*, ed. J. R. Tanner, 3 vols. (London: George Bell and Sons Limited, 1926), Vol. I, p. 265, Jackson to Pepys.

[66] *Creed's Journal of the Grand Tour, 1699–1700*, p. 23.

[67] Millicent Erskine Wemyss, *A Notable Woman and Other Sketches* (London: Eden, Remington & Co., 1893); M. A. Geoffroy, ed., *Lettres Inedites de la Princesse des Ursins* (Paris: Didier et Cie, 1859). The Princesse des Ursins exercised even more influence on behalf of Louis XIV when she went to Madrid as head of household to the new Queen of Spain during the War of the Spanish Succession.

[68] Edward T. Olszewski, "The Enlightened Patronage of Cardinal Pietro Ottoboni (1667–1740)," *Artibus et Historiae*, 23, 45 (2002), 139–165.

[69] *Creed's Journal of the Grand Tour, 1699–1700*, p. 34.

Church (San Luigi dei Francesi) that Corelli visited every year, S. Silvestro, the Monastery of Santa Chiara, Santissima Trinità dei Pellegrini twice, the Spanish Church (Santa Maria in Monserrato), and Cardinal Ottoboni's church. Creed described that church as light and very large when he attended an elaborate ceremony there with the Earl of Exeter. The countess also went to the opera. On February 6, 1700, she bought a box at the opera and six tickets along with places for two maids and footmen in the pit. At home, she rented a spinet, paid for its stringing, lining, and tuning, and hired castrati to sing, including one named Bellisome.[70] She might have seen Giovanni Bononcini's *Il trionfo di Camilla*. Written in Naples in 1696, this comic opera was first produced in Rome in 1698 and then became popular throughout Italy and Europe, and later became a hit in London.[71]

The architecture of ancient and Baroque Rome also attracted Frances. She went to see the armory and library at the Vatican, the Jew's Synagogue, the three fountains, and Castel St. Angelo. Although she visited the catacombs, she was more attracted to the palaces and villas of the Roman nobility, which displayed important collections of ancient and Renaissance and Baroque painting and sculpture. For instance she visited the famous collections at the Palazzo Borghese. It was perhaps her favorite destination with works that included "a new statue in pure white of the rape of Persepine [Persephone]. It is of the hand of Bernini."[72] Creed described the Palazzo Borghese with unabashed admiration: "There are in the first apartment ten rooms that lie together, and at the end a vista and a fountain. The floor cases are all marble . . . There are in these rooms 1,000 good pictures, all originals. There is a picture of Pope Paulus V in mosaic work that has 116,000 stones in the face and yet it is no bigger than the life."[73]

Frances saw other famous palaces and villas including the Villa Pamphili and the Gallery and Palace Farnese. The Farnese held "many fine pictures and statues," according to Creed, "but one statue of Hercules the finest in the world."[74] The Farnese Hercules was a gigantic copy of a Hellenistic sculpture. Found in the Baths of Caracalla in Rome, it was popularized throughout Europe through engravings by artists like Jacob Bol and Hendrick Goltzius.[75] Frances's accounts also record payments to see Cardinal

[70] Hatfield House Archives, Accounts 173.
[71] Oxford Companion to Music, online database: www.oxfordmusiconline.com/page/The-Oxford-Companion-to-Music.
[72] Lassels, *Voyage to Italy*, sig. H3.   [73] *Creed's Journal of the Grand Tour, 1699–1700*, p. 35.
[74] *Creed's Journal of the Grand Tour, 1699–1700*, p. 34.
[75] "Farnese Hercules," Hendrick Goltzius, Jacob Bol, Metropolitan Museum of Art (www.metmuseum.org/search-results#!/search?q=FARNESE%20HERCULES).

Ottoboni's Palace, that is the Cancellaria, and what her account book called
Prince Justinian's Palace, the Palace of the Duke of Florence, the Duke
Strozzi's palace, the Palace of the Duke at St. Benedetta, and the Palace of
Cardinal Alterieri.

In addition, Frances paid to see the Queen of Poland's lodgings at the
Palace of Don Livio Odescalchi. Maria Casimira, daughter of a French
nobleman and wife of John III Sobieski, the Queen of Poland, cut a
remarkable figure in Baroque Rome. Richard Creed described her at length.
Her guard consisted "of 20 Turks, who always attend her with their Pole-
axes." With many rich coaches and a very large retinue, "she is a woman that
loves show and glory very much." Creed also criticized what he thought her
ostentatious display of religiosity. "She is a very zealous and religious,
bigoted, priest-rid woman, which makes this court respect her very much.
She goeth very often to church, and kneels very long before the Sacrament,
and when she goeth it is in very great pomp and state, but then she takes care
to bow to and salute everybody. And sometimes she will go to church almost
quite by herself a lit candle in her hand, to show her great humility." The
Queen of Poland's theatrical presentation of self became one of the sights to
see in Baroque Rome.[76]

Gardens, along with art, sculpture, and music captured the Countess of
Salisbury's attention. The grand gardens of Baroque Rome combined
antique sculpture, waterworks, and formal patterns with tree-shaded walks
and vistas of the city. They were often very extensive.[77] Visitors who dined in
and paraded through the gardens were as much on display as the flora. Some,
such as the Villa Ludovisi, were so large, that the visitor might get lost in
them. The Countess of Salisbury frequently visited and walked in Roman
gardens belonging to the pope, nobility, and cardinals, visiting at least
fifteen. In warmer weather, in June 1700, her accounts record payments
for visits to the garden of Cardinal Negroni, Duke Strozzi's garden where she
saw its waterworks, Villa Ludovisi, palace, garden and waterworks, "seeing
and walking in Pamphili's garden," "walking in the Duke of Parma's garden,
(Palazzo Farnese)," which had fountains, "seeing the Prince of Borghese's
palace and garden;" for walking in the Strozzi garden; and "my Lady's

---

[76] *Creed's Journal of the Grand Tour, 1699–1700*, p. 30. In addition to her religiosity, the Queen
of Poland was a member of the Arcadia, a learned academy founded by Queen Christina of
Sweden that held meetings at her court, and a patron of Scarlatti. Elisabetta Graziosi, "Revising
Arcadia: Women and Academies in Eighteenth-Century Italy," in *Italy's Eighteenth Century,
Gender and Culture in the Age of the Grand Tour*, ed. Paula Findlen, Wendy Wassyng Roworth,
and Catherine Sama (Stanford, CA: Stanford University Press, 2009), pp. 29–30.

[77] On Roman gardens, see David R. Goffin, *Gardens and Gardening in Papal Rome* (Princeton, NJ:
Princeton University Press, 1991).

walking in Villa Madama." The sixteenth-century Villa Madama was known for its waterworks and grand view of the city. In July, Frances returned to the Duke of Parma's garden, in August, the Borghese garden, the garden of Matheya (Villa Mattei), and Cardinal Negroni's garden. She also saw the Duke Strozzi's Palace and paid "the Duchess of Sora's gardener." The Duchess of Sora, Olimpia Ippolita Ludovisi, later Princess of Piombino, was a close friend of the Princesse des Ursins with whom Frances had established a friendship.[78]

Even as the weather grew cooler, the countess continued to visit Roman gardens. In October she again walked in the Villa Madama, visited the Pope's garden at the Vatican, and saw the Pope's Palace at Monte Cavallo. In December she went to see the Belvedere, the papal palace that included the Sistine Chapel, and the Ludovico Ludovisi palace and waterworks and paid for seeing the Duke of Modena's palace. Unfortunately, the accounts don't identify those who accompanied her on her garden walks.

As the year progressed, Frances also continued to exchange gifts with the Princesse des Ursins, worked on her Italian with an Italian master, bought Italian books, and repeatedly paid customs for chocolate, and then, perhaps because they were afraid they were eating too much, paid for "a pair of scales from the Customs House to weigh my Lady, Mrs. Lee, and Mr. Cecil." She sent a pudding to Sir Robert Gayer, a Jacobite and non-juror whose first wife was her cousin, Sir Thomas Rich's daughter, and whose second wife was the sister of Thomas, Earl of Ailesbury. His kinsman was a member of Frances's entourage in Rome.

Unlike her husband, the Countess of Salisbury never became a Roman Catholic. Nevertheless, during her travels, she had connections with non-jurors at home and Roman Catholics in Rome. She maintained social relationships with English Catholic churchmen, often dining with Bishop Philip Ellis of the English College at Rome, James II's former chaplain and former secretary to Cardinal Philip Howard.[79] Benjamin Conway, Frances's chaplain, whom she had appointed to a Hatfield living in 1696, accompanied her to Rome. In August 1700, Conway wrote to Hilkiah Bedford, a non-juring cleric and later Bishop of the non-juring clergy in England. Conway described Cardinal Sacriponte's visit to the Countess of Salisbury and her decision to stay in Rome until Christmas before moving to Venice for Carnival. Conway sent regards from Captain Cecil and another member of

---

[78] *Archivio Digitale Boncompagni Ludovisi*: www.villaludovisi.org.
[79] Michael E. Williams, *The Venerable English College Rome: A History 1579–1979* (London: Associated Catholic Publications, 1979), pp. 44–45.

the household, Sir John Gayer, who was also in touch with Hilkiah Bedford, expressing the hope of seeing him before he left Rome.[80]

The Roman Catholic Church and its ritual continued to attract the countess, who visited relics at various churches and met with several cardinals, especially Cardinal Sacriponte.[81] The Cardinal helped her gain access to the ceremony surrounding the election of a new pope. Thus in October, she paid to see the body of the dead Pope Innocent XII, and the anointing of a new pontiff. In October 1700, she had a standing place "for my lady's seeing the Cardinals into the conclave."[82] In November she tipped "Cardinal Sacriponte's servant that brought my Lady the news of Cardinal Albani being made Pope under the name of Clement the Eleventh and paid for a bench to see the papal coronation."[83] Later, going to see the Porta Sancta shut up, she purchased gold medals with Porto Sancta, on one side and the Pope's visage on the other.[84] Before leaving Rome, the countess held grand dinners to treat Bishop Ellis, James Forbes, SJ, Father Rector of the Scotch College, and Father Baker of St Peter's.

The Countess of Salisbury's extraordinary travels in Italy did not end with her farewell to Rome. In January 1701 she moved to Venice for five months. To announce her presence, she paid for six liveries for four gondoliers and two footmen and, shortly after her arrival in January, entertained the English Consul and his Lady and the Duke of Grafton and his governor. Grafton was the eighteen-year-old son of Isabella Bennet, Countess of Arlington, daughter of Henry Bennet, Earl of Arlington, Frances's cousin. The Countess of Salisbury repeatedly went to the opera. While musical entertainment was held privately in Rome, opera was commercial in Venice.[85] The countess again hired boxes in January and February 1701 for herself and friends, and paid for tickets for her servants in the pit. At home she had the spinet strung and tuned.

Like today's tourists, Frances was drawn to San Marco, the Palazzo Ducale, the Great Council, Library, the Treasury, and the Armoury, all of them described in detail in Lassels's *Voyage of Italy*. As in Rome, she visited several palaces, including that of Signor Barbarigo, a well-known palazzo on the Grand Canal built in the sixteenth century. In addition to attending Easter ceremonies and seeing the Jesuits' church and San Rocco, she

---

[80] CCED, "Benjamin Conway." EMLO, Bodleian, Rawlinson Mss., Letter 42, F. 30, Conway to Bedford, Aug. 17, [1700].

[81] Hatfield House Archives, Accounts 173.   [82] Hatfield House Archives, Accounts 173.

[83] Hatfield House Archives, Accounts 173, f. 160.   [84] Hatfield House Archives, Accounts 173.

[85] On Venetian opera, see Beth L. Glixon, *Inventing The Business of Opera: The Impresario and His World in Seventeenth-Century Venice* (Oxford and New York: Oxford University Press, 2006)

entertained clerics and made presents to a religious order. But Lassels lists many more churches than Frances went to see. Frances did continue her Italian lessons with the Italian master and bought more Italian books. She had new clothes and new headdresses made, wore masks, and bought a "brace" of Flanders lace to "kick out my Lady's heads." Frances created relationships with members of the local elite; in April "ladies and noblemen ... stood in our house to see the entry of the Spanish Ambassador." As she did everywhere, she repeatedly bought chocolate and coffee. She also bought a pair of scales to weigh gold.

But the delights of her travel continued to be darkened by disease. As we saw, the countess had contracted smallpox in Rome, and Benjamin Conway, her chaplain, died. In Venice Charles Cecil fell ill. The cook was paid for extraordinary dishes for six nights for "my Lady Alberta and Signor Garolemus supping with my Lady in the time of Charles Cecil's sickness." The countess entertained them on several other occasions. An express was sent to George Cecil in Rome to bring him to Charles who was placed in an iron bedstead in a darkened room. Payments were now made "for 20 'brasses' holding Mr. Charles Cecil in bed when distracted." George joined the countess's entourage, which now ranged from ten to fourteen people.[86] He drew on funds from Hatfield as they continued to travel, but not toward home.[87]

War and Travel

By 1701, the Countess of Salisbury's travels were shaped not only by guidebooks but also by the rumblings and then the outbreak of battle in the War of the Spanish Succession. Charles II of Spain died late in 1700 and named Louis XIV's grandson his heir. Alliances now formed for and against France. Although England did not declare war until May 1702, the Holy Roman Emperor, who opposed France, began a campaign against Savoy, a territory with ties to France in May 1701. Now the countess traveled from Venice to Genoa to escape the Italian battles. While war might have signaled to some that it was time to return home, the Countess of Salisbury was not one of them. Instead, she continued on from Genoa to the south of France.

---

[86] Hatfield House Archives, FP10/164a; SFP 3/321. George Cecil had left for Europe before Frances, "to travel beyond the seas for his further accomplishments and education and, having occasion for more money than the interest on the £2600 will amount to, he hereby agrees that whatever he receives during the time of his travels, beyond the interest due, shall be accounted part of the principal sum."

[87] Hatfield House Archives, Accounts 75/12, George Cecil's accounts.

She settled down in Montpellier, a university town, perhaps to enjoy the excellent air, medical treatment, and nearby antiquities.[88]

Unlike most travelers who avoided France with the outbreak of hostilities in 1701,[89] the Countess of Salisbury moved to Paris where she lived for almost eight months, from February to the end of September 1702, although England declared war on France in May. In Paris, as in each city she stayed in for any length of time, Frances took a house, ordered a coach, and a musical instrument. In Paris it was a harpsical or harpsichord. She had French servants and footmen and three chaises. The accounts record payment for black liveries for four footmen and coachmen. While in Paris, she saw comedies, walked in the King's Gardens and in the Tuileries, and had dinner at Versailles on several occasions. Frances bought gloves and scarves, headdresses and patches and had bills from an apothecary and mantua maker or dressmaker as well as making more routine expenditures for wine and groceries. She also bought a "silver minute pendulum watch," a luxurious as well as technically advanced purchase because minute hands had only been added to watches since the 1670s.

The court of James II in exile was at St. Germaine des Pres near Versailles. During her long stay in Paris, did Frances also visit the Jacobite court and the large Jacobite community there? The evidence is unclear because her accounts for Paris are not as detailed as those for Rome where we have already seen that she met with Jacobite sympathizers. She dined in Versailles on February 9 and February 24. On February 20, 1702, the countess sent thirty-five pounds of beef to the "Blue Nunns" "where my lady dined this day. Sent also here 3 partridges, 3 capons, a lamb, 2 neat tongues, 6 lbs. of Palmasan cheese [sic], 12 casks of wine." The English order, the Blue Nuns, ran a convent school favored by the Jacobite community.[90] Jeremy Black points out, however, that Protestant travelers visited Catholic nunneries, "particularly convents of British nuns."[91]

The Countess continued her interest in the French court and her connections to French aristocrats. In March she went to see the review held by the

[88] Tobias Smollett, *Travels through France and Italy. Containing observations on character, customs, religion … arts, and antiquities …* (London: Printed for R. Baldwin, in Pater-noster-row, 1766), Letter IX, Montpellier, Nov. 5, 1763. "I longed to try what effect the boasted air of Montpellier would have upon my constitution; and I had a great desire to see the famous monuments of antiquity in and about the ancient city of Nismes [sic] which is about eight leagues short of Montpellier." See Black, *The British Abroad*, pp. 23, 26–27.

[89] Black, *The British Abroad*, p. 168.

[90] Nathalie Genet-Roussiac, "Jacobites in Paris and Saint Germain en Laye," in *The Stuart Court in Exile*, ed. Eveline Cruickshank and Edward Corp (London and Rio Grande: The Hambledon Press, 1995), pp. 15–38.

[91] Black, *The British Abroad*, p. 263.

King of France. In April "to the Swish" at Marshal D'Large[92] and on April 4
her steward "paid at St Cloud by my Lady's orders." St. Cloud, overlooking
the Seine west of Paris, was the grand palace of the Duke of Orleans, brother
of Louis XIV and Henrietta Stuart, daughter of Charles I, with wonderful
gardens and waterworks by Andre Le Notre.

From February to May, the countess's household continued to read
Dutch and French gazettes while Frances received gifts of strawberries and
peas from French aristocrats, Lady De Loge and Mr. Beauvoir. In June,
Frances visited the Petit Maison and sent a saddle of sirloin of beef to the
English Blue Nuns. In July she visited Versailles again. When she fell ill, her
servants went into the country to get a doctor. Water was brought from the
river for her bathing and asses' milk to make a posset.

Finally, four months after the English declared war on France, the
countess decided it was time to think of returning home. On September 2,
1702, Frances, George Cecil, Sarah Lee, and her steward, footmen, cham-
bermaid, and servants received a license to return to England from France by
way of the Southern Netherlands and the Dutch Republic.[93] Soon after, the
accounts note payment "to Mr. Daniel Arthur for carriage of letters." Sir
Daniel Arthur was no mere postman but an important Jacobite banker.
Although the Countess of Salisbury probably had contacts among the
English Jacobite exile community, none other than Arthur is specifically
named in her accounts.

Now the Countess of Salisbury purchased a new coach with springs for
660 livres or just over £43 pounds. In September she paid for a "root" of the
way from Paris to Brussels, and on September 29 the Countess of Salisbury
and her retinue left the capital. The Countess did not, however, return home
for another ten months. First, she visited Brussels for two months where she
received "a pair of harpsical," bought Spanish and French books, and purchased a great deal of lace. Two months later, on November 29, her steward
noted "560 lbs weight of goods to be transported from Brussels to Liege."[94]
Then, she moved to Ghent. From there she arranged two side trips, the first to
Bruges, the second to Antwerp, enabling her to see all three historic cities. Led
by a guide, each trip brought the company to an inn where they ate dinner,
stayed the night, and returned to Ghent the next day. They returned once
more to Brussels before setting off on the journey to Liege in part by boat.

[92] The *OED* states that the definition of swish as elegant and fashionable dates to the mid eighteenth
century. The date of this usage is 1701.
[93] TNA, SP44/387/ff. 204-205, Sept. 2, 1702, Licence granted by Queen Anne to Countess
Dowager of Salisbury, called "cousin," George Cecil, Sarah Lee, and named servants to return
from France by way of Holland. *CSPD, 1702–1703*, p. 411.
[94] Hatfield House Archives, Accounts 173, f. 172a.

The Countess and her entourage arrived in Liege on December 17, two months after the Duke of Marlborough successfully laid siege to that city.[95] On the 19th she signed the papers for the house she planned to rent for the next four months from December 24, 1702 to April 1, 1703. She furnished it and hired both a harpsical and harpsical master. As we saw earlier, Thomas Bruce, Earl of Ailesbury, lived in exile at Brussels. Now he was in Liege. Shortly after arriving, Frances paid Ailesbury's steward "for services done."

While in Liege, Frances attended concerts, Sarah Lee and George Cecil played cards, and Frances herself received ten Louis d'or, presumably for spending or gambling. She purchased materials for a new outfit: "Black crape to make her Honour a suit and black silk for the lining of it." As elsewhere, she bought Queen of Hungary water, the popular perfume. In April 1703, Frances visited Liege churches, and paid "a French master for teaching French to Mrs. Lee, Mrs. Throgmorton and Mme. Bollet" for three months. The Countess and her entourage moved on to Aix-la-Chappelle for the summer season. There Frances saw the town, saw the relics in the great Church, had her clogs mended, and bought a blue silk lute string gown. A French master continued to teach the three ladies of her household.

The accounts show that letters were posted throughout the entire journey. Sixty-five letters were dispatched from January 12 to May 13, 1703 from Liege and Aix. None of the letters from the Countess of Salisbury or George Cecil appear to have survived. Two earlier letters, one from Sarah Lee from Versailles and one from Benjamin Conway have, however, survived.

From Aix the countess went to Amsterdam, hub of global trade, where in the short time remaining, the countess bought Indian silks and calico. She did vigorous sightseeing up to the last moments of her journey in Amsterdam, Rotterdam, The Hague, Leiden, and Delft. She saw the college at Leiden, the oldest university in the Netherlands, and several palaces and gardens, secured her passports, and bought books in Amsterdam. She saw Lord Portland's house at Zorgvliet near The Hague, and on July 25 she paid to see "the house of the Kings." Anthony Stanhope, the English agent at The Hague, provided a coachman to take Frances to Delft. There she saw the Arsenal.

Finally, the Countess of Salisbury took the packet boat from Brill on July 30, 1703.[96] George Stepney wrote from Vienna to the Duke of Shrewsbury who was in Rome that "the Countess of Salisbury is got to the Hague at last,

---

[95] TNA, SP87/2/15, Marlborough to Nottingham, Oct. 12, 1702.

[96] BL, Stowe 244, ff. 219–220, July 16/27, 1703, Letters of Anthony Stanhope, agent at The Hague. While two ships and princes waited for better convoy, Stanhope wrote to Secretary of State Hedges that "My Lady Salisbury is more courageous who has parted hence this evening in order to embarque tomorrow on the packet boat."

and after so long absence seems impatient to be in England, and will take the packet boat rather than wait for the convoy." Upon leaving, Frances had her hair "done into locks." Her steward recorded the tips to the porters for transferring the entourage's goods and the wine and tips to the captain of the pacquet boat taking them home. From the pacquet boat they transferred to another vessel: the accounts record the sum given "to the captain and crew of the man of war which carried my Lady on shore."[97]

Conclusion

Frances, Countess of Salisbury, came back to England after more than four years of intrepid traveling through France, Italy, and the Low Countries. Now thirty-three, she had embraced continental culture, aristocratic social networks, and learned French and Italian. She came home to a new monarch and a culture of patriotism that questioned the cosmopolitanism in which she had been immersed for so long. England and her allies were at war with France, a war that would continue until 1713, the year of her death. Frances may have been impatient to be back in England, but once there, was she happy? The next chapter provides one answer as well as the hidden story of Frances's travels that her accounts do not tell.

[97] HMC, *Buccleuch and Queensberry*, p. 669, George Stepney to the Duke of Shrewsbury, July 24/ Aug. 4, 1703. Hatfield House Archives, Accounts 173.

CHAPTER 8

"A Seventh Son and Beau Major Shall Gain My Lady Salisbury:" Courting the Countess
George Jocelyn

In August 1699 George Jocelyn, a handsome cavalry officer, had a request to make of John Ellis, Under Secretary of State. Writing with the ease of a friend to a confidant who knew of his hopes and plans, he asked Ellis for details of the Countess of Salisbury's trip to Rome.

If you write tomorrow to your brother at Paris and don't think it improper, pray desire him to send you an account of the route Lady Salisbury intends to take. I hear she takes the Grand Tour of France cross the Alps and so to Rome. The particulars of this account may be had from her chaplain Mr. Conway with whom I suppose your brother may have an acquaintance according to the old saying of Birds of a feather etc. [Both were clerics and graduates of Cambridge] I shall steer that way as soon as I have any rule to take my measures by.[1]

In our study of money and marriage we have seen the transmutation of merchant wealth into marriage portions, arranged marriages, and upward mobility. Despite patriarchal norms, the Bennet and Morewood women – strong characters all – charted their own lives over the generations. Whether as wives or widows, they fought for their inheritances, invested in property, sought out new opportunities to study and travel, lived in London or hoarded their wealth in the country. One became a philosopher, one was murdered, and one lived in Europe for four years. Now it is time to turn our attention to romance. The story of "my affair," as George Jocelyn called it, is one that the Dowager Countess of Salisbury's accounts do not tell. It too, in its own way, is a story of money and marriage among the Stuart elite.

When the Countess of Salisbury contracted smallpox in Rome in December 1699, it looked as though her travel had ended in tragedy: a secret departure accompanied by few servants, perhaps an elopement, her whereabouts unknown, a terrible illness ... Instead, it had the makings of a

---

[1] BL, Add. Mss. 28884, f. 203, Colonel George Jocelyn to John Ellis, Aug. 27, 1699.

Figure 8.1 Photograph of Portrait of Brigadier General George Jocelyn, ownership unknown. Heinz Archives, National Portrait Gallery. Jocelyn is shown in Roman armor before a cavalry charge.

Restoration comedy. As we would expect, the countess had many suitors, one of whom was an attractive officer. As we will see, contemporaries offered commentary akin to a theatrical chorus. The countess and Jocelyn became the objects of voyeuristic comment that adapted the theatrical theme of the wealthy widow and the rake to the site of the Grand Tour.[2] Furthermore, the countess's relationship with Jocelyn offers detailed evidence on courtship in the late seventeenth and early eighteenth centuries, specifically about female independence, masculine desire, and male friendship.

As we saw in the previous chapter, the countess departed, many commentators assumed, to join or run away from a lover. The newsletter writer quoted earlier suggested that she was meeting Thomas Bruce, Earl of Ailesbury. But Ailesbury, a widower and Jacobite exile, was already planning to

---

[2] On love and sex on the Grand Tour, see Jeremy Black, *The British Abroad: The Grand Tour in the Eighteenth Century* (Stroud: Sutton Publishing, 1992).

court a young Flemish countess, although he did not marry her until April
1700.[3] Although Ailesbury was in Calais in May 1699, there is as yet no
evidence that the Countess of Salisbury met him there.[4] Later, in 1702, the
Countess of Salisbury did meet Ailesbury in Liege.[5]

Frances was certainly trying to avoid Thomas Neale, who was apparently
courting her in England. Neale, a 58-year-old widower, was Groom of the
Bedchamber to Charles II, Member of Parliament, and investor in the East
India Company as well as projector and organizer of lotteries. But Neale
never arrived on the continent. Ill in autumn 1699, he died in December
having asked, it was said, to be buried with Frances's picture.[6] One diplomat
thought Neale's attentions had hastened the countess's departure from
England. "We shortly expect to see my Lady Salisbury in her return to
London where she hopes to be at rest since Mr. Neale is so."[7] Similarly,
George Jocelyn commented on February 5, 1700, "Lady Salisbury is well
recovered and I believe much better since she has heard of Neale's will."[8]

"The Knight Errant"

In fact, George Jocelyn was the countess's most faithful suitor and, by
1699, had already courted the countess for over six months. We know that
because Lady Rachel Russell gossiped to her daughter Lady Roos on
November 19, 1698, five months before the countess left: "the report of
the town is that Mr. Joslin, a seventh son and beau major shall gain my
Lady Salisbury and there is this reason for the belief it will be a match, that
she permits his visits more than she has done any man's else, has let him be
a fortnight at her house in the country, and is often found with her now
she's come to town."[9]

Jocelyn was a younger son of Sir Robert Jocelyn, Baronet, whose family
had been settled at Hyde Hall, Hertfordshire, since the thirteenth century.

---

[3] *Memoirs of Thomas, Earl of Ailesbury*, ed. W. E. Buckley, 2 vols., Roxburghe Club Publications
(Westminster [London]: Nichols and Sons, 1890), Vol. II, pp. 473, 487–492.

[4] BL, Add. Mss. 28903, J. Swinford to Ellis, May 24, 1699, "I found here my Lord Ailesbury who
came hither to meet my Lord Jersey, he returned this afternoon to Brussels."

[5] Earl of Cardigan, *The Life and Loyalties of Thomas Bruce* (London: Routledge & Kegan Paul Ltd,
1951). After a summer spent in Liege, the Earl moved to Aix-en-Chapelle, for the season as did
the Countess of Salisbury, *Memoirs of Thomas, Earl of Ailesbury*, Vol. II, pp. 527–528.

[6] Narcissus Luttrell, *A Brief Historical Relation of State Affairs from September 1678 to April 1714*, 6
vols. (Oxford: At the University Press, 1857), Vol. IV, p. 543, Aug. 1, 1699. Mr. Neale "desires in
case of death, the Countess of Salisbury's picture may be put into the coffin with him."

[7] BL, Add. Mss. 28904, f. 291v, Mr. Lewis to Ellis, Jan. 6, 1699/1700.

[8] BL, Add. Mss. 28904, f. 340, Jocelyn to Ellis, Rome, Feb. 5, 1700. Ellis marks it 1699/1700.

[9] HMC, *Rutland*, Vol. II, p. 164, Lady Rachel Russell to Lady Roos, Nov. 19, 1698.

Descended from Lord Mayors of London in the fifteenth century,[10] his grandfather had served as sheriff of Hertfordshire between 1645 and 1647 and his father served as sheriff in 1677/1678. Hyde Hall at Sawbridgeworth was not far from Hatfield House.

George was one of the youngest of nine sons and four daughters.[11] Unlike his older brothers, he did not attend university but instead went into the army. His patron is a familiar figure: James Butler, 2nd Duke of Ormond, who as Lord Ossory was a possible match for Frances in 1682. Having inherited his grandfather's title, Ormond became a senior military commander leading troops on the continent for William III in the Low Countries and in Ireland, including at the Battle of the Boyne. Jocelyn received his first commission in the cavalry in 1689 and also served at the Battle of the Boyne. Wounded near Castle Cuff in 1690, he fought at several battles in Ireland and, in 1693, at Landen in modern Belgium as part of William's Nine Years' War against France.

After the peace of Ryswick, Jocelyn entered the Life Guards, a regiment commanded by the Duke of Ormond.[12] But in 1699 Jocelyn requested a furlough from the army in order to pursue the Countess of Salisbury.[13]

Throughout the seventeenth century and earlier, Britain's Secretaries of State collected extensive information about foreign affairs. John Ellis's many correspondents, diplomats, friends, and family relayed news to the government on continental politics, alliances, and war. They also kept an eye on the English abroad, including the Countess of Salisbury.

George Jocelyn's fifteen-month long campaign to win the countess is richly documented in the letters he wrote to John Ellis who had served as

---

[10] Walter C. Metcalfe, ed., *The Visitations of Hertfordshire Made by Robert Cooke, Esq. Clarencieux, in 1572, and Sir Richard St. George, Kt., Clarencieux, in 1634 with Hertfordshire Pedigrees from Harleian Mss. 6147 and 1546* (London: Ye Wardovr Press, 1886), pp. 14, 69, where the name is spelled Joscelin. The name can also be spelled Josselyn as well as Jocelyn. In his letters George Jocelyn signs his name with an *e* at the end.

[11] *Complete Baronetage*, ed. George E. Cockayne, 6 vols. (Exeter: W. Pollard & Co. 1900–1909), Vol. IV, p. 16, where the name is spelled Jocelyn. The family later received a baronage and became Earls of Roden in the Irish peerage.

[12] Richard Cannon, *Historical Records of the British Army, the Fourth or Royal Irish Regiment of Dragoon Guards* (London: Printed by Authority, Longman, Orme and Co. and William Cowes and Son, 1839), p. 85. *ODNB*, "James Butler, 2nd Duke of Ormond;" Emily Georgiana Susanna Reilly, *Historical Anecdotes of the Boleynes, Careys, Mordaunts, Hamiltons, and Jocelyns* (1839), p. 108, describes Jocelyn as "a Colonel in the guards and for his services in the armies of King William and Queen Anne, was given a regiment in May 1706, and made a brigadier general in 1710." Cf TNA, SP41/4/113.

[13] BL, Add. Mss. 28904, f. 181, George Jocelyn to John Ellis, Nov. 7, 1699. "When you see Mr. Crawford pray do me the favor to ask him if its necessary I should have a furlough to hinder my being respited if so pray order Mr. Calcot accordingly." On the letter Ellis noted "a furlough."

the Duke of Ormond's secretary before becoming Under Secretary of State. These letters, which have never been cited before, provide a picture of European travel from the point of view of a soldier rather than a tutor or young country gentleman. John Ellis's brother, Charles, a Cambridge graduate and cleric at Waddesdon, Buckinghamshire, was in the midst of conducting a rather difficult pupil on the Grand Tour through the Spanish Netherlands, France, and Italy.[14] Charles's letters to John provided information not only about the countries he visited but also on the English he encountered, including the countess and Jocelyn. In addition, John Jackson, Samuel Pepys's nephew, was on the Grand Tour. He corresponded with Pepys and Dr. John Shadwell, the physician son of the Restoration playwright. All three provided pointed comment on the Countess of Salisbury and Jocelyn. Yet, without letters from the countess herself or her household, we do not know if she encouraged Jocelyn. Nevertheless the extensive correspondence of others provides a detailed picture of cultural attitudes and gender relations in 1700.

After Charles Ellis arrived in Paris on July 31, 1699, he filled his letters with news of the English abroad and, for Jocelyn's benefit, the Countess of Salisbury. He described the illness sweeping Paris and reported that Louis XIV had ordered the waterworks to play "this day" at Versailles "for the entertainment of the English strangers." He added "almost all the English are setting forward for Italy. My Lady Salisbury will do so in a few days."[15] Responding to Jocelyn's inquiry, he detailed her route:

The Countess of Sarum had advice on the 3rd instant that a house was hired and ready for her at Rome. The route she designs at present is by Orleans, Lyons, Avignon, and Marseille and so to Genoa from thence to Turin and from Turin back to Florence and then directly to Rome, but I find by my author she is very uncertain in her proceedings only she is sure frighted from the Alps and will take the way of Marseille, if she should alter this progress will acquaint you as soon as I can learn it.[16]

In virtually every letter, Charles Ellis reported the countess's travel plans.[17] Despite his claim that she was "sure frighted," she eventually took the route over the Alps.

---

[14] A young man named Backwell, perhaps a grandson of Edward Backwell, the goldsmith and public financier.

[15] BL, Add. Mss. 28931, f. 286, Charles Ellis to John Ellis, Paris, Aug. 30, 1699; f. 293, Sept. 6, 1699. Charles Ellis insisted to the English Ambassador in Paris that he was not a mere tutor.

[16] BL, Add. Mss. 28931, f. 293. He had heard from John Ellis on August 28 and 31, "I perceive she has procured recommendations to Phil. from his relation here." This may refer to Philippe, Duc D'Orleans.

[17] BL, Add. Mss. 28931, f. 296. A week later, on September 13, Charles Ellis reported that "The Countess of Sarum does not propose to be stirring this fortnight at least as I can understand,"

Jocelyn himself arrived in Paris at the end of September 1699. The crossing to the continent had gone well and he immediately sought out Charles Ellis who was extremely cordial. "I addressed me to your brother as soon as I arrived from whom I have had a great deal of civility more that I should have expected from any body who was not a relation." Thereafter Jocelyn and Ellis became fast friends. Like Ellis, he described the illness sweeping Paris, but it did not keep him from seeing some of the sights including the College of Invalids. The next day he hoped to wait on "our Ambassador to Versailles where we are to see all the curiosities of that place."[18] Charles Ellis informed his brother that "Major Jocelyn came hither on 24th [September] and designs to Knight Errant it into Italy with the Lady . . . I shall do him all the service that lies in my power."[19]

As we have seen, the countess delayed her trip to Italy until the arrival of the Earl of Exeter and his large entourage. As a result the seats for her retinue on the "Diligence," the riverboat to Lyons, had been put up for sale in inns all over Paris. Charles Ellis was interested in some of the seats for his own journey, but the boat was leaving too soon.[20] Jocelyn waited too: "the colonel . . . will hardly be going quickly for I don't know my Lord of Exeter is yet arrived at Paris and they are said to stay for him."[21] Erasmus Lewis, employed by the English Ambassador in Paris, linked the countess and Jocelyn when he wrote to John Ellis from Paris on October 11: "the Countess of Salisbury sets forward tomorrow morning so it is no strange thing that Mr. Jocelyne and the rest of our English gentlemen should all bend the same way."[22]

Having crossed the Alps and arrived in Turin, Jocelyn continued to be in great good humor:

f. 296. On September 16, he wrote that "The Countess of Sarum's journey is fixed for the 12th of October according to the route designed before," f. 298. On September 20, he noted that "The Countess's progress stands as yet tied to the time and route before mentioned, and I hear nothing new relating to it but that my Lord of Exeter is expected to go along with her," f. 301. On September 22, "My Lady Sarum sets forward on Monday come sevennight," f. 303.

[18] BL, Add. Mss. 28904, ff. 104–4v. George Jocelyn to John Ellis, Oct. 7, [1699] ns.
[19] BL, Add. Mss. 28931, f. 304. Charles Ellis calls Jocelyn variously colonel and major; John Ellis refers to him as major.
[20] BL, Add. Mss. 28931, f. 309, Sept. 30, 1699.
[21] BL Add. Mss. 28931, f. 313, Paris, Oct. 11, 1699. Charles's own trip was scheduled for October 16 for Lyons by the Diligence. "I shall desire Colonel Jocelyn to forward such letters as you shall favor me with whilst he stays here to Marseilles where I hope to be in about 15 days after which our next stay will be at Leghorn where our credit lies with Mr. Ball an England merchant." He commented that "the business of Darien is very disagreeable to the Scots gentlemen who are here in great numbers and there is a very malicious book upon that subject." Darien referred to the project to create a Scottish colony in the Isthmus of Panama. Begun in 1698, it had failed by 1699, and the colony was surrendered to Spain in 1700. Richard Cavendish, "The Founding of the Darien Colony," *History Today*, 48 (Nov. 1998).
[22] BL, Add Mss. 28904, f. 145, Erasmus Lewis to Ellis, Paris, Oct. 1, 1699.

I have had the most pleasant journey imaginable to Lyons as to the weather, and country I passed through, but a very great misery and want in everybody's looks. I stayed two days, to satisfy my curiosity and there left your brother who was to go next day to Avignon by water with Mr. Bruce, Mr. Backwell etc. and don't expect to see him anymore till I come to Florence. I can't complain of my journey . . . These frightening hills which make such a noise in all travelers' accounts were (I thought) tolerable. I heard not one squeak from any of the company . . . This town will take up but little of our time, it falls very much short of what I expected and tomorrow for Milan and so to Rome.[23]

Smallpox

The Countess of Salisbury fell ill with smallpox when she returned from Naples to Rome in early December 1699. Smallpox had moved from Asia to Europe with the movement of populations at the time of the Crusades. Becoming endemic, by 1500 most people had contact with the disease even if they did not fall ill. Smallpox deaths increased in the seventeenth and eighteenth centuries and by the mid and late eighteenth centuries between 25 percent and 32 percent of those who contracted the disease died. Others were left blind. The process of infection, which took several days to appear, produced early symptoms that were like the flu followed by a rash within the mucus membranes in the respiratory tract. As pustules came out of the skin, inside and out, drinking became difficult and patients became dehydrated. Over the course of the disease, the pustules turned into scabs and the scabs into scars. The disease ran its course in a month, often leaving the patient with some or a great deal of disfigurement but also with lifelong immunity to the disease. Lady Mary Wortley Montagu, like the Countess of Salisbury a great traveler, contracted smallpox several decades later and was disfigured. She became an advocate of inoculation, placing small amounts of smallpox under the skin to create a mild case of the disease and, thereafter, immunity. Inoculation was replaced at the end of the eighteenth century by Edward Jenner's use of cowpox to vaccinate.[24] Today, with the disease declared eradicated, the general public is no longer vaccinated; there is no cure but vaccination given within the first four days can help.[25]

---

[23] BL, Add Mss. 28904, ff. 181–182v. Jocelyn to Ellis, Turin, Nov. 7, 1699.

[24] Elizabeth A. Fenn, "The Great Smallpox Epidemic," *History Today*, 53, issue 8 (2003); Peter Razell, *The Conquest of Smallpox: The Impact of Inoculation on Smallpox Mortality in Eighteenth-Century Britain*, rev. 2nd edn. (London: Caliban Books. 2003); E. Fenner, D. A. Henderson, L. Avita, I Arita, Z. Jezek, and I. D. Ladner, *Smallpox and Its Eradication* (Geneva: WHO, 1988), pp. 213, 229; *ODNB*, "Lady Mary Wortley Montagu."

[25] Fenner et al., *Smallpox.*

In 1700, while there were different strains of the disease, some of which were milder, smallpox was a serious and widely feared disease. Yet when, in December 1699, the Countess of Salisbury was struck with smallpox, some observers used her illness as an occasion to comment on her wealth, her lover, and her beauty – or lack of it. Charles Ellis was the first to report the countess's illness. He wrote to his brother on December 16: "Lady Sarum was taken ill on the 11th and yesterday the smallpox appeared of which she is said to be very full but in a way to do well." By January 6, 1700, he reported, "Lady Sarum is passed all danger though soundly peppered and blind with them but they are scaling off and her sight returning."[26] When word reached Paris, Abraham Stanyon, an English agent, commented to Matthew Prior, "I hear from Rome that my Lady Salisbury is fallen sick of the smallpox; what danger there is of her life is not said, but I'm sure you'll agree with me there's none of her beauty."[27] There is no portrait of the countess after she contracted smallpox and therefore how much she might have been disfigured is unknown.

John Jackson, Samuel Pepys' nephew, was among the many sightseers in Rome in December 1699. Jackson, Pepys, and Dr. John Shadwell, son of the Restoration playwright, Thomas Shadwell, exchanged humorous commentary on the Countess of Salisbury's luxurious lifestyle and the major's intentions.[28] When Jackson reported that the countess was said to be dangerously ill with smallpox,[29] Pepys with *schadenfreude* replied: "As little concerned as I am in it, I can't but lament my Lady Salisbury's misfortune in falling ill at the point of her whole life when she had at most cost and payne prepared for the making it most pleasurable to her."[30] Pepys criticized the countess for using her wealth to travel, identifying it with conspicuous consumption in general and love of fashion by "English ladies" in particular.

We would not, I find, my Lady Salisbury should have miscarried with her fortune so far from home; and yet whether she will think her country worth returning to is doubted, under the infelicity our English ladies are at this day very apprehensive of, from our parliament's avowed resolution to forbid the wearing of any more Indian silks and calicoes.[31]

[26] BL, Add. Mss. 28931, f. 329, Dec. 16, 1699; BL, Add. Mss. 28932, ff. 3–4, January 6, 1699/1700.

[27] HMC, *Calendar of the Manuscripts of the Marquis of Bath, preserved at Longleat, Wiltshire*, 5 vols. (London: Printed for HMSO by Mackie & Co. Ltd., 1904–1980), Vol. II, p. 395, Abraham Stanyon to Matthew Prior, Jan. 20, 1669/1700 ns.

[28] *Private Correspondence and Miscellaneous Papers of Samuel Pepys 1679–1703*, ed. J. R. Tanner, 3 vols. (London: George Bell and Sons Limited, 1926).

[29] *Private Correspondence*, Vol. I, p. 257, John Jackson to Mr. Pepys, Rome Christmas Day, Dec. 15 os/25 ns, 1699.

[30] *Private Correspondence*, Vol. I, p. 271, Pepys to Jackson, Jan. 11, 1699–1700.

[31] *Private Correspondence*, Vol. II, pp. 287–288, Pepys to Jackson, Thursday, Feb. 8, 1699–1700.

In fact, after her recovery, the countess did buy Indian silks, calicos, and lace in Brussels.[32]

Pepys, of course, had his own elaborate shopping list of cultural commodities. He found no contradiction in chastising the countess while at the same time providing Jackson with an extensive number of prints to buy, specifying "very good ones only." Pepys wanted single prints of "public processions, cavalcades, canonizations or any other solemnities extraordinary relating to the church, antiquities, or town of Rome . . . Nor even of single prints would I have any of greater size than will, when put into frames, be commodiously hung within an ordinary panel of our modern wainscoting, such as those of Paris and London in my low study."[33] Pepys wanted Jackson to appropriate Baroque Rome and bring it back to him so he could hang it on his study wall.

Meanwhile the countess could only dream of Rome. As she lay in a darkened room, the covers drawn up to keep her warm in order to bring out the pox, Jackson reported that her suitor amused himself with cards. "Our English gentlemen have of late plied their Bassett [a game resembling Faro] very warmly, and the famous Colonel Josselin and Sir Philip Moneux [Baronet of Wotton] lost above their 100*l.* a piece, the greatest part of which Sir G. Maxfield (of St. Germains) has won."[34] Later in the month, writing to James Houblon, Jackson increased the amount Jocelyn had lost to 200*l* and described the activities of the English gentlemen in more detail. The Countess of Salisbury, although fully recovered, had not yet appeared in public nor had the Earl of Exeter. Sightseeing was in abeyance, Jackson reported:

All has remained so quiet here that divers of our less-curious English gentlemen have been at a loss to know how to spend their time, and for want of other employment have been driven to make a business of Bassett . . . But the carnivals of Venice and Naples have now broke this knot of gamesters, some being gone to the one and some to the other. Those who design for the Holy Week here, which are much the greater number go for Naples, these last 4 or 5 days past not less than 30 or 40 gentlemen.[35]

In the meantime, John Shadwell responded to the news of the countess's smallpox not with alarm but with risqué humor and by sending Jackson a letter of introduction to the invalid.

I hope you'll forgive the trouble of the enclosed, which is from my Lady Manchester, [wife of Charles Montagu, Earl of Manchester, English Ambassador

---

[32] Hatfield House Archives, Accounts 173.   [33] *Private Correspondence*, Vol. I, pp. 287–288.

[34] *Private Correspondence*, Vol. I, p. 274, Jackson to Pepys, Jan. 16, 1699–1700 os/Jan. 26, 1700 ns [Maxfield may have been a relative of the Earl of Macclesfield].

[35] *Private Correspondence*, Vol. I, pp. 277–278, Jan. 23, 1699–1700 os/Feb. 2, 1700 ns.

Extraordinary at Paris.] since it will give you an opportunity if you please of being introduced to the most adored, and though her Ladyship has lately had a distemper that is generally an enemy to the fair sex, she may perhaps be the better for it, since it often mends indifferent faces as tobacco does an ill breath. 'Tis a sign I'm at such a distance that I dare be so profane, but I know you'll keep my counsel. Mr. Joslaine I suppose thinks her much handsomer than ever; if he could have got the physicians to have prescribed his going to bed to her to make the smallpox come out, he had done his own business as well as hers, but I'm afraid he'll return *re infecta*.[36]

The Countess of Salisbury was no beauty, perhaps, but still "most adored" by Jocelyn in Shadwell's raillery. All of the male gossips, with the exception of Charles Ellis, made cutting remarks about the countess even during her illness. Meanwhile Major Jocelyn's conquest remained to be completed.

Throughout January 1700, as the countess recovered, Shadwell trawled for gossip about the couple. "I shall be glad to hear of the letter I sent to you for the Lady Salisbury, and what is become of Major Joselin."[37] When he heard of Jocelyn's losses at cards, he looked on the brighter side, "I'm sorry to hear our English gentlemen have been so unlucky; as for Major Joselin, he hopes to have the fruits of the proverb, and to made amends in a rich wife."[38]

John Jackson used Lady Manchester's letter of introduction to meet the Countess of Salisbury who was still recovering.

At present she keeps in the dark; Dr. Shadwell . . . gave me an occasion of waiting on her Ladyship on Sunday last, but the light was so shutout I could hardly see her; only by accident had one glimpse of her nose, which I perceive has suffered. She lamented mightily her malicious distemper seizing her at so extraordinary a juncture, and feared she should be driven to quit Rome before she had had any pleasure or satisfaction in it; she designing for the Ascension at Venice. Under this melancholy, I thought it pity to oppress her with the more afflicting tidings of the prohibition of Indian silks, etc. I lament this part for her and all English ladies.[39]

Pepys responded, "I should be sorry you should come away, notwithstanding your sight of my Lady Salisbury's nose, without seeing the Pope's Tiara and kissing his Toe."[40] Despite such satirical comment, as we saw in the previous

---

[36] *Private Correspondence*, Vol. I, p. 275, Dr. Shadwell to Jackson, Paris, Jan. 19, 1699–1700 os/ Jan. 29, [1700] ns; "re infecta" in Latin means the business being unfinished. Did Shadwell intend a double entendre?

[37] *Private Correspondence* Vol. II, p. 280, Dr. Shadwell to Jackson, Paris Jan. 28, 1699–1700 os/ Feb. 7, 1700 ns.

[38] *Private Correspondence*, Vol. I, p. 289, Shadwell to Jackson, Paris, Monday, Feb. 12, 1699–1700 os/Feb. 22, 1700 ns.

[39] *Private Correspondence*, Vol. I, pp. 303–304, March 12, 1699–1700 os/March 23, 1700 ns, Jackson to Pepys. Jackson sent greetings to friends including John Evelyn.

[40] *Private Correspondence*, Vol. II, p. 321, Pepys to Jackson, April 12, 1700.

chapter, Frances, once fully recovered, reemerged enthusiastically into Roman society.

While people gossiped, Jocelyn wrote to John Ellis that he was about to part with his brother Charles, expressed concern about the lack of letters from his friends, especially the Duke of Ormond, worried about his debts, and saw the sights.

I'm very sorry to tell you that your brother and I must part in two or three days though I hope but for a little time, he goes to Naples sooner than my affairs will give me leave in which journey without making any great compliment to myself I think he's very much to be pitied being confined to the most unsociable awkward youth I ever saw ... The company thins apace some to Naples, others to Venice, and the rest to Jerusalem. We have been everyday to see the ruins of this once glorious place, by which we may easily guess at the alteration time has made here.[41]

Jocelyn's long courtship proved costly. He wrote to Ellis repeatedly of his need for money and asked him to handle his creditors through Edward Pauncefort, deputy paymaster in Ireland and in England between 1700 and 1705, who had a sideline in moneylending. For instance, on February 5, 1700, Jocelyn wrote that he had had "a very melancholy letter about Mr. Wat [his creditor] and the other not being paid yet which I am extremely sorry for, and had not Mr. Pauncefort gave me his word to have done it in a fortnight I would contrived some other way to have satisfied them who I'm sure are in great want of it."

To add to his concerns, the Italian post proved very uncertain. Although in Paris in December 1699, Jocelyn said that he was one "loves writing so little," he had written faithfully to his English friends. But as Jocelyn moved further south to Rome and his stay lengthened, his letters to Ellis, his other friends, and especially to the Duke of Ormond went unanswered. Jocelyn increasingly worried that he was "forgot." Thus, in January he had not had any letters from Ellis since October 15 and

has met with the same fate from most of the rest of my friends in England and were it not for your brother and some other good company which keep up my spirits a little it might be of dangerous consequence. I must impute it to the miscarriage of the post for I can't believe all my friends would agree to forget me at once. I have wrote several times to his Grace [Ormond] (to whom pray give my duty) but have received none since my bill.[42]

---

[41] BL., Add. Mss. 28902, f. 273–273v, Jan. 16 1699–1700 ns, Jan. 6, 1699–1700 os. [Note that these are in the wrong volume – Oct 1698–Feb 1699]. "I have found all manner of civility where you are very oft remembered with respect." BL, Add Mss. 28904, f. 340, Jocelyn to Ellis, Rome, Feb. 5, 1700. Ellis marks it 1699/1700.

[42] BL, Add. Mss. 28902, ff. 273–273v, Jan. 16, 1699/1700. Ellis marks it Jan. 6, 1699/1700.

A long way from home, his quest to marry the Countess of Salisbury now seemed a lonely one. He repeated his complaint to John Ellis two weeks later on February 5 and went on to describe his travel plans:

Your brother is gone to Frescati and Tivoli will return tomorrow and three days at furthest goes to Venice, and from thence homewards. In two days I go towards Naples where I shall stay till the end of the Carnivale . . . from thence, hither, to Venice, and so towards Whitehall. Lord Exeter is very ill of the gout and has not stirred out of his chamber since he came. Lady S is well recovered . . . I hope to see you in a little time.[43]

Jocelyn did go to Naples in March, returning to Rome after six weeks for Holy Week to find the shocking news that Charles Ellis had died in Venice. He wrote compassionately to John Ellis telling him "I'm sure the death of any of my own brothers could not have concerned me more having as many good qualities to recommend him to a friend as any I ever met with all."[44] In February and March, then, Jocelyn was planning to leave Rome and return to London shortly. But his stay continued.

In June, as Ellis wondered at Jocelyn's lengthy stay in Rome, Jocelyn claimed that he had sent good word "of my designs of staying some time at Rome but that I find like other designs has miscarried."[45] Disturbed to hear that his Italian journey was the topic of gossip back in London, he complained:

Malice and ill nature is what most people are subject to especially at so great distance . . . so many subjects at home for these gentlemen to exercise their talent upon that they should take so much pains to come to the jubilee for one . . . Lord Exeter and his whole family decamped about five days since. Lady S has taken his house and designs to stay here this summer if her mind does not alter, which is not of most steady.[46]

---

[43] BL, Add. Mss. 28904, f. 340, Jocelyn to Ellis, Rome, Feb. 5, 1700. Ellis marks it 1699/1700.

[44] BL, Add. Mss. 28904, f. 422, Rome, April 1, 1700. Jackson also wrote to Pepys about Charles Ellis's death: Private Correspondence, Vol. I, p. 301, Jackson to Pepys, March 12, 1699–1700 os/ March 23, 1700 ns, "we have news of his brother's being lately dead at Venice: a very ingenious gentleman, and governor to one Mr. Backwell, with whom he went from hence not above 6 weeks ago."

[45] BL, Add. Mss. 28905, ff. 49–50v, Jocelyn to Ellis, Rome, June 6, 1700.

[46] BL, Add. Mss. 28905, ff. 49 50v, June 6, 1700, Ellis's letter of March 29th had traveled from Leghorn to Florence to Venice and back. He reported on the position of a leading Cardinal and the health of the pope: "The news here is about Cardinal Bouillon's sudden recall and confinement to his abbey which is no small affliction to one of his ambitious temper. The pope goes out every day. No likelihood a sede vacante in the time I design to stay here, it begins to be very hot no stirring out but mornings and evenings. I should be glad you'd charge me with any commands from hence. Pray inclose the letters in a direction to Mr. Brown the Taylor at this place."

He planned to come home by September. Jocelyn had obviously changed his plans to coincide with those of the Countess of Salisbury.

As we saw in the previous chapter, once recovered, the countess became a great sightseer. She attended concerts all over the city, visited palazzi, and walked in Rome's beautiful gardens. One might assume that the major attended her and her retinue on these outings. Yet his letters to John Ellis in July and August complained of Rome's heat, so hot that he saw straw in the street spontaneously burst into flame. Jocelyn repeatedly said that he was about to depart waiting only for the arrival of money. Could his courtship have been inhibited by lack of funds? In June he requested £100 as he sent Ellis Greek wine. In September his money woes were even worse: a writ was threatened against him although Jocelyn had tried to keep up his payments and appears to have owed £140 to Mr. Pauncefort too.[47] The Pauncefort brothers, Edward and Tracy, were accused by parliament of corruption in keeping funds from officers in the 1690s.[48] Still Jocelyn stayed on, but his letters do not mention the Countess of Salisbury.

Finally, on November 12, 1700, it had been fourteen months since Jocelyn arrived in Paris in September 1699 to "knight errant" it after the countess, and he still remained in Rome. With every letter he told Ellis he intended to return. Noting that he had just received Ellis's of September 20, he explained to Ellis in his fullest and frankest letter that he now had his best opportunity to secure the countess although gossip continued to threaten his chances. Was he right or was he clutching at straws?

I am very sensible of the pains and trouble you have taken to the finishing my affair . . . Tis my misfortune that I should find so much difficulty in getting money now when I have most occasion for it having at present a fairer opportunity and more hopes to succeed in an affair I had almost given over then I have had since I left you by her brother and guardian's being gone to Constantinople, her chaplain dead and no body with her here but her steward where she designs to stay three months longer. And I should be very sorry to miscarry in an affair of this consequence for want of a little further application. The greatest difficulty that may have hindered my succeeding has come in letters from England which has furnished her with falsities about herself that should come from me and my friends, the particulars of em, I can't well tell nor from where but suppose it the fruitful invention of some whose interest is to prevent such a proceeding . . . I don't question but having opportunity to make clear a discovery of the whole by degrees and having removed the prejudice I think it will be no small point gained. But you know the sex lyes subject to change very much and consequently not extreamely to be depended on

[47] BL, Add. Mss. 28905, ff. 185, 240, 336.
[48] History of Parliament, "Edward Pauncefort," "Tracy Pauncefort."

even where there is the greatest hopes. [Yet] in all humane probability and something of her own confession I may have more reason to expect such a happeness than any other. She sayd lately in confidence to a friend that had the good nature to tell me that though she did design me that favour my own friends did what they could to hinder it. What she meant by that I can't imagine unless as before mentioned the contrivance of the enemy.[49]

Jocelyn's letter underlines important aspects of this story. First, there was some planning and financing that went into the courtship of the countess and a number of people supporting Jocelyn's efforts. Second, there was an opposing force, suggested by "letters from England," that furnished Frances "with falsities about herself," which supposedly came from Jocelyn's friends. We have already seen that there were several people making cutting remarks about the Countess of Salisbury and Major Jocelyn both on the continent and at home. Lady Rachel Russell had gossiped that the countess was on the verge of marrying Jocelyn even before she left for the continent. Thus, speculation about the couple already existed. The many jocular letters circulating in 1699 and 1700 may have come back to Frances. Hostility to Jocelyn's marrying the countess was most likely based on rank and money. Jocelyn's status as a younger son of a baronet made him inferior in status to the Countess of Salisbury. At the same time, the Countess of Salisbury herself was the subject of ridicule perhaps because she was a rich heiress whose wealth came from finance or because her travels were thought eccentric. Nevertheless, Jocelyn had support not only from Ellis but also from his patron, Ormond, who, Jocelyn told Ellis in the same letter, offered all assistance and "advised me not to quit her until she returns."[50]

The countess's wealth came in two forms, her jointure and her half of her father's estate, which would be inherited by her children. Thus if she remarried, children of the second marriage would share in the Bennet inheritance. Therefore, members of the Cecil family and the Cecil men of business might not support Frances's remarriage. Jocelyn's emphasis on the absence of her brother-in-law suggests not only an opening for him but also the removal of an obstacle. It is possible that Frances's sister Grace too might not have supported her remarriage. Had Frances died on the Grand Tour, her half of the estate would immediately go to Grace for life before going to all their children. Grace might well oppose her marrying a possibly imprudent soldier who would handle her money before it was inherited by the next generation, which might include more children by a second marriage to Jocelyn.

[49] BL, Add Mss. 28906, f. 191, Jocelyn to Ellis, Rome Nov. 12, 1700 ns.
[50] BL, Add Mss. 28906, ff. 191–192.

Finally, we don't know what Frances thought about Major Jocelyn. On the one hand, she had encouraged his attentions for a long time in England; on the other, she enjoyed traveling. Used now to making her own choices, perhaps she enjoyed the company of her cousin Sara Lee and her brother-in-law Charles Cecil and later, George Cecil, on the road. In any case she was not ready to commit herself to marriage.

In January 1701 Jubilee was over. One observer noted: "The holy doors being shut yesterday puts the nation upon motion, most of them to the Carnival at Venice. Lady Salisbury, followed at a modest lover's distance by Colonel Josselyn."[51] The countess now went off to the Carnival at Venice that she had missed the previous year because of smallpox. But the courtship was at an end. Because of the poor post, Jocelyn did not receive Ellis's letter of support until February 1701. Jocelyn told him of the outcome. "I am very thankful for your good wishes that I may succeed in my affair which has had more changes then the month of March and had at last quite tired me. And I am very near resolving never to meddle with that nor any uncertainty of that kind any more. She left that place a month ago and is now at Venice."[52] Jocelyn had gambled that romance in Italy would seal his proposals to Frances, Countess of Salisbury, and lost.

War

Although his plans for the countess failed, Jocelyn continued to provide Ellis with information about the prospects for war, forces, and fortifications and prepared to send him books on Italian courts and diplomacy. Ellis's other correspondents around Europe also discussed the possibility of war. In March 1701 Jocelyn was still in Rome, claiming that he had been bitten by a dog,[53] and wrote that "wars and rumors of wars fill this court and they have no hopes of its being prevented but by the wise proceedings of the gentle parliament of England."[54] By June he was in Leghorn, still having

---

[51] HMC, *Bath*, Vol. III, p. 432, Charles Jervas to Matthew Prior, Rome, Christmas Day 1700 ns.

[52] BL, Add. Mss. 28904, ff. 363–364v, Rome, Feb. 26, 1700 ns [it seems clear that it must be 1701 since the countess was recovering from smallpox in Feb. 1700; no mark by Ellis].

[53] BL, Add. Mss. 28904, ff. 388–389v, March 12, 1700–1701. "If you received mine by the last post you'll wonder that I date my letter from this place, which is more accidental than designed, having met with ill usage from a dog, and am not in condition to undertake so great a journey but hope to do it in a very few days."

[54] BL, Add. Mss. 28904, ff. 388–389v, March 12, 1700–1701. "They have begun to make levies here, designing to make up the number of 6000 foot, and dragoons, but if they go on as they have begun they don't seem to threaten mischief to any country but their own. [388v] They to be composed of Italians only and consequently not that have seen any service, one Irish officer by a particular interest has an ensign's post and is the only stranger that is or is to be preferred amongst

problems with bills of exchange. He wrote to Ellis: "At last I have found credit from a friend for L150 payable in 3 months." It would enable him to travel home. He was now on his way to Genoa.[55] Once in Genoa, he wrote that war had been declared and therefore he had to choose a different route home. Frances herself arrived in Genoa, but whether their paths crossed we do not know. He told Ellis, "I have directed a small chest of what books and other collections I have made at Rome which I value very much."[56]

By August 15 Jocelyn had reached Paris. Over two years Jocelyn's mood had varied from high spirits on his first arrival in Paris and his eager travels to Rome, sadness at the death of Charles Ellis, to melancholy as his hopes of winning the Countess of Salisbury seemed to ebb away and there were no letters from his friends. When he left Rome, troubled by debt on the long trip back to London in the midst of the outbreak of war, the Countess of Salisbury seemed to have been forgotten. Two letters to Ellis suggest that he continued to be dispirited and that Ellis sought to reassure or comfort him. On August 17, he told Ellis he planned to stay in Paris for ten days "to visit those places, and things I left unseen when I passed by this way before ... The nearer I come to London the more I desire to be there with my friends of which number with a great deal of reason I put you at the head."[57] Two weeks later, Jocelyn thanked Ellis for his kind letter welcoming him to Paris: "as you know everything tends naturally to its centre I hope in a little time to reach mine."[58]

But political crisis in Paris and war now seized center stage in Jocelyn's letters. Jocelyn wrote that James II had fainted at Mass on September 2. James II's health and his heir were crucial to his son-in-law William III and his daughter Anne, heir to the British throne. On September 10, the king was so ill he was thought to be dying, and Louis XIV visited him for three-quarters of an hour. James bade farewell to his family but then recovered. Jocelyn

---

them. The couriers are continually going between this place and Ienna in hopes to reconcile matters, but most people think ineffectively. The generality of the country seem to wish for that party. They don't care to own, since they have been frighted with the news of the arrival of so many troops in the Milanese. Yet when the contrary party are on this side the 5 hills which they seem to expect the news of here daily, I believe twill puzzle the most politick amongst them to know which side to wish success, to being equally danger to them both. The Duke of Berwick is still here. [The Duke of Berwick was the illegitimate son of James II and Arabella Churchill] And is very diligent about I know not what though I believe would guess it without any difficulty. The Duke of Grafton arrived here last Saturday and two days after [he] went to Naples. From whence he'll return in about ten days. He is grown an inch taller than myself and much bigger and if he continues growing, he'll soon be a giant.

[55] BL, Add. Mss. 28908, f. 307, Jocelyn to Ellis from Leghorn, June 4, 1701.
[56] BL, Add. Mss. 28908, f. 321, Jocelyn to Ellis from Genoa, June 7, 1701, "a world of news of all sorts here but most of it being disputable, I shall trouble you with it no more.
[57] BL Add Mss. 28909, f. 153, Jocelyn to Ellis, Aug. 17, 1701.
[58] BL Add Mss. 28909, f. 210, Jocelyn to Ellis, Sept. 3, 1701.

reported on September 14 that James II was almost dead, that Louis XIV continued his frequent visits, and finally on September 17 that James had died the day before. "The King of France who has made Declarations in favor of the Young Gentleman [James III known in England as the Young Pretender] in which I hope he'll be as successful as he has been hitherto in Italy from whence we have not lately had any news."[59] As for his sightseeing, he told Ellis "I have been to wait on Lady Kildare [Elizabeth, Countess of Kildare, 1665–1758] at Versailles and Mendon this week which are both wonders of their kind but liberty and property is better."[60] Gloom gave way to engagement. By October 1701 Jocelyn was on his way home from Calais. "People are here about extremely alarmed with this sudden recalling of the Ambassador and believe it threatens present war which God grant being in my opinion absolutely necessary for the good of Old England."[61] (See Plate 13.)

War meant employment for Jocelyn. In 1702 he was appointed Adjutant-General of the Duke of Ormond's task force against Spain and was issued a warrant to go to Portsmouth on May 31, 1702.[62] On the *Ranelagh* in Portsmouth, waiting to join the Duke of Ormond's troops to Cadiz, he called attention to the terrible conditions of the ships."[63] Once under way, Jocelyn described the campaign in a series of letters from June through October.[64] Although the campaign was a failure, by mid-October Ormond's fleet were in Galicia, recompensing the unsuccessful battle with an attack on Spanish treasure ships at Vigo Bay.[65]

---

[59] BL, Add Mss. 28909, f. 210, 240, 276, 291, Jocelyn to Ellis.

[60] BL, Add Mss. 28909, f. 240, Jocelyn to Ellis, Sept. 10, 1701.

[61] BL, Add. Mss. 28909, f. 399, Jocelyn to Ellis, Oct.14, 1701.

[62] *CSPD, 1702–1703,* p. 401, Commissions for the English Army, 1702.

[63] BL, Add. Mss. 28888, f. 336, Jocelyn to Ellis, June 16, 1702, "to think that so many good men should perish as they are like to do on board for want of common necessaries the conveniences are so ill contrived that I'm afraid every ship will be an hospital one in 10 days and three of the ships had no manner of provisions for the men were twenty-four hours without eating from whence these neglects come I can't tell." See also BL, Add. Mss. 38159, Duke of Ormond's journal of the expedition to Spain in 1702 and J. H. Owen, *War at Sea under Queen Anne, 1702–1708* (Cambridge: Cambridge University Press, 1938), pp. 82–86.

[64] BL, Add. Mss. 28888, ff. 336, 339, 381; f. 381, Jocelyn to Ellis, from on board the Ranelagh at Spithead, June 24, 1702, "We hear favors are heaped upon some people. And Lord [ ] commands the army in Flanders. I hope he'll have better luck than his predecessors. I have such a noise of all kinds near me that I can't promise you'll understand I've writ." By July 1, 1702, they were under sail, BL, Add. Mss. 28889, ff. 5–6v, 31–32v, 33, 54–55v, 56–57v. At the end of August, he wrote to Ellis from the camp before Port St. Mary's, f. 145. By the end of September, they were returning from the campaign and he wrote some 20 leagues off of Lisbon and he hoped soon to kiss Ellis's hand. BL, Add. Mss. 28912, ff. 88–89v, Sept. 30, 1702.

[65] BL, Add. Mss. 28926, f. 159–160v. Ormond had landed two hours earlier with 2,000 men. From the Ridondella on October 16, Jocelyn wrote to Ellis "I never saw so much firing in my life. "The Admiral ship set on fire and immediately blown up."

By December 1702, Jocelyn was back in England and apparently concerned again about gossip. On December 1 he wrote to Ellis, "I desire you'd not forget writing to your correspondent at Amsterdam to find out if possible by what means the Gazeteer come by that Illustrious piece of scandal, and to oblige him to a malinformer and ask pardon in his next of your very much injured humble servant, G. Jocelyne. Likewise to let his Grace know when there is orders for a commission for major of the foot guards."[66]

George Jocelyn enjoyed continuing success in his career with Ormond's patronage. In the Life Guards he rose to the rank of lieutenant colonel of the Second Troop. He became a colonel in the army in 1706 and in 1712 a brigadier general. After Ormond was promoted to Captain General of the Forces, Jocelyn become Colonel of the 5th Horse. Ormond was removed from his post in 1714 by George I, and Jocelyn retired from the army in 1715.[67] In 1713, he married Catherine Withers, daughter of a Justice of the King's Bench and widow of Sir Thomas Twysden, Baronet, shortly after the death of her husband. The couple had three children together in addition to her two. Her property in Linton, Kent, became one of their homes. The Jocelyn baronets, descendants of George's older brother Thomas, continued to rise in the eighteenth century. George's nephew Robert was named Lord Chancellor of Ireland in the 1730s and created Viscount Jocelyn in 1755. His son Robert was made Earl of Roden in 1770.[68]

What sort of man was George Jocelyn? If the Countess of Salisbury had Kneller paint her as a widow in 1696, Jocelyn had himself painted in Roman military dress pointing to a cavalry charge. While the date and artist are uncertain, the three-quarter length portrait that marks his entrance into or command in the guards represents Jocelyn wearing an elaborate high arched wig, which surrounds his sweet if somewhat mannered face.[69] Did

[66] *Gazette d'Amsterdam*, CD Rom (Oxford: Voltaire Foundation, 2000), Vol. 1, 1691–1703; BL, Add. Mss. 28889, f. 435v, Dec. 1, 1702. He added, "I hope youle excuse this trouble."

[67] TNA, SP34/18/32; SP41/4/113, Lansdowne to the secretaries of estate, Lieutenant Colonel George Jocelyne has been given a backdated colonelcy and appointed brigadier, and he requests that the commissions be prepared. Dated at Whitehall, April 4, 1712. Cannon, *Historical Records of the British Army, the Fourth or Royal Irish Regiment of Dragoon Guards*, p. 85.

[68] *Debrett's Peerage and Baronetage* (London: Debrett's Peerage Ltd.; Detroit: Distributed by Gale Research Co. 1980); Edward Hasted, "Parishes: Linton," in *The History and Topographical Survey of the County of Kent*, Vol. IV (Canterbury: W. Bristow, 1798), pp. 365–371. *British History Online*: www.british-history.ac.uk/survey-kent/vol4/pp365-371 [accessed May 26, 2018], "Catherine Withers Twysden:" Cannon, *Historical Records of the British Army, the Fourth or Royal Irish Regiment of Dragoon Guards*, pp. 19, 20, 85; TNA, PROB 11/640/51, Will of Catherine Twisden alias Jocelyne alias Jocelyn, widow of Maidstone, Kent, Sept. 12, 1730.

[69] Heinz Archive, National Portrait Gallery, *c.* 1690–1710. Jocelyn's wife left the portrait in a gold frame to her son George Jocelyn. TNA, PROB11/640/51, Sept. 12, 1730. The portrait was part of the Earl of Arran's collection until 1971.

Jocelyn resemble the Restoration rake, the protagonist of late seventeenth-century plays and eighteenth-century novels? Or did he have some of the traits of the brave and steadfast officer who a hundred years later became Jane Austen's Captain Wentworth? There are similarities. Handsome and high-spirited like Wentworth, a brave officer eager to make his mark in war and just as lacking in fortune, Jocelyn thought he had been encouraged in his romance by the Countess of Salisbury. Jocelyn's high hopes at the beginning of his journey to Rome gradually gave way to depression as his many months of attendance proved fruitless. Masculine notions of power and aristocratic honor crumbled in the face of female independence and contemporary gossip about his steadfast devotion, real or contrived. Male friendship for the Ellis brothers and the Duke of Ormond became more important in Jocelyn's letters than courtship of the Countess of Salisbury. Male desire melted in the hot sun of Rome's summer and froze in the bleak winter without army command.

Twenty years after her parents had rejected Lord Ossory (now Duke of Ormond) when she was twelve, Frances refused to marry his client. Why did the Countess of Salisbury leave George Jocelyn behind? According to Jocelyn, damaging ridicule retold in letters from London made her give him up. Had the chatter of Ellis and his European agents, or Pepys, Shadwell, and Jackson and the gossip of the town that Jocelyn complained of reach the countess and her friends? Did the Cecil network or her sister keep her from marrying? Or did she decide to remain a widow with all the freedom that it provided? In the late seventeenth century, fewer widows remarried than had earlier in the sixteenth and early seventeenth centuries.[70] What we do know is that Frances never married again and neither did Jocelyn until the year of her death in 1713. While that may suggest an undying love, Jocelyn's father died the year before in 1712, which may have improved Jocelyn's fortune and enabled him to marry.

The countess's life abroad, as much an expatriate's as a Grand Tourist, was criticized both as she traveled and once she was at home. After her return in July 1703, Lady Rachel Russell, the Whig doyenne, sniffed that "Lady Salisbury was at High [Hyde] Park a Sunday night, mighty Frenchified in her dresse as your brother says. She went first to Hatfield for two or three days. I think t'was Thursday Mr. Beaumont was upon that road and met two coaches and six horses, and the lady lifted up a curtain, and, in French spoke to ask how far t'was to Hatfield."[71] Although the cosmopolite was both

---

[70] Patricia Crawford and Laura Gowing, eds., *Women's Worlds in Seventeenth-Century England: A Sourcebook* (London: Routledge, 2000), p. 4.

[71] HMC, *Rutland*, Vol. II, p. 176, Lady Rachel Russell to Lady Granby at Belvoir Castle

lauded and chastised in the seventeenth century,[72] "Mighty Frenchified" in 1703 placed the countess alongside England's enemies, Louis XIV and Roman Catholicism. Anti-French sentiment ballooned after the declaration of the War of the Spanish Succession in May 1702.

Cosmopolitanism

The Countess of Salisbury returned to England on July 30, 1703. Three months later, she posed extraordinary questions to her receiver-general and lawyer that were as startling as her abrupt departure four years earlier. Ebenezer Sadler wrote to William Dobyns:

Sir I am dayly tormenting you and now I have 2 or 4 queries to consult upon in order for a conference tomorrow with our Lady: they are

1. About selling her jointure
2. About delivering over the Earl to the next Guardian[73] in hopes of avoiding prosecution
3. About going abroad

and to consult further if any other way may be to be taken for hitherto she says we tell her what will not do but offer nothing for her comfort or help.[74]

The urgency of the Countess of Salisbury's desire to return to the continent, perhaps even to live there, and the extraordinary lengths to which she was willing to go to achieve that end command our attention. She wanted to raise a very large capital sum from the sale of her substantial dower and surrender the guardianship of her son.

Why did the countess want to return to the continent so quickly? The possible reasons range from politics and religion, to a known or an unknown love, a desire to return to a continental aristocratic lifestyle, and a more general wanderlust. We may also speculate that her cosmopolitan identity and political and religious views made it difficult to settle down in England. Her fear of prosecution suggests that she may have wanted to live openly as a

---

[72] *OED,* "Cosmopolite."

[73] The next guardian specified in the Earl of Salisbury's will of 1694 was Lady Mary Cecil who had married William Forester, a strong Whig MP, one of the Rye House Plotters of 1683, who had escaped execution. Lady Mary had ties to Queen Mary, and their daughter Mary was placed in the Queen's Household while Forester was appointed to court office. Their son and heir, born in 1690, was a year older than his cousin, the 5th Earl of Salisbury. Turning over the guardianship of the twelve-year-old Earl of Salisbury to these well-connected Whigs might have protected his interests. In court proceedings, another guardian might have been named. Robert Cecil, esq. had been named in Frances's dower proceedings in the Court of Common Pleas.

[74] Hatfield House Archives, General 24/18, E. Sadler to Mr. Dobyns, Nov. 2, 1703.

nonjuror or Roman Catholic or that she may have been in touch with the court in exile. Indeed, her husband's Jacobite history hung heavily over her. Still, her motive may have been simpler. Her longing for her life in Paris and Rome, or perhaps a yearning for new adventures may have made her wish to be off again. Did she regret giving up George Jocelyn or did Lord Ailesbury and other Jacobites offer models for living an expatriate life? In any case, whether the countess could not "sell" her dower because it was based on Hatfield rents, or gain official approval to travel because of the war, she never traveled abroad again.[75]

Like so many other travelers, the Countess of Salisbury's journey must be placed in the larger context of seventeenth-century curiosity, material culture, and cosmopolitanism. The Grand Tour and Giro d'Italia continued to attract the Stuart elite in the early eighteenth century. At the same time, Glorious Revolution politics and religion, and the outbreak of the War of the Spanish Succession created a complex setting for those travels. Spending four years abroad, wearing French dress and speaking French in 1703, was a presentation of self at odds with English opinion. William III's statute of 1697–1698 had prohibited aid to James II and his adherents. The Countess of Salisbury did not avoid France; she spent a year there. The countess may have appeared "mighty Frenchified" in the eyes of the government as well as in the eyes of Lady Russell.[76] Furthermore, Louis XIV's recognition of James III or the Old Pretender on the death of James II in September 1701 caused an outpouring of addresses and petitions to William III and parliament. These became more numerous and strident in 1702 with the death of William III in March and the declaration of war against France in May. Queen Anne's accession speech to parliament "declared her heart to be entirely English."[77]

In contrast, before she returned to England, Frances, Countess of Salisbury, met with supporters of the deposed King James and Louis XIV in France, Italy, and the Low Countries. She visited Roman Catholic religious houses everywhere she went, although this may in part have been

---

[75] John Ingamells, *A Dictionary of British and Irish Travellers in Italy, 1701–1800* (New Haven, CT, and London: Yale University Press, 1997), p. 838, mentions that she was in Rome and Venice but does not notice the rest of her European travels. The countess's son, the 5th Earl of Salisbury, took up her interests, traveling for a few years on the continent with Dr. John Savage, who held a Hatfield living.

[76] "Wm. III, c. 1, 1697–1698: An Act against Corresponding with the late King James and his Adherents," in *The Statutes at Large of England and Great Britain from Magna Carta to the Union of Great Britain and Ireland*, ed. John Raithby, 20 vols. (London: G. Eyre and A Strahan, 1811), Vol. VI, p. 88.

[77] Mark Knights, *Representation and Misrepresentation in later Stuart Britain: Partisanship and Political Culture* (Oxford: Oxford University Press, 2005), pp. 124–125.

an aspect of the Grand Tour. She spent a year in Rome and over a year all told in Paris even after war was declared. Yet, more prudent than her Jacobite husband, there is no direct evidence that she was in contact with the court in exile. That she was pro-French and admiring of Roman Catholicism seems clear from her connections and her travels. But the lack of evidence makes it impossible to determine the extent to which the countess remained in touch with her continental contacts once she was at home. Not a practicing Roman Catholic, she continued to use her ecclesiastical patronage to appoint Anglican clergy to Cecil livings while her son, the 5th Earl, was a minor.

Conclusion

For four years the Countess of Salisbury had spent her jointure and Bennet inheritance on conspicuous consumption and luxury goods. She rented houses and coaches, saw antiquities in situ, artworks in palazzi, and walked in famous gardens, at times probably with the long-suffering George Jocelyn. She learned French and Italian, listened to Baroque music, made donations to monasteries, churches, and nunneries, and formed connections to Italian and French aristocratic networks. Had she been a young man on the Grand Tour, this would have been seen as an investment in a future career, perhaps as a diplomat although most became cultivated country gentlemen. In the eighteenth century, Frances might have written a book about her travels. But Frances's travels yielded a different result: through her unique four-year journey, she created a new identity for herself both in Europe and at home.

The countess made the most of the independence her wealth and position gave her to flout convention, gossip, and even law. She flirted with love but chose to remain single. Satirized for both her wealth and her supposed lack of beauty, "the richest match in England" refused to allow herself to be defined by such categories. During her four-year journey, the countess immersed herself with enthusiasm in the sights, sounds, views, and tastes of the places she visited and the people she met, rich and poor, who find a place in her accounts. In his memoirs, the Earl of Ailesbury described her best, calling Frances "the Countess of Salisbury that loved traveling."[78]

When she returned to England, the countess continued to make Dover House in London her home. For her, the metropolis not the country provided the cosmopolitan setting for the life she wanted to lead. In contrast, her sister Grace did not have her opportunities or direct access to her

---

[78] *Memoirs of Thomas, Earl of Ailesbury*, Vol. II, pp. 398–399.

inheritance. As we shall see in the next chapter, while Frances traveled in Europe on her Grand Tour, Grace suffered from a husband who, although a Member of Parliament, was deeply in debt and refused to support her. Indeed, the countess aided Grace financially in the years before she left for the continent. We turn now to John and Grace Bennet and how, finally, Grace was able to join her sister in fashionable Mayfair.

CHAPTER 9

"Diverse Great Troubles and Misfortunes:" Losing a Fortune

John and Grace Bennet

At the turn of the eighteenth century, the Bennet heiresses faced widely different dilemmas. Even as Frances, Dowager Countess of Salisbury, unsuccessfully sought to return to Europe, her sister Grace had deeper financial, social, and marital problems. Although Simon Bennet's daughters had inherited their father's real estate and other property at his death in 1682, their husbands controlled these assets during their lifetimes. With the death of the Earl of Salisbury in 1694, Frances, as a widow, gained control of her half of the Bennet fortune and guardianship of her son, the young 5th Earl of Salisbury. In addition, when Ralph Lee, the executor of her father's estate, made his will in 1695, he named the Countess of Salisbury the new executor.[1] As a result the countess and, under her direction, her Hatfield officials handled both Cecil and Bennet business and lawsuits.

In contrast, Grace, although her father's co-heir, had no access to her inheritance. Under the common law doctrine of coverture, her husband, John Bennet, acted in her name in legal and financial matters. In 1697 Grace wrote to one of her sister's administrators at Hatfield claiming that her husband "refused to furnish her with meat or clothes."[2] Within months in 1698 John Bennet, deeply in debt to a variety of creditors, was arrested and sent to debtors' prison. Despite the fact that John was, variously, in the Fleet and King's Bench prisons, he continued to collect the rents on the substantial properties that Simon Bennet had left Grace in his will. Instead of using the funds for his family's benefit, John diverted them to himself or his creditors.

In 1703, in need of money for herself and her eleven-year-old son, Grace Bennet turned to the law. The equity and ecclesiastical courts offered venues in which women might more easily bring suits. Grace sued fourteen people in the Court of Chancery, including her husband John Bennet, his creditors,

---

[1] TNA, PROB11/426, Will of Ralph Lee, June 20, 1695.
[2] Hatfield House Archives, SFP 3/275–282. General 93/28, R. Dowker to Ebenezer Sadler, 1697.

her sister, the Countess of Salisbury, and her underage son for the right to collect her own rents from the land she had inherited. John Bennet's mother Elizabeth sued too. In her petition, Elizabeth Bennet sought the arrears of her jointure due from the death of her husband decades before in 1663.[3]

John and Grace Bennet paint a picture of a gentry family in great disarray: a husband in prison, creditors in full cry, a mother in debt, and a wife without sufficient funds for herself, her household, and her child. Grace Bennet found herself forced to turn to her wealthy and titled younger sister when credit ran out. Finally, Grace had to sue her husband to regain the right to the income from her own property.

Some explanations for this ruinous outcome are clear; others are more mysterious. John Bennet's career, which began well, illuminates important changes in agriculture, credit, and risk at the end of the seventeenth century. As we shall see, while income from property, loans, and mortgages had been at the heart of Simon Bennet's wealth, it was the ruin of his son-in-law's. His wife Grace, however, was able to successfully assert her legal and property rights. In the end, John and Grace Bennet reveal a fortune lost and a fortune found.

Agricultural Improvement

Born in 1656, John Bennet was only seven when his father died and left him Little Abington, Cambridgeshire. His mother Elizabeth held Greater Abington for life.[4] From his childhood, John Bennet aspired to join the upper ranks of the county and identified with the aristocracy. He pursued an advantageous marriage, money, additional land, and a seat in parliament, gaining all four through family networks and social and political connections. Yet his success was short-lived. Imprisoned in the Fleet for debt in 1698 at the age of forty-two, some of his land was foreclosed on because he had not paid sufficient amounts of his past due mortgages. He died in debtors' prison fourteen years later. The legal doctrine of the equity of redemption allowed property owners to repay their mortgages and regain their property even when they had missed payments, provided they repaid the principal in a reasonable period of time. But the doctrine did not protect Bennet. His career as a landowner reveals more of the financial risks than the rewards for landowners at the end of the seventeenth century.[5]

---

[3] TNA, C6/376/83, Bennet *v.* Pelyne, 1703–1704; Cambridgeshire Archives, K619/E20, Mortlock Family of Abington.

[4] History of Parliament Online, "John Bennet."

[5] On business failure, see Julian Hoppit, *Risk and Failure in English Business 1700–1800* (Cambridge: Cambridge University Press, 2002).

John was the great grandson of Sir Thomas Bennet, the Lord Mayor. As we saw in Chapter 1, Sir Thomas, had four sons, Sir Simon, Ambrose, Richard, and John. John, the youngest, like Sir Thomas and his brother Richard, was a merchant. His son John was born in 1628 and inherited his father's estate in 1631 as well as that of his uncle Ambrose. Bennet's contacts went well beyond the City merchant community. He bought a Cambridgeshire estate in 1652 next to some Bennet cousins.[6] It may have been through the influence of his cousin Henry Bennet, later Earl of Arlington, that this John secured position within the royal household, becoming a gentleman pensioner in 1660 and a gentleman of the Privy Chamber in 1662. His marriage to Elizabeth Whitmore, daughter of Sir Thomas Whitmore of Apley Park, Shropshire, brought him property in Rotherhithe near Bermondsey and aided his political career. He sat for Bridgnorth for the Convention and Cavalier parliaments. He also served as a justice of the peace and as a commissioner for assessment and corporations in Cambridgeshire. When he died at the early age of thirty-five in 1663, he was buried in the Mercers' Chapel, like his grandfather, Sir Thomas, returning to his family's merchant roots.[7]

The adjoining parishes of Great Abington and Little Abington were just a few miles from the city of Cambridge, but in the sixteenth century they still had large open fields farmed in common and sown with the traditional grains of wheat, rye, and barley. Great Abington was somewhat larger in both acreage and population. In 1686 it had had almost 1600 acres and 205 inhabitants, while Little Abington had just over 1300 acres with only two-thirds of its neighbor's inhabitants.[8] In the later seventeenth century, county landscapes were changing. During and after the Civil War, agricultural incomes contracted, affected by heavy taxation on land. Anti-enclosure legislation had lapsed and, after the Restoration, enclosure by consent through Chancery decree became common. Larger landowners bought up properties and enclosed them, with the result that by the end of the seventeenth century many counties had fewer landowners with larger land holdings. Common fields were dwindling.[9] If City Bennets had made a fortune in trade and finance in the early seventeenth century, country Bennets faced challenges and opportunities in late seventeenth-century agriculture, specifically land purchase, credit, enclosure, and improved crops and irrigation.

---

[6] Buckinghamshire Record Office, Bulstrode Estate, D-RA/1/39, March 24, 1676/1677.

[7] History of Parliament Online, "John Bennet:" TNA, C6/376/83, Bennet *v.* Pelyne, 1703–1704.

[8] VCH, *Cambridge and the Isle of Ely*, Vol. VI, pp. 3–19, "Great and Little Abington Parishes."

[9] Joan Thirsk, ed., *Agrarian History of England and Wales*, Vol. V, *1640–1750* (Cambridge: Cambridge University Press, 1985), Part 2, pp. 318, 378–379; Christopher Clay, "The Price of Freehold Land," *The Economic History Review*, 27, 2 (May 1974), 173–189.

The Bennets also had lands in Rotherhithe on the south bank of the Thames that came to John Bennet's father through his marriage to Elizabeth Whitmore. Incorporated into London in the later seventeenth century, Rotherhithe was the site of docks, ship builders, gardens and fields. In 1688 a handsome map was drawn up by a surveyor detailing John Bennet's holdings: "A Map of land in Redriss parish in the County of Surrey being part of the estate of John Benet esq. surveyed in anno 1688."[10] The courts were held in his name until 1706 when they were taken over by his creditor Benjamin Morrett and others.[11]

We know little about John Bennet's early years. His widowed mother encouraged the education of her sons. In 1673, when he was seventeen, John went to Trinity College, Cambridge, the richest college at the university. His mother gave him Great Abington a year after he came of age in 1678, and the next year he bought the advowson, the right to recommend the vicar of the church. As we saw in Chapter 1, his younger brother Thomas went to University College, Oxford, at age fifteen in 1674, received his BA in 1678, and his MA in 1681. While at University College, Thomas held the Sir Simon Bennet Fellowship, which had been endowed by his great-uncle. After he became Bachelor of Divinity in 1689, Thomas became rector of Winwick in Lancashire, a valuable preferment of which the Earl of Derby was patron and to which he was named by his brother John. He became Master of University College, Oxford in 1690. John Verney commented after his death, "If Mr. [Thomas] Bennet had not Wigan he had some other great living in Lancashire with eight or nine hundred pounds per annum in the Earl of Derby's gift."[12] The Bennets' connection with the Earl of Derby proved useful when John sought a seat in parliament.

John Bennet wanted to marry the daughter of his very rich cousin, Simon Bennet, a match that would both bring him a very large marriage portion and enhance his political connections. He had the strong support of his cousins Henry Bennet, Earl of Arlington and Henry Capel, brother of the Earl of Essex. As we saw, Arlington claimed that John Bennet was actually

[10] TNA, E178/5663, Surrey: Rotherhithe plan of land late of John Bennet, esquire.
[11] Edward Joselyn, *Memorials to Serve as a History of the Parish of St. Mary Rotherhithe* (Cambridge: Cambridge University Press, 1907), p. 28; Daniel Lysons, "Rotherhithe," in *The Environs of London*, Vol. I, *County of Surrey* (London: T. Cadell and W. Davies, 1792), pp. 470–477. The court of the manor of Rotherhithe, held by the 3rd and 4th Earls of Salisbury seems to have been alienated to John Bennet in the 1690s.
[12] BL, Verney Mss. Microfilm 63645, John Verney to Ralph Verney, May 18, 1692; *Alumni Oxonienses: The Members of the University of Oxford, 1500-1714*, rev. and annotated by Joseph Foster, 4 vols. (Nendeln/Liechtenstein: Kraus, 1968; orig. publ. Oxford: Parker & Co., 1891–1892), Vol. I, "Thomas Bennet:" VCH, *Lancaster*, Vol. IV, pp. 122–132.

"the heir in remainder ... to the estate, which is above £6,000 per annum, with at least £100,000 pounds in ready money."[13]

John Bennet was indeed the eldest surviving male relation of Sir Thomas Bennet, the Lord Mayor. Had Simon's estate been entailed on his male heirs, the fact that he had two surviving daughters would not have mattered. Simon's large estate would have passed to the next male heir, that is, John Bennet. But he did not have an entailed estate and his daughters could inherit the estate. John Bennet therefore would have to marry one of the sisters to gain access to their fortune. Simon and Grace, however, were most interested in making upwardly mobile marriages for their daughters. They had already married the eldest, Elizabeth, to Viscount Latimer. Grace and Frances Bennet remained to be married. Both young teenagers, their parents were eager to find noble partners; the attraction of Bennet kinship was not compelling.

John Bennet's courtship of Grace junior was stormy. Both Grace Bennet and, by report, her daughter Grace, the potential bride, opposed it. Simon Bennet vividly described John's climbing a ladder to see Grace and receiving a bucket of water on his head for his pains.[14] The elder Grace no doubt opposed John Bennet because of his lack of rank. With noblemen seeking to marry her youngest daughter Frances, she was not impressed with their cousin, who threatened to steal away both her daughter and her fortune. To her shock, Grace eloped with John in 1681. John's ladder should have been a warning sign! Her daughter may not have shared her mother's aversion to her persistent and persuasive cousin; she may have wished to escape her parents; marrying at sixteen and eloping to Europe may have sounded romantic and exciting to the sixteen-year-old Grace. Although Arlington claimed that the marriage had ultimately been accepted, their European honeymoon ended in uncertainty. Upon their return, John and Grace found, according to Arlington, that no portion had yet been settled on the young couple because of the anger of his mother-in-law.[15] A lawsuit filed many years later indicated that John Bennet himself never agreed to jointure or a marriage settlement for his wife and that instead she had to claim her dower from his estate after his death.[16]

[13] HMC, *Ormonde*, Vol. VI, p. 440, Arlington to Ormond.
[14] HMC, *Ormonde*, Vol. VI, pp. 54–55, Simon Bennet to Arlington, May 2, 1681.
[15] HMC, *Ormonde*, Vol. VI, p. 191, Arlington to Ormond, Oct. 16, 1681, Euston Hall; pp. 242–243. History of Parliament Online, "John Bennet 1656–1712."
[16] TNA, C6/376/83, Bennet *v.* Pelyne, 1703–1704; TNA, C110/175, Morrett *v.* Paske, "Particulars of John Bennet's estate, Great Abington and Little Abington," 1726–1733; TNA, C6/383/72, Grace Bennet *v.* Countess of Salisbury, John Bennet, John Bennet infant etc. Jointure was a contract made usually at the time of marriage providing financially for the surviving spouse and child or children. Dower was a common law custom by which a widow received one-third or more of her husband's estate.

After their European sojourn, the couple returned to live in Abington House, a substantial manor house which had twenty-four chimneys and as many as five bays.[17] They settled down to a life in Cambridgeshire and London. John Bennet lived in Bloomsbury Square and in Leicester Fields as well as in Great Abington. In the early 1690s, Grace gave birth to a son named John.

If John and Grace had a rather uncertain start to their marriage in 1681, the death of Simon Bennet in 1682 brought the promise of greater financial stability. In his will, Simon left each of his daughters £20,000 provided that they did not marry before the age of sixteen and had the consent of their mother and Ralph Lee, the London merchant whom they called cousin. Simon Bennet also divided his real estate between his two daughters. John Bennet certainly used his expectation of Grace's marriage portion and real estate to begin his strategy of extending his Cambridgeshire holdings by buying up land and copyholds around his Abington estates in 1683.[18]

Between 1683 and 1690, Bennet bought the copyholds of at least nine properties that ranged in size from 30 acres to a tiny rood. Almost all were arable. The size of many of these holdings – 2 and 3 acres or smaller – suggest the patchwork of land holdings before enclosure. The largest of 35 acres belonged to Thomas Amye, a longtime Great Abington farmer who also "surrendered an acre and 10 perch called Darchouse Yard."[19] Altogether John Bennet bought some 100 acres in Great Abington and enclosed his holdings there.[20] As a result two-thirds of the 636 acres of his manorial holdings were enclosed. On part of the 35 acres around the Hall he sowed sainfoin, a crop for improved grazing. Although he enclosed lands in Greater Abington, Little Abington remained relatively unenclosed. But the numbers of landowners in the area declined between the sixteenth and eighteenth century from ten to three.[21] John Bennet sought to irrigate 100 acres of his newly enclosed lands, bringing in large pumps and pipes to water it. Unfortunately for Bennet, the pipes under the fields broke, making this investment useless with unfortunate results.[22]

---

[17] VCH, *Cambridge and the Isle of Ely*, Vol. VI, pp. 3–19, "Great and Little Abington Parishes."
[18] Christopher Clay, in Thirsk, ed., *Agrarian History of England*, Vol. V, Part 2, pp. 193–194, 196.
[19] Cambridgeshire Archives, K619/E11.
[20] VCH, *Cambridge and the Isle of Ely*, Vol. VI, "Great Abington."
[21] VCH, *Cambridge and the Isle of Ely*, Vol. VI, "Great Abington."
[22] Cambridgeshire Archives, K619/E20; K619, manorial records of the Mortlock estates in Great and Little Abington.

Suing for Simon Bennet's Estate

John Bennet repeatedly sought to enhance his assets by increasing his control of the Bennet inheritance. In 1682, after Simon Bennet died, John sued his brother-in-law, the Earl of Salisbury, claiming that he was not entitled to a marriage portion of £20,000 but only £10,000 because his wife Frances was under sixteen when Salisbury married her. Were John Bennet to win in court, Salisbury would only receive £10,000 from Simon Bennet's estate; the rest would be invested in land as part of the general estate to be divided between the two heiresses and their husbands. Therefore Bennet would control additional land and income.

This case and its iterations continued from 1682 to 1691 as it moved from Chancery to the House of Lords to which John Bennet appealed. Bennet argued that the words of Simon's will were clear, that the maker of a will was "his own Chancellor," and a court of equity should not review his intent. The judges presented the facts:

Simon Bennet by will devised £20,000 to his daughter so as she married after the age of 16 and with the consent of the trustees named in the said will. But if she married before she was 16, or without the consent of the trustees then he devised to her £10,000 and no more, and that the other £10,000 should go into the bulk of his personal estate and be laid out in the purchase of lands and settled as he had directed.[23]

The Lord Commissioners in Chancery decided that Salisbury had married Frances "with the consent of the trustees ... Mr. Bennet the Testator had in his lifetime made some overtures of marrying this daughter to the said Earl. And thereupon the court decreed that the Earl should have the portion, (viz) £20,000." When the decision in Chancery was appealed to the House of Lords in 1691, the ruling was upheld. Grace Bennet, mother-in-law to both men, testified on behalf of Salisbury that Simon Bennet had supported the marriage of the Earl and Frances despite her young age.[24] She obviously preferred her lordly son-in-law, as did the House of Lords.

Even as Bennet sued Salisbury throughout the 1680s, Salisbury and Bennet joined together to sue others to protect the property their wives

---

[23] *English Reports*, Nelson 170, Earl of Salisbury *v.* Bennet, Lords Commissioners, Mich. Term 1691, p. 818; *English Reports*, 2 Venn 223, pp. 744–745.

[24] HLRO, HL/PO/JO/10/3/184/18 and 19, Petition and Appeal of John and Grace Bennet; Answer of Earl and Countess of Salisbury; *English Reports*, 2 Freeman 119. C. 135, Mr. Bennet. Appellant *v.* Lord Salisbury, Respondent. [1691] Appeal to the House of Lords, pp. 1097–1098, 1689.

had inherited from Simon Bennet.[25] Bennet also tried to use his position as Simon Bennet's son-in-law to claim an unpaid debt from the Crown. In 1690 he presented a petition stating that his father-in-law had loaned £10,000 to Charles II in 1676 to be repaid at 6 percent interest. Because much of the principal and interest remained unpaid, Bennet himself requested repayment,[26] a claim that was contested in the 1704 lawsuit between the Countess of Salisbury, Grace Bennet, and John Bennet.

Member of Parliament

As his land holdings grew in the late 1680s, Bennet sought a seat in parliament, a traditional gentry aspiration. His mother referred to her husband and son as "parliament men."[27] She testified that her husband had lived both at Great Abington and in town at her mother's house in Great Lincoln's Inn Fields. Another witness testified that her son John Bennet lived in Bloomsbury Square and Leicester Square Fields.[28] Elections in the 1670s and 1680s tended to be contested along political and religious lines, but kinship and family connections continued to be important. With a small elite it was not surprising to find extended cousinage among the candidates. Some small boroughs with small electorates fell under the influence of the lords of the manor. John Bennet did not choose to stand for the county of Cambridgeshire, a sign that he did not have strong enough support from the great county families. Instead he stood for Cambridge University in 1690, gained support from the Whigs, but lost to James II's former Attorney General Robert Sawyer and Edward Finch.[29]

John Bennet tried again for a parliamentary seat in 1691. This time he gained one of the borough seats in Newton, Lancashire, where the Lords of the Manor, the Leghs, maintained great influence, often taking one of the seats themselves. The election was a conflict not about religion but about who was entitled to vote. Thomas Brotherton, a Whig, wanted to expand the electorate by allowing under tenants to participate, thereby raising the electorate from 104 to 167 and diluting the Legh family's influence. As soon as he heard that the incumbent had died, Bennet mobilized a network of kin and favor to gain Legh's support. He wrote to the baronet and MP, Sir Robert

---

[25] See such cases as TNA, C6/262/37, Earl of Salisbury *v.* Bornford, Earl of Salisbury, Frances Cecil his wife, John Bennet, Grace Bennet his wife *v.* Richard Bornford, Thomas Brand, and William Brand. Subject: property in Carlton, Bedfordshire, Chellington, Bedfordshire, 1689.

[26] BL, Add. Ms. 33057, f. 17, John Bennet to the King [*c.* 1690].

[27] Cambridgeshire Archives, K619/E20.   [28] Cambridgeshire Archives, K619/E20.

[29] History of Parliament Online, "Edward Finch." Finch, Fellow of one of the Cambridge colleges, was son of Heneage Finch, Earl of Nottingham, Simon Bennet's stepbrother.

Myddleton. Myddleton sat for Bridgnorth, the same seat Bennet's father had held, and he was married to Frances Whitmore, his first cousin. "Mr. John Chicheley died last night, and I was today with my Lord Cholmondeley who tells me that Frances Cholmondeley has the only interest with Mr. Legh so as if you please to send me to him as soon as you can it will be a very great obligation."[30] Bennet, claimed "one of my greatest designs is to oppose Mr. Brotherton." Peter Legh's uncle Thomas also wrote in favor of Bennet's candidacy. "Your best friends in these parts mightily desire it, among which I am one." The Earl of Derby, Lord Lieutenant of Lancashire, also wrote on Bennet's behalf, as did Bennet's brother Thomas, Master of New College, Oxford, and rector of Winwick in Newton.[31] Derby stressed that Bennet "has friends in the House of Commons and money too perhaps sufficient to cope with Brotherton." Legh gave Bennet his support for the seat.[32]

Bennet's "friends in parliament" were a mixture of cousins, neighbors, and extended relations. They included his cousin and Cambridge neighbor Sir Levinus Bennet who was in parliament between 1689 and 1693; his cousin Sir Robert Myddleton to whom Bennet had written; and Sir William Whitmore, his uncle, who all sat in the parliament of 1690. The Earl of Derby was married to Lady Elizabeth Butler, the niece of Edward Viscount Latimer who had also been Simon Bennet's son-in-law. These in-laws knew each other: in 1682 Thomas Butler, Earl of Danby, sent news to Latimer that "your father Bennet is dead . . . I hear he has made a will, and they have sent for Jack Bennet who is at Lancaster Assizes."[33]

All these interventions with Peter Legh worked and Bennet got the seat. Although Bennet proved an inactive member of the House of Commons, membership in the Commons offered several benefits. Prestige was one: it enhanced his standing in the larger gentry community. The seat also provided immunity against his creditors. He was not, however, reelected in 1695. The money to which the Earl of Derby referred was rapidly disappearing.

Mortgages and Loans

Mortgages made one Bennet fortune and unmade another. Traditionally, common law allowed the holders of mortgages to foreclose when debtors did not pay their debts on time even when the amount owed was less than the value of the property. But as we have seen, mortgage law was changing in the

[30] Quoted in History of Parliament Online, "John Bennet" and "Newton Borough 1690."
[31] Quoted in History of Parliament Online, "Newton Borough 1690."
[32] Quoted in History of Parliament Online, "John Bennet" and "Newton Borough 1690."
[33] Andrew Browning, *Thomas Osborne, Earl of Danby and Duke of Leeds*, 3 vols. (Oxford: Blackwell, 1913), Vol. II, p. 102, Danby to Latimer, August 28, 1682.

seventeenth century even before Simon Bennet's death. In 1681 Simon Bennet's stepbrother, the distinguished judge Heneage Finch, Earl of Nottingham and Lord Chancellor, declared in Newcomb *v.* Bonham "once a mortgage always a mortgage." He argued that mortgages were taken out to secure loans not to convey property. According to the principle of the equity of redemption, borrowers had the right to repay their mortgages even if they missed a payment as long as they repaid it within a "reasonable," if undefined, period of time. Despite this doctrine, John Bennet lost his property. One of his creditors, Maximillian Western, claimed that in Bennet's case, the equity of redemption, had long since run out, suggesting that there were limits to the period in which a mortgagee could reclaim his property.[34] The Bennet family's experience displays the complexities of credit and insolvency at the turn of the century.

Why John Bennet found himself in such desperate financial straits and in debtors' prison remains unclear. He had several sources of income. His 636 acres in Great and Little Abington had rents between £450 and £600 a year.[35] He also held land in Rotherhithe, Surrey, on the edge of Bermondsey, which his mother had brought to her marriage with his father.[36] In a lawsuit of 1704, he admitted that he had received Grace's marriage portion of £20,000, as well as her inheritance from her mother, and access to Grace's half of the real estate inherited from her father. Her rents amounted to £2,000 or £3,000 a year in addition to his rents of £450 to £600.

As for expenditures, Bennet bought 100 acres in the Abingtons, which he enclosed and improved. He took out a mortgage for £6,000 for pipes and pumps to irrigate the land, but the pipes failed. How much Bennet paid for the land he bought in Cambridgeshire remains unknown except for an individual farm or small holding.[37] Like the Earl of Salisbury and many others, John Bennet had other obligations. He may have had to pay off debts left by his father. Land taxes too, which were heavy, increased with John's enlarged holdings. Perhaps Grace's large inheritance came in slowly. In fact, Frances and Grace sued the executor, Ralph Lee, because he had not collected all of the debts owed to Simon Bennet. Bennet's mother's jointure of £300 a year in addition to her living expenses were also a charge upon his

---

[34] Cambridgeshire Archives, K619/E20; TNA, C6/501/20, Westerne *v.* Bennet, 1697.

[35] TNA, C6/501/20, Westerne *v.* Bennet 1697.

[36] TNA, E 178/5663 states that Bennet received the manor of Rotherhithe from the Earl of Salisbury in 1692, while an eighteenth-century suit claims that Bennet bought the manor in 1690.

[37] On the price of freehold land in the period, see Robert C. Allen, "Price of Freehold Land and Interest Rates in the Seventeenth and Eighteenth Centuries," *The Economic History Review*, 41, 1 (Feb. 1988), 33–53; David Cannadine, "Aristocratic Indebtedness," *The Economic History Review* 30, 4 (1977), 641.

estate. When he did not pay it, it began to pile up along with 5 percent interest. Still, with the death of Grace Bennet senior in 1694, killed by the butcher of Stony Stratford, Grace and John inherited another £5,000. There should have been sufficient money from Grace's marriage portion and inheritance to pay for John's land purchases.

John Bennet began to take out mortgages on his land from 1683 until the year of his death. David Cannadine draws attention to the several reasons why aristocrats took out mortgages: family, house building, land purchase, consumption, and other ventures.

Did John Bennet develop a strategy for his finances? Did he intend to take out mortgages systematically on his new Cambridgeshire property, paying it back perhaps with the rent or capital from Grace's £20,000? Or was Bennet spending his income on other things besides land purchases, agricultural improvement, and household expenses? Was Bennet an agricultural improver and real estate investor, or a lavish consumer, a gambler, or even a wastrel?

Bennet, a country gentleman, who had noble relatives and well-to-do gentry relations, may have tried rashly to live up to those connections. For her part, his wife Grace may have aspired to the life that her sister, the Countess of Salisbury, was living. Whatever the reasons, Bennet's mortgages, even if originally conceived as part of estate management, ultimately got out of hand. Whether it was agricultural overreach, poor investments, or consumption, John Bennet apparently spent much of the £25,000 from Grace's marriage portion and her mother's estate, lost Great and Little Abington, and tried to exchange some of Grace Bennet's lands and rents for cash. Even so, there is yet one more reason for Bennet's failure. His creditors were as quick to take advantage of his necessity, as he was to take their loans.[38]

In Chancery

Three voices that emerge from the many suits over John Bennet's estate cast light on his predicament. First, in 1704 Grace said her husband John Bennet was in prison "by what means or occasions is best known to himself." Her language distanced herself from his indebtedness and its disastrous outcome. In contrast, his cousin Alice Compton, descended from his aunt and involved in suits after his death as one of his heirs in law, claimed that his creditors had

---

[38] On credit see Craig Muldrew, *The Economy of Obligation: The Culture of Credit and Social Relations in Early Modern England* (New York: St. Martin's Press, 1998); Margaret Hunt, *The Character of Credit: Personal Debt in English Culture, c. 1740–1914* (Cambridge: Cambridge University Press, 2003).

mistreated him. "John Bennet having for diverse years been a prisoner and in a very low and necessitous condition several of his creditors did take advantage thereof and of his negligence and obtain securities for much greater sums than were justly due unto them and obliged him to give them large premises for what they so lent or paid unto him."[39] One of the creditors, Thomas Paske, replied to Alice Compton's argument that Bennet's creditors had defrauded him. To those who claimed that he "imposed on the weakness or necessities of John Bennet with overcharging him with interest," he answered they were groundless and that Bennet was "very much in arrears."

Despite their differing views, Alice Compton and Thomas Paske both point to the key reason why Bennet lost his fortune: short-term loans and compound interest. From at least 1683 until 1711, John Bennet took out a series of short-term loans and mortgages at compound interest of 5 percent or 6 percent, some secured by his Cambridge land, others secured by his Rotherhithe and other properties. Benjamin Morrett claimed that Bennet had as many as thirty-nine creditors. They ranged widely from a wealthy London goldsmith to City merchants, to a member of the Grocers' Company, a cousin who was a clerk of the signet, his mother, wife, and son. When he failed to pay off the initial loans, Bennet took out further loans, which in the meantime had accumulated interest ballooning out of control. It has been argued that creditors had a difficult time in collecting their outstanding debts once debtors were in debtors' prison.[40] As we shall see, in John Bennet's case, some of his creditors were more successful in claiming money and property than others.

Bennet provides a case study in the ability of a country gentleman to get credit in the form of multiple securities and mortgages and the difficulty of paying off debt in a declining agricultural economy. Five of his creditors make the process clear, Thomas Paske, Sir Thomas Fowle, Thomas Western, Benjamin Morrett, and Sir Cholmeley Dering. At the very beginning of his purchases of land in Great Abington in 1683, Bennet bought a farm with a £950 loan from Thomas Paske. The loan required a penalty of £1,970 if the principal was unpaid by a certain date. Between 1683 and 1717, as the principal of £950 remained unpaid, Paske renegotiated the loan, now turned into a mortgage, several times over, each time increasing the amount from £3,000, to £4,000, £6,000, and, finally, over £7,000 without ever giving Bennet any more money. Paske took possession of land that stood security of the loan, part in the Abington estate and part in Rotherhithe, and collected rents from the tenants. Paske continued to claim five years after Bennet's death that he was still owed £7,000 for the original loan of £950.

[39] TNA, C11/1178/10, Morrett *v.* Gumley, 1716.   [40] Hunt, *The Character of Credit*, p. 111.

Bennet also took out two mortgages from Sir Thomas Fowle, a London goldsmith and banker. The first was for £2,000 on property in Rotherhithe, the second for £6,000 backed by Bennet's Great Abington estate. In the case of the first mortgage, Fowle passed it on to Sir Cholmeley Dering, Baronet. By the early eighteenth century, it amounted to £3,500. To pay for his pipes and pumps for irrigation on July 22, 1689, Bennet took out the second mortgage from Fowle for £6,000 in exchange for lands in Great and Little Abington. After paying back, £1,000, the principal with interest stood at £5,250.[41] In 1690 Bennet and Fowle turned over the latter mortgage to Sir Thomas Western, a member of the Grocers' Company who became one of the greatest suppliers of ordnance to William III (see Plate 14). The terms of the mortgage called for Bennet to repay Western £5,250 or Western would hold Great and Little Abington for a thousand years. Again the loan went unpaid. In 1697 Sir Thomas Western took over two-thirds of Bennet's Great Abington property.

In a lawsuit filed by Western against John Bennet, one of the tenants deposed that

He believed the complainant by virtue of the mortgage . . . is in possession of about four hundred and sixty acres of land or thereabouts in Great Abington . . . of the which above 400 acres are enclosed and that the same are of the yearly value of £230 thereabout and that the rent hath been paid at that rate except for so much of the said lands as said defendant holds of the complainant which this deponent believed to be one hundred and fifty pounds per annum but whether that rent has been paid by the defendant to the complainant the deponent knows not.[42]

John Bennet had estimated optimistically that the estate should bring in £600 a year.[43] At Western's death, he left his interest to his son Maximillian, who foreclosed on the property in 1709. In a later suit in 1720, a lawyer on behalf of the Western interests referred to John Bennet's "neglecting his affairs or his absconding" prior to his imprisonment.[44]

In 1698, the year after Western took over much of the Abington property and three years after John Bennet lost his parliamentary seat, he was taken by the bailiff to the Fleet: "John Bennet, Esq.," was "turned over before Mr. Justice Nevill to one Webster who brought him down . . . Liberty of rules per Warden on sec[urity]."[45] That Bennet was neglecting his affairs seems clear; whether he tried to physically outrun his creditors hasn't been substantiated.

---

[41] TNA, C6/501/20, Westerne *v.* Bennet, 1697; C22/211/22, Westerne *v.* Bennet, Depositions taken in the country, 1706.
[42] TNA, C22/211/22, Westerne *v.* Bennet, 1706.
[43] TNA, C6/501/20, Westerne *v.* Bennet, 1697.   [44] Cambridgeshire Archives, K619/E20.
[45] TNA, PRIS 10/157, John Bennet, Esq., March 17, 1697–1698.

Figure 9.1 "Fleet Prison," *The Microcosm of London; or, London in miniature with . . . illustrations by Pugin and Rowlandson*, 3 vols. (London: Methuen, 1904). The Folger Shakespeare Library. John Bennet was sent to the Rules outside of the Fleet in 1698.

John Bennet was not incarcerated in the Fleet prison itself but in the Rules, an area adjacent to the Fleet prison.[46] Assignment to the Rules required Bennet to find two persons of property to vouch for his good behavior.[47] He was thus able to continue to conduct business, get credit, and use Grace Bennet's rents as a means of collateral.

Two creditors who continued to loan Bennet money were Thomas Pelyne and Benjamin Morrett. These loans were especially risky for them. The statute on debt provided that creditors could take the debtor's body, but once they had done so they could no longer take his land and goods. One has to wonder whether having given over most of Great Abington to the Westerns, Bennet decided to keep Rotherhithe and go to prison since he had Grace's rents to live on. As Margaret Hunt suggests, "affluent debtors content to suffer imprisonment could – and – did subsist on rents, income and savings within the prison walls in defiance of their creditors."[48]

Yet Bennet's creditors who continued to loan him money while he was in prison did take land and rents when he failed to repay them. Benjamin

---

[46] On debtors' prisons, see Joanna Innes, "The King's Bench Prison in the Later Eighteenth Century: Law, Authority and Order in a London Debtors' Prison," in *An Ungovernable People*, ed. John Brewer and John Styles (London: Hutchinson, 1980), pp. 250–298, and Hunt, *The Character of Credit*.

[47] Hunt, *The Character of Credit*, p. 121.   [48] Hunt, *The Character of Credit*, p. 111.

Morrett, a merchant of St. Giles in the Field, loaned Bennet £750 in 1696 and then loaned him another £500. Although Bennet paid off some of the debt, he still owed Morrett £1,059. Bennet secured the loan with an indenture on half of a property in Nottinghamshire "to which he was entitled for life," probably his wife Grace's property which had a rental income of £204 a year. Morrett also paid off £145 of one of Bennet's loans to a third party. Bennet grew even more desperate while in prison and gave Morrett land as security for smaller and smaller amounts of money. According to Morrett, Bennet mortgaged the manor of Rotherhithe to him for £100 for 500 years in 1708. As a result, Morrett began to hold the Rotherhithe manorial courts. For an additional £90 that year, Bennet mortgaged two London properties to John Jolley in trust for Morrett, one half of a Cannon Street house, and a Barge Street house let at £6 pounds a year. Morrett loaned Bennett money again in 1710 and 1711.[49]

When John Bennet died in prison, he left no will and no personal estate although he apparently did still have some land of his own. The total amount of his debts to dozens of creditors was enormous inflated by compound interest. In particular, he still owed Thomas Paske £7,000 based on his original loan of £950, Benjamin Morrett more than £1,000, Thomas Pelyne £650 and Sir Cholmeley Dering £3,500.[50] Sir Cholmeley was killed in a duel in 1711, but his son inherited Bennet's debt.[51] Maximillian Western had already foreclosed on Bennet's home at Great Abington. Bennet's creditors were not all great merchants or gentlemen. A sailor named Jacob Saunders who loaned Bennet £160 in 1699 claimed a total debt of £300 that remained unpaid in 1703. Finding that Bennet had "a very great estate in lands your orator was advised to endeavor to get satisfaction by and out of some part thereof." Saunders sued out a writ to the sheriff of Surrey to secure a piece of property in Rotherhithe.[52] After Bennet's death in 1712, Benjamin Morrett and other creditors continued to sue Bennet's estate until 1741. John Bennet's financial troubles drew his wife Grace and sister-in-law Frances, Countess of Salisbury into extended litigation.

Women's Property Rights

According to the doctrine of coverture, a married woman became a *feme covert*, her legal identity joined with her husband's. Research over the last

[49] TNA, C11/1137/28, Morrett *v.* Paske, 1725.
[50] TNA, C11/1178/10, Morrett *v.* Gumley, 1716.
[51] TNA, C9/224/27, 1707, Dering *v.* Bennet. Dering was killed in a duel on May 18, 1711.
[52] TNA, C5/629/43, Saunders *v.* Benet, 1703.

twenty years has demonstrated, however, that women frequently turned to the equity and ecclesiastical courts for a variety of economic and social disputes.[53] Married women could file claims in Chancery on issues of trusts, inheritance, mortgages, and other issues. We saw earlier that Grace Bennet sued her husband John for her rents, her mother-in-law sued him for her jointure, while his sister-in-law Frances, Countess of Salisbury, acting as executor, sued John and Grace and two generations of a country gentry family, the Kirkbys, and a goldsmith family, the Fowles, for the £4,000 debt owed to the Bennets. All used Chancery for their suits.

When Grace Bennet sued her husband in Chancery, she claimed, John Bennet Esq. had been committed to the Fleet "and hath ever since continued so and is like thereto remain ... yet in all that time as well as before ... continued to receive the rents of your Orator's estate and dispose thereof ... and your Orator and her said son have been supported and maintained by supplies from your Orator's said sister."

Grace requested support from her husband to no avail. "Instead he diverts the rents ... that he collects to his supposed creditors and also sublets the rents to others." She asked the court to make her husband and his creditors pay the rents to her or on her behalf. Grace further claimed that her father Simon Bennet had made an indenture in 1679, setting up a trust that explicitly said that neither of his daughters' husbands could have anything to do with their money.

In response to Grace's complaint, Bennet's creditors claimed that they had loaned him money in good faith because he had told them that he had an estate of £2,000 or £3,000 a year that was unencumbered with debts. Benjamin Morrett, for instance, claimed that in 1696 when Bennet borrowed money to pay off debts, he understood he had an estate "in the right of his wife of £3,000 a year." Thomas Pelyne said that he gave Bennet £680 in exchange for an annuity to be paid quarterly guaranteed by land on which Bennet claimed that there were no encumbrances. He understood Bennet to be a gentleman with land worth £2,000 a year. Later Pelyne testified that he created a lease in which Bennet promised him half of Calverton and Stony Stratford (Grace Bennet the elder's Buckinghamshire manors) under certain circumstances. He had only recently heard of the 1679 indenture that created a trust leaving lands to the daughters with limitations.

---

[53] See Tim Stretton, *Women Waging Law in Elizabethan England* (Cambridge: Cambridge University Press, 1998); Laura Gowing, *Domestic Dangers: Women, Words, and Sex in Early Modern London* (Oxford: Oxford Studies in Social History, 1999); Lindsay Moore, *Women and the Law in the Anglo-American World, 1600–1800* (Manchester: Manchester University Press, forthcoming).

John Bennet replied to his wife's suit by relying on the doctrine of coverture. Grace claimed that Simon Bennet had set up what John called a "pretended trust of diverse manors" for his heirs without their husbands' interference. In response, John maintained that he was advised that he did not have to account for any rents he took while Grace was his wife and under coverture. "All the rents and profits . . . part of the said real estate during such coverture is by law in right of the said complainant and this defendant's marriage . . . legally come and vested in this defendant."[54] The doctrine of coverture specifically gave John Bennet the right to Grace's inheritance of half of Simon's Bennet's property during her lifetime.

Grace Bennet's case makes at least two interesting points. First, she claimed that Simon Bennet's trust enabled her to collect rents from her inherited property even during her marriage or at least direct how the rents could be used. We saw that Simon Bennet's mother tried to do this earlier. In 1661 Lady Finch left money to her two daughters specifying, "whereas they are both now married . . . my desire and intent is that their husbands shall have nothing to do in the disposal thereof." She directed her executors to pay out her legacies according to her daughters' wishes until their husbands died. Then, as widows, they could control it themselves. Second, incarceration in debtors' prison did not limit credit transactions, even fraudulent ones. John Bennet collected Grace's rents even while in the Fleet and King's Bench and raised loans on those rents from several creditors.

In another case in 1704, Grace sued her husband John and her sister Frances.[55] Having asked her sister and the Hatfield men of business to take over rent collection from her husband, Grace asked her sister to return the funds that she had collected. The countess answered that she would do so but only after deducting the monies she had loaned Grace since 1697. This suit, of which only the countess's answer and John Bennet's answer survive, presents a very strong statement of the countess's view of John Bennet. First, the Hatfield lawyer William Dobyns, on behalf of the countess, pointed out

---

[54] TNA, C6/376/83, Bennet *v.* Pelyne, Grace Bennet, complainant, 1703–1704, "and that the said complainant who is one of two heirs of the said Symon Bennet and this defendant in her right were and are legally seized of the complainant's moiety of the said manors, lands and hereditaments during her life."

[55] TNA, C6/383/72, Grace Bennet *v.* Countess of Salisbury, John Bennet, John Bennet infant etc., 1704. In her answer, the countess claimed that John Bennet "doth pretend that he is in some way intituled into a debt of ten thousand pounds owing to this defendant's late father from Sir Robert Viner deceased." She argued that Simon Bennet's personal estate was large enough to satisfy his debts and legacies and to leave "a very great overplus" which should be invested in land and settled in the same way as the real estate.

that John and Grace had inherited large amounts of money but that John Bennet had never made provision for Grace's financial future. Because John and Grace eloped, her parents had been unable to insist on a marriage contract that would have provided for Grace and any children that the couple had. As the lawyer Dobyns pointed out,

The complainant and husband hath received very great sums of money ... Notwithstanding the great fortune and advantages the complainant's husband has had with the complainant yet that he hath not made any settlement or provision for her either out of his own estate or otherwise howsoever not made her such allowances for her own expenses and maintenance and for servants and family either suitable to her fortune or as her necessary occasions required nor the maintenance and education of John Bennet this infant ... but on the contrary this defendant [Frances, Countess of Salisbury] hath for seven years past from time to time supplied the complainant with money and other necessaries otherwise the complainant and her son the said John Bennet the infant might have been reduced to great streights and necessities.

Grace had finally appointed her sister to collect the rents and use the money as Grace directed. Ebenezer Sadler, the Hatfield Receiver General, collected the money, and Frances was ready to account for it, but she wanted a "satisfaction" or "deduction ... for what she has so far from time to time supplied the complainant and her son either in money or otherwise."

In response, John Bennet gave an unusually direct description of his financial woes. He answered his wife's complaint by saying that her father had consented to their marriage and that Grace agreed to his collecting the rents. He did not try to minimize his assets. On the contrary, he admitted that he had received £20,000 as a marriage portion and, later, £5,000 after her mother's death. Furthermore, he claimed that in his lifetime Simon Bennet had "a very great kindness" for him. He signed over to John and Grace a great debt, a loan of £10,000 to Charles II that was due from the Exchequer.

From prison, Bennet admitted he had had "divers great troubles and misfortunes." He had sent Grace money and had tried to "contract his debts into a lesser compass" and paid off several of them. Bennet believed "that if complainant had not been prevailed with to put a stop to the payment of the said rents this defendant or his assignees in about a year's time should have brought himself and his affairs into a very good condition." In short, he suggested that the Countess of Salisbury or her Hatfield officials had pressured Grace to remove his access to her income. He hoped that his wife Grace had not appointed an administrator under Simon Bennet's trust of 1679 and emphasized her "duty of kindness" to him. To pay off his debts, he had found "the best and easiest way" was to lease out his and Grace's estate.

"Very much pressed," to pay several of his debts, "he doth confess he hath made several assignments of the rents and profits of several parts of the estate in the bill."

Thus Bennet had given an annuity drawn on the property to Mr. Pelyne for which he had received the value in ready money and secured several other debts of Mr. Morrett and others in the same way. He denied, however, that he meant to defraud or prejudice Grace Bennet but only to pay his debts. He asked the court, even if it agreed that Simon Bennet had made the trust in the interest of his daughters in 1679, not to allow Grace through the persuasion of others to take away her rents and her "duty of kindness" toward him.

Grace Bennet took action against John Bennet to claim her autonomy over her own property and sued her sister for the return of her income. John Bennet tried to woo back his wife as well as her rents even as he invoked the doctrine of coverture to claim that he had a life interest in her property. The Countess of Salisbury advanced her family's interests and her own, supporting her sister Grace against John Bennet, aligning herself with Salisbury interests, and, as executor of her father's estate, continuing to sue to recover outstanding Bennet debts.[56]

When Benjamin Morrett tried to recover monies he had loaned Bennet in 1696, he found himself confronted not only with other creditors but also with John Bennet's wife, heirs at law, and mother. Elizabeth Bennet testified that when she had married John's father, "in consideration of £5,000 she conveyed lands in Rotherhithe to his use for life." Her jointure was £300 a year. In 1703 she drew up accounts with her son John on the arrears of her jointure, which by now amounted to £2,520. Elizabeth insisted on interest on the arrears. "Her son's imprisonment and intangled circumstances" had "forced her to contract great debts for her subsistence which she still owes."[57] Although she had hoped to rent out houses for £50 per annum, Sir Cholmeley Dering, one of John Bennet's creditors, had refused her entrance because he held the mortgage on them. The elderly Elizabeth requested that her claim be paid first before all other creditors. The presiding judge agreed. At the same time, the judge put off but did not dismiss the issue of Grace's own claim of dower on John Bennet's estate.

If John Bennet continued in debtors' prison to protect his estate, in the end he lost Great Abington, the manor house, and part if not all of his

---

[56] TNA, C6/341/1, *Countess of Salisbury v. Fowle*, April 6, 1704.
[57] TNA, C11/1178/10, *Morrett v. Gumley*, July 6, 1716.

estate. His wife was unable or unwilling to help him since he had already helped himself to some of her income. His sister-in-law, the Countess of Salisbury, also did not come to his aid. John Bennet left no will and Grace Bennet claimed he had no personal estate. Having foreclosed on Abington House in 1712, Maximillian Western rebuilt it and Humphrey Repton redid its landscaping adding waterworks and a canal.[58] A few years later, Western tried to reroute the water channel that John Bennet's father had established when he had exchanged lands with his cousin Sir Thomas Bennet, in Brabraham, Cambridgeshire, in 1659. Western complained that the tenants opened the lock or sluice and flooded the land. The judge decided that the land exchange of 1659 was good and that Western would have to protect his own lands.[59]

The lawsuits about Bennet's estate continued as various creditors and relatives sought payment. John Bennet's heirs at law, most descended from his father's sister, engaged in suits with his creditor, Benjamin Morrett, and got their court costs covered with a payment of £1,000. After paying their lawyer £500 and other costs, John Bennet's surviving cousins wound up with £83-6-8 each.[60]

Conclusion

John Bennet's story runs contrary to the usual view of landowning, credit, mortgages, and debt in the late seventeenth century. He was a well-to-do landowner and MP, who sought to increase his holdings, buy up copyhold land, enclose, and improve his land in Great Abington. Unlike other landlords who undertook similar improvements, however, he was ultimately unsuccessful because of the failure of his irrigation system and his financing. Bennet's use of mortgages was not in itself unusual among the landed gentry either for investment or to release capital. But while members of the aristocracy might be able to roll their debt over several generations, Bennet was not able to do so. Either he particularly misman-aged his finances and his credit or his creditors were particularly insistent on repayment and multiplying his short-term debt or both. Changes in legal doctrine on the nature of mortgages in the late seventeenth century did not protect John Bennet when he failed to pay back his loans or paid

---

[58] Alison Taylor, *Archaeology of Cambridgeshire*, Vol. II, *South East Cambridgeshire and the Fen Edge* (Cambridge: Cambridgeshire County Council, 1998), pp. 11–13.

[59] Cambridgeshire Archives, K619 E17, 1715/1716.

[60] TNA, C110/175, Morrett *v.* Paske. The heirs in law were Thomas Copleston, Sir Nicholas Morice, Joseph Taylor and his wife Rebecca Withrow, Richard Reynel, and Brent Reynel Spiller.

them insufficiently. One outcome of the tangle of cases that emerged from Bennet's insolvency was the assertion of women's property rights against male creditors. Grace Bennet claimed her right to collect her own rents, and Elizabeth Bennet successfully claimed her right to her jointure against her son's male creditors. Yet with an estate lost and a husband assigned for many years first to the Rules of the Fleet and then of the King's Bench prison, what could life be like for his wife Grace Bennet?

CHAPTER 10

"Fortune's Darlings:" Single Women in Hanoverian London

The Countess of Salisbury and Grace Bennet

Over the course of the seventeenth century, London became the largest city in Europe. Attracting more migrants than it killed through infant mortality and infectious diseases, the metropolis continued to develop new neighborhoods and new housing. The City had been a magnet for the gentry at least since the late Middle Ages during the meeting of the law courts and parliamentary sessions; by the late seventeenth century, however, the nobility and gentry were spending months in town for a season that included marriage making as well as lawsuits and legislation. The culture of this urban gentry society continued to be marked by visiting and gossip, more interest in politics and finance and somewhat less perhaps in religious expression. "Politeness" and civic virtue animated the townhouses of the London gentry.[1] They provided an audience for newspapers and new periodical literature. Despite continuing wars with France, French taste dominated aristocratic household interiors. At the same time the East India Company, which began with the importation of spices, expanded its trade to include silks, calicos, and porcelain and, at the end of the century, introduced lacquer and Indian art to England. The metropolis now sat at the center of global networks of trade from Asia to the North American colonies and the West Indies that brought "exotic groceries," including coffee, tea, sugar, tobacco, and chocolate and their accouterments to London tables.[2]

The Bennet sisters lived in London from the 1690s to the 1730s, Frances a dowager countess and Grace the wife of a Member of Parliament who was later committed to debtors' prison where he died. Neither

---

[1] Larry Klein, "Politeness and the Interpretation of the British Eighteenth Century," *Historical Journal*, 45, 4 (2002), 869–898; Ian Warren, "The English Landed Elite and the Social Environment of London *c.* 1580–1700: The Cradle of an Aristocratic Culture?" *English Historical Review*, 126, 518 (2011), 44–74.

[2] Helen Jacobsen, *Luxury and Power: The Material World of the Stuart Diplomat 1660–1714* (Oxford: Oxford University Press 2011); Linda Levy Peck *Consuming Splendor: Society and Culture in Seventeenth-Century England* (Cambridge: Cambridge University Press, 2005).

sister remarried. This phenomenon was not unusual in late seventeenth-century London. While the practice in earlier centuries was for wealthy widows to remarry, often more than once, in the late seventeenth century they more often remained single.[3] Once in London on their own, the Bennet sisters showed remarkable independence, forging new relationships, enjoying the city's cultural life, and using their income and their investments to present and enhance identities "suitable to their fortune." While both women had country houses, they made their homes principally in the capital.

In 1695 Frances, Dowager Countess of Salisbury, ordered Salisbury House on the Strand torn down. In its place, she created Cecil Street with houses between the Strand and the Thames. Yet her role in the redevelopment of the West End, discussed below, has never been noticed. In the same year, as we have seen, she took up residence in Dover House. Located on Dover Street, a newly created street off Piccadilly near St. James, the large townhouse was her London residence between 1695 and her death in 1713.

Grace Bennet, who had sued for maintenance and the right to collect the rents on her property, had sufficient funds to buy a house nearby on Albemarle Street. Indeed, after the death of John Bennet in 1712, Grace proved to be an astute businesswoman. Not only did she gain control of her landed property, she also invested in the London stock market, buying shares in the Bank of England, the East India Company, and the South Sea Company, and so did her friends. On a small scale, Grace was also a moneylender, loaning funds to her friends, one of whom, the wife of a leading solicitor, was a friend of Sarah, Duchess of Marlborough. Grace's position represented a remarkable change from her lawsuits of 1704. How the two Bennet heiresses made their mark in London casts light on the capital's building boom, material and print culture, and the early stock market. It also allows us to see how the fortune that these women inherited, once under threat from John Bennet, could be maintained and increased. They used it to lead rich lives in eighteenth-century London where their fortune initially had been made one hundred years earlier.

---

[3] On widowhood in early modern London, see Barbara Harris, *English Aristocratic Women, 1450–1550: Marriage and Family, Property and Careers* (Oxford and New York: Oxford University Press, 2002); Susan Whyman, *Sociability and Power in Late-Stuart England: The Cultural Worlds of the Verneys, 1660–1720* (Oxford and New York: Oxford University Press, 1999), pp. 87–110; Julie Schlarman, "The Social Geography of Grosvenor Square: Mapping Gender and Politics, 1720–1760," *Journal of Architectural History*, 28, 1 (2003), 8–28.

Real Estate Development

The Strand had been one of the first areas of the West End to be developed as a grand avenue of mansions belonging to high-ranking noblemen and bishops. After the Great Fire of 1666, the City needed to be rebuilt and aristocratic owners of some of the great houses on the Strand tore them down for development as fashionable London moved further west and north.[4] Nicholas Barbon, the real estate developer, emphasized the profit from such speculative building. In his *An Apology for the Builder* (1685), he pointed out "these houses in the Strand and Charing Cross are worth now fifty and threescore pounds per annum which within this thirty years were not let for above twenty pounds." The Countess of Salisbury played a key role in the redevelopment of the Salisbury properties on the Strand. Indeed, her example suggests that other women may have played a similarly unseen role.

Following the unsuccessful efforts of the 3rd Earl of Salisbury to develop the site in the 1670s, in the early 1690s the 4th Earl decided to tear down Salisbury House and put up new houses. A private parliamentary act was passed that enabled him to lease Salisbury House and its gardens to John Hodge, a carpenter from St. Clement Danes, to build houses in exchange for an annual ground rent of £600.[5] The earl would then grant sixty-year leases to Hodge to let the houses. But when the 4th Earl died suddenly in 1694, the parliamentary act was null and void. A new private act was needed to allow the guardians of the four-year-old 5th Earl of Salisbury to lease Salisbury House to Hodge.[6]

The countess's role in the new act was essential because as guardian of her young son she had the power to give the order to create Cecil Street and issue the leases for the new houses. Her consent was also required because she was

---

[4] For instance, Henry Howard, 6th Earl of Norfolk, tore down Arundel House on the Strand sometime after 1673 and put up streets and commercial and residential buildings. Arundel Castle Mss. MD 1514.

[5] John Hodge was later named parish carpenter of Clement St. Danes on October 24, 1699. *St Clement Danes Parish: Minutes of Parish Vestries*, June 1, 1686–Oct. 24, 1699, Oct. 24, 1699. *London Lives: Poverty, Crime and the Making of a Modern City, 1690–1800* (www.londonlives.org, version 1.1), Westminster Archives Centre, Feb. 12, 2018.

[6] HL/PO/JO/10/1/473/900, Salisbury House Act, Feb. 14, 1695. "An Act to enable the Guardians of James, Earl of Salisbury, to make leases of Salisbury House and some other hereditaments in the Strand, in the County of Middlesex, for improvement thereof by building" was passed in 1695. It enabled the countess to lease Salisbury House, its gardens and houses to John Hodge for sixty years (f. 35); Hodge agreed in exchange for a ground rent of £600 pounds and individual leases on each house to build eight houses on the Strand "and to make [the] street from the Strand to the Thames and to build houses on both sides of the said street" (f. 31).

giving up some of her dower rights, including annual income from Salisbury House.[7] The act specifically drew attention to her "Right of Dower."[8]

The draft bill and the leases show Frances's role in the redevelopment of the Salisbury House site. Frances added her consent to the bill in her own hand: "I do approve of this draught of an Act of Parliament and desire the same may be enacted with such alterations as the Parliament shall think fit. F Salisbury."[9] With the passage of the bill, the countess issued and signed a series of leases for houses on Cecil Street and two on the Strand to John Hodge. The houses were aimed at well-to-do tenants. With fourteen-foot frontages and depths of fifty feet or more, the houses had leases for fifty-nine years with rents of £30 and £35 a year. They were to have "good planks for the floors" and glazing on the windows. John Strype called Cecil Street a "fair street ... having very good houses, fit for persons of repute ... And the Houses next the Strand, which are lofty and good, will no doubt be taken up by good Tradesmen."[10] The leases stated explicitly that the houses could not be rented to brewers, bakers, dyers, melters of tallow, etc.[11]

Even as Frances took part in the development of Cecil properties, she and her sister also continued to profit from the Bennet property holdings in London and elsewhere. Frances and John Bennet received accounts between 1700 and 1712, and in 1711 Frances and Grace granted a lease of land in Lamb's Conduit Fields. Ten years later, Francis's son, the 5th Earl of Salisbury, and Grace Bennet granted a piece of land in Lamb's Conduit to Nicholas Curzon.[12]

---

[7] Hatfield House Archives, Accounts 151/20, Lady Salisbury's Dower, "Particulars of London to be set out for the Countess of Salisbury's Dower, c. 1685?"

[8] HL/PO/JO/10/1/473/900, Salisbury House Act, Feb. 14, 1695, "And forasmuch as the said Frances Countess of Salisbury hath Right of Dower of in and to the said messuages lands and hereditaments Bee it enacted by the Authority aforesaid that the said Frances Countess of Salisbury shall not in respect of her said Dower impeach the said rents lease or the said leases thereby to be provided to be made but she shall be dowable only of Rents respectively reserved and to be reserved thereupon and of the reversion and the reversions expectant thereupon" (f. 39).

[9] HL/PO/JO/10/1/473/900, Salisbury House Act, Feb. 14, 1695, f. 40. Salisbury had named his wife Frances as guardian unless she remarried before his son was twenty-one; otherwise his sister Lady Mary Cecil, who was married to Sir William Forester, a leading Whig parliamentarian, would be guardian. Forester introduced the bill in the House of Commons in February 1695. It passed without amendment in either house in April 1695 and was agreed to by the king in April 1695.

[10] John Strype, *A Survey of the Cities of London and Westminster ... By John Stow, citizen and native of London ... Now lastly, corrected, improved, and very much enlarged ... by John Strype ... In six books*, 2 vols. (London: Printed for A. Churchill, J. Knapton, R. Knaplock, J. Walthoe, E. Horne, [and 5 others], 1720), Vol. II, Book 4, chap. 7, p. 120.

[11] BL, Add Charter 17179; BL, Add. Charter 17181; Indentures between Dowager Countess of Salisbury and John Hodge, Carpenter of St. Clement Danes.

[12] Hatfield House Archives, Accounts 78/5, 1700–1712, Account of Thomas Moar with the Countess of Salisbury and John Bennet; Lease Countess of Salisbury and Madame Grace Bennet

Figure 10.1 Dover House, Dover Street, Piccadilly, front elevation, 1718, drawn by William Emmett. Westminster City Archives, A15A7936, Gardner Box 48 No. 27b. Dover House became the Countess of Salisbury's home in the 1690s.

Dover House

As for herself, the Countess of Salisbury made her home in Dover House. Its owner, the Earl of Dover, was a Jacobite who joined James II in exile in France. Near smart St. James Square and the new neighborhood of Mayfair, Dover Street was itself part of the Restoration real estate boom. It had been newly created after 1686 along with Bond Street and Albemarle Street after Clarendon House, the grand mansion of Edward Hyde, Earl of Clarendon, built a mere quarter of a century earlier, was torn down.[13] The speculators ran into trouble and were unable to finish their project:

to G. Watson of land in Lamb's Conduit Fields, Dec. 22, 1711; Demise, Earl of Salisbury and Madame Grace Bennet to N. Curzon of a piece of ground in Lambs Conduit Fields, July 12, 1721.

[13] Sir Walter Besant, *London North of the Thames* (London: Adam and Charles Black, 1911), pp. 168–169. Strype, *Survey of London*, Vol. II, Book 6, chap. 5, p. 78. Albemarle Buildings was named after the Duke of Albemarle who bought the property from Clarendon.

Yet those Houses that are finished, which are towards Pickadilly, meet with Tenants. In this Building, which takes the general Name of Albemarle Buildings, are these Streets, viz. Bond-street; at the upper End of which, in the Fields, is a curious, neat, but small Chapel, serving as a Chapel of Ease for the Inhabitants of these Parts ... Albemarle-street, in the Midst, which fronts St. James's-street. Dover-street, the best of all for large Buildings, and hath the most finished and inhabited Houses for Gentry, especially the West Side.[14]

Dover Street attracted high-ranking and extremely well connected residents including John Evelyn. There, Frances expressed her cosmopolitan taste and manners.

While important articles have appeared on the aristocratic town house, few focus on the period 1690–1730.[15] The Countess of Salisbury's accounts provide significant information about interior decoration, gardens, and household organization in London. Dover House was a handsome three-story town house with three coach houses and stabling.[16] Frances spent thirty-two weeks at Dover House in 1695/1696, preferring it to her dower house. Using part of her income of over £3,000 a year, she decorated the interior and exterior of the house. Even though she did not own Dover House, she provided glazing throughout, laid marble pavement on the outside, planted flowers in the garden, and replaced two squares of glass in the great lantern. That year she paid her servants in the capital £215-7-6 in wages while spending £727-7-4 for delicacies and provisions. Her total household expenses for the year amounted to £2,529-1-6.[17] Close to St. James Palace, she also received fruit and flowers from "the Prince's garden."[18]

Then, as we saw, the countess suddenly departed secretly for Paris in 1699 and spent four years on the continent. After she returned, she once again moved back to Dover House and continued to work on the house. The staircase was one focus of Frances's decorating.[19] She put up "amberellas"

---

[14] Strype, *Survey of London*, Vol. II, Book 6, chap. 5, p. 78, "the Undertakers ... not being in a Condition to finish so great a Work, made Mortgages, and so intangled the Title, that it is not to this Day finished ... So that it lyeth like the Ruins of Troy, some having only the Foundations begun, others carry'd up to the Roofs, and others covered, but none of the Inside Work done."

[15] See Caroline Barron, "Centres of Conspicuous Consumption: The Aristocratic Town House in London 1200–1550," and M. H. Port, "West End Palaces, The Aristocratic Town House in London, 1730–1830," *The London Journal*, 20, 1 (1995); Schlarman, "The Social Geography of Grosvenor Square."

[16] *The Daily Journal* (London: Printed for T. Bickerton, 1721–1737), "Dover House, Dover Street, sold by auction, 1 February, 1727."

[17] Hatfield House Archives, SFP 3/29–31; Accounts 73/5, 1696.

[18] Hatfield House Archives, SFP 3/99.

[19] Julie Schlarman, "The Social Geography of Grosvenor Square," p. 22. Julie Schlarman points to the central role occupied by the staircase in Georgian townhouses.

(sunblinds), "making the sashes [windows] to slide on the great stairs, and setting up a white marble chimneypiece."[20] The accounts refer to Indian pictures, "hanging pictures below in my Lords' apartment" and "hanging pictures up one pair of staircases," although they do not describe the pictures or artists.[21] After spending money on upholstery and wainscoting, she paid for eighty sash lights in the sash windows. In 1704, the countess ordered "72 yards white veined and 20 yards wainscot colour" for the painter. When the house was sold in 1727, after the death of the Countess of Dover, the advertisement drew attention to its beautiful staircase, finely painted by Mr. Laguerre.[22] It is not clear who commissioned his work, the Countess of Salisbury or her landlords.

Household Ordinances and Social Life

In July 1703, shortly after she returned from Europe and took up residence in London, the Countess of Salisbury established household orders for Dover House. These may be the only surviving household ordinances for an early eighteenth-century London townhouse. Such ordinances were more characteristic of the royal household.[23] The countess's regulations and accounts show that food, its abundance and diversity, was a significant symbol of luxury and status. At the same time, the ordinances were a fiscal plan aimed at limiting costs by establishing control over servants and food and wine. The countess's household ranged from 21 or 22 to 26 if her twelve-year-old son, the 5th Earl of Salisbury, came to town. Meals were organized according to three different tables in a familiar hierarchical pattern. The countess and her companion and cousin Mrs. (Sarah) Lee dined at the first table and, "if my Lord be brought to town," they were joined by "His Lordship and his Tutor." A second table was made up of her high-ranking servants, including the steward and the housekeeper. Finally, there was a third table of what would later be called the household below stairs that included the cook, the butler, the porter, four footmen, three housemaids, a scullery maid, a laundry maid, and a kitchen maid. The young earl would also have a footman and maid. In addition there was a coachmen, postilion, and groom

---

[20] Hatfield House Archives, SFP 3/99, 113–115, "From the bills," Window sashes were a new invention in the late seventeenth century.

[21] Hatfield House Archives, SFP 3/120, 1693–1765, p. 120 (1707, 1708, 1709). Frances's order for two blunderbusses and gunpowder spoke as well of protection.

[22] Louis Laguerre (1663–1721) was a well-known French artist and decorator who worked for the highest-ranking nobility of the period.

[23] See, for instance, Brian Weiser, "A Call for Order: Charles II's Ordinances of the Household (BL Stowe 562)," *Court Historian*, 6, 2 (2001), 151–156.

who were at board wages. The countess's household appears to equal the Edwardian townhouse.

Food for the countess's table was bountiful. "Her Honour's table to be daily 4 dishes first course and 4 second at dinner, to furnish which and to make what farther provision will be necessary for the family there be allowed 5 stone of beef, mutton, veal or pork to be dressed daily- and also 30/- to be laid out daily for other provisions as lamb, fowle and fish, butter, eggs, herbs, fruit, flour, cheese and what else is necessary to be for dressing." The steward weighed the meat that the housekeeper purchased and kept track of the wine, keeping "a quantity of the cheapest wine for entertaining strangers as he shall see fitting of which a distinct account to be kept."[24] The orders aimed to prevent pilfering of food by the servants. The doors were to be shut up when dinner was brought up; the servants were to eat at their tables and not take their food to their rooms; and the cook was to see the remains wrapped up in the larder.[25]

Besides establishing her home in London, the countess also traveled within England. In 1704 she spent an extended summer and fall in Bath, perhaps for her health, for twenty-four weeks between May 24 and November 5.[26] At Bath, in addition to paying for lodging, grocery, and butcher's bills, Frances bought food and luxuries that had appealed to her when she traveled on the continent. She purchased chocolate, Hungary water, as well as tea, "three boxes of essence," snuff, and Venice treacle, a medication.[27] A sedan chair took her to the pump room thirty-seven times. She and Sarah Lee also went to see Badminton House, the home of the second Duke of Beaufort.

In London, the countess took part in a lively social life where she forged a close friendship with her neighbors on Dover Street. They included Dorothy, née Brudenell, Countess of Westmoreland, widow of the Earl of Westmoreland, and her second husband Robert Viscount Dunbar. The Hatfield House bills reflect the countess's interest in visiting, print culture, and lotteries, although they are much more scattered than the accounts for her European trip. We know more about what she spent on food and wages than whom she entertained. In 1704 she paid wages to eleven men ranging from £3 to £20 and to ten women from £4 to £15 for a total of £142-12-6.

---

[24] Hatfield House Archives, General 12/27, [Orders for Dover house] SFP3/77 78, "Orders about Dover House."

[25] Hatfield House Archives, General 12/27, SFP 3/77–78, "Orders about Dover House."

[26] Hatfield House Archives, SFP 3/87–89, Expenses at Bath, May to Nov. 1704.

[27] Venice or Venetian treacle was not a sweet but a drug dating back to the first century BC, taken up by Galen and still in the pharmacology texts until the nineteenth century. J. P. Griffin, "Venetian Treacle and the Foundation of Medicines Regulation," *British Journal of Clinical Pharmacology*, 58, 3 (2004), 317–325.

By 1705/1706 the countess was paying £230-16 in rent for Dover House as well as £3 a year for seats in Trinity Chapel.[28] The 1709/1710 bills included eleven liveries including suits and great coats as well as a livery for the countess's page. The countess had her own coach, her own chaise, and her own sedan chair for which carriers charged her 1 guinea a week to carry her about town. She also paid for periwigs, perukes, and natural wigs.[29]

The accounts do shed particular light on the contemporary print culture that appealed to the Countess of Salisbury. She and her household kept current with the news and gossip of the town, the law, and parliament. In 1704 she paid £1 for a book on popish controversies as well as transcribing the accounts of her jointure for the year.[30] In 1709–1710 her account read: "12 Tatlers, Session paper, 53 benefit tickets, Duke of Marlborough's speech, 1d, Jan. 9 for the last dying speeches of the prisoners 1d ... May 21 Mr. Thornhill's trial ... May 25 last dying speeches of the prisoners 1d."[31]

The *Tatler*, the pioneering weekly magazine written by Richard Steele using the pseudonym of Isaac Bickerstaff, satirized the social life of the elite who bought the weekly. The trial of Richard Thornhill, which Frances read about, grew out of a fracas followed by a duel with pistols in which Thornhill killed Sir Cholmeley Dering who had attacked him in May 1711. Dering was one of John Bennet's creditors to whom he owed £3,500. Frances probably bought the tract about his trial because it was a notorious case. That Dering's death might have an impact on family finances must have added extra interest to the tract. Thornhill was acquitted of murder, found guilty of manslaughter instead, and was murdered himself in August 1711.[32]

Glimpses of Frances's social life also appear in her son's correspondence while at Oxford. The letters refer to his mother and young Salisbury's relations, young John Bennet and his Gresley and Lee cousins. For instance, in 1707 Salisbury received news of the town including gossip about current marriage negotiations. The author of the letter, named Berton, began by urging "your immediate presence in town." He went on to report that "Lady Halifax and Lord Roxburgh were agreed, the Duke of Grafton and the City heiress are making a bargain, Lord Quarrenton's heartbroken." (At least the

[28] Hatfield House Archives, SFP 3/99.
[29] Hatfield House Archives, SFP 3/120–121, Bill 438, 455.
[30] Hatfield House Archives, SFP 3/87–89, Expenses at Bath, May to Nov. 1704.
[31] Hatfield House Archives, SFP 3/139, Bills 447.
[32] *A true account of what past at the Old-Bailey, May the 18th, 1711 relating to the tryal of Richard Thornhill, Esq. indicted for the murther of Sir Cholmley Deering* (London: Printed for John Morphew, 1711); *A full and true account of a horrid and barbarous murder: committed last night by one Mr. King and Mr. Smith, two Kentish gentlemen, on the body of Richard Thornhill, esq; the quarrel ... about Sir Cholmly Deering, deceas'd* ([London]: Printed by M. Holt in Fleetstreet, 1711). History of Parliament Online, "Sir Cholmeley Dering."

first two were untrue.) He went on: "I had the honour of seeing Lady Salisbury here lately, she looks and is very well. Cossine Grisley revives upon the approach of xmas, which will bring the lad from Cambridge."[33]

G[eorge] Lee wrote to Salisbury about a scandal unfolding in London. Robert "Beau" Fielding, who had had connections at the court of Charles II, became involved in a bigamy accusation. "Mr. Field ... is more gay and merry than ever, and the town say it is the conquest he has made with Lady Charles makes him so full of fine aires and dress, he visits my Lady Salisbury and they are much diverted with his comical discourse." Lee's letter also referred to the earl's cousin: "Mr. Bennet talks with a great deal of pleasure sometimes of going to Oxford and having your Lordship's company but I suppose it must be at his father's pleasure." Despite the fact that John Bennet was in debtors' prison, the letter suggests that he would have to give permission.[34]

Although Frances had supported non-juring clergy and appeared at times to have Roman Catholic leanings, she remained formally within the established church. John Evelyn wrote in 1701–1702, while Frances was on the continent, that he heard a sermon at Trinity Chapel, the small church behind the northern end of Bond Street, by "A chaplain of the Countess of Salisbury ... Sleepe surpriz'd me exceedingly which God in mercy pardon."[35] In 1712 and 1713, Frances attended Anglican churches frequently. In addition to supporting nearby Trinity chapel, she was carried to St. Martin's in the Fields, Russell Street, and often to fashionable St. James Piccadilly near her home. Frances also went to the opera. She had attended Italian opera in Rome and Venice during her European travels. Perhaps she saw *Rinaldo*, Handel's opera first staged in 1711 and revived in subsequent years[36] or the English opera of Purcell first put on in the 1680s.[37]

Legacies and Lotteries

Frances, Dowager Countess of Salisbury, died on July 7, 1713.[38] By 1711 she had been spending the late summer months in Hampstead,

---

[33] Hatfield House Archives, FP 10/196, 1690–1731; Estate Papers, Box V, 101.

[34] Hatfield House Archives, FP 10/203–204; Estate Papers, Box V, 83, G. to Earl of Salisbury at Christ Church, Oxford, [c. 1705–1707], Lee's brother and Mr. Finch had gone to Epsom for the week. Lee may have been related to Sarah Lee, Frances's companion and cousin.

[35] *The Diary of John Evelyn*, ed. E. S. de Beer, 6 vols. (Oxford: Clarendon Press, 1955), Vol. V, p. 445. Nonjurors refused to take the oath of allegiance to William III and remained loyal to James II.

[36] *The Diary of John Evelyn*, ed. de Beer, Vol. V, p. 445.

[37] *Encyclopaedia Britannica*, "Opera." Handel arrived in England in 1710.

[38] Hatfield House Archives, SFP 3/20, 4/13.

sending up Bath water and wine. In fact, her bills show work both in Hampstead and in Kensington even as she continued to pay the bricklayers at Dover House. With her fine Dutch writing paper and Dutch quills, she continued to send out letters, both domestically and internationally, which unfortunately have not been found.[39]

In her relatively brief will marked by charity and simplicity, Frances stated that she "died in charity with all the world and freely and heartily forgive all those who have in any way injured me."[40] Asking to be buried not at Hatfield but at St Giles in the Fields, an early seventeenth-century church supported by Archbishop Laud whose stained glass windows and silver had been reinstalled at the Restoration, she requested a very simple and inexpensive funeral costing no more than £50. In line with the early eighteenth-century fashion for less elaborate funerals, the countess wished it to be held at two in the morning with only two coaches and no escutcheons to identify her and as few lights as possible. She recommended the arrangement of her funeral to her friend Dorothy, Countess of Westmoreland. The countess made the Earl of Thanet one of her executors. Not only was he her son's father-in-law, he was a member of the Society for the Propagation of the Gospel in Foreign Parts (SPG) which was sending missionaries to colonies in North America to reform Anglican churches and to convert native Americans.

The countess left her son a portrait of his father, the 4th Earl of Salisbury, in enamel framed in gold but provided no bequests to any other member of her family including her sister Grace. It must be assumed that her land was already designated for her son. She asked that all her goods be sold and the money combined with her rents and "any money by her when she died" to be dispersed as she ordered, "which shall not be otherwise by me disposed of by some note in writing with my name and seal." The money was to be used to pay her debts and her executors' expenses. The rest was to go for charitable uses "relieving poor and necessitous persons," providing them with clothing and placing their children as apprentices and other charitable deeds as her executors, the 6th Earl of Thanet, the Countess of Westmoreland, and William Constable, the Countess of Westmoreland's brother-in-law, thought appropriate. She added a codicil leaving £50 each to her waiting woman and maidservant and, in a second codicil, lottery tickets to her coachman and to a Mrs. Tribe, called Mrs. Andrewes, and her son.

Lottery tickets may sound like odd legacies, but they were actually valuable bonds or annuities paying semiannual or annual interest for which there was a secondary market. Under William and Mary and Queen Anne,

[39] Hatfield House Archives, SFP 93/139, 1705, Aug.–May 1710–1711.
[40] TNA, PROB11/536/55, Will of Frances, Countess of Salisbury, Dowager, Oct. 3, 1713.

the state used lotteries to raise substantial funds. For instance in 1710, a parliamentary statute under Queen Anne raised £1,500,000 by issuing 150,000 tickets at £10 apiece. Each ticket holder received an annuity of 14 shillings a year for thirty-two years with the possibility of prizes ranging from £5 to £1,000. Similar lotteries with variations were run in 1711 and 1712, sometimes two a year up to through the 1780s.[41]

Frances had bought lottery tickets in 1710. She gave ten lottery tickets to her coachman "out of the number of my lottery tickets, which was drawn last Michelmas 1710 and in which I have either five and twenty or eight and Twenty Tickets whereof one is a benefit one of five pounds a year ... which will bring him in the yearly income of Twelve pounds of year. This I give for the maintenance of him, his wife and children and to his heirs as long as the revenue shall last." Since each of the ten tickets was worth fourteen shillings a year, ten would bring in 140 shillings or £7 a year. One of them was worth an additional £5 so that the total was £12 a year.

The countess gave "the rest of the tickets in this same lottery above mentioned" to Mrs. Tribe "commonly called Mrs. Andrewes," but only for her life. Then the tickets were to be sold and used "in the maintenance of her son Thomas Tribe either in the putting him out an apprentice or any other way which my Executors shall judge most advantageous to him." If both Mrs. Andrewes and Thomas Tribe should die "before the said tickets be sold," she left it to the executors to use the tickets for charitable purposes. She does not identify Mrs. Andrewes as a household servant and appears to want to provide as much for her children as for her. Mrs. Andrews's inheritance of fifteen or eighteen lottery tickets paying 14 shillings a year each amounted to £10-50 to £12-60 a year. On her death the tickets would be sold for a capital amount in the interest of her son Thomas Tribe.

Frances went on to provide a further benefaction to young Thomas Andrewes who had most likely been her page.

I also give and bequeath to Thomas Andrewes (who I have of late years taken into my care and who is now about nine or ten years of age) the yearly interest of a hundred pounds which I put into another lottery made after the other above mentioned not yet drawn which annual interest I will and desire my Executors shall sell for the said Thomas Andrewes's advantage as they the said Executors shall judge most conducing to that end. But if there happen to be any benefit lot or lots when the lottery is drawn the said Thomas Andrewes is to have no advantage of it or them but I leave the said lot or lots to my Executors to be laid out in what charity to the poor they shall judge best.

[41] John Ashton, *A History of English Lotteries* (London: Leadenhall Press, 1893, reissued Gage, 1969), pp. 48–55.

If Thomas Andrewes died before the interest could be sold for his benefit, then she ordered her executors to sell it for charitable deeds for the poor.

Thomas Andrewes may have been left a ticket from the lottery of 1711 in which the tickets were £100 each and the interest rate 6 percent each bringing him £6 a year. Frances did not want Thomas to win the top prize of £1,000, but she did want him to have a capital sum that would secure him a useful occupation. These legacies, which preserved social difference, rewarded the countess's servants but especially tried to benefit these children.

Frances, Countess of Salisbury, had asked for a simple funeral. The Countess of Westmoreland abided by most of her wishes, but in the end rich materials and custom marked Frances's status. Her coach and her chaise had to be painted for mourning at a cost of £70. Her large coffin, made of elm and lead, was laid with sarcenet taffeta, with a ruffle, a fabric her great grandfather Sir Thomas Bennet had imported. The body "put up with sweets" was "covered with best new velvet with a gold plate coat of arms and inscription." It had four gilt handles and nine coronets, "set off with three rows of best gilt nails." The room was "hung in deep mourning with black cloth."

As Frances had requested, there were only two coaches but there were thirteen plumes of black feathers for the horses. Ten men in black carried branch lights against the dark. Thirteen pairs of gloves for the coachmen and the light men and three fine cloaks for the principal mourners were provided. "A large achievement with supporters" spelled out her arms and her status as a countess. According to Frances's wishes, the poor of the parish of St. Giles received money. As customary, her servants went into mourning. Frances's important woman servants, Mrs. Ann Lee, Mrs. Sarah Lee, Mrs. Throckmorton, Mrs. Bulley, and Mrs. Davis wore mourning shoes, black silk scarves, "all a mode heads" gloves, and mourning hoods. Her important male servants had gloves and hatbands.

Frances was only forty-three years old when she died. Married at thirteen to a foolish young nobleman, she led a life of independence and adventure after his death using her wealth to explore France, Italy, and the Netherlands and, after her return, to create a fashionable life in England especially in London. In addition to working on Cecil real estate interests, she focused on Dover House, translating the cosmopolitan style and manners she had brought back into her home. She spent freely and lived up to her status as Countess of Salisbury, and yet her fortune based on Bennet property remained intact. Her death, then, had important consequences for both her sister and her son.

Grace Bennet: Rebuilding the Family Fortune

In contrast to the Countess of Salisbury, it might be thought that her sister, Grace Bennet, was consigned to poverty, shame, as well as an unhappy marriage because of John Bennet's long imprisonment for debt. In fact, at her death in 1732, aged 68, Grace Bennet's estate was worth over £22,000 in cash, notes and bonds, stocks, jewelry, and household furnishings. This amount did not include extensive real estate holdings worth at least £3,200 a year plus her house on Albemarle Street.

Where did this wealth come from? In 1697 Grace had claimed her husband would not provide her with maintenance; in 1704 she testified that he misappropriated her rents and later claimed that he died insolvent. Perhaps one mystery solves the other. To begin with, John and Grace's financial position at the turn of the century is unclear. It is likely that they had more assets than they presented in their various lawsuits. In any case, John Bennet could not sell Grace's real estate. Grace rebuilt her position through social connections and her fortune through inheritance, real estate, and stock market investment.

To begin with, Grace's identity as sister to the Countess of Salisbury and later aunt to the Earls of Salisbury came to the fore after John Bennet's relegation to the Rules of the Fleet. She emphasized the connection by frequently visiting her nephew, the 5th Earl of Salisbury, at Hatfield House while his mother was on the continent and received luxurious foodstuffs from him – twenty-four dozen crayfish, a swan pie with a turkey inside, four hams, hog tongues, and two brace of does in 1702.[42] Grace also enjoyed a social network that connected her to elite friends and her merchant cousins while John Bennet was in prison. Grace was a friend for many years of Lady Betty Cotton, born Elizabeth Wigston, who married Sir Robert Cotton, 5th Baronet. They went to Hatfield together to visit the young Earl of Salisbury in 1700, 1702, and 1704 and bought lottery tickets together on September 6, 1731. Grace also became friendly with the family of Sir William Parsons of Langley, Buckinghamshire, 3rd Baronet, grandson of her aunt, Lady Catherine Clifton, her father's stepsister. The Parsons' only daughter Grace, born *c.* 1720, was her goddaughter

Furthermore, from the time of the law cases of 1703 and 1704, Grace Bennet laid claim to her own income. The Hatfield accounts show that starting in 1704 one tenant at least paid his rent to her not to her husband.[43]

---

[42] Hatfield House Archives, SFP 3/69/70, 1702, Bills 400; SFP 3/70–71, Bills 401.
[43] Hatfield House Archives, Accounts 78/5. John Bennet was paid between 1700 and 1703; Grace Bennet was paid in 1704–1705 and 1708–1712.

That meant that she would potentially have £3,000 a year in rental income. Since some of the accounts still show payments to John Bennet, whether she received all of her income is unclear. Certainly, with the death of Bennet in 1712, Grace gained full control of her half of the Bennet fortune not only the rent but also the real estate itself. Just as important, in 1713, with the death of her sister, Grace gained a life interest in her sister's half of the Bennet fortune as well. Grace's financial situation had improved dramatically. She was able to buy one of the most expensive townhouses on Albemarle Street, near Dover Street, from Sir Nicholas Morice, a relative of John Bennet, where her neighbors included one of the Duke of Marlborough's generals and noblemen like the Duke of Chandos.[44] Her coach was stabled in Grosvenor Mews.

Women were very active and often successful investors in London's new stock market.[45] With fortune in hand, Grace began to buy shares in the Bank of England, the East India Company, and the South Sea Company. Founded in 1694 in the aftermath of the Glorious Revolution, the bank offered long-term loans to the Crown, invaluable to William III for his wars with France, and secure shares for public investment, backed by parliament. It tended to attract Whig investors. The East India Company, founded in 1600, was the largest joint stock company. Its successful voyages to the East Indies attracted the interest of a larger public not just international merchants. Its stocks were therefore among those that began to be traded at the end of the seventeenth century in the nascent stock trading in Exchange Alley and the London coffee houses. In the early eighteenth century, the South Sea Company attracted the most attention. Its mission was to exploit South America and the slave trade. This was not a new British interest. Guyana adventures went back to the 1580s and Gilbert Morewood, Grace's grandfather, may have invested in the "Mayflower," a ship that participated in the Guinea trade in 1647.

---

[44] TNA, PROB11/653/319, Sept. 7, 1732, Will of Grace Bennet, Widow of St. Martin in the Fields, Middlesex. Grace paid the third highest tax on Albemarle Street. The Duke of Chandos purchased Albemarle House in 1710 and sold it in 1722. P. G. M. Dickson and J. V. Beckett, "The Finances of the Dukes of Chandos: Aristocratic Inheritance, Marriage, and Debt in Eighteenth Century England," *Huntington Library Quarterly*, 64, 3/4 (2001), 309–355. Sir Nicholas Morice, 2nd Baronet, sat for a Cornish borough between 1702 and 1726. History of Parliament, "Sir Nicholas Morice." His nephew, Nicholas Morice, Clerk of the Signet, who died in 1712, was also an MP.

[45] Anne Laurence, "Women Investors, 'That Nasty South Sea Affair,' and the Rage to Speculate in Early Eighteenth-Century England," *Accounting, Business, and Financial History*, 16, 2 (2006), 245–264; Ann M. Carlos and Larry Neal, "The Micro-Foundation of the Early London Capital Market: Bank of England Shareholders during and after the South Sea Bubble 1720–1725," *The Economic History Review*, 59, 3 (2006), 498–538.

Grace Bennet bought over 15,000 shares of stock, 5,000 in the Bank of England, 5,000 in the East India Company, and 5,250 in the South Sea Company. The spectacular collapse of the South Sea Company's share price after a spectacular rise in 1720 led to what was called the South Sea Bubble. While this purchase might be thought to have been a mistake, it is now clear that those who held onto their shares in the company did not lose much of their money.[46] The Hatfield accounts show that her 5,250 South Sea shares, worth 110 percent of their value at her death in 1732, continued to pay dividends for several years thereafter and were worth at least £4,718 in 1738.[47]

Grace was now so well off by October 31, 1719, her nephew, James Cecil, 5th Earl of Salisbury, wrote to her "concerning his demand upon his aunt's share of his grandfather Bennet's estate on account of his mother's portion." Clearly he was concerned in case Grace might think of leaving his share to others. By omitting any reference to Grace's son John, the letter makes clear that he had died; otherwise she would have left him her share of the inheritance.

Grace offered Cecil a piece of property worth £2,225 for his half of the inheritance, but Salisbury claimed that offer was £1,512 less than the £3,737 he was owed, based on the accounting of John Hoskins, Master in Chancery in 1692. At that time, Simon Bennet's personal estate amounted to £14,680-19-2. By 1712 there was £6,165-8-51/4. With interest, Salisbury's half now amounted to £3,737. Cecil claimed that Simon Bennet's estate did not have sufficient funds because of the "several bad securities on which his money was lent by him and his agents." It would be necessary therefore to sell real estate in order to provide the money, a process allowed by Simon Bennet's will. Nevertheless, emphasizing the good understanding between them, Salisbury offered to accept her land or waive his demand for the money provided Grace left all of the Bennet real estate to him and his heirs after her death. She agreed to his suggestion that she execute a legal document that all of Simon Bennet's real estate would go to the Earl of Salisbury and his children.[48] In the event, Grace outlived the 5th Earl. Because of her investments, she was able to leave his heirs even more than he wanted as well as providing legacies to other friends and relations.

---

[46] Julian Hoppit, "The Myths of the South Sea Bubble," *Transactions of the Royal Historical Society*, 12 (2002), 141–165; Hatfield House Archives, Accounts 94/10. In the years after her death, Grace Bennet's estate received dividends on her shares. By May 13, 1738, "Received on £4,275 Old South Sea Annuities £4000 being sold at 110 3/4 + 275 at 110 ¼, £4718 -4-3."

[47] Hatfield House Archives, Accounts 94/10.

[48] Hatfield House Archives, General 95/19; FP 10/217.

Women and Investment

Grace had held onto much of the real estate she inherited from her mother, father, and sister as well as making her own investments in property such as the Albemarle house. Grace's wealth escaped her husband's creditors because of Simon Bennet's trust and will. Now, as we have seen, like other elite women of the period, she invested in shares on the newly developing stock market.

Grace was part of a network of well-to-do women, many of them single or widowed, that stretched socially upward to the highest echelons of the town. In addition to Grace, two women in her circle illustrate the relationship between elite women and business. One of them, Eleanor Curzon (1691–1754), was the daughter of Nathaniel Curzon, 2nd Baronet, and sister of Sir Nathaniel Curzon, 4th Baronet, who owned Keddleston Hall and a great house in Queen's Street in Bloomsbury Square. The Curzons were second in wealth in Derbyshire only to the Dukes of Devonshire.[49] Eleanor Curzon was one of the executors of Grace Bennet's will and lived on George Street, near fashionable Hanover Square.

Eleanor secured an extraordinary legal victory when she sued the South Sea Company. She bought 1,000 shares of South Sea stock in 1720 as part of the third subscription. When the stock's price began to plummet, she sued the company to regain her initial investment. The company offered to repay only what the stock was then worth, a third of its original value. Eleanor Curzon, however, wanted all of her money back. She pointed out that that the clerk who took her money had mistakenly put down her name as Edward instead of Eleanor! The company countered that this was mere scribal error. Eleanor claimed that the wrong name invalidated the transaction. She sued in the Court of Exchequer and the judges decided in Eleanor's favor in November 1722. When the South Sea Company appealed the case to the House of Lords, they too decided in Eleanor's favor in March 1723. Eleanor Curzon got all of her money back with costs.[50] Women's

---

[49] *ODNB*, "Sir Nathanial Curzon 4th Baronet."

[50] See *English Reports*, House of Lords, Vols. 1, 4, Case 2, The South Sea Company, Appellant; Eleanor Curzon, Respondent [March 11, 1722], pp. 1092–1094, The Governor and Company of Merchants of Great Britain Trading to the South-Seas and Other Parts of America and for the Encouraging the Fishery, Appellants: Eleanor Curzon, Respondent: the Appellant's case; HLRO, Main Papers, HL/PO/JO/10/6/325, Nov. 17, 1722–Jan. 18, 1723; *HLJ: Vol. 22, 1722–1726*, pp. 37–63. South Sea Company versus Curzon; Dec. 18 - South Sea Company *v.* Curzon. a. Petition and Appeal of South Sea Company ... b. Answer of Eleanor Curzon, 4 February 1723 ... "It is Ordered and Adjudged, by the Lords Spiritual and Temporal in Parliament assembled, That the said Petition and Appeal be, and is hereby, dismissed this House; and that the Order of Dismission therein complained of be, and is hereby, affirmed." Feb. 4, 1723, This Day

experience in the use of the legal system now proved a useful tool in this case of buyer's remorse.

Grace Bennet also loaned money to her friends. The amounts usually were small, ranging from £10 to £60 or in one case a series of small loans amounting to £102.[51] There was, however, one exception. Lady Ann Chesshyre, who was one of the witnesses to Grace Bennet's will, borrowed amounts from her ranging from £200 to £600 over three years, from 1725 to 1728, totaling £2,600 with interest.[52] One of these sums seems to have been for an investment in shares; others were for other investments or loans. That moneylending was an element of the sentiment of friendship as well as business, appears in a letter Lady Ann Chesshyre wrote to Sarah, Duchess of Marlborough in the 1730s.

Lady F[rancis] Shirley informed me that when she was in town she had seen Lady Hinchingbook's [*sic*] house in Dover Street that is to be sold for £1500 ... She expressed herself so as she made me inwardly grieve I was not in a capacity to shew my friendship and I wish'd for the sake of so deserving a friend, what I never did for myself, a greater aflewence of fortune.[53]

Lady Ann's husband, Sir John Chesshyre, was a leading lawyer. During the reign of Queen Anne, he became a queen's sergeant and, under George I, in 1727, the king's first sergeant with precedence over all royal counsel. Having

the Answer of Eleanor Curzon, to the Petition and Appeal of the Governor and Company of Merchants of Great Britain trading to The South Seas, and other Parts of America, and for encouraging the Fishery, &c. was brought in. *HLJ: Vol. 22*, Jan. 28, 1723, pp. 60–76; Feb. 1723, pp. 1–10. *HLJ: Vol. 22*, March 11, 1723, pp. 76–84: The South Sea Company later successfully lobbied parliament to enact a law to prevent such grounds for a suit.

[51] For a discussion of women as moneylenders, see Amy Froide, *Never Married: Single Women in Early Modern England* (Oxford: Oxford University Press, 2005) and Judith Spicksley, "Usury Legislation, Cash and Credit: The Development of the Female Investor in the late Tudor and Stuart Periods," *The Economic History Review*, 61, 2 (May, 2008), 277–301.

[52] Hatfield House Archives, Accounts 90/8, Note for Lady Chesshyre with Interest for £500, March 8, 1725; Jan. 26, 1726, Note from Lady Chesshyre for £200, July 25, 1726; Note from Lady Chesshyre for £500, June 16, 1727; Note from Lady Chesshyre for £600, 14 May 1728; Note from Lady Chesshyre for £300, July 18, 1728; Note from Lady Chesshyre for £500; Total £2,600; When she borrowed £200 on Jan. 6, 1726, the receipt said "from Lady Chesshyre for £200 to buy East India Bonds"; on March 8, 1725, it read "Lady Chesshyre's Note for £500 to be put out for interest"; on July 25, 1726, "Lady Chesshyre's note for £500 to be put out for interest"; another said on June 16, 1727, "Lady Chesshyre Note for £600 and interest."

[53] BL, Add. Mss. 61477, Vol. 378, 1732–1738, Lady Ann Chesshyre to Sarah Duchess of Marlborough, f. 157, Tuesday morning Sept. 26, 1732 or 1738. Sir John Chesshyre died in 1738, possibly the date of Lady Ann's letter to the duchess. He established a library and left other bequests as well as leaving £20,000 for an estate to be purchased for Ann's use during her lifetime. Huntingdonshire Archives, Montagu family, Earls of Sandwich of Hinchingbrooke, Marriage Settlement, Hinch 1/12, March 13, 1740, refers to Lady Elizabeth Hinchingbrooke's former house on the west side of Dover Street.

earned £3,000 a year for many years, he decided to cut back on his case load, writing, "this Michaelmas Term I reduced my business and ceased to go into other courts as formerly, and confined my attendance on the business of the Court of Common Pleas, contenting to amuse myself with lesser business and smaller gain, being in November 1725 of the age of 63." His income then declined dramatically, averaging about £1,300 a year.[54] It is probably not a coincidence that Lady Ann began to borrow money from Grace Bennet in 1725, the year her husband's income dropped from £3,000 to £1,300. Yet Sir John Chesshyre died in 1738 a very wealthy man. David Lemmings notes "his fee book shows that he had lent £20,000 to Philip Stanhope, fourth earl of Chesterfield, and the *Gentleman's Magazine* claimed he left a personal estate of £100,000." In contrast to Frances and Grace Bennet and Eleanor Curzon who controlled their own monies, Lady Ann Chesshyre appears not to have had control of hers despite her husband's wealth. Nevertheless, she had paid back £2,100 with interest to Grace Bennet's estate by 1734. Grace's accounts also suggest that she might have been investing in stocks and loaning some of the money out for interest for Lady Ann Chesshyre, in short serving as a bank or brokerage for a woman who might not have been able to make those investments on her own.

Moneylending was not new and had long taken place among women below the elite. But as Anne Laurence, Ann Carlos, Amy Froide, and Rosemary O'Day have shown, elite women from the late seventeenth century on became more and more active in business as investors in the stock market and as depositors in banks.[55] Although her sister, the Countess of Salisbury, focused almost entirely on real estate, Grace Bennet had become a shrewd businesswoman with varied financial interests.

Fortune Transferred

The newspapers posted the news of Grace Bennet's death on September 7, 1732. The *London Evening Post* announced, "On Tuesday dy'd at her House in Albemarle Street, the Hon Mrs. Bennet, she was Great Aunt to the Right

[54] This quotation and paragraph are drawn from David Lemmings, "Sir John Chesshyre," *ODNB*; Robert Cole, "Feebook of Serjeant Sir John Chesshyre," *Notes and Queries*, 2nd ser. 7 (June 1859), 492–493.

[55] Anne Laurence, "The Emergence of a Private Clientele for Banks in the Early Eighteenth Century: Hoare's Bank and Some Women Customers," *The Economic History Review*, ns, 61, 3 (Aug. 2008), 565–568; Ann Carlos, "Women Investors in Early Capital Markets, 1720–1725," *Financial History Review*, 11, 2 (2004), 197–224; Rosemary O'Day, *Women's Agency in Early Modern Britain and the American Colonies: Patriarchy, Partnership and Patronage* (Harlow: Pearson Longman, 2007); Amy M. Froide, *Silent Partners: Women as Public Investors during Britain's Financial Revolution 1690–1750* (Oxford: Oxford University Press, 2016).

Figure 10.2 *Landscape view of Hatfield House c.* 1740, painter unknown. Reproduction by courtesy of the Marquess of Salisbury. Frances Bennet went to Hatfield as a young bride when she married James, 4th Earl of Salisbury, in 1683. It was home to her grandson, James, 6th Earl of Salisbury, who inherited the Bennet–Morewood fortune in 1732.

Hon. the Earl of Salisbury, and her Estate (which we hear is about 4000 l. per annum) goes to the said Earl."[56]

Marriages had created alliances; death now brought bequests. Four days later Ann, Dowager Countess of Salisbury, broke the news to her son, the nineteen-year-old 6th Earl of Salisbury, that his great-aunt, Grace Bennet, had died.[57] Although Lawrence Stone stated that Grace Bennet died intestate, in fact she left an extensive will.[58] Ann sent glad tidings of the fortune that Grace had left the Cecils. In addition to real estate worth £3,000 per annum, Grace had provided the young earl with her house on Albemarle Street and £1,000, and made him coheir of the rest of her estate after the payment of bequests. His younger brother received a legacy composed of land worth £200 per annum (which at twenty years' purchase might amount to £4,000), plus £4,000 in movables and a pearl necklace worth £1,000,

[56] *London Evening Post*, Sept. 7, 1732.
[57] Hatfield House Archives, Box T/111, FP 11/1–3, Anne, Dowager Countess of Salisbury, to the 6th Earl of Salisbury, Sept. 11, 1732. Anne one of the daughters of the Earl of Thanet founded a charity school for the education of forty girls between the ages of nine and sixteen in the same year that Grace Bennet died.
[58] Lawrence Stone, *Family and Fortune: Studies in Aristocratic Finance in the Sixteenth and Seventeenth Centuries* (Oxford: Clarendon Press, 1973), p. 116.

while his sister Anne received £1,000. Although noting that the younger Cecils were omitted, the dowager countess acknowledged that Grace "has been extremely generous" and urged the earl immediately to go into mourning as her chief heir.[59] Grace had certainly kept her word to the 5th Earl. Grace's legacy to the 6th Earl of Salisbury of £1,000 was to be given to him at age eighteen with 4 percent interest beginning at her death. The lands she left to William Cecil in Leicester, Stafford, and Derby had belonged to "my late dear mother." His legacy of £4,000 was to be paid to him at age twenty. In the meantime it was to accrue interest at 4 percent.

Written in 1730, Grace Bennet's will provided her own voice. It was elaborate where her sister Frances's will was brief. Grace asked to be buried privately in Westminster Abbey and requested no more than four mourning coaches, twice as many as her sister Frances had had. While Frances had specified that the funeral cost no more than £50, twenty years later Grace's cost £300. Grace remembered family and friends in detail while Frances turned to charity.

As well as providing generously for the Cecils, Grace remembered members of her extended family who were descended from her father's stepsister Lady Clifton and her mother's sister Lady Gresley, especially single cousins and young people. In particular, she made her cousin Catherine Parsons, Lady Clifton's granddaughter, her chief heir after the Cecils. "A spinster" who lived at Mile End, Catherine Parsons received £2,000, Grace's house in Albemarle Street for eight months, her movables, and half of the remainder of her estate to be shared with the 6th Earl of Salisbury. Were none of the Cecils to survive, the remainder was allocated between Catherine Parsons and Lee Gresley, son of Grace's cousin, Sir Thomas Gresley.

With her parents, her husband, her son, and all her sisters dead, Grace Bennet made substantial bequests to godchildren and cousins. Sir William Parsons, Baronet, brother of Catherine Parsons, and his wife Frances, sister of Mary Dutton, Duchess of Northumberland, had named their only daughter Grace. Grace Bennet, her godmother, left her £300 at age eighteen, or when she married, and her brother another £200. She left Sir William and his mother £50 each. Barbara Clerke, whose father Sir Talbot Clerke, 4th Baronet, was dead, was another godchild to whom Grace left the handsome sum of £700.[60] In these cases these legacies were to accrue interest from three

---

59 Hatfield House Archives, Box T/111, FP 11/1–3, Sept. 11 1732, Anne, Dowager Countess of Salisbury, to the 6th Earl of Salisbury.

60 TNA, PROB11/653/319, Will of Grace Bennet, Widow of St. Martin in the Fields, Middlesex, Sept. 7, 1732. Hatfield House Archives, Box T/111, FP 11/1–3, Sept. 11, 1732. The lands left to William Cecil included Overseal and Netherseal in Leicestershire, lands in Derby and Staffordshire, estates that had belonged to her mother Grace.

months after her death to be paid semiannually for their benefit. Grace also included a provision in her will requiring parents not to interfere with these bequests to these young people. Once the girls reached eighteen and the boys reached twenty, their receipts were to be "plenary and sufficient" for the receipt of the money. "And their respective parents or relations do not interfere or concern themselves therein."

Grace also remembered the Gresleys, leaving her cousin Sir Thomas Gresley, "son of my late aunt Dame Frances Greisley" £100 and his son Lee £500 "on account of his being my near relation and for the trouble of being one of my Executors." She gave her other executors Eleanor Curzon and Sir Robert Langley £100 pounds each.

As for her household, Grace left £1,000 and a watch to Martha Eyres, her servant and cousin, as well as "all my clothes wearing apparel, lace, and linen, and all the furniture of the chamber wherein she lyes." Grace remembered several servants including her cook and coachman in her will. She left £20 each for the poor of the parish of St. George Hanover Square and the parish of Calverton and Beachampton, Buckinghamshire, her parents' home. To her household and "menial" servants not named in the will, she gave one-quarter year's wages and a suit of mourning.

Grace Bennet had managed successfully to keep the estate inherited from her mother, father, and sister as well as her own investments in real estate, movables, and stock from her husband and her husband's creditors. Grace's wealth may have escaped them because of family trusts, wills, and a series of court decisions, including Bennet *v.* Davis 1725, that held that a wife was able to receive separate property from her father even without trustees.[61]

When Grace Bennet left her land and half of the remainder of her movables to the 6th Earl of Salisbury, three generations of money made in the East India Company, imports and exports, the lead trade, the property market, and finance swelled the treasury of the Cecils and helped to reestablish the financial footing of the Earls of Salisbury. At her death Grace Bennet had achieved that fortune and status she had not always enjoyed earlier in life. Even as Benjamin Morrett continued to sue John Bennet's estate in the 1730s and 1740s, the Hatfield accountants kept track of the income from Grace Bennet's cash, shares, and rents from the extensive Bennet properties and her household goods too.

In her will, Grace stated "all jewelry, plate and China Ware, household goods, pictures, linen and other furniture" found in her house on Albemarle

---

[61] Peere Williams, *English Chancery Reports*, 2 P. Wms. 316, cited in Susan Staves, *Married Women's Separate Property in England, 1660–1883* (Cambridge, MA: Harvard University Press, 1990), p. 133.

Street was to be shared equally between Catherine Parsons and the Earl of
Salisbury. To that end almost immediately, the Hatfield men of business
inventoried her assets, drawing up "A Particular of the Money, Jewels,
Trinkets and other Valuable Things found in the House of Mrs. Grace
Bennet deceased in Albemarle Street, 6th September 1732."[62]

Grace filled her house with rich and attractive material goods, the products
of Britain's global trade. They included fashionable items such as a chocolate
pot, a teakettle, a coffee pot, jewelry, and good furniture. Anne, Countess of
Salisbury, wife of the 5th Earl, bought items from Grace's estate totaling £487
including three large "Wainscott Press," that is clothes presses with paneling,
four chairs and tables, a chafing dish, cupboard and dresser, and twenty
pounds of chocolate; Catherine Parsons, Grace's cousin and co-beneficiary
of the estate, took a chest and box, a settee, bed and bedding, a repeating clock,
two writing boxes, her own picture, a tea table, China, and a tea kettle. There
were few debts other than the bills from her doctor, apothecary, and nurse that
arrived after her death.

Along with her will, the Hatfield accounts underline three things about
Grace Bennet's wealth: First, a large portion of her wealth was in shares,
second she kept a substantial amount of money in cash like her mother and
thus had substantial capital to loan. In the house on Albemarle Street she had
£1,138 in cash on hand. Not unlike her mother, Grace kept even more cash
in the family house at Calverton, Buckinghamshire. It amounted to £3,700
in all. (Thus, the Earl of Salisbury's half of ready money found in the house
at Calverton was £1,866-3-10 1/2).[63] Third, she had been extremely generous to the Cecils. In addition to the real estate, which they expected, she left
them more than half her personal estate, which was hers to do with as
she liked.

One account laid it out clearly. It estimated that Grace's legacies amounted to
£11,160, which, along with gifts to servants, debts, and the cost of her funeral,
totaled £12,160. Her assets included £14,910 in stock; Lady Chesshyre's debt
of £2,600 which the accountants were not sure had been paid; bank notes of
£1,450, material goods including coaches worth £1,400 and outstanding rent of
£1200, amounting altogether to over £22,000. Subtracting her legacies, the
remainder of her estate amounted to just over £10,000 to be divided in half
between the 6th Earl of Salisbury and Catherine Parsons along with the legacies
they had already received from Grace.[64]

Thus, the young Earl of Salisbury would inherit £6,000 in cash and
property worth at least £3,000 a year from Grace as well as her house in

[62] Hatfield House Archives, Accounts 90/8.   [63] Hatfield House Archives, Accounts 43/6.
[64] Hatfield House Archives, Accounts 92/10.

town. As we have seen, his brother William had been left another £4,000, a pearl necklace, and property in three counties, and their sister £1,000. The Hatfield accountants tracked the income from Grace's estate for the next seven years. Some bills were outstanding, such as "Dower out of Mr. Bennet's estate not yet settled." Their initial figures did not include Grace's estate at Calverton in Buckinghamshire inherited from her mother. In the "Account of the Estate of Mrs. Grace Bennet deceased" in addition to addressing the ready money found there, the accountant listed the animals sold, horses, black cattle, sheep, hogs, as well as the corn, hay, and wool, and outstanding rents that made up the value of the Bennets' old house.[65]

The arrangement struck fifty years before by Simon Bennet the financier and his wife Grace Bennet the elder with James, 3rd Earl of Salisbury, had come to fruition. At the same time, the Bennet heiresses had achieved their own aspirations as well as those of the founders of the Bennet and More-wood fortune when they had put their wealth into marriage portions. But Frances and Grace had outlived their teenage marriages and enjoyed the cosmopolitan lives they desired.

Conclusion

In the early eighteenth century, the Bennet sisters achieved significant independence and power rather than the violence, unhappiness, and death imagined by Hogarth in *Marriage A-la-Mode*. But it was not gained easily. Efforts to control women's agency took place not only through marital arrangements and legal controls on women's property but also through contemporary comment. Ridicule about the body identified lust and disease with independence. Still, these limits failed to curtail the lives of Frances and Grace Bennet. Shaped by the women themselves through their own notable choices after their marriages, their lives were ultimately lived not only in the country house but in London, spa towns, and on the continent, while their values were molded by international travel, metropolitan and cosmopolitan interests. The Bennet sisters demonstrate the importance of changing our focus on heiresses as instruments of property transfer to women in their own right. When their marriages ended, Frances and Grace spent their long widowhood in London. The agency exercised by both sisters points not to the rise of eighteenth-century domesticity and femininity but to independent lives on the Grand Tour and in the fashionable capital.

With Grace's death the merchant fortune made in international trade, property, and finance now came into the hands of the teenaged 6th Earl of

---

[65] Hatfield House Archives, Accounts 43/6.

Salisbury. For Grace herself rank and fortune had its privileges. Thus, the *London Evening Post* reported, "Last night the Corpse of the Lady Bennet, Great Aunt to the present Earl of Salisbury, was carry'd from her House in Albemarle-Street, and interred in Westminster Abbey."[66] There Grace joined her long dead sister, Viscountesss Latimer. Seven years later in 1739 as the Hatfield accountants closed the books on Grace Bennet's estate, they noted that Lady Anne Chesshyre still owed interest on one of her loans.

[66] *London Evening Post*, Sept. 1732.

Conclusion

In 1738, even as the Hatfield men of business were winding up Grace Bennet's estate, William Hogarth painted two pictures, *The Western Family* and *The Strode Family*, that had some connections to the Bennets. Indeed, over two decades between 1720 and 1747 Hogarth, artist and moralist, commented on issues that mattered to the Bennet family, from the founder of the fortune, Sir Thomas, to his great-granddaughter, Grace. In *Industry and Idleness*, Hogarth contrasted the idle apprentice, who wound up on the gallows, with the industrious apprentice, a moral, hardworking church attender who made a good marriage and reached the position of Lord Mayor of London, rather like the philanthropic Sir Thomas Bennet more than a century before. *Marriage A-la-Mode* strongly attacked the practice of arranged marriages symbolized by the union of the daughter of a wealthy London alderman and a debt-ridden earl, not unlike the marriages of the Bennet heiresses in the 1670s and 1680s. In *The Emblematical Print on the South Sea Scheme*, the artist satirized the South Sea Company in whose shares Grace Bennet, her friend Eleanor Curzon, and many others had invested.[1] Hogarth thus addressed issues that were both timely, such as the stock market crash, and traditional, such as social mobility through apprenticeship and arranged marriage that had taken place in the previous century and even earlier.

In the 1730s, Hogarth turned to "conversation pieces," scenes of domestic hospitality and luxury, in which he portrayed well-to-do families at the tea table accompanied by their relatives and friends.[2] The arrival of tea in England from Asia dated back to the 1650s or before and, in the home,

---

[1] William Hogarth, *The South Sea Scheme, c.* 1721, Etching and engraving on paper; *Marriage A-la-Mode*, 1743–1745, series of six oil paintings, National Gallery, London; *Industry and Idleness*, 1747, a series of twelve engravings.

[2] Ching-Jung Chen, "Tea Parties in Early Georgian Conversation Pieces," *The British Art Journal*, 10, 1 (Spring/Summer 2009), 30–39.

tea was served with sugar, an import that burgeoned with the transportation of Africans to West Indies plantations around the same time. Through luxurious accessories, including the sugar bowl or sugar chest, tea caddy, silver or porcelain teapot, silver salver, and tea table, the well-to-do exhibited their cultivation and wealth and placed England's global trade on display. It may be recalled that in 1662 Grace Bennet the elder had requested the largest silver sugar chest that the goldsmiths in London had on hand and reminded her husband Simon that his mother, Lady Finch, had had one, too. Whether Lady Finch and Grace Bennet were using it to sweeten tea, sugar wine, or for other purposes, the handsome piece took its place on their table or buffet. Seventy years later, Grace Bennet the younger had a tea table and teakettle that her heir Catherine Parsons bought from Grace's estate. Tea was moving from an exotic import to a necessity.

Hogarth's portrait *The Western Family* (see Plate 14) presents Thomas Western just returned from hunting. His wife stands beside him as tea is served on a silver table to his family, a clergyman, and a child, in a handsome room filled with paintings and a keyboard instrument. Thomas Western was the great-grandson of Thomas Western, the grocer and government contractor to William III, who lent over £5,000 to Grace Bennet's husband John secured by a mortgage on Great Abington, Cambridgeshire. In 1697 Thomas Western took over most of the property. His son Maximillian completed foreclosure proceedings in 1709, throwing the Bennets off their Cambridgeshire land and making Great Abington their family's residence.[3] The Thomas Western who was about to drink tea in Hogarth's portrait was Maximillian's younger cousin.

I

Women of Fortune has traced a story of fortunes and families over 150 years. Sir Thomas Bennet and Gilbert Morewood, younger sons of minor gentry who went to London to make their way, did not become part of a new middle class. Instead, the economic expansion of the late sixteenth and seventeenth centuries, in which they participated, helped shape a new Stuart elite that blended land, finance, and international trade. The Bennets and Morewoods, who became part of that new elite, exemplified this phenomenon. They also displayed the use of large marriage portions to aid their families' aspiration to move into the aristocracy.

The Bennet–Morewood fortune was made from the cloth trade, Crown finance, moneylending, rents, the East India Company, and the American

[3] VCH, *Cambridge and the Isle of Ely*, Vol. VI, pp. 3–19, "Parishes: Great and Little Abington."

interloping trade. Later, Simon Bennet's mortgage, loan, and rental business, based on his large property portfolio, increased their fortune through an expansive form of private banking. John Bennet's agricultural and real estate losses appeared to have reduced their wealth. By 1732, however, Grace Bennet, the last of the family, invested in shares. She left land yielding £3,000 a year as well as her London house to her great nephew James, 6th Earl of Salisbury, and property worth £200 a year to his brother. In addition, she had an estate of almost £23,000. She left legacies of £11,160 with a further £10,000 to be divided between the residual heirs, Salisbury and Catherine Parsons.[4] The Bennet fortune was key in paying off debts of the 3rd and 4th Earls and adding new properties to the Hatfield estate.[5]

Three generations of Bennet and Morewood women, who inherited the merchant and financial fortune, demonstrate the permeability of the English elite in the early modern period through their marriages into the aristocracy and the nobility. Furthermore, Elizabeth, Lady Finch, her daughters, Viscountess Conway and Lady Clifton, her daughter-in-law Grace and Lady Gresley, and her three granddaughters, Viscountess Latimer, the Countess of Salisbury, and Grace Bennet, belie historiographical claims about heiresses that have narrowly objectified them as transmitters of property. They also challenge views of women that omit them from the historical record altogether or picture them as victims.

Elizabeth, a rich City widow, outwitted her many suitors, and through her two marriages, her negotiations with courtiers, and lawsuits protected the interests of her son Simon Bennet, and her two daughters, Lady Clifton and Anne, Vicountess Conway. The well-educated Lady Clifton used the law to fight to protect her property and to provide marriage portions through a parliamentary statute for her daughters despite the debts left by her husband. Her sister Ann Conway, a brilliant philosopher who corresponded with important thinkers of the period, wrote an analytical study of Hobbes and Spinoza. Frances, Lady Gresley, daughter of Gilbert Morewood, the East Indian merchant, was not a philosopher but knew her own mind as she sought to place her sons in London apprenticeships, marry off her daughters, preserve her own timber rights, and control her family. Even her sister Grace Bennet the elder, Simon Bennet's wife, murdered by the local butcher, turned out to have had a strong sense of her own property rights which she pursued against her minister, her steward, and her neighbors. She questioned the tradition of tithes and its expansion to new types of

---

[4] Hatfield House Archives, Accounts 92/10.
[5] Lawrence Stone, *Family and Fortune: Studies in Aristocratic Finance in the Sixteenth and Seventeenth Centuries* (Oxford: Clarendon Press, 1973), p. 158.

agriculture in the seventeenth century. Grace's daughters too traced new paths for themselves.

Frances, Countess of Salisbury, made the best of her arranged marriage to the 4th Earl. After his death, she lived in London and then made an extraordinary four-year journey through Western Europe, arguably the longest Grand Tour of any aristocratic woman in the seventeenth century. Her cultural interests in art, architecture, and music are reflected in her detailed accounts, while her long romance with Major George Jocelyn was significant enough to be recorded in diplomatic dispatches. Back in London, she used her role as executor of the Salisbury estates to create Cecil Street on the Strand and to establish a new home for herself in Dover House in Mayfair. At her death her half of the Bennet estate passed to her sister Grace.

Grace survived a bad marriage and financial distress to become an investor in shares and moneylender to her aristocratic friends. Grace Bennet's funeral was neither as large as her great-grandfather Sir Thomas Bennet's in Cheapside in 1627 nor as lavish as her mother's at Hatfield House in 1694. Nevertheless, its setting in Westminster Abbey and her rank as aunt to the 6th Earl of Salisbury reinforced her secure position in the early Hanoverian social elite despite a mother who was murdered and a husband who died in debtors' prison.

The Bennet women's stories celebrate independence, education, curiosity, individual choice, and ambition for both married women and widows. They and many of their contemporaries overcame obstacles of youthful marriages to forge their own paths. Anne Conway had to choose how to pursue her life as a philosopher while married and suffering constantly with debilitating headaches. The Countess of Salisbury had to carry on her European journeys in the midst of war and Grace Bennet had to sue her husband for years for her own rental income. Advantaged by having money, they preserved their fortune for the next generation.

Unsung, the Bennet women's stories provide a strikingly different picture of women, social relations, legal rights, and the economy over the seventeenth and early eighteenth centuries. They confirm that coverture could be less restrictive in practice, even if not in theory. Opportunities for women expanded along with the growth of the English economy. Women could hold property separate from their husbands if their fathers established trusts for them. Nevertheless, as we have seen, as the Bennet and Morewood women got richer, their age of marriage got younger, so that by the 1670s, Simon Bennet's youngest daughter married the Earl of Salisbury at the age of thirteen. Yet by the late seventeenth century, widows did not remarry in the same numbers as they had in the sixteenth century. The Bennet and Morewood women have much to tell us about changes in the seventeenth-century English economy and society and women's role in it.

By the early eighteenth century, London was the largest city in Europe and its financial hub. The capital grew in population from 1550 to 1750 from approximately 80,000 to 700,000.[6] It also played a continuing role in the lives of the elite, including the Bennets and Morewoods. Sir Thomas and his wife Mary Bennet lived in the City in St. Olave Old Jewry, and Elizabeth and Richard Bennet took over their City house while they also had a house in Gloucestershire. Sir Simon and Elizabeth, Lady Bennet, lived in Beachampton, Buckinghamshire, a house later inherited by Simon Bennet who also maintained an office in London. As the City grew westward so the Bennets moved too. With her second marriage, Elizabeth Finch moved to Kensington House in the village of Kensington. Her daughter Anne often stayed with her even after she was married to Viscount Conway whose home was at Ragley Warwickshire. After she married, Lady Anne's sister, Lady Clifton, lived at Clifton Hall, Nottinghamshire, but once she was widowed she lived six months a year in Bloomsbury. Similarly, Lady Finch's granddaughter, the Countess of Salisbury, lived in London as a widow, in Dover House on Dover Street, while the countess's sister lived on Albemarle Street, in Mayfair, one street away. Lady Gresley spent most of her time in the country in Drakelowe, Derbyshire, but she wished to place her sons in London as apprentices and apparently yearned for the City as she maintained her decades-long correspondence with the Mayor of London, Sir John Moore.

Women, whether married or widowed, were able to use their assets in new ways and for new purposes. From Lady Finch, whose handsome widow's portion was much in demand, to the Bennet sisters, two of whom were buried in Westminster Abbey, the women of the Bennet and Morewood families sought not only to protect their property rights but also to extend them. Lady Finch's prenuptial agreement with Sir Heneage Finch called for £10,000 in land for her, the guarantee of the varied assets she brought into the marriage, and the protection of her young son's inheritance. She negotiated for Simon Bennet's wardship with one of Charles I's courtiers and after Heneage's death added to the property adjoining Kensington House. As executor of her husband's will, Elizabeth, Lady Bennet sought to ensure that University College, Oxford would commemorate his major endowment and carry out his wishes.

Lady Gresley not only insisted on her timber rights but also defended herself in two suits brought against her by her son. He claimed that because she was under coverture during her marriage, any money she had saved was due to the estate. He also argued that, after her husband's death, Frances had

[6] "People in Place: Families, Household, and Housing in London 1550-1720," Project 2003–2006, The Institute of Historical Research, London (www.history.ac.uk/cmh/pip/index.html).

kept gold, books, and lumber that also belonged to the estate. Despite the wide-ranging demands of her son, Lady Gresley agreed only to return some books and heritage wood. Grace Bennet used her family's fortune made in international trade and mortgages to invest in shares in the Bank of England, the East India Company, and the South Sea Company. She also loaned money from the considerable cash she had on hand.

As we have seen, like other well-to-do contemporaries, the Bennet and Morewood women owned luxurious material objects and some aspired to an aristocratic lifestyle. Lady Finch had Kensington House, living there with her family for over thirty years. Devoted to her daughters, Lady Finch left her very rich son Simon a diamond ring, but she divided her estate between her two married daughters and forbade their husbands from having control over the monies. Her daughter, Lady Clifton, who focused on her children's advancement, not only raised portions for her daughters through a private act of parliament but also tried to provide for their education with Lady Diana Bruce while optimistically requesting that her son marry the daughter of the Duke of Newcastle. Lady Gresley used the strict Calvinist language of her upbringing in her letters to Sir John Moore even as she requested a pearl ring that she heard that he wanted to give her. Her sister, Grace Bennet senior, wanted fine gold coins from Simon Bennet's business and was quoted in a lawsuit as saying that she would rather let the fruit of her orchard rot than pay her tithes to William Carpender.

Frances, Countess of Salisbury presented herself in portraits, both as a newly married young woman and as a grieving young widow. She loved foreign travel, spent more than £11,000 during her four years in Europe between 1699 and 1701, and, once home, was willing to give up the guardianship of her child if she could return to Europe. When that proved impossible, she surrounded herself in her London house with the elegant and the new, including Indian paintings on her handsome staircase. Frances's sister Grace, with her well-furnished and expensive house on Albemarle Street, identified herself with her high-ranking circle of women friends and had warm relations with her extended family including her godchildren and her nephew, the 5th Earl of Salisbury. At the same time, the Bennet women in the third generation continued their connections to relations and friends in the City.

Women of Fortune began in the middle of Queen Elizabeth's reign in 1570 before the Armada; it ends in the reign of George II and the rule of Walpole in 1739. In 1570 England had no transatlantic colonies. By 1739 Britain had a global trading empire, North American colonies, and control of several islands in the Caribbean. We have seen how merchant wealth made in international trade and finance was transferred to members of the nobility, some debt-ridden, through strategic investment in upwardly mobile marriages. England's social and political elite now included those who made their money in the City.

At the same time, *Women of Fortune* has told a series of stories about woman who used their mercantile fortunes and their positions as heiresses to exercise their independence despite a set of legal and social structures intended to contain them. It is clear, however, that several of these women did not control their own marital choices despite the contemporary circulation of ideas of companionate marriage. The arranged marriage of the thirteen-year-old Frances Bennet to the 4th Earl of Salisbury may have gratified the aspirations of her parents but left her consigned to a foolish man. When Grace Bennet eloped with her cousin John Bennet, it left her married to an incompetent landowner who mortgaged her land for personal loans. These marriages ended only with the deaths of their husbands although, once John Bennet was arrested, Grace was unable or refused to help get him out of prison. Violence against women did not disappear because of the growth in women's property rights and agency. In the case of Grace Bennet the elder, because she was unprotected, her wealth may have attracted her murderer.

II

What happened to the Morewoods and the Bennets and their kin after our story closes in 1739? The London Morewoods who descended from Gilbert Morewood's stepdaughter Frances and Peter Salmon appear to have stayed in London. The Yorkshire Morewoods remained minor gentry, but the Derbyshire Morewoods of Alfreton Hall became wealthy after finding coal on their property. George Romney painted their portraits in the late eighteenth century. Sir Thomas Bennet's older brother Richard had many descendants, who included Sir John Bennet, the civil law judge who was impeached in 1621, many Members of Parliament, in addition to the Earl of Arlington and the Earls of Tankerville. The Gresleys continued to serve in parliament. Drakelowe, the Gresleys' home, remained in the family until 1927 when it was sold at auction. Sir Nigel Gresley, the famous engineer, was a member of a cadet branch of the family. George Jocelyn, ultimately a brigadier general, married but his line died out by the end of the seventeenth century. His older brother became ancestor to the Earls of Roden. Catherine Parsons, granddaughter of Lady Clifton and Grace Bennet's cousin, shared in the remainder of Grace Bennet's estate. Catherine's niece, Grace Parsons, was Grace Bennet's goddaughter, and her nephew William Parsons became a highwayman, hanged in 1751. The Cecils, Earls of Salisbury, paid off many of their debts with their marriage to Frances Bennet, and the Bennet inheritance in 1732 put their finances on a more secure footing, which has lasted to the present.

As we have seen, there were a few paintings of the Bennet women. These include Mary Taylor, wife of Sir Thomas Bennet, by Hieronymus Custodis (see Plate 2), her daughter-in-law, Elizabeth Ingram, wife of Sir Simon Bennet (see Plate 1), Frances, Countess of Salisbury, as a young woman by Willem Wissing and as a widow by Godfrey Kneller (see Plate 12), and Anne, Countess of Salisbury, by Charles Jervas (see Plate 15). There is another portrait. Frances, Countess of Salisbury's granddaughter, Lady Anne Cecil, was left £1,000 by the countess's sister, Grace Bennet, in 1732. Lady Anne married William Strode in 1736. After they returned from Europe, William commissioned Hogarth to paint *The Strode Family* to celebrate their marriage, their travels, and the impending birth of their first son (see Plate 16).[7]

The Strode Family is a conversation piece showing the couple having tea with Colonel Strode, and William's European traveling companion Dr. Arthur Smyth.[8] It reflects several of the themes discussed earlier in the book. First, their marriage displays the continuing connection between City and country and the integration of land and trade in England's social and political elite. Lady Anne Cecil, sister to the 6th Earl of Salisbury, did not marry a nobleman, a baronet, or a knight. She married a rich country gentleman whose father, Samuel Strode, was a member of the Barber Surgeons of London and represented the South Sea Company and the Bank of England.

Samuel Strode, won £5,000, the largest prize, in the lottery of 1712, a lottery that Frances, Countess of Salisbury, may also have invested in. With his winnings Strode purchased a country house in Ponsbourne, Hertfordshire, near Hatfield in 1718.[9] Lady Anne's grandmother, Frances Bennet, had married into the nobility when she married the 4th Earl of Salisbury; in contrast Lady Anne married into recently arrived country gentry with roots in the City.[10] The Strodes nevertheless quickly became part of the political and social elite. William Strode was elected to parliament in 1740, where he served until 1755.

The Strode Family also displays the couple's cultivation and refinement and the expanding taste for the Grand Tour. Lady Anne's grandmother Frances spent four years in Europe. Her son, the 5th Earl of Salisbury, spent time on the Grand Tour as part of his education. William Strode spent two

---

[7] Their son, William Strode, was born on July 23, 1738.
[8] Elizabeth Einberg and Judy Egerton, *The Age of Hogarth: British Painters Born 1675–1709* (London: Tate Gallery Collections, 1988).
[9] History of Parliament Online, "William Strode."
[10] She had two sisters, one married the 2nd Earl of Egmont, and the other remained unmarried.

years in France, Italy, and the Low Countries between 1730 and 1732 instead of going to university, and the Strodes went to Europe on their honeymoon. Hogarth includes Italian paintings on the wall in *The Strode Family* to represent the art they would have seen.

Finally, as in *The Western Family* (see Plate 14), Hogarth presents the Strode family having tea. Among the luxury accessories on the tea table is a sugar bowl, a reminder again of Grace Bennet's request for a sugar chest. More prominent are a porcelain teapot and, on the floor, a large tea caddy. This tea caddy, however, is a real artifact belonging to the Strodes. It remained in the Strode family until 1930.[11] Along with civility and refinement, *The Strode Family* celebrates wealth created in City business now transmuted into country property and aristocratic aspirations realized.

The Cecils did not forget the Bennet name. In 1789, fifty years after Grace Bennet's estate had been accounted for, the 1st Marquess of Salisbury, son of the 6th Earl of Salisbury to whom Grace Bennet had left the bulk of the Bennet fortune, and the Marchioness, a leading eighteenth-century social and political figure, named their second daughter Emily Anne Bennet Elizabeth Cecil. Emily Anne married William Nugent, 1st Marquess of Westmeath, in 1812. Although women's property rights had expanded in practice, coverture still remained common law doctrine and divorce remained restricted. In the case of Lady Emily Cecil, years of marital violence and deprivation by her husband were followed by separations and reconciliation. Finally, she sued Westmeath for divorce, claiming cruelty and denial of food and maintenance. Grace Bennet had made a similar claim about her husband John. In Lady Emily's case, her maid testified that in Ireland, early in their marriage, Westmeath had refused her even her own pin money and that in addition she was often unable to send for tea and sugar. Westmeath beat her on several occasions, once while she was eight months pregnant. The issues in Westmeath *v.* Westmeath included whether or not her reconciliation with the violent Westmeath invalidated her separation agreement and provision for maintenance and custody of their daughter. The ecclesiastical court in 1825 ordered her to return to her husband while a common law court decision in 1827 decided that her separation agreement was void because the couple had reconciled. In the end, however, Lady Emily won her divorce, and her deed of maintenance was upheld in 1831.[12] The outcome of

---

[11] Chen, "Tea Parties in Early Georgian Conversation Pieces," 30–39.

[12] Lawrence Stone, *Broken Lives, Separation and Divorce in England 1660–1887* (Oxford: Oxford University Press, 1993), pp. 284–344; Emily Anne Bennet Elizabeth Nugent, Marchioness of Westmeath, *A Narrative of the Case of the Marchioness of Westmeath* (London: James Ridgeway, 1857), pp. 13, 16.

Westmeath v. Westmeath ultimately contributed to the passage of the Custody of Infants Act of 1839 and the Matrimonial Causes Act allowing women to divorce for cruelty in 1857. This statute also gave married women control of their own property even while separated.[13]

Earlier, the Bennet and Morewood women had turned to the law to uphold their rights. Elizabeth Bennet made a prenuptial agreement with her second husband, Sir Heneage Finch; Lady Frances Clifton sued William Sacheverell over his accounts; Grace Bennet the elder defended her orchard against her tithe-seeking minister; Grace Bennet the younger successfully sued her husband for her rents; the Countess of Salisbury, as executor, sued Simon Bennet's debtors; Lady Gresley defended her right to her timber and her portion of her husband's estate against her own son. They did so not only as widows but also as wives. Success did not always come easily or completely. It was a fight that continued into the nineteenth century. Neither Lady Emily's divorce in *Westmeath v. Westmeath* nor the Matrimonial Causes Act of 1857 settled the issue of married women's property rights. Even the Married Women's Property Act of 1882 left questions unanswered.[14] Instead, over centuries, in each generation, women like the Bennets and Morewoods fought for their rights for themselves, their children, and their families within the interstices of a decaying system of coverture and the patriarchal claims that upheld it.

---

[13] Act of the Parliament of the United Kingdom, 20 & 21 Victoria, c. 85, 1857. Amy Louise Erickson, *Women and Property in Early Modern England* (New York: Routledge, 1993, 1995, 2002). On nineteenth-century divorce law and literature, see Kelly Hager, *Dickens and the Rise of Divorce* (New York: Routledge, 2010); Mary L. Shanley, *Feminism, Marriage, and the Law in Victorian England, 1850–1895* (Princeton, NJ: Princeton University Press, 1989).

[14] Act of the Parliament of the United Kingdom, 45 & 46 Victoria, c. 75, 1882.

Hatfield House Accounts 92/10 Computation of Mrs. Bennet's Personal Estate

"Mrs. Bennet by her will gave"

> To the Earl of Salisbury £1,000
> To William Cecil Esq. £4,000 and the Pearl Necklace
> To Lady Anne Cecil £1,000
> To Master John Parsons £200
> Miss Grace Parsons £300
> Miss Barbara Clarke £700
> Catherine Parsons £2,000
> Thomas Griesley £100
> Lee Griesley £500
> Sir Robert Lowley £100
> Mrs. Curson £100
> Lady Parsons £50
> Sir William Parsons £50
> Mrs Martha Eyres £1,000
> To Sir Georges Parish and Beachampton
> £20 a piece to the poor

$$£11,160$$

To the servants a years wages and for mourning about	£ 200	
The Funeral about	£ 300	£1,000
Servants wages and Debts owing	£ 500	
	£12,160	

"Computation of Mrs. Bennet's Personal Estate"

5600 Bank Stocks at 150 per cent	£ 8,400
500 India Stock at 158 per cent	£ 790
5200 South Sea Annuities at 110 percent	£ 5,720
	£14,910

My Lady Chessyre's Notes uncertain whether all is paid £2,600
Bank Notes £1,450

In Cash in Several parcels	£	120
	£	1,330
Notes that are good about	£	130
Plate trinkets and other little things	£	500
Household goods, linen, horses		
coaches, other things about	£	1,400
Arrears of Rent	£	1,200

	£22,190
To be paid	− 12,160
	£10,030

Dower out of Mr Bennet estate not yet settled.

Bibliography

Manuscript Sources

Arundel Castle

Arundel Castle Mss. MD 1514.

British Library

Add. Charter 6221, Bond of Edward Duckett, Mercer of London, to Thomas Bennet, 1615.

Add. Charter 17179, Indenture between Dowager Countess of Salisbury and John Hodge, Carpenter of St. Clement Danes.

Add. Charter 17181, Indenture between Dowager Countess of Salisbury and John Hodge, Carpenter of St. Clement Danes.

Add. Mss. 3057, f. 17, John Bennet to the king. [c. 1690?].

Add. Mss. 28050, f. 7, Edward, Viscount Latimer, to unknown, presumably his wife, Elizabeth Bennet, Feb. 8, 1679.

Add. Mss. 28050, f. 73, Edward, Viscount Latimer, to his sister.

Add. Mss. 28087, ff. 1–1v, Edward Osborne, Viscount Latimer, to his father, the Earl of Danby, n.d.

Add. Mss. 28884, f. 203, Colonel George Jocelyn to John Ellis, Aug. 27, 1699.

Add. Mss. 28888, f. 336, Jocelyn to Ellis, June 16, 1702.

Add. Mss. 28888, f. 339, Jocelyn to Ellis.

Add. Mss. 28888, f. 381, Jocelyn to Ellis, from on board the *Ranelagh* at Spithead, June 24, 1702.

Add. Mss. 28889, ff. 5–6v, 31–32v, 33, 54–55v, 56–57v, 145, letters to John Ellis, July 1701–1702.

Add. Mss. 28889, f. 435v, Jocelyn to Ellis, Dec. 1, 1702.

Add. Mss. 28902, f. 273–273v, Jan. 16 1699–1700 ns Jan. 6, 1699–1700. os. [Note that these are in the wrong volume – Oct. 1698–Feb. 1699].

Add. Mss. 28903, J. Swinford to Ellis, May 24, 1699.

Add. Mss. 28904, ff. 104–4v, George Jocelyn to John Ellis, Oct. 7, [1699] ns.

Add Mss. 28904, f. 145, Erasmus Lewis to Ellis, Paris, Oct. 1, 1699.

Add Mss. 28904, ff. 181–182v, Jocelyn to Ellis, Turin, Nov. 7, 1699.

Add. Mss. 28904, f. 191v, George Broughton to John Ellis, Nov. 13, 1699.

Add. Mss. 28904, f. 291v, Mr. Lewis to Ellis, Jan. 6, 1699/1700.

Add Mss. 28904, f. 340, Jocelyn to Ellis, Rome, Feb. 5, 1700. John Ellis marks it 1699/
     1700.
Add Mss. 28904, ff. 363–364v, Rome, Feb. 26, ns 1700 or 1701.
Add. Mss. 28904, ff. 388–389v, March 12, 1700–1701.
Add. Mss. 28904, f. 422, Rome, April 1, 1700.
Add. Mss. 28905, ff. 49–50v, Jocelyn to Ellis, Rome, June 6, 1700.
Add. Mss. 28905, ff. 185, 240, 336.
Add Mss. 28906, f. 191, Jocelyn to Ellis, Rome, Nov. 12, 1700 ns.
Add. Mss. 28908, f. 307, June 4, 1701 Jocelyn to Ellis from Leghorn.
Add. Mss. 28908, f. 321, June 7, 1701.
Add Mss. 28909, f. 153, Jocelyn to Ellis, Aug. 17, 1701.
Add. Mss. 28909, f. 210, Jocelyn to Ellis, Sept. 3, 1701.
Add. Mss. 28909, f. 240, Jocelyn to Ellis, Sept. 10, 1701.
Add Mss. 28909, f. 276, Jocelyn to Ellis.
Add Mss. 28909, f. 291, Jocelyn to Ellis.
Add. Mss. 28909, f. 399, Jocelyn to Ellis, Oct. 14, 1701.
Add. Mss. 28912, ff. 88–89v, Sept. 30, 1702.
Add. Mss. 28926, f. 159–160v.
Add. Mss. 28931, f. 286, Charles Ellis to John Ellis, Paris, Aug. 30, 1699; f. 293,
     Sept. 6, 1699.
Add. Mss. 28931, f. 293.
Add. Mss. 28931, f.296.
Add. Mss., 28931, f. 304.
Add. Mss., 28931, f. 309, Sept. 30, 1699.
Add. Mss., 28931, f. 313, Oct. 11, 1699.
Add. Mss. 28931, f. 329, Dec.16, 1699.
Add. Mss. 28932, ff. 3–4, Jan. 6, 1699/1700.
Add. Mss. 33057, f. 17, John Bennet to the King [*c.* 1690].
Add. Mss. 33572, f. 376, Frances Cecil, wife of James, Earl of Salisbury, Letter to her
     brother-in-law, R. Cecil, *c.* 1690.
Add. Mss. 38159, Duke of Ormond's journal of the expedition to Spain in 1702.
Add. Mss. 41806, f. 217, Dr. Salmon's case against the Hamburgh Company 1672.
Add. Mss. 61477, Vol. 378, 1732–1738, Lady Ann Chesshyre to Sarah Duchess of
     Marlborough, f. 157, Tuesday morning, Sept. 26, 1732 or 1738.
Add. Mss. 71131E, Sir Thomas Bennet's funeral.
Add. Mss. 71131D, Sir William Cokayne's funeral.
Egerton 3352, ff. 72, 74, Symon Bennet, declaration in regard to marriage settlement of
     Elizabeth Bennet and Edward Viscount Latimer.
Sloane Ms. 2812, f. 50, John Metford, MD of Northampton, Medical case book,
     medical prescription for Grace Bennet, wife of Simon Bennet of Beachampton
     of Buckinghamshire, 1655.
Sloane Mss. 3203, ff. 103–108v, "Dr. Salmon's receipts."
Stowe 244, ff. 219–220, Letters of Anthony Stanhope, agent at The Hague, July 16/
     27, 1703.
Verney Mss. Microfilm 63645, John Verney to Ralph Verney, May 18, 1692.

Cambridgeshire Archives

Cambridgeshire Archives, K619/E11.
Cambridgeshire Archives, K619 E17, 1715/1716.
Cambridgeshire Archives, K619/E20, Mortlock Family of Abington.

Centre for Buckinghamshire Studies

BP13/1/1, Parish register, Beachampton, p. 143.
PR13/25/4, Copy of probate of will of Sir Simon Bennet of Beachampton, Baronet, Aug. 15, 1631.
Chester Family of Chicheley, D-C/3/10, Nov. 26, 1689.
Bulstrode Estate, D-RA/1/39, March 24, 1676/1677.

Derbyshire Record Office

D77/1/16/5, Bundle D21, Feoffment by Sir George Gresley of Drakelowe, 1626, Bart, and Thomas his son, Callingwood Saunders of Caldwell, Robert Radford of Lullington and Thomas Gresley of Lullington to John Bludworth of London, vintner, and Gilbert Morewood of London, grocer, of the manor of Overseal, Netherseal and Seal Grange. Consideration, £1,000. June 27.
D77/1/16/5, Bundle D22, to Morewood. Consideration £2,560; Dated Nov. 11.
D77/1/16/5, Bundle D23, Indenture of defeasance, Morewood–Gresley, March 7, 1626/1627.
D77/1/16/6, Bundle E2, Bargain and Sale by Zacharie Johnson of Netherseal, clerk to Gilbert Morewood, citizen and grocer of London of the advowson of Netherseal, Aug. 2, 1630.
D77/1/16/7, Particular of Mr. Gresley's manor house of Netherseal with the demesne and realty there unto belonging, *c.* 1650s.
D77/1/16/7, June 20, 1650.
D77/1/16/7, Schedule of Morewood's goods around Seale.
D77/1/16/9, Bundle H3, 1690–1698. Some time after 1712 or 1713, Grace Bennet the younger and Sarah Frowde wife of Ashburnham Frowde struck an agreement with Thomas Gresley and Richard Moor and various freeholders concerning disputes over Mill Green in Netherseal.
D77/1/16/10, Bundle J7, Lady Gresley sells wood and timber to her son Thomas for £3,000, Oct. 11, 1710.
D77/1/16/11, Bundle K, August 16 (after 1713, death of Frances Countess of Salisbury).
D77/1/23/10, "Review of landed estate and income of Sir Thomas Gresley prior to marriage." Pre 1650.
D77/1/23/11–17, Deeds relating to Seal, Overseal, Netherseal and Overseal.
D77/1/23/13, Rough draft of agreement between the Gresleys, Bennets and Salmons drawn up by Mr. Woodbridge of Grey's Inn, July 19, 1652.

DD77/1/23/27–28, Two copies of agreements between Dame Frances Gresley, widow of Sir Thomas Gresley, and Thomas Gresley, second son and sole executor of Sir Thomas's' will.

D77/2/1/374, Netherseal Estate rental.

D77/4/5/2, Dame Frances Gresley to Thomas Gresley, "For Mr. Thomas Gresley at Mr. John Nuberry's house at Blackfriars," n.d.

D77/18/4, 1703.

D5054/12/3, Letter book of merchants trading to Alicante, Spain, 1648–1652.

Folger Shakespeare Library

Folger, V.b. 25, Gresley Mss. Twenty-four autograph letters from Frances Gresley and Sir Thomas Gresley to Sir John Moore between 1672 and 1696.

Gloucestershire County Council

D678/1 F3/1–5.

Guildhall Library

Guildhall Ms. 00507, ff. 96–98, Frances Lady Gresley to Sir John Moore, Feb. 28, 1692/1693.

Guildhall Ms. 4423/1, St. Christopher le Stocks, Churchwarden Accounts, 1575 to 1660, ff. 165, 176, 180v, 182, 184, 188v.

Guildhall Ms. 11571, Grocers' Company, Wardens' Accounts.

Guildhall Ms. 11592A, Grocers' Company Admissions Etc. 1345–c. 1670, Alphabet Book.

Guildhall, Grocers' Company, Calendar of Court Minutes, Vol. IV, Pt. I, 1640–1649.

Guildhall Ms. 29445/1, f. 25 a, Thomas Finch to Sir John Moore, April 6, [1678].

Guildhall Ms. 29445/1 f. 44, Thomas Finch to Sir John Moore, March 4, 1678–1679.

Hatfield House

Hatfield House Archives, Accounts 43/6.

Hatfield House Archives, Accounts 73/5, Household Account of the Dowager Countess of Salisbury, 1696

Hatfield House Archives, Accounts 75/11, Account of Hugh Hawker, Steward of Household from Michelmas 1698 to May 2, 1699.

Hatfield House Archives, Accounts 75/12, George Cecil's accounts.

Hatfield House Archives, Accounts 76/2.

Hatfield House Archives, Accounts 78/5, 1700–1712, including Account of Thomas Moar with the Countess of Salisbury and John Bennet; Lease Countess of Salisbury and Madame Grace Bennet to G. Watson of land in Lamb's Conduit

Fields, Dec. 22, 1711; Demise, Earl of Salisbury and Madame Grace Bennet to N. Curzon of a piece of ground in Lambs Conduit Fields, July 12, 1721.

Hatfield House Archives, Accounts 90/8, includes Lady Chesshyre's notes to Grace Bennet and inventory of Grace Bennet's goods.

Hatfield House Archives, Accounts 92/10.

Hatfield House Archives, Accounts 94/10.

Hatfield House Archives, Accounts 108/405, Payment for paintings and frames, 1687.

Hatfield House Archives, Accounts 115/24, Trial of Barnes.

Hatfield House Archives, Accounts 125/24.

Hatfield House Archives, Accounts 139/3, Oct. 1649.

Hatfield House Archives, Accounts 142/12.

Hatfield House Archives, Accounts 142/12A.

Hatfield House Archives, Accounts 151/20, "Particulars of London to be set out for the Countess of Salisbury's Dower, *c.* 1685?"

Hatfield House Archives, Accounts 162/3.

Hatfield House Archives, Accounts 162/6, April 15, 1657.

Hatfield House Archives, Accounts 162/6, June 6, 1657.

Hatfield House Archives. Accounts 162/6, June 18, 1657.

Hatfield House Archives, Accounts 162/6, June 30, 1658.

Hatfield House Archives, Accounts 162/6, Aug. 26, 1658.

Hatfield House Archives, Accounts 173, Expenses while the Countess of Salisbury was in Europe.

Hatfield House Archives, Accounts, Box T/111, FP 11/1–3, Anne, Dowager Countess of Salisbury, to the Sixth Earl of Salisbury, Sept. 11, 1732.

Hatfield House Archives, Bills 107, 1617.

Hatfield House Archives, Bills 360, Grace Bennet's funeral.

Hatfield House Archives, Bills 369.

Hatfield House Archives, Bills 387, "Disbursements after my Lady came to Paris before she went to housekeeping, Account of James Lowen."

Hatfield House Archives, Cranborne Papers Supp. 6/13, S. Percivall to G. Stillingfleet mentions £3,000 per annum as the jointure of Frances, Countess of Salisbury, Jan. 5, 1685

Hatfield House Archives, Deeds 74/7, Dame Grissell Woodroffe, security for debt to Sir Thomas Bennet, 1604.

Hatfield House Archives, Deeds 106/20, Lady Mary Chandois, security for debt to Sir Thomas Bennet, 1606.

Hatfield House Archives, Deeds 89/20, Simon Bennet's release for Lady Finch, Oct. 20, 1649.

Hatfield House Archives, Deeds 94/10, Nov. 21, 1712.

Hatfield House Archives, Deeds 152/9, Lady Finch's release for Simon Bennet, Oct. 25, 1649.

Hatfield House Archives, Deeds 160/21, Assignment by W. Steward to Sir R. Wynn and Sir W. Uvedale of wardship and marriage of Simon Bennet, 1628.

Hatfield House Archives, Estate Papers, Box V, 83, G. to Earl of Salisbury at Christ Church, Oxford, [*c.* 1705–1707].

Hatfield House Archives, Estate Papers, Box V, 101.

Hatfield House Archives, Estate Papers and Private Mss., p. 204, Samuel Percivall to George Stillingfleet, Michaelmas, 1690.

Hatfield House Archives, FP9, 1678 to 1689.

Hatfield House Archives, FP10/118a.

Hatfield House Archives, FP10/124, Case of the Countess of Salisbury's dower, 1694.

Hatfield House Archives, FP10/164a.

Hatfield House Archives, FP10/196, 1690–1731.

Hatfield House Archives, FP10/203–204.

Hatfield House Archives, FP10/217.

Hatfield House Archives, FP10/230a

Hatfield House Archives, General 12/27, Orders for Dover House.

Hatfield House Archives, General 19/19, Percivall to Dobyns, about Grace Bennet's answer, Feb. 8, 1683.

Hatfield House Archives, General 20/23.

Hatfield House Archives, General 21/13, Margaret, Countess of Salisbury to John Fisher re Mr. Bennet's business, May 29, 1682.

Hatfield House Archives, General 22/35, Ebenezer Sadler to William Dobyns, July 29, 1686.

Hatfield House Archives, General 24/18, E. Sadler to Mr. Dobyns, Nov. 2, 1703.

Hatfield House Archives, General 25/31, April 15, 1687.

Hatfield House Archives, General 72/27, Henry Capel to Simon Bennet from Kew, Dec. 7, 1679.

Hatfield House Archives, General 72/35, Grace Bennet to Simon Bennet, May 5, 1662.

Hatfield House Archives, General 74/8, [the letter is not dated] Aug.–Nov. 1685.

Hatfield House Archives, General 92/7, Roger Chapman to Simon Bennet, Oct. 2, 1672.

Hatfield House Archives, General 92/38, Ralph Lee to Madam Grace Bennet at Calverton, Dec. 20, 1687

Hatfield House Archives, General 93/26, William Gifford to the Earl of Salisbury at his house in Gerrard Street, Oct. 23, 1694.

Hatfield House Archives, General 93/28, R. Dowker to Ebenezer Sadler, 1697.

Hatfield House Archives, General 95/19.

Hatfield House Archives, General 101/14. G. Lowe & Co. to Richard Bennet, at Antwerp.

Hatfield House Archives, General 127/12, Fr stile [May 28, 1699] Mrs Sarah Lee to Mr. Sadler, June 7, 1699.

Hatfield House Archives, General 131/121.

Hatfield House Archives, General, Samuel Percivall to George Stillingfleet, Feb. 10, 1689/1690.

Hatfield House Archives, Legal 12/12, E. Scott's bill of complaint against Richard Bennet about an East Indian Adventure.

Hatfield House Archives, Legal 11/13, 1669, papers re a judgment for debt.

Hatfield House Archives, Legal 29/21b.

Hatfield House Archives, Legal 38/4, 52/10, 237/11, Richard Bennet's business, 1620.

Hatfield House Archives, Legal 64/6, 1627. A man named Cole sued Bennet for non-payment of wages for Mrs. Cole who had served as "milch nurse to his son."

Hatfield House Archives, Legal 120/4, Judgment for security of £38, Feb. 11, 1674/1675.

Hatfield House Archives, Legal 124/12, E. Scott *v.* Dame Elizabeth Finch, 1632.

Hatfield House Archives, Legal 169, May 10, 1687.

Hatfield House Archives, Legal 177, Answer of Leonard Thomson in Grace Bennet *v.* Leonard Thomson for the use of the complainant, 1691.

Hatfield House Archives, Legal 184/6.

Hatfield House Archives, Legal 184/7, Bill, Thomson *v.* Bennet, Feb. 26, 1691.

Hatfield House Archives, Legal 247/10.

Hatfield House Archives, SFP "notes from the bills" (particularly SFP 3/69–70). These cover expenses while the Countess of Salisbury was in Europe and her sister Grace Bennet dined with the young Earl of Salisbury.

Hatfield House Archives, SFP 3/2.

Hatfield House Archives, SFP 3/20.

Hatfield House Archives, SFP 3/26, 1695.

Hatfield House Archives, SFP 3/29–31, 1693–1765.

Hatfield House Archives, SFP 3/29–30, SFP 3/40.

Hatfield House Archives, SFP 3/48, Visits to Sir Edward Mansel and Lord Rutland.

Hatfield House Archives, SFP 3/59, April 2, 1699, "Hire of a good coach and three sets of fresh horses 4 at each time to carry 6 persons from London to Dover on Tuesday next between 4 in the morning and 8 at night for 6 persons to Dover and 5/ for carrying my Lady from Dover House to the coach."

Hatfield House Archives, SFP 3/69/70, Bills 400, 1702.

Hatfield House Archives, SFP 3/70–71, Bills 401.

Hatfield House Archives, SFP 3/77–78, "Orders about Dover House."

Hatfield House Archives, SFP 3/87–89, Expenses at Bath, May to Nov. 1704.

Hatfield House Archives, SFP 3/99, 113–115, "From the bills."

Hatfield House Archives, SFP 3/120, 1693–1765 (1707, 1708, 1709).

Hatfield House Archives, SFP 3/120–121, Bill 438, 455.

Hatfield House Archives, SFP 3/139, Bill 447.

Hatfield House Archives, SFP 3/139, 1705, Aug.–May 1710/1711.

Hatfield House Archives, SFP 3/237, Expenses at Calverton.

Hatfield House Archives, SFP 3/275–282.

Hatfield House Archive, SFP 3/299, E. Sadler, Death of abortive child and churching of my Lady, Dec. 18, 1694,

Hatfield House Archives, SFP 3/300.

Hatfield House Archives, SFP 3/321.

Hatfield House Archives, SFP 4/13.

Hertfordshire Record Office

Skippe Family of Ledbury, B38/132. Quitclaim for the remainder, subject to redemption.

House of Lords Record Office

HLRO, L/PO/JO/10/1/340/310, Salmon *v.* The Hamburgh Company, Nov. 7, 1670.
HLRO, HL/PO/JO/10/1/341/320, "Amended Draft of an Act for the better payment of the debts of Sir Clifford Clifton, Knight, deceased, and raising portions for his daughter, 18 Nov. 1670."
HL/PO/JO/10/1/473/900, Salisbury House Act 14, Feb. 1695, "An Act to enable the Guardians of James, Earl of Salisbury, to make leases of Salisbury House and some other hereditaments in the Strand, in the County of Middlesex, for improvement thereof by building," 1695, enabling the dowager countess to lease Salisbury House, its gardens and houses to John Hodge for 60 years.
HL/PO/JO/10/3/184/18 and 19, Petition and Appeal of John and Grace Bennet; Answer of Earl and Countess of Salisbury.
HL/PO/JO/10/6/325, Main Papers, Nov. 17, 1722 – Jan. 18, 1723.

Hull History Centre

Hull University Archives, Brynmor Jones Library, Papers of the Forbes Adam/Thompson/Lawley (Barons Wenlock) Family of Escrick, U DDFA2/24/1, Marriage Settlement: Symon Benet of Beachampton, co. Bucks. esq. (son and heir of Richard B. of London dec'd) to Gilbert Morewood of London esq: Prior to marriage of Symon Benet and Grace Morewood, daughter of Gilbert, Oct. 9, 1649.

Huntingdonshire Archives

Montagu family, Earls of Sandwich of Hinchingbrooke, Marriage Settlement, Hinch 1/12, March 13, 1740.

Lincolnshire Archives

2 THOR HAR 3/8/33, John Broking of London, merchant, with Charles Thorold of London, esq: sale of 95 tuns of oil, and the repayment of £2,060 and interest, Aug. 5, 1685.

London Metropolitan Archives

Orphans Deeds 33 CLA/002/04/033.
CLA/071/AD02/001006.

The National Archives

C2/Chas I/M23/2, Morewood *v.* Wynn.
C2/Chas I/W44/35, Wynn *v.* Morewood.

C3/390/76, Wharton *v.* Bennet, Lord Philip Wharton, knight, Dame Dorothy Wharton and others *v.* Sir Thomas Bennet and Richard Bennet, 1621.

C3/402/53, Sir Heneage Finch and Dame Elizabeth Finch *v.* Sir Simon Bennet re personal estate of deceased Sir Thomas Bennet knight in London, 1631 or before.

C5/71/86, Earl of Salisbury and Frances Countess of Salisbury *v.* John Bennet and Grace Bennet, 1690 and HLRO 1691.

C5/186/183, Earl of Salisbury *v.* Chapman, 1693.

C5/218/46, Countess of Salisbury *v.* Chapman, 1695, regarding personal estate of Simon Bennet.

C5/266/4, Earl of Salisbury *v.* Countess of Salisbury, 1698.

C5/629/43, Saunders *v.* Bennet, 1703.

C6/262/37, Earl of Salisbury *v.* Bornford, Earl of Salisbury, Frances Cecil his wife, John Bennet, Grace Bennet his wife *v.* Richard Bornford, Thomas Brand and William Brand. Subject: property in Carlton, Bedfordshire, Chellington, Bedfordshire, 1689.

C6/275/19 Bennitt *v.* Bennett, 1682.

C6, 275/25, Bennet *v.* Bennet, 1683.

C6/341/1, Countess of Salisbury *v.* Fowle, April 6, 1704.

C6/376/83, Bennet *v.* Pelyne, Grace Bennet, complainant, 1703–1704.

C6/383/72, Grace Bennet *v.* Countess of Salisbury, John Bennet, John Bennet infant etc., 1704.

C6/501/20, Westerne *v.* Bennet, 1697.

C9/22/78, Griesley *v.* Rich, Eyre and Morewood, 1654.

C9/172/27, Gresley *v.* Gresley, 1700.

C9/224/27, 1707, Dering *v.* Bennet. Dering was killed in a duel on May 18, 1711.

C9/473/73 Gresley *v.* Gresley, 1702.

C11/1137/28, Morrett *v.* Paske, 1725.

C11/1178/10, Morrett *v.* Gumley, 1716.

C22/211/22, Westerne *v.* Bennet, Depositions taken in the country, 1706.

C110/175, Morrett *v.* Paske, Particular of John Bennet's estate, 1726–1733.

C 142/435/116, Sir Thomas Bennet, Inquisition Post Mortem, 1627–1628.

C142/446/80, Richard Bennet, Gloucester, Inquisition Post Mortem, 1627–1628.

E44/484, Assignment of an obligation by Lady Elizabeth Finch of Kensington, widow, June 13.

E115/142/57, Various taxation certificates show Elizabeth Finch's residence in Middlesex rather than in Gloucestershire.

E115/143/54, Certificate of Residence showing Sir Heneage Finch to be liable for taxation in London, and not in the city of Westminster, etc., Middlesex, the previous area of tax liability, 1629.

E115/151/171, Certificate of Residence showing Sir Heneage Finch to be liable for taxation in London and not in (county unknown), the previous area of tax liability, 1628.

E134/2Jas2/Mich.23, Carpender *v.* Bennet.

E134/4W&M/Mich9, William Carpender, clerk *v.* Grace Bennett, widow, 1692.

E178/5663, Surrey: Rotherhithe plan of land late of John Bennet, esquire. E 178/5663 states that Bennet received the manor of Rotherhithe from the Earl of Salisbury in

1692 while an eighteenth-century suit claims that Bennet bought the manor in 1690.

E199/28/40, London and Middlesex Schedule of Goods of Richard Bennet, 22 James I.

Letters Patent to Sir Simon Bennet, Chief Justice of the Forests South of the Trent, Handley within the Forest, Whittlewood Forest, Northamptonshire and Buckinghamshire, March 27, 1629–March 26, 1630.

P.C. 2/38, 325 ff.

PRIS 10/157, John Bennet, Esq., March 17, 1697/1698,

PROB4 17737, Engrossed Inventories, Oct. 30, 1679.

PROB11/151/286, Will of Sir Thomas Bennet, Alderman of Saint Olave Old Jewry, City of London, Feb. 20, 1627.

PROB11/153/479, Will of Richard Bennet, May 7, 1628.

PROB11/160/369, Will of Sir Simon Bennet.

PROB11/160/764, Sentence of Heneage Finch, Recorder of London, of Saint Bartholomew the Great, City of London, Dec. 7, 1631.

PROB11/204/281, Will of John Morewood of the Oaks, May 11, 1648.

PROB11/206/461, Will of Andrew Morewood, Dec. 29, 1648.

PROB11/212/751, Will of Gilbert Morewood, June 21, 1650.

PROB11/238/74, Will of Anthony Morewood, April 22, 1654.

PROB11/307/365, Will of Elizabeth Bennet, Feb. 27, 1662.

PROB11/325/394, Will of Sir Thomas Rich, Sonning Berkshire, Nov. 20, 1667.

PROB11/349/164, Will of Peter Salmon of Saint Martin in the Fields, Middlesex, Nov. 18, 1675.

PROB11/359/541, Will of Anne, Viscountess Conway, 1679.

PROB11/364/424, Will of Dame Frances Clifton, Nov. 29, 1680.

PROB11/371/283, Will of Symon Bennet of Calverton, Buckinghamshire

PROB11/423/102, Will of James, 4th Earl of Salisbury.

PROB11/426, Will of Ralph Lee, June 20, 1695.

PROB11/458/22, Sentence of Sir Thomas Gresley of Drakelowe, Derbyshire, Feb. 1700.

PROB11/458/42, Will of Sir Thomas Gresley, May 11, 1700.

PROB11/523/198, Will of Dame Frances Gresley, Oct. 1, 1711.

PROB11/536/55, Will of Frances, Countess of Salisbury, Dowager, Oct. 3, 1713.

PROB11/640/51, Will of Catherine Twisden alias Jocelyne alias Jocelyn, widow of Maidstone, Kent, Sept. 12, 1730.

PROB11/653/319, Will of Grace Bennet, Widow of St. Martin in the Fields, Middlesex, Sept. 7, 1732.

SP16/281, f. 143, "Considerations touching the settlement of Sir Simon Bennett's foundation in University College, Oxford," [undated]

SP17/H/12, Grant to Anne Stewart, Lady Saltoun, to search for rents in arrears in the Exchequer and Duchy of Lancaster, June 17, 1630.

SP29/406/227, Conway Papers, Dame Frances Clifton to Anne, Vicountess Conway, Oct. 3, 1678.

SP29/407/41, Conway Papers, Dame Frances Clifton to Anne, Vicountess Conway, Oct. 17, 1678.

SP29/407/132, Conway Papers, Dame Frances Clifton to Anne, Viscountess Conway, Nov. 2 [1678].

SP29/411, f. 293, Conway Papers, Christopher Cratford to Viscount Conway, April [8?], 1679.

SP29/411, f. 301, Conway Papers, Christopher Cratford to Viscount Conway, London, April 15, 1679.

SP29/411, f. 305, Conway Papers, Dame Frances Clifton to Viscount Conway, April 22, 1678.

SP29/413, f. 65, Conway Papers, Christopher Cratford to Viscount Conway, London, March 2, 1680.

SP29/414, f. 59, Conway Papers, Christopher Cratford to Viscount Conway, July 22, 1680.

SP32/15, f. 346, James Vernon to Lord Ambassador Williamson.

SP34/18/32, Jocelyn's army appointment.

SP41/4/113, Jocelyn's army appointment.

SP44/387/ff. 204–205, Licence granted by Queen Anne to Countess Dowager of Salisbury, called "cousin," George Cecil, Sarah Lee, and named servants to return from France by way of Holland, Sept. 2, 1702.

SP46/101, Report by William Clerk and Thomas Exton, Admiralty Judges, on the petition of Samuell Vassall, Roger Vivian, Richard Shute, Gilbert Morewood, and other merchants of London, concerning the *Concord*, taken as prize by the Dutch in 1648. Doctors' Commons, Nov. 3, 1649.

SP87/2/15, Marlborough to Nottingham, Oct. 12, 1702.

Court of Wards, WARD 7/77/75, IPM Richard Bennet: Gloucester, 4 Charles I.

Court of Wards, WARD 7/81/208; IPM Sir Simon Bennet: Buckingham, 7 Charles I (c. 1632).

Nottinghamshire Archives

DD4P, Portland of Welbeck (4th Deposit), Deeds and Estate Papers, DD4P/36/7, Copy of the Will of Dame Frances, widow of Sir Clifford Clifton of Clifton, Feb. 6, 1679/1680

University of Nottingham MSS.

Cavendish Papers, Pw1/335–337, 1685.

Cavendish Papers, Pw1/548, Newcastle to his wife Frances, Oct. 26, 1687.

Cavendish Papers, Pw1/550, Jean Beaumont to Henry 2nd Duke of Newcastle, Oct. 9, 1686.

Cavendish Papers, Pw1/635, Duke of Newcastle to the Duke of Albemarle, Dec. 21, 1684.

Cavendish Papers, Pw1/636, Duke of Newcastle to the Duke of Albemarle, Jan. 22, 1685.

Cavendish Papers, Pw1/662, Latimer to Danby, Oct. 4, 1687.

Clifton Papers, Cl C 96, Sir Clifford Clifton to Mr. Hodgson, Feb. 7, 1669/1670.
Clifton Papers, Cl C 97, Lady Frances Clifton to Gervase Holland, July 1, 1673.
Clifton Papers, Cl C 98, Lady Frances Clifton to Gervase Holland, n.d.
Clifton Papers, Cl C 167 Elizabeth and Francis Finch to Sir Gervase Clifton, June 1650.
Clifton Papers, Cl C 170, Francis Finch to Frances Finch, April 8, 1650.
Clifton Papers, Cl C 171, Francis Finch to Frances Finch, April 15, 1650.
Clifton Papers, Cl C 173, Francis Finch to Frances Finch, 1650.
Clifton Papers, Cl C 174, Francis Finch to Lady Frances Clifton, Oct. 11, 1650.
Clifton Papers, Cl C 177, 178, 179, Heneage Finch to Frances Finch, from Rouen, Oct. and Nov., 1643.
Clifton Papers, Cl C 180, Heneage Finch to Frances Lady Clifton, June 23, 1670.
Clifton Papers, Cl C 252, 1, 4, Trinity Term, 21 Charles I, 1645, Court of Wards and Liveries.
Clifton Papers, Cl L 261/8, Printed case of Dame Frances Clifton and William Clifton and Catherine and Arabella Clifton.
Clifton Papers, Cl C 333, Henry More to Frances Finch.
Clifton Papers, Cl C 334, Henry More to Frances Finch.
Clifton Papers, Cl C 371, Francis Pruitan to Mrs. Clifton Sept. 24, 1661.
Clifton Papers, Cl C 391, L. Rugeley to Lady Frances Clifton, May 15, 1679.
Clifton Papers, Cl C 555, Clifford Clifton to Sir Gervase Clifton, May 11, 1650.
Clifton Papers, Cl C 556, Clifford Clifton to Sir Gervase Clifton, May 28, 1650.
Clifton Papers, Cl C 557, Clifford Clifton to Sir Gervase Clifton, June 11, 1650.
Clifton Papers, Cl C 716, Lady Frances Clifton to Gervase Holland, Saturday, n.d.
Clifton Papers, Cl D 1504, Copy of will of Sir Clifford Clifton of Clifton, 1669.

Oxford University, Bodleian Library

Bodleian, E. Edwards, "Calendar of the Carte Manuscripts," vol. 66, f. 402, Newsletters to Theophilus Hastings, Earl of Huntingdon, April 19, 1699, f. 409, [May 1699].
Bodleian, MS Carte 216, f. 49, Longford to Arran, May 13, 1682.
Bodleian MS Carte 216, f. 75, Fitzpatrick to Arran, June 9, 1682.
Bodleian, MS Carte 219, f. 198, No. II, Ormond to Arran, Jan. 6, 1681.
Bodleian, MS Carte 70, ff. 552–552v, Duke of Ormond to Mathew, June 10, 1682.
Bodleian, MS Carte 219, ff. 334–335, June 10, 1682.
Bodleian, Oxford Ms. Eng. Hist. c478/f. 8–9, Lady Wharton to her cousin Sir William Heyricke, Nov. 26, 1617.
Bodleian, Rawlinson Mss., Letter 42, F. 30, Conway to Bedford, Aug. 17, [1700].

Oxford University, College Archives

www.univ.ox.ac.uk/about/archives
UC: E14, The Estate of Handley Park, Northamptonshire: Sir Simon Bennet's donation to University College
UC: E14/L1 and L2, Lawsuits with the Bennet family
UC: E14/L5, Settlement of Bennet estate

UC: MA26, Papers of former Master, Thomas Walker

UC: MA32, Papers of former Master, Thomas Bennet

UC: P164/L2/1, 2, and 3 Handley Park and Bennet donation from Sir Arthur Ingram's papers at Temple Newsam, n.d. (late 1630s or early 1640s?)

Sheffield Archives

Crewe Muniments, CM, 1686, William Lambton and Dame Katherine, his wife, Lyndley Richardson and Henry Byngley *v.* John Moseley, Anthony Morewood, Joshua Ballard and others concerning the non-payment of tolls for carrying lead and other commodities on the river Idle, November 13, 1629.

Printed Primary Sources

A full and true account of a horrid and barbarous murder: committed last night by one Mr. King and Mr. Smith, two Kentish gentlemen, on the body of Richard Thornhill, esq; the quarrel … about Sir Cholmly Deering, deceas'd ([London]: Printed by M. Holt in Fleetstreet, 1711).

A True and Exact Account of all the ceremonies observed by the Church of Rome, at the opening, during the progress, and at the conclusion of the next approaching Jubilee, in the year 1700 (London: Printed by D. Edwards in Fetter-Lane, 1699).

Abstracts of Gloucestershire inquisitions post mortem in the reign of Charles I, part 4 no. 80, Volume 9 (London: British Record Society, 1893–1914).

Accomptes of the church wardens of the parishe church of St. Christofers nere the Stocks in the City of London, ed. Edwin Freshfield, 3 vols. in 1. (London: Rixon and Arnold, 1882).

Acts of the Parliament of the United Kingdom, 20 & 21 Victoria, c. 85, Matrimonial Causes Act.

Acts of the Parliament of the United Kingdom, 45 & 46 Victoria, c. 75, Married Women's Property Act.

Alumni Oxoniensis: The Members of the University of Oxford, 1500–1714, rev. and annotated by Joseph Foster, 4 vols. (Nendeln/Liechtenstein: Kraus, 1968; orig. publ. Oxford: Parker & Co., 1891–1892), Vol. I, "Thomas Bennet."

Analytical Index to the Series of Records Known as the Remembrancia: 1579–1664, ed. W. H. Overall and H. C. Overall (London: E. J. Francis, 1878).

Anonymous, *The Unfortunate Lady: A Brief Narrative of the Life, and Unhappy Death of the Lady Bennet, Late of Buckinghamshire; Who was Most Barbarously and Inhumanly Murthered at her own House, on Wednesday the 19th of September, 1694, by a Butcher of Stony-Stratford* … (London: Printed for H. Maston, in Warwick-Lane, 1694).

Bacon, Francis, *The Essayes or Counsels, Civill and Morall*, ed. Michael Kiernan (Oxford: Clarendon Press, 2000).

Barbon, Nicholas, *A discourse concerning coining the new money lighter in answer to Mr. Lock's Considerations about raising the value of money* (London: Printed for Richard Chiswell, 1696).

A Discourse of Trade (London: Tho. Milbourne for the author, 1690).

Baron and Feme: A treatise of the common law concerning husbands and wives (London: Printed by the assigns of Richard and Edward Attykns, Esqs. for Jon Walthroe, 1700).

Behn, Aphra, *Poems upon Several Occasions: With a Voyage to the Island of Love* (London: Printed for R. Tonson and I. Tonson, at Gray's-Inn-Gate Next Gray's-Inn Lane, and at The Judges-Head at Chancery Lane End Near Fleetstreet, 1684).

Birch, Thomas, *The History of the Royal Society, 4 vols.* (London: A. Millar, 1756–1757).

ed., *The Court and Times of Charles the First, 2 vols.* (London: Henry Colburn, 1848).

Blackstone, Sir William, *Commentaries on the Laws of England in Four Books*, 12th edn. (London: A. Strahan and W. Woodfall, 1793–1795).

Blackstone, Sir William, *The Commentaries of Sir William Blackstone, Knight, on the Laws and Constitutions of England* (Chicago: American Bar Association, 2009).

Blunt, Charles, *The Sale of Esau's Birthright or the New Buckingham Ballad* (1679), EEBO.

Burke, John, and John Bernard Burke, *A Genealogical and Heraldic History of the Extinct and Dormant Baronetcies of England, Ireland, and Scotland*, 2nd edn. (London: J. R. Smith, 1844).

Calendar of Buckinghamshire Quarter Sessions, ed. William Le Hardy, Buckinghamshire Record Society (Aylesbury: Buckinghamshire County Council, 1933).

A Calendar of the Court Minutes, etc. of the East India Company, 1635–1639, ed. Ethel Bruce Sainsbury (Oxford: Clarendon Press, 1907).

A Calendar of the Court Minutes, etc. of the East India Company, 1640–1643, ed. Ethel Bruce Sainsbury (Oxford: Clarendon Press, 1909).

A Calendar of the Court Minutes, etc. of the East India Company, 1644–1649, ed. Ethel Bruce Sainsbury (Oxford: Clarendon Press, 1912).

A Calendar of the Court Minutes, etc. of the East India Company, 1650–1654, ed. Ethel Bruce Sainsbury (Oxford: Clarendon Press, 1913).

Calendar of State Papers, Domestic Series, of the Reigns of Edward VI, Mary, Elizabeth, and James, 1547–1625, ed. Mary Anne Everett Green and Robert Lemon (London: Longman, 1856–1872).

Calendar of State Papers, Domestic Series, during the Commonwealth, 1649–1660, ed. Mary Anne Everett Green (London: Longman, 1875–1886).

Calendar of State Papers, Domestic Series, of the Reign of Charles II, 1660–1685, ed. Mary Anne Everett Green (London: Longman, 1860).

Calendar of State Papers, Domestic Series, of the Reign of William III, 1689–1702 (London: HMSO, 1908–1937).

Calendar of State Papers, Domestic Series, of the Reign of Anne, 1702–1703, ed. Robert Pentland Mahaffy (London: HMSO, 1916).

Calendar of State Papers, Colonial, Vol. III, 1617–1621, ed. W. N. Sainsbury (London: Longman, 1860–1905).

Calendar of State Papers, Colonial, Vol. IV, 1622–1624, ed. W. N. Sainsbury (London: Longman, 1860–1905).

Calendar of State Papers, Colonial, Vol. VI, 1625–1629, ed. W. N. Sainsbury (London: Longman, 1860–1905).

Calendar of State Papers, Colonial, Vol. VIII, 1630–1634, ed. W. N. Sainsbury (London: Longman, 1860–1905).

Calendar of State Papers, Treasury Books, Vol. II, 1667–1668, ed. W. A. Shaw (London: Longman, 1868–1889).

Cannon, Richard, *Historical Records of the British Army, the Fourth or Royal Irish Regiment of Dragoon Guards* (London: Printed by Authority, Longman, Orme and Co. and William Cowes and Son, 1839).

Cardigan, The Earl of, *The Life and Loyalties of Thomas Bruce* (London: Routledge & Kegan Paul Ltd, 1951).

Catholic Encyclopedia, "Jubilee."

Chester, Joseph Lemuel, ed., *Marriage, Baptismal and Burial Register of the Collegiate Church of St. Peter Westminster* (London: Mitchell and Hughes, 1876).

Cokayne, George E., *The Complete Peerage of England, Scotland, Ireland, Great Britain and the United Kingdom: Extant, Extinct or Dormant*. Revised. V. Gibbs. 13 vols. (London: St. Catherine Press, Ltd., 1910–1959).

Cokayne, George E., *Some Account of the Lord Mayors and Sheriffs of the City of London during the First Quarter of the Seventeenth Century* (London: Phillimore and Co., 1897).

Complete Baronetage, ed. George E. Cokayne, 6 vols. (Exeter: W. Pollard & Co. 1900–1909)

Coryat, Thomas, *Coryat's Crudities* (London, 1611).

Creed, Richard, *Richard Creed's Journal of the Grand Tour, 1699–1700 to Rome with the 5th Earl of Exeter*, ed. Alice Thomas (Oundle, Peterborough: Oundle Museum, 2002).

The Daily Journal (London: Printed for T. Bickerton, 1721–1737), "Dover House, Dover Street, sold by auction, Feb. 1, 1727."

Debrett's Peerage and Baronetage (London: Debrett's Peerage Ltd.; Detroit: Distributed by Gale Research Co., 1980).

Encyclopedia Britannica, "Opera."

English Reports, 2 Freeman 119–120, C. 135, Mr. Bennet. Appellant *v.* Lord Salisbury, Respondent. [1691] Appeal to the House of Lords, pp. 1097–1098, 1691.

English Reports, Nelson 170, Earl of Salisbury *v.* Bennet, Lords Commissioners, Mich. Term 1691, p. 818.

English Reports, 2 Venn 223, pp. 744–745.

English Reports, House of Lords, Vols. 1, 4, Case 2, The South Sea Company, Appelant; Eleanor Curzon, Respondent [March 11, 1722], pp. 1092–1094.

The Entring Book of Roger Morrice, ed. Mark Goldie et al., 6 vols. (London: Boydell and Brewer, 2009).

F., A., *The travels of an English gentleman from London to Rome: on foot. Containing a comical description of what he met with remarkable in every city, town, and religious house in his whole journey*, 4th edn. (London: Printed for A. Bettesworth, 1718).

Fiennes, Celia, *Through England on a Side Saddle in the Time of William and Mary* (London: Field and Tuer, The Leadenhall Press, 1888).

Gazette d'Amsterdam, CD Rom, Oxford, Vol. I, 1691–1703.

Geoffroy, M. A., ed., *Lettres Inedites de la Princesse des Ursins* (Paris: Didier et Cie, 1859).

Great Britain: Royal Commission on Historical Manuscripts (HMC)

The Manuscripts of the Marquis of Bath preserved at Longleat, Wiltshire, 5 vols. (London: HMSO, 1904–1980).

Report on the Manuscripts of the Duke of Buccleuch and Queensberry . . . preserved at Montagu House, Whitehall . . . (London: HMSO, 1899–1926).

The Manuscripts of the Earl Cowper . . . preserved at Melbourne Hall, Derbyshire, 3 vols. (London: HMSO, 1888–1889).

The Manuscripts of Allan George Finch, esq., of Burley-on-the-Hill, Rutland, 5 vols. (London: HMSO, 1913–1965).

The Manuscripts of the Marquis of Ormonde [formerly] preserved at the castle, Kilkenny, 8 vols. (London: HMSO, 1885–1920).

The Manuscripts of His Grace the Duke of Rutland . . . preserved at Belvoir Castle, 4 vols. (London: HMSO, 1888–1905).

The Manuscripts of Major-General Lord Sackville . . . preserved at Knole, Sevenoaks, Kent, ed. A. P. Newcombe, 2 vols. (London: HMSO, 1940–1966).

The Manuscripts of the Most Hon. The Marquess of Salisbury . . . preserved at Hatfield House, Herefordshire, 24 vols. (London: HMSO, 1883–1976).

Tenth Report of the Royal Commision on Historical Manuscripts, Part IV, Captain Stewart's Mss., p. 132. (1906, Reissue of 1885 edition).

Gordon, Thomas, and John Trenchard, *Cato's Letters or Essays on Liberty, Civil and Religious, and Other Important Subjects*, ed. and annotated by Ronald Hamowy, 2 vols. (Indianapolis: Liberty Fund, 1995).

Green, Mary Anne Everett, ed., *Diary of John Rous: Incumbent of Santon Downham, Suffolk, from 1625 to 1642*, Camden Society, Series 1, no. 66 (London: Printed for the Camden Society, 1856).

Grosart, Reverend Alexander B., ed., *De Jure Maiestatis, or Political Treatise on Government (1628–1630) and the Letterbook of Sir John Eliot (1625–1632)*, 2 vols. (London: Printed for Earl St. Germans, 1882).

Hasted, Edward, "Parishes: Linton," in *The History and Topographical Survey of the County of Kent*, Vol. IV (Canterbury: W. Bristow, 1798), pp. 365–371.

History of Parliament: The House of Commons 1660–1690, ed. Basil Duke Henning, 3 vols. (London: Secker and Warburg, 1983).

The History of Parliament: The House of Commons 1690–1715, ed. D. Hayton, Evelyn Cruickshanks, and S. Handley, 5 vols. (Cambridge: Cambridge University Press, 2002).

Hogarth, William, *Emblematical Print on the South Sea Scheme*, 1721, *Marriage A-la-Mode*, 1743–1745, *Industry and Idleness*, 1747.

Howell, James, *Instruction for Forreine Travel* (London, 1642).

Hunter, Joseph, *Familiae Minorum Gentium*, Vol. III, ed. John W. Clay, Harleian Society, vol. 39 (London, 1895).

Hallamshire: The History and Topography of the Parish of Sheffield (London, 1819).

Journal of the House of Commons: Vol. 2, 1640–1643 (London: HMSO, 1802).

Journal of the House of Commons: Vol. 4, 1644–1646 (London: HMSO, 1802).

Journal of the House of Commons: Vol. 6, 1648–1651 (London: HMSO, 1802).

Journal of the House of Commons: Vol. 9, 1667–1687 (London: HMSO, 1802).

Journal of the House of Lords: Vol. 22, 1722–1726 (London: HMSO, 1767–1830).

King, Gregory, "Natural and Political Observations upon the State and Condition of England, 1696," in *Two Tracts by Gregory King*, ed. G. E. Barnett (Baltimore: John Hopkins University Press, 1936), pp. 11–56.

Lassels, Richard, *The Voyage of Italy, or a Compleat Journey through Italy: In two parts. With the characters of the people, and the description of the chief towns, churches, monasteries, tombs, libraries, pallaces, villas, gardens, pictures, statues, and antiquities* (Newly printed at Paris, and are to be sold in London, by John Starkey, 1670).

Lipscomb, George, *The History and Antiquities of the County of Buckinghamshire*, 4 vols. (London: J. and W. Robins, 1847).

List of the Principal Inhabitants of the City of London 1640, from Returns Made by the Aldermen of Several Wards, ed. W. J. Harvey (London: Mitchell and Hughes, 1886).

Locke on Money, ed. Patrick Hyde Kelly, 2 vols. (Oxford: Oxford University Press, 1991).

The London Evening Post (London [England]): Printed by R. Nutt, September 7, 1732).

Luttrell, Narcissus, *A Brief Historical Relation of State Affairs from September 1678 to April 1714*, 6 vols. (Oxford: At the University Press, 1857).

Makin, Bethsua, *An Essay To Revive the Antient Education of Gentlewomen, in Religion, Manners, Arts & Tongues. With An Answer to the Objections against this Way of Education* (London: Printed by J. D. to be sold by Tho. Parkhurst, at the Bible and Crown at the lower end of Cheapside, 1673).

Memoirs of Thomas, Earl of Ailesbury, ed. W. E. Buckley, 2 vols., Roxburghe Club Publications (Westminster [London]: Nichols and Sons, 1890).

Metcalfe, Walter C., ed., *The Visitations of Hertfordshire Made by Robert Cooke, Esq. Clarencieux, in 1572, and Sir Richard St. George, Kt., Clarencieux, in 1634 with Hertfordshire Pedigrees From Harleian Mss. 6147 and 1546* (London: Ye Wardovr Press, 1886).

Minutes of the Vestry Meetings and Other Records of the Parish of St. Christopher le Stocks, ed. Edwin Freshfield (London: Printed by Rixon and Arnold, 1886).

Miscellanea Genealogia et Heraldica, ed. Joseph Jackson Howard, Vol. I, 3rd ser. (London: Mitchell Hughes, and Clarke, 1896).

Nichols, John, *The Progresses, and the Processions of Queen Elizabeth*, 3 vols. ([London]: Printed by and for the editor, 1788–1805).

Nicholson, Marjorie, and Sara Hutton, eds., *The Correspondence of Anne, Viscountess Conway, Henry More and Their Friends, 1642–1684* (Oxford: Clarendon Press, 1930, 1992).

ODNB, "Sir John Chesshyre," "Frank Melton," "Thomas Grey of Groby," "Sir Edward Hopton," "Sir Robert Vyner," "Sir Paul Pindar," "Sir John Jacob," "Sir Maurice Abbott," "William Courten," "Matthew Cradock," "Elizabeth, Viscountess Lumley of Waterford," "Sir Heneage Finch," "Heneage Finch, Earl of Nottingham," "Sir John Finch," "Edward Conway, Earl Conway," "Sir John Moore," "Jane, Lady Burdett," "James Butler, Earl of Ormond," "James, 4th Earl of Salisbury," "Sir Francis Wheler," "James Butler, 2nd Duke of Ormond," "Lady Mary Wortley Montagu," "Sir Nathanial Curzon fourth baronet."

Owen, John Hely, *War at Sea under Queen Anne, 1702–1708* (Cambridge: Cambridge University Press, 1938).

Private Correspondence and Miscellaneous Papers of Samuel Pepys 1679–1703, ed. J. R. Tanner, 2 vols. (London: George Bell and Sons, Limited, 1926).

Proceedings, Principally in the County of Kent, in connection with the Parliaments called in 1640, and especially with the Committee of Religion appointed in that year. Ed. by the Rev. Lambert B. Larking, M. A., from the collections of Sir Edward Dering, Bart., 1627–1644, with a preface by John Bruce ([Westminster]: Printed for the Camden Society, 1862).

The Records of the Honorable Society of Lincoln's Inn ... Admissions Register, Vol. I, *Admissions from 1420–1799* ([London] Lincoln's Inn: Printed by H. S. Cartwright, 1896).

The Records of the Virginia Company of London, ed. Susan Myra Kingsbury, 3 vols. (Washington: Government Printing Office, 1906–1935).

The Register Book of the Parish of St. Christopher le Stocks in the City of London, ed. Edwin Freshfield, Vol. I (London: Printed by Rixon and Arnold, 1882)

Registers of Bradfield in the Diocese of York, 1550–1722, transcribed and ed. Arthur B. Browne (Sheffield: A. MacDougall and Sons, 1907).

Reilly, Emily Georgiana Susanna, *Historical Anecdotes of the Boleynes, Careys, Mordaunts, Hamiltons, and Jocelyns* (1839).

Smollett, Tobias, *Travels through France and Italy. Containing observations on character, customs, religion ... arts, and antiquities ...* (London: Printed for R. Baldwin, in Pater-noster-row, 1766).

St. Clement Danes Parish: Minutes of Parish Vestries, 1st June 1686 – 24th October 1699, 24th October 1699. *London Lives: Poverty, Crime and the Making of a Modern City, 1690-1800* (www.londonlives.org, version 1.1), Westminster Archives Centre, Feb. 12, 2018.

Strype, John, *A Survey of the Cities of London and Westminster ... By John Stow, citizen and native of London ... Now lastly, corrected, improved, and very much enlarged ... by John Strype ... In six books*, 2 vols. (London: Printed for A. Churchill, J. Knapton, R. Knaplock, J. Walthoe, E. Horne, [and 5 others], 1720).

Taylor, Alison, *Archaeology of Cambridgeshire*, Vol. II, *South East Cambridgeshire and the Fen Edge* (Cambridge: Cambridgeshire County Council, 1998).

A true account of what past at the Old-Bailey, May the 18th, 1711 relating to the tryal of Richard Thornhill, Esq. indicted for the murther of Sir Cholmley Deering (London: Printed for John Morphew, 1711).

Victoria History of the County of Buckingham, ed. William Page, 4 vols. (London: Constable and Co. Ltd., 1905–1927). Vol. IV, 1927.

Victoria History of the County of Cambridge and the Isle of Ely, ed. A. P. M. Wright, Vol. VI (London: Published for the University of London, Institute of Historical Research by Oxford University Press, 1978).

Victoria History of the County of Lancaster, ed. William Farrar and J. Brownbill, 8 vols. (London: Constable and Co. Ltd., 1906–1914). Vol. IV, 1911.

Victoria History of the County of Nottingham, ed. William Page, Vol. II (London: Constable and Co. Ltd., 1910).

Victoria History of the County of York North Riding, ed. William Page, 2 vols. (London: Constable and Co. Ltd., St. Catherine Press, 1914–1923). Vol. I 1914, Vol. II 1923.

Victoria History of the Country of York East Riding, ed. K. J. Allison, 7 vols. (London: Published for the Institute of Historical Research by Oxford University Press, 1969–1989). Vol. I, 1969.

Webb, Clifton, *London Livery Company Apprenticeship Registers*, Vol. 48, *Grocers Company, Apprenticeships, 1629–1800* (London: Society of Genealogists Enterprise Limited, 2008).

Westmeath, Marchioness of, Emily Anne Bennet Elizabeth Nugent, *Marchioness of Westmeath, A Narrative of the Case of the Marchioness of Westmeath* (London: James Ridgeway, 1857).

"Wm. III, c. 1, 1697–1698: An Act against Corresponding with the late King James and His Adherents," in *The Statutes at Large of England and Great Britain from Magna Carta to the Union of Great Britain and Ireland*, ed. John Raithby, 20 vols. (London: G. Eyre and A Strahan, 1811).

Willis, Browne, *The History and Antiquities of the Town, Hundred, and Deanry of Buckingham* (London: Printed for the author, 1755).

Secondary Works

Alleman, Gilbert, *Matrimonial Law and the Materials of Restoration Comedy* (Wallingford, PA: Published privately, 1942).

Allen, D., "The Political Function of Charles II's Chiffinch," *Huntington Library Quarterly*, 39, 3 (1975–1976), 277–290.

Allen, Robert C., "Price of Freehold Land and Interest Rates in the Seventeenth and Eighteenth Centuries," *The Economic History Review*, 41, 1 (Feb. 1988), 33–53.

Andrewes, Kenneth, *Ships, Money and Politics: Seafaring and Naval Enterprise in the Reign of Charles I* (Cambridge: Cambridge University Press, 1991).

Appleby, Joyce Oldham, *Economic Thought and Ideology in Seventeenth Century England* (Princeton, NJ: Princeton University Press, 1978).

"Locke, Liberalism, and the Natural Law of Money," *Past and Present*, 71 (May 1976), 43–69.

Ashton, John, *A History of English Lotteries* (London: Leadenhall Press, 1893, reissued Gage, 1969).

Ashton, Robert, *The Crown and the Money Market* (Oxford: Clarendon Press: 1960).

Bailey, Joanna, *Unquiet Lives: Marriage and Marriage Breakdown in England, 1660–1800* (Cambridge: Cambridge University Press, 2003).

Barbour, Violet, "Marine Risks and Insurance in the Seventeenth Century," *Journal of Economic and Business History*, 1 (1928–1929), 561–596.

Barnard, Toby, and Jane Fenlon, *The Dukes of Ormonde, 1610–1745* (Woodbridge, and Rochester, NY: Boydell Press, 2000).

Barron, Caroline, "Centres of Conspicuous Consumption: The Aristocratic Town House in London 1200–1550," *The London Journal*, 20, 1 (1995), 1–16.

Baumann, Wolf-Rudiger, *The Merchant Adventurers and the Continental Cloth Trade, 1560s–1620s* (Berlin: Walter de Gruyer, 1990).

Beckett, J. V., *The Aristocracy in England 1660–1914* (Oxford: Blackwell, 1986).

Besant, Sir Walter, *London North of the Thames* (London: Adam and Charles Black, 1911).

Black, Jeremy, *The British Abroad: The Grand Tour in the Eighteenth Century* (Stroud: Sutton Publishing, 1992).

Botelho Lynn, and Pat Thane, eds. *Women and Aging in British Society since 1500* (Harlow: Longman, 2000).

Boulton, Jeremy, "London Widowhood Revisited: The Decline of Female Remarriage in the Seventeenth and Early Eighteenth Centuries," *Continuity and Change* 5, 3 (1990), 323–355.

Boxer, C. R., *The Dutch in Brazil, 1624–1654* (Oxford: Clarendon Press, 1957).

Boydston, Jeanne, "Gender as a Question of Historical Analysis," *Gender and History*, 20 (Nov. 2008), 558–583.

Brenner, Robert, *Merchants and Revolution: Commercial Change, Political Conflict, and London's Overseas Traders, 1550–1653* (Princeton, NJ: Princeton University Press, 1993).

Broadberry, Stephen, *British Economic Growth 1270–1870* (Cambridge: Cambridge University Press, 2015).

Brook, Benjamin, *The Lives of the Puritans: Containing a Biographical Account of Those Divines Who Distinguished Themselves in the Cause of Religious Liberty, from the Reformation under Queen Elizabeth, to the Act of Uniformity in 1662,* 3 vols. (London: Printed for J. Black, 1813).

Brown, Keith, *Noble Society in Scotland* (Edinburgh: Edinburgh University Press, 2004).

Browning, Andrew, *Thomas Osborne, Earl of Danby and Duke of Leeds, 1632–1712,* 3 vols. (Oxford: Blackwell, 1913).

Cannadine, David, "Aristocratic Indebtedness," *The Economic History Review*, 30, 4 (1977), 624–650.

Cannon, John, *Aristocratic Century: The Peerage of the Eighteenth Century* (Cambridge: Cambridge University Press, 1984).

Carlos, Ann M., "Women Investors in Early Capital Markets, 1720–1725," *Financial History Review*, 11, 2 (2004), 197–224.

Carlos, Ann M., and Larry Neal, "The Micro-Foundation of the Early London Capital Market: Bank of England Shareholders during and after the South Sea Bubble 1720–1725," *The Economic History Review*, 59, 3 (2006), 498–538.

Cass, Frederic, *Monken Hadley* (Westminster: J. B. Nichols and Son, 1850).

Cavendish, Richard, "The Founding of the Darien Colony," *History Today*, 48 (Nov. 1998).

Cecil, David, *The Cecils of Hatfield House* (London: Constable and Co. Ltd., 1973).

Chaney, Edward, *The Evolution of the Grand Tour* (London: Frank Cass, 1998).

——— *The Grand Tour and the Great Rebellion: Richard Lassels and "Voyage of Italy" in the Seventeenth Century* (Geneva: Saltine, 1985).

Chard, Chloe, *Pleasure and Guilt on the Grand Tour, Travel Writing and Imaginative Geography 1600–1830* (Manchester: Manchester University Press, 1999).

Chard, Chloe, and Helen Langdon, eds., *Transports: Travel Pleasure and Imaginative Geography, 1600–1830* (New Haven, CT: Yale University Press, 1996).

Charlton, Kenneth, *Women, Religion, and Education in Early Modern England* (London and New York: Routledge, 1999).

Chaudhuri, K. N., "The East India Company and the Export of Treasure in the Early Seventeenth Century," *The Economic History Review,* ns, 16, 1 (1963), 23–68.

   The English East India Company: The Study of an Early Joint-Stock Company, 1600–1640 ([London]: Frank Cass and Company, 1965).

Chen, Ching-Jung, "Tea Parties in Early Georgian Conversation Pieces," *The British Art Journal,* 10, 1 (Spring/Summer 2009), 30–39.

Churches, Christine, "Women and Property in Early Modern England: A Case Study," *Social History,* 23 (May 1998), 165–180.

Clay, Christopher, *Economic Expansion and Social Change: England 1500–1700,* 2 vols. (Cambridge: Cambridge University Press, 1984).

   "The Price of Freehold Land," *The Economic History Review,* 27, 2, (May 1974), 173–189.

Claydon, Tony, *Europe and the Making of England* (Cambridge: Cambridge University Press, 2007).

Clucas, Stephen, "The Duchess and the Viscountess: Negotiations between Mechanism and Vitalism in the Natural Philosophies of Margaret Cavendish and Anne Conway, *In-Between: Essays & Studies in Literary Criticism,* 9 (2000), 125–136.

Coates, Ben, *The Impact of the English Civil War on the Economy of London, 1642–1650* (Aldershot: Ashgate, 2004).

Cole, Robert, "Feebook of Serjeant Sir John Chesshyre," *Notes and Queries,* 2nd ser. 7 (June 1859), 492–493.

Cox, A. D. M., "Handley Park," *University College Record,* 6, 1 (1971), 57–63.

Crawford, Patricia, and Laura Gowing, eds., *Women's Worlds in Seventeenth-Century England: A Sourcebook* (London: Routledge, 2000).

Cressy, David C., *Birth, Marriage and Death, Ritual, Religion and the Life-Cycle in Tudor and Stuart England* (Oxford: Oxford University Press, 1997).

Darwall-Smith, Robin, *The History of University College Oxford* (Oxford: Oxford University Press, 2008).

de Roover, Florence Edler, "Early Examples of Marine Insurance," *Journal of Economic History,* 55, 2 (Nov. 1945), 172–200.

The Diary of John Evelyn, ed. E. S. de Beer, 6 vols. (Oxford: Clarendon Press, 1955).

Dickson, P. G. M., and J. V. Beckett, "The Finances of the Dukes of Chandos: Aristocratic Inheritance, Marriage, and Debt in Eighteenth Century England," *Huntington Library Quarterly,* 64, 3/4, (2001), 309–355.

Dolan, Brian, *Ladies of the Grand Tour, British Women in Pursuit of Enlightenment and Adventure in Eighteenth-Century Europe* (New York: Harper Collins, 2001).

Durston, Chris, "'Unhallowed Wedlocks': The Regulation of Marriage during the English Revolution," *Historical Journal,* 31 (1988), 45–99.

Ebert, Christopher, "Early Modern Atlantic Trade and the Development of Maritime Insurance to 1630," *Past and Present*, 213, 1 (Nov. 2011), 87–114.

Einberg, Elizabeth, and Judy Egerton, *The Age of Hogarth: British Painters Born 1675–1709* (London: Tate Gallery Collections, 1988).

Elliot, David, "Some Slight Confusion: A Note on Thomas Andrewes and Thomas Andrewes," *Huntington Library Quarterly*, 47, 2 (1984), 129–132.

Erickson, Amy Louise, "Common Law versus Common Practice: The Use of Marriage Settlements in Early Modern England," *The Economic History Review*, ns, 43, 1 (1990), 21–39.

   Women and Property in Early Modern England (New York: Routledge, 1993, 1995, 2002).

Farnell, James, "The Navigation Act of 1651: The First Dutch War and the London Merchant Community," *The Economic History Review,* ns, 16, 3 (1964), 439–454.

Fenn, Elizabeth A., "The Great Smallpox Epidemic, *History Today*, 53, 8 (2003).

Fenner, E., D. A. Henderson, L. Avita, I. Arita, Z. Jezek, and I. D. Ladner, *Smallpox and Its Eradication* (Geneva: WHO, 1988).

Firth, C. H., and R. S. Rait, *Acts and Ordinances of the Interregnum, 1642–1660*, 2 vols. (London: HMSO, Printed by Wyman and Sons, Ltd., 1911).

Fletcher, J. S., *A Picturesque History of Yorkshire*, 6 vols. (London: Caxton Publishing, *c.* 1901).

Forsyth, Hazel, *London's Lost Jewels: The Cheapside Hoard* (London: Museum of London, 2013).

Foyster, Elizabeth, *An English Family History, 1660–1857* (Cambridge: Cambridge University Press, 2005).

French, J. Milton, "George Wither's Verses to Dr. John Raven," *Publications of the Modern Language Association*, 63 (1948), 749–751.

Froide, Amy M., *Never Married: Single Women in Early Modern England* (Oxford: Oxford University Press, 2005).

Froide, Amy M., *Silent Partners: Women as Public Investors during Britain's Financial Revolution 1690–1750* (Oxford: Oxford University Press, 2016).

Fryman, Olivia, ed., with contributions by Sebastian Edwards, Joanna Marschner, Deirdre Murphy, and Lee Prosser. *Kensington Palace* (New Haven, CT: Yale University Press, in association with the Paul Mellon Centre for Studies in British Art, forthcoming).

Gauci, Perry, *The Politics of Trade: The Overseas Merchant in State and Society, 1660–1720* (Oxford and New York: Oxford University Press, 2001).

Genet-Roussiac, Nathalie, "Jacobites in Paris and Saint Germain en Laye," in *The Stuart Court in Exile*, ed. Eveline Cruickshank and Edward Corp (London and Rio Grande: The Hambledon Press, 1995), pp. 15–38.

Glixon, Beth L., *Inventing The Business of Opera: The Impresario and His World in Seventeenth-Century Venice* (Oxford and New York: Oxford University Press, 2006).

Goffin, David R., *Gardens and Gardening in Papal Rome* (Princeton, NJ: Princeton University Press, 1991).

Gowing, Laura, *Domestic Dangers: Women, Words, and Sex in Early Modern London*, Oxford Studies in Social History (Oxford: Clarendon Press, 1999).

Grassby, Richard, *The Business Community of Seventeenth-Century England* (Cambridge: Cambridge University Press, 1995).

Graziosi, Elisabetta, "Revising Arcadia: Women and Academies in Eighteenth- Century Italy," in *Italy's Eighteenth Century, Gender and Culture in the Age of the Grand Tour,* ed. Paula Findlen, Wendy Wassyng Roworth, and Catherine Sama (Stanford, CA: Stanford University Press, 2009), pp. 103–124.

Griffin, J. P., "Venetian Treacle and the Foundation of Medicines Regulation," *British Journal of Clinical Pharmacology*, 58, 3 (2004), 317–325.

Groenveld, Simon, "The English Civil Wars as a Cause of the First Anglo-Dutch War, 1640–1652," *Historical Journal*, 30 (1987), 541–566.

Habakkuk, Sir John, *Marriage, Debt, and the Estates System: English Landownership, 1650–1950* (Oxford: Clarendon Press, 1994).

Hager, Kelly, *Dickens and the Rise of Divorce* (New York: Routledge, 2010).

Harris, Barbara J., *English Aristocratic Women 1450–1550: Marriage and Family, Property and Careers* (Oxford and New York: Oxford University Press, 2002).

 English Aristocratic Women's Religious Patronage, 1450–1550: The Fabric of Piety (Amsterdam: Amsterdam Press, 2018).

Hill, Christopher, *The Economic Problems of the Church* (Oxford: Clarendon Press, 1956).

Hindle, Steve, "Work, Reward and Labour Discipline in Late Seventeenth-Century England," in *Remaking English Society: Social Relations and Social Change in Early Modern England,* ed. Steve Hindle, Alexandra Shepard, and John Walter (Woodbridge: Boydell and Brewer, 2013), pp. 255–280.

Hollingsworth, T. H., *The Demography of the British Peerage, Supplement to Population Studies*, 18, 2 (London: London School of Economics, 1964).

Hoppit, Julian, "The Myths of the South Sea Bubble," *Transactions of the Royal Historical Society*, 12 (2002), 141–165.

 Risk and Failure in English Business 1700–1800 (Cambridge: Cambridge University Press, 2002).

Houlbrooke, Ralph A., *The English Family, 1450–1700* (New York and London: Longman, 1984).

"The Huguenot Family in England: III, The Vandeputs," *The Ancestor*, 4 (1903), 32–43.

Hunt, Margaret, *The Character of Credit: Personal Debt in English Culture, c. 1740–1914* (Cambridge: Cambridge University Press, 2003).

 The Middling Sort: Commerce, Gender and the Family in England 1680–1780 (Berkeley and Los Angeles: University of California Press, 1996).

Hutton, Sarah, "Anne Conway, Margaret Cavendish and Seventeenth Century Scientific Thought," in *Women, Science and Medicine 1500–1700: Mothers and Sisters of the Royal Society*, ed. Lynette Hunter and Sarah Hutton (Stroud: Sutton Publishing, 1997), pp. 218–234.

 Anne Conway: A Woman Philosopher (Cambridge: Cambridge University Press, 2004).

Impey, Edward, *Kensington Palace: The Official Illustrated History* (London: Merell, 2003)

Ingamells, John, *A Dictionary of British and Irish Travellers in Italy, 1701–1800* (New Haven, CT, and London: Yale University Press, 1997).

Innes, Joanna, "The King's Bench Prison in the Later Eighteenth Century: Law, Authority and Order in a London Debtors' Prison," in *An Ungovernable People*, ed. John Brewer and John Styles (London: Hutchinson, 1980), pp. 250–298.

Jacobsen, Helen, *Luxury and Power: The Material World of the Stuart Diplomat 1660–1714* (Oxford: Oxford University Press 2011).

Johnson, A. M., "Buckinghamshire 1640–1660, A Study in County Politics," Appendix II, "A List of Yearly Estate Values as Recorded in Richard Grenville's Ms. Note Book" (MA thesis, University of Wales, 1962–1963).

Joselyn, Edward, *Memorials to Serve as a History of the Parish of St. Mary Rotherhithe* (Cambridge: Cambridge University Press, 1907).

Kenny, Shirley, *The Works of George Farquhar*, 2 vols. (Oxford: Clarendon Press, 1988).

Klein, Larry, "Politeness and the Interpretation of the British Eighteenth Century," *Historical Journal*, 45, 4 (2002), 869–898.

Knights, Mark, *Politics and Opinion in Crisis, 1678–1681* (Cambridge: Cambridge University Press, 1994).

   Representation and Misrepresentation in later Stuart Britain, Partisanship and Political Culture (Oxford: Oxford University Press, 2005).

Kriz, Kay Dian et al. "Grand Tour Forum," *Eighteenth Century Studies*, 31 (1997), 87–114.

Lake, Peter, "Popular Form, Puritan Content? Two Puritan Appropriations of the Murder Pamphlet from Mid-Seventeenth-Century London," in *Religion, Culture, and Society in Early Modern Britain, Essays in Honour of Patrick Collinson*, ed. Anthony Fletcher and Peter Roberts (Cambridge: Cambridge University Press, 1994), pp. 313–334.

Lang, Robert G., "The Greater Merchants of London in the Early Seventeenth Century" (D. Phil. thesis, Oxford University, 1963).

   "Social Origins and Social Aspirations of Jacobean London Merchants," *Economic History Review*, ns, 27, 1 (Feb. 1974), pp. 28–47.

Laurence, Anne, "The Emergence of a Private Clientele for Banks in the Eighteenth Century: Hoare's Bank and Some Women Customers," *The Economic History Review*, ns, 61 (2008), 565–586.

   "Women Investors, 'That Nasty South Sea Affair,' and the Rage to Speculate in Early Eighteenth-Century England," *Accounting, Business, and Financial History* 16, 2 (2006), 245–264.

Lawson, Philip, *The East India Company: A History* (London: Longmans: 1993).

Liu, Tai, *Puritan London: A Study of Religion and Society in the City Parishes* (Newark: University of Delaware Press, 1986).

London Past and Present: Its History, Associations, and Traditions, ed. Henry Benjamin Wheatley and Peter Cunningham (Cambridge: Cambridge University Press, 2011).

Lysons, Daniel, "Rotherhithe," in *The Environs of London*, Vol. I, *County of Surrey* (London: T. Cadell and W. Davies, 1792), pp. 470–477, *British History Online*: www.british-history.ac.uk/london-environs/vol1 [accessed 13 May 2018].

MacFarlane, Alan, ed., *The Diary of Ralph Josselin, 1616–1683*, Records of Social and Economic History, New Series (Oxford: Oxford University Press for the British Academy, 1976).

McIntosh, Marjorie, "Money Lending in the Periphery of London, 1300–1600," *Albion*, 20 (1988), 557–571.

McLay, K. A. J., "Sir Francis Wheler's Caribbean and North American Expedition, 1693: A Case Study in Combined Operational Command during the Reign of William III," *War in History* 14 (2007), 383–407.

Maczak, Antoni, *Travel in Early Modern Europe, trans. Ursula Phillips* (Cambridge: Polity Press, 1995).

Madan, Falconer, *The Gresleys of Drakelowe* (Oxford: Printed for subscribers by [H. Hart], 1899).

Melton, Frank T., *Sir Robert Clayton and the Origins of Deposit Banking* (Cambridge: Cambridge University Press, 1986, 2002).

Mendelson, Sara, and Patricia Crawford, *Women in Early Modern England 1550–1720* (Oxford: Clarendon Press: 1998).

Meyer, Liam, "'To Rise and Not to Fall': Representing Social Mobility in Early Modern Comedy and Star Chamber Litigation" (Ph.D. thesis, Boston University, 2014).

Monod, Paul, *Jacobitism and the English People 1688–1788* (Cambridge: Cambridge University Press, 1993).

Moore, Lindsay, *Women and the Law in the Anglo-American World 1600–1800* (Manchester: Manchester University Press, forthcoming).

Morris, Christopher, ed., *The Journeys of Celia Fiennes* (London: Cresset Press, 1949).

Morton, Richard, and William Peterson, "The Jubilee of 1700 and Farquhar's 'The Constant Couple,'" *Notes and Queries*, 200 (1955), 521–525.

Muldrew, Craig, "Credit and the Courts: Debt Litigation in a Seventeenth Century Urban Community," *The Economic History Review*, ns, 46 (1993), 23–38.

The Economy of Obligation: The Culture of Credit and Social Relations in Early Modern England (London: Palgrave Macmillan, 1998).

O'Day, Rosemary, *Cassandra Brydges (1670–1735), First Duchess of Chandos: Life and Letters* (Woodbridge: Boydell and Brewer, 2007).

Women's Agency in Early Modern Britain and the American Colonies: Patriarchy, Partnership and Patronage (Harlow: Pearson Longman, 2007).

Olszewski, Edward T., "The Enlightened Patronage of Cardinal Pietro Ottoboni (1667–1740)," *Artibus et Historiae*, 23, 45 (2002), 139–165.

Outhwaite, R. B., *Clandestine Marriage in England, 1500–1800* (London and Rio Grande: Hambledon, 1995).

"Marriage as Business: Opinions on the Rise in Aristocratic Bridal Portions in Early Modern England," *Business Life and Public Policy, Essays in Honour of D. C. Coleman*, ed., Neil McKendrick and R. B. Outhwaite (Cambridge: Cambridge University Press, 1985), pp. 21–37.

Owen, J. H., *War at Sea under Queen Anne, 1702–1708* (Cambridge: Cambridge University Press, 1938).

Parsons, Philip, *The Monuments and Painted Glass of Upwards of One Hundred Churches Chiefly in the Eastern Part of Kent* (Canterbury: Simmons, Kirkby and Jones, 1794).

Paulson, Ronald, *Hogarth: His Life, Art and Times,* 2 vols. (New Haven, CT: Yale University Press, 1991).

Peck, Linda Levy, "A Consuming Culture," Program for Philip Massinger's *The City Madam,* (Stratford on Avon: Royal Shakespeare Company, 2011).

    Consuming Splendor: Society and Culture in Seventeenth-Century England (Cambridge: Cambridge University Press, 2005).

Pincus, Steven C. A., "Popery, Trade and Universal Monarchy: The Ideological Context of the Outbreak of the Second Anglo-Dutch War," *English Historical Review,* 422 (1992), 1–29.

Polnitz, Aysha, *Princely Education in Early Modern Britain, Cambridge Studies in Early Modern British History* (Cambridge: Cambridge University Press, 2015).

Port, M. H., "West End Palaces: The Aristocratic Town House in London, 1730–1830," *London Journal,* 20, 1 (1995), 17–46.

Probert, Rebecca, *Marriage Law and Practice in the Long Eighteenth Century: A Reassessment* (Cambridge: Cambridge University Press, 2010).

Rabb, Theodore K., *Enterprise and Empire: Merchant and Gentry Investment in the Expansion of England, 1575–1630* (Cambridge, MA.: Harvard University Press, 1967).

Razell, Peter, *The Conquest of Smallpox: The Impact of Inoculation on Smallpox Mortality in Eighteenth-Century Britain, rev. 2nd edn.* (London: Caliban Books. 2003).

Redford, Bruce, *Venice and the Grand Tour* (New Haven, CT: Yale University Press, 1996).

Rosen, Adrienne B., Susan M. Keeling, and C. A. F. Meekings, "Parishes: Great and Little Abington," in *A History of the County of Cambridge and the Isle of Ely,* ed. A. P. M. Wright, Vol. VI (London, 1978), pp. 3–19. *British History Online*: www.british-history.ac.uk/vch/cambs/vol6/ pp. 3–19 (accessed July 19, 2017).

Roth, Randolph, "Homicide in Early Modern England, 1549–1800: The Need for a Quantitative Synthesis," *Crime, History & Societies,* 5, 2 (2001), 33–67.

Rudolph, Julia, "Property and Possession: Literary Analyses of Mortgage and Male Folly," in *A Cultural History of* Law, Vol. IV, *A Cultural History of Law in the Age of Enlightenment,* ed. Rebecca Probert and John Snape (Bloomsbury: London, forthcoming).

Schlarman, Julie, "The Social Geography of Grosvenor Square: Mapping Gender and Politics, 1720–1760," *Journal of Architectural History,* 28, 1 (2003), 8–28.

Schutte, Kimberly, *Women, Rank, and Marriage in the British Aristocracy, 1485–2000: An Open Elite?* (Basingstoke: Palgrave Macmillan, 2014).

Seddon, P. R., "Marriage and Inheritance in the Clifton Family during the Seventeenth Century," *Transactions of the Thoroton Society,* 84 (1980), 33–43.

Shanley, Mary L., *Feminism, Marriage, and the Law in Victorian England, 1850–1895* (Princeton, NJ: Princeton University Press, 1989).

Smith, Hilda, *Reason's Disciples: Seventeenth-Century English Feminists* (Champaign-Urbana: University of Illinois Press, 1982).

Spicksley, Judith, "Usury Legislation, Cash and Credit: The Development of the Female Investor in the Late Tudor and Stuart Periods," *The Economic History Review,* 61, 2 (May, 2008), 277–301.

Staves, Susan, *Married Women's Separate Property in England 1660–1833* (Cambridge, MA: Harvard University Press, 1990).

Stenhouse, William, "Visitors, Display, and Reception in the Antiquity Collections of Late-Renaissance Rome," *Renaissance Quarterly*, 58 (2005), 435–465.

Stone, Lawrence, *Broken Lives: Separation and Divorce in England, 1660–1857* (Oxford: Oxford University Press, 1993).

   Family and Fortune: Studies in Aristocratic Finance in the Sixteenth and Seventeenth Centuries (Oxford: Clarendon Press, 1973).

   Uncertain Unions: Marriage in England, 1660–1753 (Oxford: Oxford University Press, 1992).

Stone, Lawrence, and Jeanne C. Fawtier Stone, *An Open Elite? England 1540–1880* (Oxford: Oxford University Press, 1984).

Stoye, J. Walter, *English Travellers Abroad 1604–1667* (London: Jonathan Cape, 1952).

Stretton, Tim, *Women Waging Law in Elizabethan England* (Cambridge: Cambridge University Press, 1998).

Stretton, Tim, and Krista J. Kesselring, eds., *Married Women and the Law: Coverture in England and the Common Law World* (Ithaca, NY: McGill University, 2013).

Sutton, Ann F., *The Mercery of London: Trade, Goods and People, 1130–1578* (Aldershot: Ashgate, 2005).

Sweet, Rosemary, "British Perceptions of Italian Cities in the Long Eeighteenth Ccentury," in *British History, 1600–2000: Expansion in Perspective*, ed. Kazuhiko Kondo and Miles Taylor (London: IHR, 2010), pp. 153–176.

Tague, Ingrid H., *Women of Quality: Accepting and Contesting Ideals of Femininity in England, 1690–1760* (Woodbridge: Boydell and Brewer, 2002).

Tarzia, Wade, "The Hoarding Ritual in Germanic Epic Tradition," *Journal of Folklore Research*, 26, 2 (1989), 99–121.

Taunton, Nina, *Fictions of Old Age in Early Modern Literature and Culture* (New York and London: Routledge, 2007).

Teague, Frances, *Bethsua Makin, Woman of Learning* (Lewisburg, PA: Bucknell University Press, 1998).

Thirsk, Joan, ed., *Agrarian History of England and Wales, Vol. V, 1640–1750* (Cambridge: Cambridge University Press, 1984–1985.)

Thompson, E. P., "The Moral Economy of the English Crowd in the Eighteenth Century," *Past and Present*, 50 (1971), 76–131.

Tyacke, Nicholas, *The History of the University of Oxford, Vol. IV, Oxford in the Seventeenth Century* (Oxford: Oxford University Press, 1997).

Upton, Anthony F., *Sir Arthur Ingram, c. 1565–1642* (Oxford: Oxford University Press, 1961).

Van Bochove, Christiaan, Heidi Deneweth, and Jaco Zuijderduijn, "Real Estate and Mortgage Finance in England and the Low Countries, 1300–1800," *Continuity and Change*, 30, 1 (2015), 9–38.

Wallis, Patrick, "Labor, Law and Training in Early Modern London: Apprenticeship and the City's Institutions," *Journal of British Studies*, 51, 4 (2012), 791–819.

Warren, Ian, "The English Landed Elite and the Social Environment of London c. 1580–1700: The Cradle of an Aristocratic Culture?" *English Historical Review*, 126, 518 (2011), 44–74.

Wemyss, Millicent Erskine, *A Notable Woman and Other Sketches* (London: Eden, Remington & Co., 1893).

Whyman, Susan, "Land and Trade Revisited: John Verney, Merchant and Baronet," *London Journal*, 22 (1997), 16–32.

    Sociability and Power in Late-Stuart England: The Cultural Worlds of the Verneys, 1660–1720 (Oxford and New York: Oxford University Press, 1999).

Weiser, Brian, "A Call for Order: Charles II's Ordinances of the Household (BL Stowe 562)," *Court Historian*, 6, 2 (2001), 151–156.

Williams, Michael E., *The Venerable English College Rome, A History 1579–1979* (London: Associated Catholic Publications, 1979).

Women's Studies, 26, 5 (1997), Special issue on women and travel.

Zahedieh, Nuala, "An Open Elite? Colonial Commerce, the Country House and the Case of Sir Gilbert Heathcote and Normanton Hall," in *Slavery and the British Country House*, ed. Madge Dresser and Andrew Hann (Swindon: English Heritage 2013), pp. 71–77.

Zupko, Ronald E., *A Dictionary of Weights and Measures for the British Isles* (Philadelphia: American Philosophical Society, 1985).

Websites

"The Acquisition of the Estate," in *Survey of London: Volume 39, The Grosvenor Estate in Mayfair, Part 1 (General History)*, ed. F. H. W. Sheppard (London, 1977), pp. 1–5, *British History Online*: www.british-history.ac.uk/survey-london/vol39/pt1/pp1-5 [accessed Oct. 3, 2009].

Archivio Digitale Boncompagni Ludovisi: www.villaludovisi.org

The British Museum: www.britishmuseum.org/research/search_the_collection_data base/term_details.aspx?bioId=77938, "Thomas Tompion."

CCED, Clergy of the Church of England Database: http://db.theclergydatabase.org .uk/jsp/search/index.jsp, "William Carpender," "Calverton," "Benjamin Conway."

Dale, T. C., "Inhabitants of London in 1638: St. Bartholomew Exchange," in *The Inhabitants of London in 1638* (London: The Society of Genealogists, 1931), pp. 36–37. *British History Online*: www.british-history.ac.uk/no-series/london-inhabitants/1638 [accessed April 28, 2018].

"Farnese Hercules," Hendrick Goltzius, Jacob Bol, Metropolitan Museum of Art (www .metmuseum.org/search-results#!/search?q=FARNESE%20HERCULES).

Historic England: Broad Marston Manor, List Entry 1350112. www.historicengland .org.uk/listing/the-list/list-entry/1350112.

History of Parliament Online: www.historyofparliamentonline.com: "Sir Nathanial Barnardiston," "John Bennet," "John Bennet senior," "James Cecil, Fourth Earl of Salisbury," "Sir Clifford Clifton," "Sir Cholmeley Dering," "John Ferrar," "Edward Finch," "Francis Finch," "Sir Christopher Hatton," "Newton Borough 1690," "Sir John Nulls," "Edward Osborne, Viscount Latimer," "Edward Pauncefort," "Tracy Pauncefort," "Sir Thomas Rich," "William Strode," "Sir John Wolstenholme."

Oxford Companion to Music, online database: www.oxfordmusiconline.com/page/ The-Oxford-Companion-to-Music.

Pelling, Margaret, and Frances White, *Physicians and Irregular Medical Practitioners in London 1550–1640 Database* (London: Originally publ. by Centre for Metropolitan History, 2004). *British History Online*: www.british-history.ac.uk/no-series/london-physicians/1550-1640 [accessed Oct. 31, 2016].

"People in Place: Families, Household, and Housing in London 1550-1720," Project 2003–2006, The Institute of Historical Research, London (www.history.ac.uk/cmh/pip/index.html).

Royal College of Physicians, Lives of the Fellows: http://munksroll.rcplondon.ac.uk/, "Sir John Finch."

University College Archives, University College, "Oxford Main Buildings": www.univ.ox.ac.uk/college_building/main-quad/ [accessed August 18, 2016].

Index

Note: Page numbers in italic refer to Figures

Salisbury, James Cecil, 3rd Earl of 140, 254
Salisbury, James Cecil, 4th Earl of *139*
    conversion to Roman Catholicism 141, 182
    death (1694) 141, 172, 185
    gambling 182–183
    gossip about 183–184
    Grand Tour 182
    imprisonment for treason 184
    marriage to Frances Bennet 8–9, 138–141,
        182–187
    and trial of Barnes for murder 153
    will 185
Salisbury, James Cecil, 5th Earl of 141, 180, 255
    correspondence 260
    Grace Bennet and 265, 267
    legacy from mother 262
Salisbury, James Cecil, 6th Earl of, Grace
        Bennet's legacy 10, 271–272, 274
Salisbury, Margaret, Countess of 139
Salisbury, Robert Cecil, 1st Earl of 22, 49
Salisbury, earls and marquesses of 283
    and Bennet inheritance 285
    see also Cecil; Hatfield
Salmon, Dr. Peter 64–65
    legacy from Gilbert Morewood 67
    marriage to Joan Henson 64
    physician to Charles I 64
Salmon, Joan (Henson) 108
    daughter of Frances 63, 69
    death 110
    and Frances, Lady Gresley 107
    legacy from Gilbert Morewood 67
    marriage to Peter Salmon 64
Saunders, Jacob, seaman 245
Savoy 196, 203
Sawyer, Robert 238
Scarlatti, Alessandro, composer 198
Scott, Edmund, grocer 26
scriveners, as bankers 35, 164
Seal, manor of *see* Netherseal; Overseal
Shadwell, Dr John 212, 215–216
Shadwell, Thomas 215
Shaftesbury, Earl of 125
Sheffield, lead merchants 48
Sherfield Manor 23
Shirley, Sir Robert and Lady 181
Shrewsbury, Earl of 146
Shute, Richard, partner in *Concord* venture
        57, 60
silver
    intrinsic value of 165
    wealth held in 77, 99

slave trade 19, 57, 60
Sligh, Sir Samuel 111
smallpox 214–215
    inoculation and vaccination 214
Smyth, Dr. Arthur 284
social mobility 3–4, 72, 76, 121
    and marriage portions 122
    and new Stuart elite 278–279
    and status differences 137
Solemn League and Covenant (1643) 56
Somerset, Duchess of, investment with 94
Sora, Olimpia Ippolita Ludovisi, Duchess
        of 201
South Sea Company 164, 166, 277
    collapse 267
    Eleanor Curzon and 268–269
    investment in 266
Spa, Liège 181
spices
    imports 49
    Morewood's trade in 51–52, 71
    reexport of 51–52
Stanhope, Anthony 206
Stanyon, Abraham 215
Stawell, Ursula 103
Steele, Sir Richard 260
Stepney, George 206
Steward, William, and wardship of Simon
        Bennet 30, 82–83
Stillingfleet, George 171
stocks (investment)
    Bank of England 266
    East India Company 164, 266
    South Sea Company 266, 268–269
Stone, Nicholas 85
Stony Stratford, Bennet property 27, 34, 66
Strode, Lady Anne (née Cecil) 284. *See* color
        plate 16
Strode, Samuel 284
Strode, William 284. *See* color plate 16
Strode family 284–285. *See* color plate 16
Strype, John 65, 255
sugar, and luxurious accessories 278
sugar box, silver 1, 2, 159, 278
sugar trade 19
sumptuary laws 20
Swale, Mr, cheesemonger 37

tapestries, in Finch houses 88
The Tatler magazine 260
Taylor, Mary, m. Sir Thomas Bennet *see* Bennet
tea, luxury accessories 277, 285